CASE STUDIES IN WORK, EMPLOYMENT AND HUMAN RESOURCE MANAGEMENT

CASE STUDIES IN WORK, EMPLOYMENT AND HUMAN RESOURCE MANAGEMENT

Edited by

TONY DUNDON

Professor of Human Resource Management and Employment Relations, Kemmy Business School, University of Limerick, Ireland and Visiting Professor, Work and Equalities Institute (WEI), University of Manchester, UK

ADRIAN WILKINSON

Professor of Employment Relations and Human Resource Management and Director of the Centre for Work, Organisation and Wellbeing, Griffith University, Australia and Visiting Professor, University of Sheffield, UK

Cheltenham, UK • Northampton, MA, USA

© Tony Dundon and Adrian Wilkinson 2020

All rights reserved. No part of this publication may be reproduced, stored in a retrieval system or transmitted in any form or by any means, electronic, mechanical or photocopying, recording, or otherwise without the prior permission of the publisher.

Published by
Edward Elgar Publishing Limited
The Lypiatts
15 Lansdown Road
Cheltenham
Glos GL50 2JA
UK

Edward Elgar Publishing, Inc.
William Pratt House
9 Dewey Court
Northampton
Massachusetts 01060
USA

A catalogue record for this book
is available from the British Library

Library of Congress Control Number: 2019952388

ISBN 978 1 78897 557 5 (cased)
ISBN 978 1 78897 558 2 (paperback)
ISBN 978 1 78897 559 9 (eBook)

Printed and bound in Great Britain by TJ International Ltd, Padstow, Cornwall

CONTENTS

About the editors and contributors   viii

1   Work, employment and human resource management: Case study applications   1
Tony Dundon and Adrian Wilkinson

SECTION I   PEOPLE RESOURCING

2   Fishing for diversity in legal talent pools: Recruiting early talent at Pinsent Masons   7
Dora Scholarios and Scott A. Hurrell
3   Rethinking the selection process in Saltire Brokers   14
Scott A. Hurrell, Giuliana Mazzoni and Dora Scholarios
4   Defending wellbeing at work: A case study on autism   20
Alan Roe and Alexandra Athelstan-Price
5   Flexibility in recession and recovery   25
Stewart Johnstone and Stephen Procter

SECTION II   HR STRATEGY, REWARDS AND PERFORMANCE

6   Determinants of human resource management strategy in a franchise   32
Ashlea Kellner
7   Contribution based pay in local government   39
Mathew Johnson
8   A high performance work system in a multi-stakeholder context   45
Eva Knies, Peter Leisink and Paul Boselie
9   Performance management: Rewarding for performance at Sprooker Inc.   52
Ryan B. Gould and Wayne O'Donohue
10   Gender pay gaps at Southside University Hospital Trust   59
Carol Woodhams, Sheila Wild and Carol Atkinson
11   The campaign for a 'real Living Wage'   67
Peter Prowse, Tony Dobbins and Ray Fells

SECTION III   WORKPLACE RELATIONS AND VOICE

12   Employee voice and transnational regulation: Double-breasting at BritCo   76
Niall Cullinane, Tony Dundon, Jimmy Donaghey, Eugene Hickland and Tony Dobbins
13   Is Ryanair the Southwest Airlines of Europe?   80
Geraint Harvey and Peter Turnbull
14   Uber and the problem of regulatory arbitrage   90
Michael Walker

15	Public sector employee engagement initiatives and employee voice results	95
	Russell Robinson	
16	Resistance, mischief and misbehavior @ The Jad-Gin Co. (JGC)	100
	Caroline Murphy, Lorraine Ryan and Tony Dundon	
17	The divided workforce: Zero hours work at Sports Direct	105
	Michelle O'Sullivan	

SECTION IV HUMAN RESOURCE DEVELOPMENT, DIVERSITY, SKILLS AND TRAINING

18	Learning from doing and telling at work	112
	James Brooks, Irena Grugulis and Hugh Cook	
19	For some or all? Debating the value of inclusive and exclusive approaches to talent management	118
	Sharna Wiblen	
20	What is competence? Theory, policy and practice	123
	Jonathan Winterton and Travis Turnbow	
21	Gender at Victoria Police: A long way travelled	129
	Georgina Caillard and Julie Wolfram Cox	
22	Workplace bullying at Neptune Plc	137
	Ria Deakin and Helge Hoel	
23	New forms of worker organising: Sex work in Argentina	142
	Kate Hardy	

SECTION V CULTURE AND JOB QUALITY

24	System error, restart? Allegations of sex discrimination at Microsoft Corp.	148
	Anthony Rafferty	
25	Changing organisational hierarchies: KnowledgeLtd	156
	Rory Donnelly	
26	Worker wellbeing at Jacaranda House	161
	Susan Ressia, Adrian Wilkinson and Paula K. Mowbray	
27	What makes a good job for low-waged workers?	166
	Chris Warhurst and Sally Wright	
28	Organizing project-based work in the games industry: Two contrasting cases	172
	Wike Been and Noëlle Payton	
29	Human resource management and relationship marketing: How two organizations leveraged tattoos to build their brand	178
	Andrew R. Timming	

SECTION VI LEADERSHIP AND CHANGE

30	Meaningless leadership	184
	Leo McCann	

31	Amazon: HRM and change in the house of neo-liberalism *Brian Harney and Tony Dundon*	191
32	Leadership and change at Ford Motor Company *Dan H. Langerud and Peter J. Jordan*	201
33	Implementing performance management in a public sector organisation in a developing country *Thuraya Farhana Haji Said*	207

SECTION VII INTERNATIONAL HRM

34	HR function at MNC subsidiary level: Mediating challenges and tensions *Jonathan Lavelle, Patrick Gunnigle and Sinead Monaghan*	216
35	Implementing HRM within multinational corporations: Localisation or global standardisation? *Anastasia Kynighou*	222
36	Global talent and mobility in a decentralised multinational enterprise *Anthony McDonnell, Stefan Jooss and Hugh Scullion*	230
37	Strategy and people management in China – Haier as an example *Fang Lee Cooke*	239
38	Emiratization: Benefits and challenges of strategic and radical change in the United Arab Emirates *Rachid Zeffane and Linzi Kemp*	245
39	Survival and outsourcing in the South African clothing and textiles industry: The changing fortunes of ClothTran *Christine Bischoff and Geoffrey Wood*	254
40	Cultural and logistical preparation of expatriates *William Despotovic*	261

SECTION VIII GLOBAL LABOUR RIGHTS

41	Labor practices in Apple's supply chains in China *Jenny Chan*	266
42	Framing workers' rights internationally: The case of Volkswagen and transnational collective agreements *Stephen Mustchin, Miguel Martínez Lucio, Michael Whittall, Fernando Rocha and Volker Telljohann*	272
43	Labour rights and global standards: What the Ali Enterprises fire tells us about social accountability and labour conditions in an international supply chain *Jean Jenkins*	277

Index 285

ABOUT THE EDITORS AND CONTRIBUTORS

EDITORS

Tony Dundon is Professor of Human Resource Management and Employment Relations, Kemmy Business School, University of Limerick, Ireland and Visiting Professor at the Work and Equalities Institute (WEI), Alliance Manchester Business School, the University of Manchester, UK. He is a Fellow of the Academy of Social Sciences (AcSS), a Fellow of the Chartered Institute of Personnel and Development (CIPD) and former Chief Examiner for the CIPD. He has published in a range of journals, including the *British Journal of Management*, *Human Relations*, and *Work Employment & Society*. His other books include: *Routledge Companion to Employment Relations* (2018, Routledge); *A Very Short, Fairly Interesting and Reasonably Cheap Book about Employment Relations* (2017, Sage); *Human Resource Management: Cases and Texts*, 5th edn (2017, Pearson); *Handbook of Research on Employee Voice* (2014, Edward Elgar Publishing); *Global Anti-Unionism* (2013, Palgrave); and *Understanding Employment Relations*, 2nd edn (2011, McGraw-Hill).

Adrian Wilkinson is Professor and Director of the Centre for Work, Organisation and Wellbeing at Griffith University, Australia and Visiting Professor at the University of Sheffield, UK. He has authored, co-authored and edited 30 books and more than 160 articles in refereed journals. His recent books include *The Oxford Handbook of Employment Relations* (2014, Oxford University Press); *Handbook of Research on Employee Voice* (2014, Edward Elgar Publishing); *HRM at Work: People Management and Development*, 6th edn (2016, CIPD); *The Oxford Handbook of Management* (2017, Oxford University Press); *A Very Short, Fairly Interesting and Reasonably Cheap Book about Employment Relations* (2017, Sage); *Human Resource Management: Cases and Texts*, 5th edn (2017, Pearson); *The Routledge Companion to Employment Relations* (2018, Routledge). He is a Fellow and Accredited Examiner of the Chartered Institute of Personnel and Development in the UK and a Fellow of the Australian Human Resource Institute. He is an Academician (now Fellow) of the Academy of Social Sciences (AcSS) in the UK and the Australian Academy of Social Sciences. He has been shortlisted by *HR Magazine* for the award of HR's Most Influential International Thinker.

CONTRIBUTORS

Alexandra Athelstan-Price is Researcher and Consultant, University of Leeds, UK.

Carol Atkinson is Professor of HRM and Associate Dean for Research for the Faculty of Business and Law, Manchester Metropolitan University, UK.

Wike Been is Researcher, Amsterdam Institute for Advanced Labour Studies (AIAS-HSI) of the University of Amsterdam (UvA), the Netherlands.

EDITORS AND CONTRIBUTORS

Christine Bischoff, Wits City Institute, University of Witwatersrand, South Africa.

Paul Boselie is Professor of Public Administration and Organization Science and Head of Department at the Utrecht University School of Governance, the Netherlands.

James Brooks is Post-Doctoral Research Fellow, Leeds University Business School, UK.

Georgina Caillard is a Teaching Associate, Department of Management, Monash Business School, Monash University, Australia.

Jenny Chan is Assistant Professor of Sociology at The Hong Kong Polytechnic University and elected Vice President of the International Sociological Association's Research Committee of Labor Movements.

Hugh Cook is Lecturer in Employment Relations and HRM, Leeds University Business School, UK.

Fang Lee Cooke is Professor and Coordinator of Monash Business Digitalisation Research Network, Monash Business School, Monash University, Australia.

Niall Cullinane is Senior Lecturer, Queen's University Management School, Belfast, UK.

Ria Deakin is Senior Lecturer in HRM, MMU Business School, Manchester Metropolitan University, UK.

William Despotovic is Lecturer, Department of Employment Relations and Human Resources, Griffith University, Brisbane, Australia.

Tony Dobbins is Professor of Employment Relations and HRM, Birmingham Business School, University of Birmingham, UK.

Jimmy Donaghey is Professor, Monash University, Australia.

Rory Donnelly is Professor of HRM and Organisational Behaviour, University of Liverpool Management School, UK.

Ray Fells is Professor in Negotiation and Workplace Relations, University of Western Australia Business School, Perth, Australia.

Ryan B. Gould is Scholarly Teaching Fellow, Department of Employment Relations and Human Resources, Griffith University, Australia.

Irena Grugulis is Professor of Work and Skills, Leeds University Business School, UK.

Patrick Gunnigle is Emeritus Professor of Business Studies, Department of Work and Employment Studies, Kemmy Business School, University of Limerick, Ireland.

Kate Hardy is Lecturer, Leeds University Business School, UK.

Brian Harney is Associate Professor of Strategic HRM, Dublin City University Business School, Ireland.

Geraint Harvey is Professor and Director of the Centre for People and Organisations, School of Management, Swansea University, UK.

Eugene Hickland is Assistant Professor of Employment Relations and Human Resource Management, Dublin City University Business School, Ireland.

Helge Hoel is Emeritus Professor, Alliance Manchester Business School, University of Manchester, UK.

Scott A. Hurrell is Senior Lecturer in Human Resource Management and Organisational Behaviour, Adam Smith Business School, University of Glasgow, Scotland.

Jean Jenkins is a Reader in Employment Relations, Cardiff Business School, and a member of the Wales Institute of Social and Economic Research, Data & Methods (WISERD), Cardiff University, UK.

Mathew Johnson is Lecturer in Employment Studies at the Work and Equalities Institute, Alliance Manchester Business School, University of Manchester, UK.

Stewart Johnstone is Senior Lecturer in HRM and Employment Relations, Newcastle University Business School, UK.

Stefan Jooss is Lecturer in Management, Cork University Business School, University College Cork, Ireland.

Peter J. Jordan is Professor of Organisational Behaviour, Griffith Business School, Griffith University, Australia.

Ashlea Kellner is Research Fellow, Centre for Work, Organisation and Wellbeing, Griffith University, Australia.

Linzi Kemp is Associate Professor of Management & Organizational Behavior at the American University of Sharjah, United Arab Emirates.

EDITORS AND CONTRIBUTORS

Eva Knies is Professor of Strategic Human Resource Management at the Utrecht University School of Governance, the Netherlands.

Anastasia Kynighou is Senior Lecturer in HRM and Programme Leader for the Global Online MSc in International HRM, Manchester Metropolitan University, UK.

Dan H. Langerud is a Doctoral Candidate, Griffith Business School, Griffith University, Australia.

Jonathan Lavelle is Senior Lecturer in Employment Relations, Department of Work and Employment Studies, Kemmy Business School, University of Limerick, Ireland.

Peter Leisink is Emeritus Professor of Public Administration and Organization Science at the Utrecht University School of Governance, the Netherlands.

Miguel Martínez Lucio is Professor of International HRM and Comparative Industrial Relations, Work and Equalities Institute, Alliance Manchester Business School, University of Manchester, UK.

Giuliana Mazzoni, Adam Smith Business School, University of Glasgow, UK.

Leo McCann is Professor of Management, The York Management School, University of York, UK.

Anthony McDonnell is Professor of Human Resource Management and Head of the Department of Management and Marketing, Co-Director of the HR Research Centre at Cork University Business School, University College Cork, Ireland.

Sinead Monaghan is Assistant Professor in International Business, Trinity Business School, Trinity College Dublin, Ireland.

Paula K. Mowbray is Lecturer, Department of Employment Relations and Human Resources, Griffith University, Australia.

Caroline Murphy is Lecturer in Employment Relations, Department of Work and Employment Studies, Kemmy Business School, University of Limerick, Ireland.

Stephen Mustchin is Senior Lecturer in Employment Studies, Work and Equalities Institute, Alliance Manchester Business School, University of Manchester, UK.

Wayne O'Donohue is Senior Lecturer, Department of Employment Relations and Human Resources, Griffith University, Australia.

Michelle O'Sullivan is Senior Lecturer in Industrial Relations, Department of Work and Employment Studies, Kemmy Business School, University of Limerick, Ireland.

Noëlle Payton is Researcher, Amsterdam Institute for Advanced Labour Studies (AIAS-HSI) of the University of Amsterdam (UvA), the Netherlands.

Stephen Procter is the Alcan Professor of Management, Newcastle University Business School, UK.

Peter Prowse is Professor in Human Resource Management and Employment Relations, Sheffield Business School, Sheffield Hallam University, UK.

Anthony Rafferty is Senior Lecturer in Employment Studies, Work and Equalities Institute, Alliance Manchester Business School, University of Manchester, UK.

Susan Ressia is Lecturer, Department of Employment Relations and Human Resources, Griffith University, Australia.

Russell Robinson is Director of Training and Engagement for a United States federal government agency, Founder of Amplified Research and Consulting, LLC, and Adjunct Professor at the University of Louisville, USA.

Fernando Rocha is Director of the Department of Studies at the Fundación 1º de Mayo, Research Institute to the Trade Union Comisiones Obreras, Spain.

Alan Roe is Lecturer in Work and Employment Relations, Leeds University Business School, UK.

Lorraine Ryan is Lecturer in Employment Relations, Department of Work and Employment Studies, Kemmy Business School, University of Limerick, Ireland.

Thuraya Farhana Haji Said is Lecturer at UBD School of Business and Economics (UBDSBE), Universiti Brunei Darussalam, Brunei.

Dora Scholarios is Professor of Work Psychology at University of Strathclyde Business School, Glasgow, UK.

Hugh Scullion is Professor in International HRM, Hull University Business School, University of Hull, UK.

Volker Telljohann is Senior Researcher, IRES Emilia-Romagna, Italy.

EDITORS AND CONTRIBUTORS

Andrew R. Timming is Associate Professor of Human Resource Management, University of Western Australia Business School, Australia, Deputy Head of the Department of Management and Organisations and Director of Business and Community Engagement.

Travis Turnbow is Senior Business Development Manager with Workday, based in Paris, France.

Peter Turnbull is Professor of Management and Industrial Relations, the New School of Management, University of Bristol, UK.

Michael Walker is a PhD Candidate at the University of Technology Sydney, Australia.

Chris Warhurst FRSA is Professor and Director of the Institute for Employment Research at the University of Warwick, UK.

Michael Whittall is Research Fellow at Friedrich-Alexander Universität, Germany and Nottingham Trent University, UK.

Sharna Wiblen is Assistant Professor (Lecturer), Sydney Business School at the University of Wollongong, Australia.

Sheila Wild is a leading expert on gender pay issues, with over 30 years' experience in the field. She now runs EqualPayPortal.

Jonathan Winterton is Professor and Head of Department of Management, Huddersfield Business School, UK, and was formerly Executive Dean of the Faculty of Business & Law at Taylor's University, Malaysia.

Julie Wolfram Cox is Professor, Management, Department of Management, Monash Business School, Monash University, Australia.

Geoffrey Wood is Professor and DanCap Chair of Innovation, as well as Head of Dan Management, at Western University, Canada.

Carol Woodhams is Professor of HRM and Head of the People and Organisations Department, Surrey University, UK.

Sally Wright is Senior Research Fellow, Institute for Employment Research at the University of Warwick, UK.

Rachid Zeffane is Professor of Management (OB & HRM) at the University of Sharjah, United Arab Emirates.

In addition to the case studies in the main text, an accompanying 'tutor manual' is provided to those lecturers who want to use any of the cases for in-class teaching, student projects, formative and summative student assessment exercises, and/or for the cases to be used for formal examinations. Guidance on the best use for each case, together with suggested solutions to the questions asked and issues the case raises are contained in the accompanying 'tutor manual' and can be found here: https://e-elgar.com/textbook-resources/case-studies-in-work-and-employment-and-human-resource-management

1
Work, employment and human resource management: Case study applications

Tony Dundon and Adrian Wilkinson

Many textbooks on HRM and Industrial Relations combine discursive, prescriptive, theoretical and sometimes a critical synthesis of the practical applications of abstract concepts and ideas. As a field of study, HRM covers a wide remit associated with work, employment and organisational studies. Academic disciplines overlap between sociology, economics, law, history or industrial and organisational psychology (among others) (Boxall and Purcell, 2016; Wilkinson et al., 2017, 2019; Bratton and Gold, 2019). Most approaches have the admirable aim of synthesising information and concepts to impart a degree of knowledge. Some even seek to contrast alternative or differing interpretations of such knowledge with demonstration through models, frameworks, contemporary innovations that relate to evolving contexts and scenarios for application.

However, these are not neutral or *apolitical* applications of knowledge (Dundon et al., 2017). Understanding the antithesis of alternative knowledge paradigms is an important part of scholarship and learning, and unpacking various discourses can underscore particular managerial or other corporate vested-interests (Bridgman et al., 2016). In HRM this relates to what Legge (1995) famously described as contrasting rhetoric and realities in the world of work. Contemporary debates might include, for example, the '#996 approach' to work and employment. For some business leaders – key among them being Jack Ma, the co-founder of giant online shopping platform Alibaba – the #996 approach is to encourage 12-hour working days (9am–9pm), 6 days a week.[1] For corporate leaders such an approach can open up new opportunities for increasing the earning capacity for millions of poor people, many in less developed parts of the world. However, it is probable that increasing low paid jobs will generate even more wealth for business leaders than it does in uplifting the share in national income or wealth distribution for workers. The narrative of offering new earnings opportunities, or claims for more efficient flexibility, typically means exploiting others lower down the hierarchy and the workers required to labour 9am-to-9pm, 6 days a week. Indeed, extending critical synthesis and research knowledge may illustrate that not only does #996 benefit a few at the top, at the expense of workers, it is also unsustainable and counter-productive to long-term productivity (Batt, 2018). For instance, long hours runs against the research evidence about employee well-being, mental health, organisational productivity and individual stress (Guest, 2017).

The purpose of this book is to provide a bank of *evidence-based* case studies that offer critically informed applications for students and educators. Taken together they represent a set of developed materials in which knowledge generation can be extended through application and critical analysis, reflection and synthesis. In part, the demand for the book arose from conversations about the difficulties of integrating critical analysis and engagement for students because of the way much university learning has been developing, particularly in business school environments. Many texts and modules present very brief scenarios of ideas and theories, with condensed hypothetical situations for students to consider the concepts and theories they are studying. Large student numbers mean that seminars and tutorials are less frequent as spaces for debate and discussion, and even when they do exist, the increasing numbers in such groups means that student reflection is more difficult to sustain.

The cases in this volume have been derived from scholarly research into one or more specific work, employment, HR and/or organisational analysis topics. They lend themselves as supplementary learning materials with the specific aim of encouraging students to apply knowledge and debate alternatives to those of the more prescriptive managerial and vested-interest language. For the majority, the cases in this volume are anchored from ongoing research projects and analysis of the respective chapter authors. In other words, these case studies are first and foremost real world situations, written by leading scholars from the fields of industrial relations, HRM, work and employment studies, work sociology, organisational psychology, labour economics, the law, and organisational analysis. The audience is students and educators seeking materials for critical analysis and reflection at higher or advanced levels of study and those interested in the world of work, employment and/or organisational analysis. It is relevant for those on a range of cognate masters' programmes in human resource management, work and organisation studies, industrial relations, and related MBA modules found at many educational institutions. They are NOT puff pieces for organisations but are research based and critical in their approach.

STRUCTURE OF BOOK AND CASES

The cases vary and are presented in the book by related thematic content, concerned with the world of work and the management and application of organisational practices and ideas.

In Section I there are four case studies covering in some detail what may be defined as 'people resourcing'. Several debatable issues surround how corporations recruit and select employees for jobs. Scholarios and Hurrell and Hurrell, Mazzoni and Scholarios cover these issues in Chapters 2 and 3, respectively, drawing on research from a case in legal services (recruitment) and the finance sector (selection). Following this, Roe and Athelstan-Price, in Chapter 4, report a case about well-being policy along with how representation can function to support workers with autism. These 'people resourcing' dynamics include not only how companies recruit, select and manage well-being, but also the challenges and pressures surrounding flexibility and issues about people exiting an organisation during times of austerity. In Chapter 5 Johnstone and Procter report on the case of flexible working in recession and recovery.

Section II then shifts attention to cases reporting on 'HR strategy, rewards and performance'. Six cases report debates across multiple organisational types; for example, implementing HR strategy in small firms (e.g. the coffee shop club) in Chapter 6 by Kellner, and pay and remuneration in a public sector authority, from Johnson in Chapter 7. These debates are captured and extended further with a case about High Performance Work Systems (HPWS) in Chapter 8, from Knies et al.

Performance management is presented in a case by Gould and O'Donohue in Chapter 9. Next, in Chapter 10, gender pay and pay gaps are addressed by Woodhams et al.; and in Chapter 11, issues about pay equality and public policy debates are discussed by Prowse et al. with a case about living wage campaigns.

Section III then directs attention to some of the key complexities in 'workplace relations and voice', with six case studies that offer plenty to discuss and debate. For example, in Chapter 12 Cullinane et al. outline the use of double-breasting voice and transnational employment regulations. Related is the case in Chapter 13 that contrasts Ryanair in Europe with Southwest Airlines in the US, capturing issues of union recognition from long established research in this sector by Harvey and Turnbull. In Chapter 14 Michael Walker reviews the phenomenon that is the so-called Uberization of employment issues and labour market legal reform. The issues that link employee engagement with alleged voice outcomes is reported in Chapter 15 by Robinson, followed in Chapter 16 by a case of workplace resistance in a bespoke small batch gin manufacturer, from Murphy et al. Contemporary developments and important debates about insecurity and employment precariousness can be found in the case in Chapter 17, from O'Sullivan, reporting on zero hours work and attendant employment contracts in the well-known retail outlet Sports Direct.

Section IV groups together six cases capturing 'Human resource development, diversity, skills and training'. The core issue of skill and how 'learning by doing and telling' is delivered in the fire service is reported in Chapter 18 from Brooks, Grugulis and Cook. Next, the challenges associated with 'developing talent' are covered in Chapter 19 by Wiblen, followed by a case that opens up debate on the meaning of 'competence', from Winterton and Turnbow in Chapter 20. How the Victoria State Police in Australia manage gender diversity is shown in Chapter 21 by Georgina Caillard and Julie Wolfram Cox. A number of these underlying themes are picked up more specifically by Deakin and Hoel in Chapter 22, when debating bullying in the workplace. Next, Kate Hardy, in Chapter 23, provides a platform to evaluate issues of labour (de)commodification and inclusion for groups of workers that are typically missing in mainstream texts, namely the concerns of sex workers.

Section V includes another six cases that address themes of 'culture and job quality'. In Chapter 24 Rafferty reviews a well-known class-law suit at Microsoft Corp, contrasting the masculinity of HR control and its impact on diversity and the issues of stereotyping. Culture features as a key issue in Donnelly's case in Chapter 25 about changing organisational hierarchies and boundaries, with particular relevance to knowledge-intensive type environments. Cultural facets pervade workplace well-being in Chapter 26 from Ressia et al. Warhurst and Wright provide a case in which public policy in Scotland is used to promote an active agenda to enrich job quality cultures for lower paid occupations. In Chapter 28 Been and Payton chart new terrain with a case about freelancers and work quality issues unique to the gaming industry, providing contrasting insights across computer gaming programmers. Then, in Chapter 29, Timming presents two case comparisons to show how body art (tattoos) can enhance corporate brand and culture.

Next there are four chapters in Section VI, that between them tackle critically the meanings and applications of 'leadership and change'. In the first of these, in Chapter 30, McCann explains that while being a leader is difficult and a thankless challenge, it can nonetheless have a sinister and highly controlling motive. Important from McCann's case is the need to unpack what are often 'meaningless' pockets of espoused wisdom from management leadership gurus. Next, in Chapter

31 by Harney and Dundon, the case of Amazon shows the 'ideology of hard leadership' and the HR impacts from neo-liberalism on employees' working lives. In Chapter 32 Langerud and Jordan review ideas of transformational leadership by examining the specific case of the Ford Motor Company. Next, in Chapter 33, Said draws distinctions between micro and macro leadership facets when outlining the performance change from a New Public Management (NPM) leadership agenda in a developing country context.

Section VII directs attention to 'international HRM', with seven chapters. Lavelle, Gunnigle and Monaghan in Chapter 34 report a case about the HR function at a multinational subsidiary. It draws on challenges of change and continuity and how processes are mediated across complex organisational layers. In Chapter 35 Kynighou draws on expatriate HR issues and competing demands between local and global contextual pressures. McDonnell et al., in Chapter 36, address several issues concerned with how multinational corporations manage international staff mobility. Extending the global HR dimensions in Chapter 37, Lee Cooke provides some insight about the transformation of one of China's fastest growing and redeveloped MNCs, Haier, focusing on the implementation of people management strategy. Next, specific country of origin approaches provide further opportunities to contrast related HR and employment issues in the United Arab Emirates (Chapter 38, by Zeffane and Kemp), South Africa (Chapter 39, by Bischoff and Wood) and Australian expats (Chapter 40, by Despotovic).

The final section includes three chapters that extend debates and issues related to globalisation, with a particular concern with 'global labour rights' and labour standards across multinational corporations and supply chains. In Chapter 41 Chan provides a case of labour degradation and how workers have been treated in Foxconn, one of the largest suppliers of components that feature in smartphones and other electronic devices. Next, in Chapter 42, Mustchin et al. provide evidence from their research into the negotiation of framework agreements at Volkswagen, debating the important role of trade union actors. Finally, Chapter 43 concludes the section with an important case about worker safety and the power of collective organisation. In this chapter, Jenkins provides case evidence to showcase to students how power asymmetries remain permissive alongside (or because of) voluntary enforcement codes, offering critical analysis of corporate responsibility narratives. Taken together, the cases in Section VIII illustrate that issues of workplace safety, hazardous employment and labour agency are not isolated incidents but pervade countries, continents and multinational organisational types.

CONCLUSION: THEMES AND STRUCTURE

All the cases in this volume are contemporary, relevant and cover different sectors, countries, occupations and experiences. As a bank of evidence-based cases, the collection in its own right is significant and unique. In an era when academics are pressurised to publish in top journals in addition to (in some countries) having to demonstrate impact reports from their research, it is important not to lose sight of the important impact we, as educators, have on students. These cases may help to stimulate and inform students of research-focused approaches to scholarship and the application of research in teaching.

The cases are also important given the timing of many of the research enquiries from which they are drawn, including the synthesis of work and employment debates that extend beyond the global financial recession. While the sections provide some order, there are overlapping themes and issues between these, and educators may find a case in one particular section can be used for issues they want to address in another. Given the field of study, many of the cases illustrate the *capacity-building power* and *role of agency* as a collective dynamic for change and improvement for people. Second, *structures of accumulation* matter. How corporate enterprises respond to and shape global forces amplifies the political tensions that shape work, employment and organisational analysis. These issues extend to a *policy-driven agenda* from research engagement. Finally, the collection of case studies shows how a *multi-disciplinary* approach can inform knowledge to those issues and concerns that extend beyond a single organisation or groups of actors.

The aim has been to include case studies that are specific, critical and focused and do NOT invite students to walk in the shoes of managers, by trying to fix some presumed corporate problem for a managerial class or other corporate vested-interest group. Instead, they are cases that apply social science analysis of issues of a field of study to review, to discuss concepts, and to debate impacts on and for a wider stakeholder groups and agency interests.

END NOTES

1 Jack Ma defends the 'blessing' of a 12-hour working day, *BBC News*, 5th April 2019 (https://www.bbc.co.uk/news/business-47934513).

REFERENCES

Batt, R. (2018), 'The financial model of the firm, the "future of work", and employment relations', in A. Wilkinson, T. Dundon, J. Donaghey and A. Colvin (eds), *The Routledge Companion to Employment Relations*, London: Routledge.

Boxall, P. and Purcell, J. (2016), *Strategy and Human Resource Management*, 3rd edn, New York: Palgrave Macmillan.

Bratton, J. and Gold, J. (2019), *Human Resource Management: Theory and Practice*, 6th edn, Basingstoke: Palgrave.

Bridgman, T., Cummings, S. and Mclaughlin, C. (2016), 'Re-stating the case: How revisiting the development of the case method can help us think differently about the future of the business school', *Academy of Management Learning*, **15**(4), 724–41.

Dundon, T., Cullinane, N. and Wilkinson, A. (2017), *A Very Short, Fairly Interesting and Reasonably Cheap Book About Employment Relations*, London: Sage.

Guest, D. (2017), 'Human resource management and employee well-being: Towards a new analytic framework', *Human Resource Management Journal*, **27**(1), 22–38.

Legge, K. (1995), *Human Resource Management*, Basingstoke: Macmillan Business.

Wilkinson, A., Redman, T. and Dundon, T. (2017), *Contemporary Human Resource Management: Text and Cases*, 5th edn, London: Pearson.

Wilkinson, A., Bacon, N., Snell, S. and Lepak, D. (2019), *The Sage Handbook of Human Resource Management*, 2nd edn, New York: Sage.

SECTION I
PEOPLE RESOURCING

2
Fishing for diversity in legal talent pools: Recruiting early talent at Pinsent Masons

Dora Scholarios and Scott A. Hurrell

COMPANY BACKGROUND

Pinsent Masons is a Top 15 UK law firm and Top 100 international law firm. Today's firm was created in 2012 from the merger between international law firm Pinsent Masons and UK Top 50 law firm McGrigors, with the combined firm operating worldwide under the brand of Pinsent Masons (PM). The firm has a global network of offices with multiple locations in the UK and Europe, the Asia-Pacific region, Dubai, Qatar and Johannesburg. At the time of the merger, McGrigors' managing partner, Richard Masters, described the new firm as providing a 'solid platform for growth' which would 'allow them to become market leaders in strategically key sectors' (Pinsent Masons press release, 2012).

Today, the firm defines itself as more than a law firm with the aim of working alongside their clients as business partners to help solve their sector-specific problems. Trainee solicitors are therefore encouraged to get to know their clients' business to become both legal and business advisors. 'Our lawyers are also commercially-minded individuals who understand their clients' business needs and who use legal expertise as a tool to develop business solutions and deliver real client service'. (Graduate Brochure).

New trainees will go through six-monthly rotations in four practice areas of which there are at least 11; for example, banking and finance, corporate, dispute resolution and litigation, insurance and reinsurance, employment, pensions, and construction and engineering.

DIVERSITY CONTEXT

As with other professions, law has been in the spotlight over its lack of diversity and the existence of barriers to entry for some under-represented groups. The profession's traditional patriarchal dominance at senior levels, its lack of ethnic diversity, and the high proportions of individuals from more advantaged social backgrounds are particular issues (Sutton Trust, 2009; SMCPC, 2014). This profile of the legal profession is just as distinct in other national contexts, such as the United States, as it is in the UK (2018 Law360 Diversity Snapshot).

In the UK, ensuring a diverse pool of talent, particularly through 'enabling apprenticeship excellence', has become a strategic priority for many top firms, and for the Institute of Student

Employers (ISE).[1] Apprenticeships, which imply recruitment straight from school rather than university, have become a more prominent issue for many businesses following the government's introduction of the Apprenticeship Levy in 2017.[2] As a result, one of the ISE's goals is to support and enable its membership to navigate the apprenticeship landscape, which is complex and evolving. The ISE's current chair happens to be PM's Head of Early Talent, Deborah McCormack. As Deborah notes:

> Historically, many in roles like mine have focussed on graduate recruitment and development strategy. That focus has evolved to be far broader in scope, with the introduction of professional apprenticeship pathways. Strategically, many firms are now looking far more holistically at 'Early Talent' management and how this underpins the succession plan.

The legal profession has already gone to some lengths to create a level playing field for talented young people trying to enter the profession, regardless of their background.

PM is a market leader amongst legal firms promoting diversity as a core business strategy. The firm prides itself in being 'a champion of diversity and development' (www.pinsentmasons.com/en/careers/) and this is reflected in the leading role it plays in a number of initiatives. These include the following:

- Schemes to raise student aspirations to study law include the Aspiring Solicitors programmes and Pathways to Law, a programme established by social mobility promoting organisations, the Sutton Trust and the Legal Education Foundation, to widen access to the legal profession (see, for example, the Sutton Trust, 2009).
- Being one of the top ranked law firms in the 2017 and 2018 Social Mobility Employer Indexes (41 out of 136 participating employers in 2018). This scheme enables employers to share any initiatives they have to encourage talent from all backgrounds. PM's ranking indicates that they are dedicated to removing hurdles in recruitment which disproportionately affect individuals from lower socio-economic groups (Social Mobility Foundation, 2018); for instance, encouraging applications from a wide range of universities rather than targeting those often considered more elite, such as the Russell Group and Oxford and Cambridge ('Oxbridge').[3]
- PM was one of the founder members of the PRIME alliance (which now includes over 60 law firms) intended to provide legal work experience and pre-placement advice to underprivileged children aged 14–18 attending state-funded schools. These may include children who qualify for free school meals, have been in local authority care, those who have been carers, refugees or asylum seekers.
- PM is one of several global law firms offering alternative qualification pathways into professional service roles, including apprenticeship programmes (introduced in November 2017 for paralegal apprentices and business operations apprentices). These represent an 'earn as you learn' pathway which combines academic study with work-based learning.
- Equality initiatives concerned with gender, race and sexual orientation are also a prominent feature of the company's overall culture. For example, PM was the No. 1 ranked employer in Stonewall's 2019 UK Workplace Equality Index (second in 2017 and 2018), which benchmarks

employers' progress on lesbian, gay, bi and trans (LGBT) inclusion in the workplace (https://www.stonewall.org.uk/our-top-employer-2019). Employers who enter the Index present evidence of their practice in 10 areas, including how employees are engaged in LGBT inclusion through attraction, recruitment, retention and development.

DIVERSITY AND INCLUSION AS RECRUITMENT STRATEGY

Defining talent

Recruiting for diversity and inclusion is an organisational priority. A significant driver for the firm has been the increasing importance of its global client portfolio. A more global and diverse client base has required the firm to offer a range of skills. One example of this demand is that clients routinely request information about the diversity of teams who will act on their matters.

The firm is also considering the nature of talent required to represent 'Tomorrow's Lawyer' as part of a strategy to identify the key strengths of candidates globally. Given the variety of professional services offered by the firm, senior partners believe that future talent will be required to reflect a range of strengths, including innovation potential and client-relationship skills, as well as the more technical legal skills. These concerns within the firm mirror not only the changing business environment for professional services, but also wider debates about the status of professions in the future. Susskind and Susskind's (2015) book, *The Future of the Professions: How Technology Will Transform the Work of Human Experts*, argues that expertise traditionally assumed to be held uniquely by professionals such as doctors, teachers, accountants, architects and others will increasingly be distributed more widely and at low cost given advances in artificial intelligence and internet technology. The type of jobs available and the definition of talent for future professionals, therefore, is likely to change.

Diversity as best practice

External business pressures and the decision to position themselves as market leaders means that recruiting for diversity has become a best practice norm for PM. The Head of Early Talent, who spends a significant amount of energy ensuring the firm takes diversity seriously, described their approach as trying to 'level the playing field' for candidates from all types of backgrounds.

Crucial to this process is the Early Talent team, comprising the Head of Early Talent, one Graduate Recruitment Manager, three Graduate Recruitment officers, two Graduate development officers, one International Graduate Recruitment and Development Officer, one Apprenticeships Officer, and three Administrative Assistants. Most of the team have been with the firm (or one of the firms before the merger) for over 10 years. This team plays a crucial gatekeeping role in how diversity goals are achieved. It manages recruitment across the UK and for the Middle East offices, taking responsibility for preparing marketing collateral, social media content (e.g., Instagram,

Twitter) and building networks with schools and universities across the UK (e.g., attending Law Fairs and career or recruitment events). They intentionally, and personally, visit a wide range of higher education institutions rather than focusing on a select elite group, as described above, where there tends to be low proportions of students from socially disadvantaged backgrounds. They also develop unique relationships with some universities' careers services, even providing mentoring and coaching of candidates to allow them to prepare stronger applications.

Internally, the team works closely with partners and senior staff who are involved in recruitment. They ensure a diverse pool of assessors (different assessors are allocated to different selection stages to ensure candidates see at least three different assessors) and train assessors to avoid unconscious bias. Partner attitudes and behaviour with regard to doing favours for friends and family have also shifted; for example, it is now not acceptable to find friends'/family's children work placements. PM's own successful HR Network TV service is evidence of their commitment to a professional approach to HR.

Several aspects of the firm's current recruitment practice can be highlighted.

1. PM works with a number of diversity and social mobility organisations to identify and engage with talent from a wider pool.
2. 2017 diversity data indicates that 64.6 per cent of trainees had attended a UK state school and 26.9 per cent a fee-paying school; 43.8 per cent were from the first generation in their family to attend university; and 70.8 per cent were female (https://www.pinsentmasons.com/PDF/2017/Diversity-Statistics-2017.pdf).
3. Contextualised recruitment allows candidate achievements to be 'contextualised' against personal circumstances. A leader in this area is external provider Rare who are specialists in building social mobility metrics into companies' applicant tracking systems by drawing from their database which contains information about candidates' school and university results and UK postcodes. For those applying for graduate roles, this additional information on socio-economic background and personal circumstance can then be considered at the initial screening stages and again in the final decision-making wash-up sessions where all assessment information is considered for each candidate.
4. 'Authentic' and 'transparent' attraction aligns recruitment messages with the strengths required for the role/organisation and employer brand. This approach projects the company values and culture effectively, helping candidates decide themselves if the firm is a good 'fit' for them. In its graduate brochure, PM describes its values as follows: respect and cooperation, ambition and excellence, and openness and approachability.
5. Recent steps to opening up alternative talent pools include removing screening based solely on minimum levels of academic qualifications, and placing more emphasis on processes which identify candidate strengths and future potential. This is being looked at by the firm as a transformational global project. Although minimum entry qualifications are still required for graduates, there is more emphasis on an individual's innate strengths and behaviours. The ISE's 2018 Annual Student Recruitment Survey confirms this is a wider trend, with a growing proportion of employers adopting 'strengths-based' (43 per cent) and 'values-based' (32 per cent) recruitment and selection as well as the more common 'competency-based' (79 per cent) approach.

6. Unlike some legal firms, PM makes a point of looking for wider work experience, even if it is unrelated to law. Many law firms require legal work experience; however, this is unlikely to be as common amongst candidates from more disadvantaged backgrounds. PM also access a more diverse pool of talent through their own placement scheme, as this can be an entry route to a traineeship with the firm. Feedback on an intern's performance on a placement is an important indicator of future potential.

CHALLENGES

Despite being champions of diversity, having a dedicated team and the strong brand linked to widening access to professional services jobs, there are still challenges in ensuring equal access for all qualified talent.

1. There is a limited number of positions to offer deserving candidates. There are 68 trainee solicitor positions per year in the UK and c. 3000 applicants for these positions. Candidates pursuing vacation placements or training contracts, therefore, are competing for relatively few opportunities. Attracting the appropriate skills profile during early talent recruitment also remains an issue. Some partners still identify gaps in certain skills at the assessment centre stage; for example, flexibility and resilience.
2. While staff recognise the importance of the firm's apprenticeship programmes, in many cases there is a significant amount of pastoral support – and hence staff resources – required for these candidates compared to the support required by graduates. Although PM have a dedicated Apprenticeship Officer in place to support apprentices, the level of resources required will increase as the number of apprentices in the business increases.
3. PM recognises that they cannot impose a 'one size fits all' approach to diversity across their international offices. The HR team's strong message is that it is essential to ensure that the profile of those offered jobs reflects the cultural norms of the local labour market and the profile of applicants received by the firm. BAME (Black, Asian and minority ethnic) representation, for example, is a more salient issue in some parts of the UK than others. Equal opportunity data may not be held in some locations, such as Johannesburg; and a 'connected candidate' recruitment model based on an individual's networks may still be more attractive in some international locations, such as Dubai. Moreover, definitions of 'desirable attributes' can vary. 'Modesty' for example, is a more valued candidate quality in Asia or Dubai than it is Europe.
4. There has been a shift in gender balance towards women in law, who now represent the majority of applications and trainees (see the 2017 diversity data mentioned above). This trend reflects the proportions choosing to study and continue with a career in law. Nevertheless, the firm has noticed that male applicants seem to be more attracted to higher-paying City of London firms, especially the Magic Circle[4] or US firms, which emphasise progression. PM's more development-focused, agile and work–life balance brand seems to be a more attractive option for women. Subtle shifts in recruitment messaging though have recently made a difference in the number of applications from male candidates.

SUMMARY

Increasingly, large employers are realising that a homogeneous workforce of graduates is no longer sufficient for meeting the business needs of a diverse client base. Alongside employers' strategic business concerns, there is also wider recognition that some professions tend to be dominated by individuals from more privileged backgrounds. This has prompted efforts to change hiring practices to recruit more diverse pools of potential applicants. PM are one of the leaders in this respect amongst professional services firms, as shown by their involvement in various diversity and inclusion initiatives and their Early Talent team which is dedicated to 'levelling the playing field' for certain under-represented groups in the profession.

QUESTIONS

1. In what ways is PM's recruitment strategy aligned (or not) with its external context? Is this an example of a 'best practice' or 'best fit' strategy?

2. Considering the challenges identified in the case, what tensions can you identify with respect to achieving diversity and inclusion goals?

3. From the perspective of the Early Talent team, what difficulties can you see in implementing the recruitment strategy?

4. Are the issues reported with attracting male recruits actually a problem for PM?

END NOTES

1. The ISE is a member organisation of leading employers dedicated to all aspects of student recruitment and development. It promotes 'best practice' and provides data to its members (see ISE, 2019).
2. Since the introduction of the Levy in 2017, businesses with annual payrolls over £3 million are required to set aside 0.5 per cent of their wage bill to be spent on apprenticeships or work-based learning.
3. The Russell Group is a self-selected association of 24 publicly funded UK universities dedicated to ensuring research intensity. Although these universities are associated with high levels of prestige (see, for example, 'Universities vie for the metric that cannot be measured: prestige', *The Guardian*, 29 March 2016) they do not have any specifically different student entry requirements.
4. The Magic Circle comprises five leading London firms: Allen & Overy, Clifford Chance, Freshfields Bruckhaus Deringer, Linklaters, and Slaughter and May (*The Economist*, 2012).

REFERENCES

The following readings relate to recruitment practice, HRM, or to recruitment in professions and professional service firms, including law. These can be used to explore further how recruitment is used with respect to under-represented groups related to race, gender and class.

Ashley, L. (2010) Making a difference? The use (and abuse) of diversity management at the UK's elite law firms. *Work, Employment and Society*, **24**(4), 711–27.

Ashley, L. and Empson, L. (2013) Differentiation and discrimination: understanding social class and social exclusion in leading law firms. *Human Relations*, **66**(2), 219–44.

Bolton, S. and Muzio, D. (2008) The paradoxical processes of feminization in the professions: the case of established, aspiring and semi-professions. *Work, Employment and Society*, **22**(2), 281–99.

Bowen, D. and Ostroff, C. (2004) Understanding HRM–firm performance linkages: the role of the 'strength' of the HRM system. *Academy of Management Review*, **29**(2), 203–21.

Cook, A.C., Faulconbridge, J.R. and Muzio, D. (2012) London's legal elite: recruitment through cultural capital and the reproduction of social exclusivity in city professional service fields. *Environment and Planning A*, **44**(7), 1744–62.

Hurrell, S.A. and Scholarios, D. (2016) Recruitment, in A. Wilkinson, T. Redman and T. Dundon (eds) *Contemporary Human Resource Management*, Harlow: Pearson, 5th edn.

Institute of Student Employers (ISE) (2019) *About ISE*, accessed at https://ise.org.uk/page/AboutISE.

Parry, N. and Jackling, B. (2015) How do professional financial services firms understand their skill needs and organise their recruitment practices? *Accounting Education*, **24**(6), 514–38.

Social Mobility and Child Poverty Commission (2014) *Elitist Britain?* London: SMCPC.

Social Mobility Foundation (2018) The Social Mobility Employer Index 2018: key findings. Accessed at http://www.socialmobility.org.uk/wp-content/uploads/2018/07/Social-Mobility-Employer-Index-2018-Key-findings.pdf.

Susskind, R. and Susskind, D. (2015) *The Future of the Professions: How Technology Will Transform the Work of Human Experts*, Oxford: Oxford University Press.

Sutton Trust (2009) *The Educational Backgrounds of Leading Lawyers, Journalists, Vice Chancellors, Politicians, Medics and Chief Executives*. Submission to the Milburn Commission on Access to the Professions, London: Sutton Trust.

The Economist (2012) *Taking the Magic Abroad*, 7th July.

3
Rethinking the selection process in Saltire Brokers

Scott A. Hurrell, Giuliana Mazzoni and Dora Scholarios

Please note, whilst the organisation has been anonymised, the case study is a real company where two of the authors were invited to provide consultancy and make suggestions on the issues below. The case has been written in the present tense as readers are asked to take on the role of consultants when undertaking the task at the end.

BACKGROUND AND CONTEXT

'Saltire Brokers' (SB) is a successful financial services SME in Glasgow, providing insurance services. SB employ approximately 40 people. The company has been expanding fast in terms of both new staff and business. The CEO has noted some issues and has called your team of HR consultants to meet with him and the HR/Accounts manager (HRAM) (the manager has a dual role) to try and solve them.

Staff in SB are organised around two main functional areas: insurance brokers (a technical role involving financial knowledge and expertise) and account handlers (a less technical role which predominantly involves managing relationships with customers). Within each function there are three levels: A. Trainee (where graduates, and occasionally apprentices, typically start); B. standard; and C. Senior. In addition to the two main functions, there are also staff specialising in IT and technology, innovation and growth, and administration. There is also a senior management team comprised of the CEO, the COO and the heads of the brokering and account handling departments.

Despite staff generally performing well the CEO reports some issues with whether some staff 'care' and/or issues relating to 'common sense' or 'intelligence'. Some staff make recurring mistakes leading to performance issues. The CEO also reports that some are unwilling to put in effort beyond their job descriptions, for example by working overtime. There are also issues of high staff turnover amongst recent graduate recruits, and a number have left recently.

Despite the above issues, the CEO recognises that not all people may want to be 'ultra-ambitious, high performers'. This is not reported as a huge issue, but everyone needs to have the base level of competence at least, and some do not quite meet this expectation. He does, however, state that the senior management team in the organisation are all high achievers and do not understand/are not used to dealing with those who are not, or who are less driven than they are. The CEO and HRAM report that managers and senior employees are short on time and it is difficult for them always to find time for 'people management' type activities (e.g. around understanding performance and helping people to improve).

There are also potential issues with succession planning for future business needs and growth. The changing nature of the business means that new skills such as web coding and social media marketing (to design customer solutions and attract more customers) are also going to be needed, and these roles are currently being developed for advertisement.

Pay is not a huge issue for SB in recruiting staff, as they are able to offer competitive rates, although they cannot always compete with industry leaders. They can usually find people for trainee positions due to strong relationships with local universities. However, it can be difficult to recruit more experienced people from within the industry, especially in the most senior and specialised broker positions, due to supply of suitable people and the reputation and dominance of bigger and more established firms. Because of this difficulty in attracting more experienced brokers, SB sometimes recruit more generally from the insurance industry, as well as recent graduates, at trainee level and provide post-hire training. There is also a tendency, in the wider industry, for people in more senior positions to often walk into jobs straight away, with little formal selection process, due to their skills and reputation. The industry can sometimes be a little 'cliquey' and word of mouth is important, especially for more senior positions. For these reasons, the CEO is not keen to lengthen the selection process (e.g. by adding in candidate presentations to assess interpersonal skills and technical knowledge).

The CEO and HRAM think that the problems they have with some staff may be solved at the selection stage and want to know how the process might be improved. Your team's job is to review the current process and provide suggestions.

CURRENT PROCESS AS OUTLINED BY CEO AND HRAM

At present all vacancies are advertised on the company website, through specialist insurance recruitment websites, and through links with universities (internships, contacts with careers services and links with academics teaching relevant degrees). SB are also keen to try and use apprenticeships where possible, and recently successfully hired an apprentice to work in administration, after they completed their qualification in SB. Headhunting and direct approaches are sometimes used for more senior positions.

In terms of the intended selection process, all applicants (apart from the most senior positions recruited by word of mouth) send a CV and fill in a standardised application form. If they are invited to the next stage, they then all fill in a personality 'colours' test and learning styles questionnaire. Those applying for brokering roles also need to complete a technical job knowledge test. Candidates then have two, or more, interviews.

Pre-interview tests

The colours test is frequently used by businesses, and seen as an easily accessible way of determining how people interact with others, process information and tend to behave in the workplace. It assigns everyone to one of four colour 'types'. The technical details of the various versions of the colours test that exist are not easily available as it is provided by commercial organisations. The test seems predominantly based on the Myers–Briggs Type Indicator, combined with elements of the Big Five personality inventory. A typical version of the colours test can be found here (a publicly available example from the care sector) (https://www.skillsforcare.org.uk/Documents/Leadership-and-management/well-led/Day-1-17/1.4.1-Colour-Personality-Test-FULL.pdf). The CEO and HRAM report that the personality profile is not used for selection decisions per se, but for guiding interviews. After hire, some employees decide to display 'their' colour, on computers or at their work station, although this is not compulsory.

The typical learning style questionnaire used in organisations differentiates people along two continua, depending on whether they prefer to learn through experience/abstract conceptualisation (dimension 1) or reflection/active experimentation (dimension 2) (Swailes and Senior, 1999). The HRAM reports that little is done with the learning styles questionnaire, in either selection or post-hire, and she is unsure what role it plays.

The technical test for brokering roles is based around job knowledge, specific to insurance and financial services, such as risk and probability calculations and regulatory knowledge. Those getting below a certain value can only be hired at a trainee level, or may not be hired at all.

Interview process and types

Interview questions are structured around the personality test, applicants' CV and prior experience, the job description and some other more general questions. Questions are also sometimes used to gauge how applicants respond to unexpected situations. 'Forward looking' questions are used in the interviews to assess candidates' motivation and how they see their future. Competency questions are not generally used in the interviews as the CEO feels answers might be 'faked' and not reveal much. There are generally two people at each interview, usually involving the applicant's prospective line manager, although the exact composition of panels is changeable. Interview questions are not currently standardised for each position, and different interviewers approach interviews differently.

Candidates successful at the first interview stage are invited back for a second or even a third interview, where they meet the CEO. This second interview is less formal than the first and takes the form of a 'chat'. There is no standard number or sequence of interviews for each position. For non-technical roles, the CEO reports that it can be hard to tell candidates why they do not have a second interview, whereas the test can be referred to for technical positions.

The HRAM reports that she would like to see greater use of competency questions and greater standardisation of interviews. The CEO reports that he would like to see more, or different, tests in the process.

ISSUES REVEALED BY WORKPLACE INVESTIGATION

You have decided to go and interview employees who have been through the selection process, and some managers, to work out where the process is working well and what issues there might be.

Issues that spill over into the workplace have also been revealed. From this investigation you have found the following:

- Recruitment advertising is very much based upon the technical detail of the job rather than the company. Adverts are technical, impersonal, lengthy and based around the job description. Employees report that the opportunity for career development and progression – as well as SB's focus on company growth and process innovation – are very attractive features of the organisation, but these only became apparent once they started their SB careers.
- Many reported that once they met the CEO at their final interview, his passion convinced them they wanted the job, but his vision is expressed personally and only to those meeting him at the final interview.
- Not all candidates had the same number or type of interviews, even for the same type of role. Some candidates did not complete tests at all; some completed tests during the first interview and some completed them afterwards. The number of interviews was also not correlated with experience; that is, more experienced applicants did not always equate to less interviewing and vice versa. People reported differing levels of structure in interviews depending on who was interviewing. There was general confusion over the process, how the number of interviews was decided upon, and how methods were combined to select candidates. This confusion was apparent in both employees and managers.
- Many brokers found that they were unable to answer many of the technical test questions before their interviews, because they lacked knowledge or expertise in the area. Staff were also not given feedback on their test score and some apparently did badly but were still hired at a trainee level, with the test not used for development purposes post-hire. It was felt that a 'cut-off' score in the test was inappropriate for those without brokering experience, although it was not clear whether all of those hired had reached a 'cut-off' score. It seemed staff were a little confused over how this was used for the various levels of brokering, but that those not scoring highly enough were only hired as trainees.
- Managers reported that brokering skills could be acquired through training and that prior knowledge is not necessary to eventually become proficient in brokering.
- Employees are a little unclear why the personality 'colours' test is used during selection. Some employees chose to display their colour on their monitor, but many could not see the value of it. It was reported that some employees might have used their supervisors' or managers' colours to determine how quickly they should need to get work done (i.e. who would be more/less forgiving of work being late). It was not clear whether the colours were used to assign people to roles that suited them, although employees and managers noted that different roles (e.g. account handling vs. brokering) had different demands and that teams needed a mix of various types of people. Neither employees nor managers made reference to the learning styles questionnaire.
- Some managers felt that SB might be better off rethinking the selection process.

QUESTIONS

You have been tasked, as HR consultants, with helping SB review, and possibly redesign, their selection process. The CEO and HRAM are also open to other suggestions regarding how HR practices may be improved. In undertaking your task please consider the following questions:

1 How valid are the various methods used by SB? Might different methods be valid for different roles?

2 What alternatives might SB consider? Do they need all stages of the selection process?

3 Taking the above into account, might SB redesign their selection process? How and why? Would this be the same for all positions?

4 Might SB want also to focus on changes to the recruitment process?

5 Might SB want to look at changing some internal HR processes too?

6 Are SB likely to face any constraints in implementing the above?

REFERENCES

The following readings (including some 'classics') will help in answering the questions.

Barrick, M.R., Mount, M.K. and Judge, T.A. (2001) Personality and performance at the beginning of the new millennium: What do we know and where do we go next? *Personality and Performance*, **9**(1/2), 9–30.

Hurrell, S.A. and Scholarios, D. (2014) The people make the brand: Reducing social skills gaps through person–brand fit and HRM practices, *Journal of Service Research*, **17**(1), 54–67.

Hurrell, S.A. and Scholarios, D. (2016) Recruitment, in A. Wilkinson, T. Redman and T. Dundon (eds) *Contemporary Human Resource Management*, Harlow: Pearson, 5th edn.

Kristof-Brown, A. (2000) Perceived applicant fit: Distinguishing between recruiters' perceptions of person–job and person–organization fit, *Personnel Psychology*, **53**(3), 643–71.

Le, H., In-Sue, O., Shaffer, J. and Schmidt, F. (2007) Implications of methodological advances for the practice of personnel selection: How practitioners benefit from meta analyses, *Academy of Management Perspectives*, **21**(3), 6–15.

Michael, J. (2003) Using the Myers–Briggs Type Indicator as a tool for leadership development? Apply with caution, *Journal of Leadership and Organizational Studies*, **10**(1), 68–81.

Moscoso, S. (2000) Selection interview: A review of validity evidence, adverse impact and applicant reactions, *International Journal of Selection and Assessment*, **8**(4), 237–47.

Pittenger, D.J. (2005) Cautionary comments regarding the Myers–Briggs Type Indicator, *Consulting Psychology Journal: Practice and Research*, **57**(3), 210–21.

Schmidt, F.L. and Hunter, J.E. (1998) The validity and utility of selection methods in personnel psychology: Practical and theoretical implications of 85 years of research findings, *Psychological Bulletin*, **124**(2), 262–74.

Scholarios, D. (2016) Selection, in A. Wilkinson, T. Redman and T. Dundon (eds) *Contemporary Human Resource Management*, Harlow: Pearson, 5th edn.

Swailes, S. and Senior, B. (1999) The dimensionality of Honey and Mumford's learning styles questionnaire, *International Journal of Selection and Assessment*, **7**(1), 1–11.

4
Defending wellbeing at work: A case study on autism

Alan Roe and Alexandra Athelstan-Price

INTRODUCTION

An analysis of the British Workplace Behaviour Survey by Fevre et al. (2013) found that 'employees with disabilities and long-term illnesses were more likely to suffer ill-treatment in the workplace and experienced a broader range of ill-treatment. Different types of disability were associated with different types of ill-treatment' (p. 288). The authors concluded that such treatment was 'embedded in the social relations of the workplace' and came from co-workers, supervisors and managers. Furthermore, they found that people with 'invisible disabilities' were as likely, if not more likely, to suffer from ill-treatment or discrimination (p. 303).

According to Brugha et al. (2012) more than 1 in 100 people are on the autism spectrum in the UK – 700 000 people. The National Autistic Society (2016) also points out that only 16 per cent of autistic adults are in full-time paid work and 32 per cent are in 'some kind' of paid work. This paints a pretty bleak picture in terms of opportunity for people on the autism spectrum. Despite increasing awareness about neurological conditions over the past decade there has been little change in the employment prospects for autistic people during that time. The percentage of those in work was almost unchanged between 2007 and 2016 (p. 8). However, those fortunate enough to find employment would find that 'employers… are worried about getting things wrong for autistic employees and that they don't know where to go for advice' (National Autistic Society, 2016, p. 5). In response to increasing public awareness, but little progress achieved by Human Resource (HR) professionals, the Chartered Institute for Personnel and Development (CIPD) published a neurodiversity guide in order to 'spur on action from employers to create more inclusive workplaces where neurodivergent individuals can thrive' (CIPD, 2018a, p. 2).

Public discourse around autism (and sometimes disability in general) has been largely shaped by a medical model of disability – the focus on a cure or a treatment to eradicate an 'impairment'. According to Booth (2014) this has largely shaped discourse in politics and law. Writing for the Trade Union Congress (TUC), the author highlights that there is a distinct approach that locates questions associated with autism within the concept of the social model of disability. This model identifies the barriers faced by people; barriers that limit participation, whether they be practical or attitudinal. From this perspective it is quite logical to pursue the concept of 'reasonable adjustment', established with the Disability Discrimination Act, 1995 and built on in the Equality Act 2010. In summary: 'The social model identifies attitudes which may impede disabled people's participation and equality. There is prejudice and ignorance surrounding autism. There are also workplace practices, procedures, cultures, unwritten rules and communication forms which do not take account of people on the autistic spectrum' (Booth, 2014, p. 7).

Public discourse around autism and work has helped develop understanding about the connection between workplace stress and its consequences (O'Dell et al.). However, autism is also sometimes associated with mental health issues. Autism is not a mental illness but people on an autistic spectrum are often more vulnerable to developing mental health issues, sometimes brought on by 'social conflict, sensory overload, misunderstandings, discrimination and other factors' (Wales TUC, 2017, p. 10). The wellbeing of employees is often claimed to be a top priority for employers. According to ACAS (2012), there is a growing recognition of wellbeing issues in the workplace. HR professionals have also raised the profile of mental health issues and the wellbeing of employees (CIPD, 2018b). Nevertheless, work-related stress and mental health issues are clearly increasing; work-related stress and mental illness now accounts for more than half of work absences in the UK (HSE, 2018). Furthermore, the 'contradictory policy requirements, weaknesses in training, lack of support from relevant internal and external specialists and various work and budgetary pressures' have made the task of the line-manager difficult when there is an expectation that they will be the one that delivers policy at the operational level (Cunningham et al., 2004, p. 273). Developing an approach to such complex workplace issues is therefore extremely important for both the employer and the individual worker.

BACKGROUND

This case study is set in an educational institution in the UK that has 30 000 students and 6000 staff in academic, administrative, support and service roles. The organisation is divided into separate schools and departments which enjoy a certain amount of independence in terms of their Human Resource Management, but within the context of an organisation-wide set of strategies, policies and processes. HR are to an extent decentralised and have a certain amount of autonomy. Likewise, the main union for academic and academic-related staff (University and Colleges Union) is organised around the school structure. One consequence of traditions and arrangements within this institution, along with many others, is that 'caseworkers' from the union do not normally represent union members in their own school for grievance and disciplinary cases.

THE CASE

Kate is a 32-year-old woman with a PhD in Business and Management. She acquired her doctorate at the same institution, and was published whilst completing her studies in collaboration with her supervisor and another academic. On completion of her studies she had a number of short contracts doing research but could not obtain a research fellowship or a more permanent post. After more than two years on fixed-term contracts Kate's contract was again coming to an end. By this time Kate, who had always experienced communication differences with other people, also started to experience anxiety and depression, which was exacerbated by sleep loss.

Kate discussed her medical issues with her doctor and also availed herself of the employers' counselling services, mental health support services and 'access to work' (a government scheme to support people with disabilities at work). Kate made a difficult decision to apply for a Grade 4 administrative role despite having been working as a researcher and teacher at Grade 7. Kate was poorly informed by management and HR about the Redeployment Policy, which would have serious consequences. This was a big decision for Kate at a time when she could have been better supported. However, in the light of her deteriorating mental health and recognition that she had an unidentified neurological spectrum condition, she decided that job security was her priority. Kate secured some temporary employment in a Grade 4 administrative role and at this point consulted her union about her situation, which had become extremely distressing.

Because of her length of service and employment status Kate was eligible for redeployment within the organisation into another 'suitable' post. This would be completed by a process of matching a candidate's qualifications, skills, knowledge and experience with current vacancies across the organisation. Redeployment is a process that allows the employer to keep staff with knowledge, skills and experience of working within the organisation. It also provides an opportunity to retain staff who are familiar with the culture of the organisation and can provide an easier and more cost-effective way of filling a vacancy. Her union representative explained the process. However, because of the strict interpretation of this policy Kate now found herself in a very upsetting situation.

The employer would only match her against work in a Grade 4 post, regardless of her qualifications, skills and experience of working in Grade 7 posts. It is clear that the 'choices' Kate was faced with were ones which were not entirely determined out of free will, but were made within the context of some quite strict institutional boundaries within the policy on redeployment. Kate had not been adequately supported or advised by the line manager and HR locally in terms of her options. Although this process provided a way forward out of a terribly precarious situation, Kate felt that applying for an administrative role rather than a research one was never really a free choice; it was a necessity. She felt the need to prioritise stability (regular income) over research (the career she had trained for).

Kate applied for and was successful in securing a Grade 4 role as an administrative assistant in the library. This was a considerable step down from her previous roles and was not as well paid but would ensure some financial stability and hopefully, she thought, be less stressful than working on a zero hours contract, and at least secure. Kate planned to seek some stability in her circumstances whilst looking for more 'ideal' roles without the financial and mental pressures she had felt.

Because Kate had already raised issues that she had around autism and mental health (anxiety and depression) it was agreed that her trial period, which mirrors the process for probation, would be five months long instead of the normal three. This was agreed and Kate started work in the September and met with her new line manager in order to set objectives for the trial period and establish a training and development plan. A mid-term review was set for November and the final 'continuation' document was to be signed at the end of February.

Although Kate enjoyed her new role and was enthusiastic, there were occasions when expectations and instructions were not clear to her and this would cause anxiety and confusion and sometimes result in short periods of absence. Kate's manager struggled to understand the situation but nevertheless tried to support her and encouraged her to seek advice and support from HR. After some discussion it was agreed that Kate would seek an appointment with Occupational Health and that consideration would be given in terms of some reasonable adjustment.

The report from Occupational Health was helpful for all and supportive of Kate in terms of suggestions for reasonable adjustments and clear recognition of her condition. The report stated that Kate was fit for work and the organisation had to try and adjust its expectations of what was reasonable. Some of the clear advisory points were to extend flexibility in terms of hours and attendance; to ensure that communications were clear and explicit as well as regular; to ensure an open channel of communication between Kate and her manager; to understand that the normal process for reporting sick was not helpful – Kate could often be well enough to return to work within hours but sickness policy made this approach impossible; and to provide Kate with a neurodiversity coping strategy trainer as well as access to counselling. Very importantly the report stated that, due to autism, states of 'meltdown' or 'shutdown' could be triggered in situations where a high state of anxiety is reached.

It was agreed that Kate would be asked to work on specific duties, with clear priorities that she would email her line manager each day to report what hours she had worked, she would have a regular meeting each week with her line manager and that objectives for the following week would be agreed. It was also agreed that even if Kate had reported in sick in the morning she could still attend work if she felt well enough, within any period of time.

The set of adjustments recommended was slightly unusual but was agreed and supported by the line manager and HR. The mid-term review reflected on this information and Kate's progress and aims and objectives were set and agreed. At that meeting it was agreed to extend the trial period for another month. Although Kate agreed to this she became increasingly anxious about why this had been done but did not feel she could raise the issue. Nevertheless, Kate's manager indicated during their regular catch-up meetings that there were no foreseeable problems about the trial period being completed successfully.

After a very stressful week in the office where someone had made an aside about Kate's 'attitude and behaviour' over a minor incident with booking a room, Kate's manager said in passing that 'we need to talk about your continuing trial period'. Kate was convinced this meant a further extension and left work that day. Kate subsequently phoned in sick and contacted her union asking for help. The union allocated a 'caseworker' who arranged a meeting between the manager, HR and Kate.

After a considerable period of instability and a deterioration in her mental health as a consequence of stress at work, Kate finds herself on sick leave and feeling that she will not pass her trial period in her new job. The organisation's policies are supportive of disabled staff and following disclosure have provided an occupational health assessment, access to counselling services, and some reasonable adjustments. However, the manager is trying to provide a service and has to consider the wellbeing of all staff in the workplace and the running of the department. The caseworker thought that the question of the trial period needed to be resolved before any other discussions took place. To all intents and purposes the trial was ready to sign off at the end of February and it was quickly established with the line manager that Kate's employment position was confirmed. With this obstacle resolved, all parties could now try to establish the level and detail of the reasonable adjustment necessary to support Kate in her post.

QUESTIONS

1. In light of the literature mentioned in the introduction to this case study, what issues and concepts are raised?

2. How would you advise Kate if you were the caseworker?

3. What would you consider a reasonable outcome?

REFERENCES

ACAS (2012), Health, work and wellbeing, London: ACAS.

Bewley, H. and George, A. (2016), Neurodiversity at work, Research Paper, London: NIESR, ACAS, available at http://m.acas.org.uk/media/pdf/2/m/Neurodiversity_at_work_0916(2).pdf.

Booth, J. (2014), Autism in the workplace, London: TUC.

Brugha, T., Cooper, S.A., McManus, S., Purdon, S., Smith, J., Scott F.J., Spiers, N. and Tyrer, F. (2012), Estimating the prevalence of autism spectrum conditions in adults: extending the 2007 Adult Psychiatric Morbidity Survey, Leeds: NHS Information Centre for Health and Social Care.

CIPD (2018a), Mental health in the workplace, London: CIPD.

CIPD (2018b), Neurodiversity at work, London: CIPD, accessed at https://www.cipd.co.uk/Images/neurodiversity-at-work_2018_tcm18-37852.pdf.

Cunningham, I., James, P. and Dibben, P. (2004), Bridging the gap between rhetoric and reality: line managers and the protection of job security for ill workers in the modern workplace, *British Journal of Management*, **15**, pp. 273–90.

Equality Act (2010), accessed at https://www.legislation.gov.uk/ukpga/2010/15/pdfs/ukpga_20100015_en.pdf.

Fevre, R., Robinson, A., Lewis, D. and Jones, T. (2013), The ill-treatment of disabled employees in British workplaces, *Work, Employment and Society*, **27**(2), 288–307.

Health and Safety Executive (2018), Health and safety at work: summary statistics for Great Britain 2018, London: HSE.

National Autistic Society (n.d.), Managing an autistic employee (Website), accessed at https://www.autism.org.uk/professionals/employers/information-for-employers/managing.aspx.

National Autistic Society (2016), The autism employment gap: too much information in the workplace, London: The National Autistic Society.

O'Dell, L., Bertilsdotter Rosqvist, H., Ortega, F., Brownlow, C. and Orsini, M. (2016), Critical autism studies: exploring epistemic dialogues and intersections, challenging dominant understandings of autism, *Disability and Society*, **31**(2), 166–79.

Wales TUC (2017), Autism awareness in the workplace: Wales toolkit, Cardiff: Wales TUC.

Wales TUC (2019), Autism awareness in the workplace: a toolkit for trade unionists, Cardiff: Wales TUC, accessed at https://www.tuc.org.uk/autism-awareness-workplace.

5
Flexibility in recession and recovery

Stewart Johnstone and Stephen Procter

BACKGROUND AND CONTEXT OF THE ORGANISATION

AutoParts designs and manufactures automotive components for heavy duty commercial vehicles, including trucks, buses and agricultural equipment. Production began at the site in the 1990s, and has grown significantly since its inception, in terms of both employment numbers and production output. Manufacturing activity is focused around two main business streams. First, the assembly of automotive components supplied to vehicle manufacturers for installation in new vehicles, and secondly the production of aftermarket components which must be replaced by users at regular intervals through the life of vehicles. While demand for new parts closely reflects volatile automotive markets, demand for replacement components is generally more stable and predictable.

THE FLEXIBLE EMPLOYMENT MODEL

Given the overall variability of demand patterns, the production workforce has traditionally comprised permanent employees on open-ended contracts, and a proportion of temporary staff provided by an employment agency. This helps the business scale up during peak demand (by sourcing additional agency staff and offering overtime), and to scale down during a lull (by reducing agency staff and overtime). The flexible employment model thus allows the company to easily adjust the number of workers and hours worked, and this was believed to help protect both the business and permanent employees from market fluctuations.

A flexible employment model was believed to be essential to allow the business to align staffing levels with seasonal patterns, such as the decline in demand during European factory shutdowns in summer, as well as more unpredictable changes linked to changing market conditions. Senior managers agreed that the utilisation of a proportion of agency workers was common practice in the automotive industry.

However, due to the general trajectory of overall growth, the policy had resulted in a sizeable number of long-serving 'temporary workers'. Managers acknowledged the ethical questions around such arrangements, and also commented that it might not make business sense to pay an ongoing premium for agency workers on a long-term basis. As one manager reflected, 'would it actually be cheaper to employ some of these people directly and pay them a severance payment should they be made redundant?'

BACKGROUND TO THE 2008 RECESSION

Prior to the recession, the financial performance of the business had been strong for several years, and the site had expanded and invested heavily in new technology. By 2007, production output had reached record levels and forecasts suggested this upward trajectory would continue. Senior management noted the challenges becoming evident in several US and European organisations in the second half of the year but the order book at AutoParts remained strong. In 2008, however, the uncertainty around the 'credit crunch' in financial markets and spectre of a major economic downturn had begun to emerge, and by September a senior manager noted how:

> I was in a meeting and while we had seen demand fall over the summer we were still okay, doing reasonably well, people were still pretty confident. And I remember it was during that meeting that someone announced that Lehman Brothers had gone bust. And then I was concerned. Really concerned. Were we about to fall off a cliff? And I think it was within 30 days of that happening it was quite literally a crash.

An Operations Manager recounted how by October:

> I was in my office and someone came in and asked if our systems were down as orders had disappeared. And when we investigated, several orders had been cancelled and others postponed until the following year. You'd have TruckCo normally making 20,000 engines a month but in November 2008 they only sold 72 trucks. They didn't want anything at all from us – they had inventory. People simply stopped buying new trucks.

Fortunately, while demand for new components seemed suddenly to disappear, the aftermarket business stream is generally more stable, and it was believed that it could provide some level of insulation from the sharp decline in demand for new parts. Nevertheless by the end of 2008, and following over a decade of growth, production output had fallen by 50 per cent.

RESPONSES TO THE RECESSION (2008–2009)

In line with the flexible employment model, around one third of the production workforce were employed by an external employment agency. The first response was therefore to remove all agency workers from the business. A senior manager explained how in a downturn:

> The tough reality is that you shed your temps. It's like an insurance policy I guess. Yes, you pay an upfront premium for temps, but you can also let them go in an inexpensive and swift manner when a downturn comes. And so in this case that's exactly what we did.

Having quickly reduced the size of the production workforce, other measures were then considered, including the introduction of short-time working and a compulsory pay cut. However, given the lack of work, a decision was made to reduce the number of shifts from three to one. The suspension of the shift system meant that workers would no longer be entitled to shift premia, worth 20 per cent of their pay, and therefore allowed the company to cut the wage bill significantly. In addition, it was decided that the senior management team would adopt a four-day week.

As a senior manager explained:

> Officially it was short-time working for us, a four-day week, and we were able to share this with the workforce. Of course, in reality it was a salary sacrifice or pay cut as everyone was still in 5 or 6 days. And in the grand scheme of things, a leadership pay cut is going to make very little difference to the bottom line. But it was highly significant and symbolic. We're in this together and it's hurting us all. The workforce could see that management weren't just sitting in their ivory towers but were sharing the pain.

Having removed agency workers and reduced the number of shifts, many of the remaining workers in the beleaguered New Build business were then redeployed to the Aftermarket production areas where market demand was stronger. As the downturn continued to bite, further cost saving measures were then considered (see Table 5.1). As the HR Manager explained:

> We crunched the numbers again and worked out that we still needed to lose people. Now you can't always avoid compulsory redundancies but there was a deliberate move to avoid compulsory redundancies by any means necessary. People were able to enquire about what their package might be, no questions asked. Our view was that we should try and let the people who want to leave go, rather than focusing upon what they were doing. And to be honest if that meant long nights brainstorming how to sort things out then so be it.

Twenty members of staff left the business as part of the voluntary redundancy programme, from both production and administrative roles.

RECOVERY FROM RECESSION (2009–2011)

By spring there were signs of recovery in the New Build business as some orders began to be received. This was followed by a sudden surge of orders in Aftermarket, believed to reflect that users were servicing older vehicles rather than upgrading their fleets. The impact of the recession at AutoParts was therefore described as 'deep and quick', with a significant fall in demand during 2008 and 2009, followed by the beginning of a slow recovery later that year. By 2011, conditions in both business streams had improved significantly, and the company organised an end of year party to celebrate the recovery. For the company, the experience of the recession was believed to demonstrate the effectiveness of their flexible employment model, as it allowed the business to expand and contract relatively easily, reflecting changing market conditions, and to protect the employment of a 'core' workforce.

Table 5.1 Company labour flexibility strategies at AutoParts (2008–2014)

	Numerical (Flexibility in the number of employees)	Working time (Flexibility in working hours)	Functional (Flexibility in work organisation)	Consequences for business	Consequences for workers
The flexible employment model (–2008)	Agency staff in most cyclical areas but with regular and generally stable work. Most highly experienced. Allow organisation to flex down during quiet months by temporarily laying off agency staff (e.g. summer) and to flex up in times of high demand. 'Stable flexibility'	Overtime (extended hours or extra shifts) regularly offered to all staff during busy periods.	Limited functional flexibility. Staff generally work in a particular production area.	Buffer of experienced agency workers. Ability to better align production demand/hours with staffing levels. Reduce slack. Control costs. Protect 'core'.	Segmentation of workforce into core/periphery with different levels of employment security. Some evidence of 'temp to perm'. Some long-serving 'stable agency' workers unable to obtain permanent contracts.
Responses to recession (2008/9)	All agency staff removed from the business. Protection of the 'core' workforce but nevertheless a small number of voluntary redundancies.	Reduce number of shifts and implementation of standard working week. Loss of shift pay. No reduction in working hours. Elimination of overtime working. Short-time working for leadership team only.	Some permanent staff redeployed from New Build to Aftermarket following downturn in New Build demand	Ability to reduce costs by rapidly and easily reducing workforce size. Ability to reduce costs by eliminating overtime and shift allowance. Minimise redundancies. Protect 'core'.	All agency staff leave the business. Some remaining permanent workers expected to carry out different roles. Remaining permanent staff adopt different working patterns and lose shift allowance. Some voluntary redundancies for permanent staff.
Recovery (2009–2011)	Agency staff return to business.	Overtime offered to all staff during busy periods. Increase number of shifts. Return of shift pay.	Limited functionality flexibility. Staff generally work in same role. Agency staff sourced to fill vacancies.	Ability to scale up workforce to meet rising production demand	Some former agency staff re-join the business. Permanent workers continue in their new roles.
Responses to recovery (2011–)	Increased use of agency staff across production. Redevelopment of a buffer of 'stable temps'. Develop new layer of 'ad hoc temps' use to fine-tune staffing levels.	Overtime in times of peak demand. New group of ad hoc agency workers with no guaranteed hours provide daily/hourly flexibility.	Limited functional flexibility. Staff generally work in same role.	Ability to scale workforce up and down on a monthly, weekly, daily and hourly basis. Further reduce slack. Further reduce costs.	Further segmentation of workforce into core, 'stable temps' and 'ad hoc temps' with varying degrees of uncertainty. Limited evidence of 'temp to perm'. Some long-serving 'stable agency' workers unable to obtain permanent contracts. 'Ad hoc' agency workers unable to obtain regular work.

RESPONSES TO RECOVERY (2011–)

Yet despite the broadly positive assessments of how the business had navigated recession, a review of the flexible employment model was deemed necessary. As a senior manager explained: 'Following the recession, we realised we'd really felt our way through and we needed to look at things differently going forward. I think it was a wakeup call for a number of people. There's a lot of volatility out there.'

Since the crisis a number of changes to the flexibility strategy were noted. First, prior to the recession staffing levels were normally decided locally by line managers, based on their prior experience and personal judgements. New policies have since been implemented which mean that local managers must obtain various approvals before increasing staffing levels. Also, rather than relying on managerial judgement, a computer programme now determines the optimum number of operatives required based upon production levels. As a line manager explained: 'In the past, I could ring up the agency, say I want 10 more people. Now you plan all your work, feed it into an Excel spreadsheet, and it tells you straightaway how many people you need. Before it was much more rough cut.'

Second, there have been changes in the composition of the workforce. Prior to the recession there was a segmentation between the permanent staff and a buffer of 'stable temps' employed by an agency, and who would typically account for around one third of the workforce. Since the recession, however, the proportion of agency workers has increased to around 50 per cent of the workforce. An HR Manager also admitted that 'temp to perm' conversions are now much rarer than before, and that as permanent staff have left the business voluntarily, they have usually been replaced by an agency worker. However, as well as the increase in the number of agency staff, there has also been a change in their utilisation. As a production operative explained:

> We used to have two groups of workers and now we have three. There are those with permanent contracts. Then you've got your 'permanent agency', been here for years, very skilled. Then you've got your temporary agency who just come in and out. None of this officially exists but it's how we see it on the shopfloor.

As these flexible workers are not guaranteed any work, the HR manager explained that this now gives the business daily and even hourly flexibility. Agency workers can also be sent home if there is no work, due for example to a production outage. This clearly contrasts with the dominant model prior to the recession where most agency workers benefited from stable, predictable ongoing employment. For the business this was believed to allow the site to be 'leaner and more robust', though some questioned the ethical dimension of this approach. As a manager noted: 'One week they're in and the next they're not. It's really difficult. You're wondering when your next work is coming. It may be a sound business strategy but it's not nice to people. You could say it's selfish of the business.' However, as the HR Manager concluded: 'It's simply something we need to do and means we can protect the business and permanent workforce going forward. The stuff we have to do from a business perspective can be hard.'

QUESTIONS

1 What are the challenges and benefits of the approach taken in this organisation?

2 How can this case study be explained in terms of models of the 'flexible firm' (for example Ackroyd and Procter, 1998; Atkinson, 1984; Lepak and Snell, 2002; Wright and Snell, 1998)?

3 Why are companies in the UK, where employment protection legislation is relatively weak, so keen to employ temporary workers?

4 How would you evaluate the outcomes of the approach taken at AutoParts for the business?

5 How would you evaluate the outcomes of the approach taken at AutoParts for workers? Consider in particular the psychological contract from the perspective of (a) protected core workers; (b) 'permanent' temporary workers; (c) 'flexible' temporary workers.

REFERENCES

Ackroyd, S. and Procter, S. 1998. British manufacturing organization and workplace industrial relations: some attributes of the new flexible firm. *British Journal of Industrial Relations*, **36**(2), 163–83.

Atkinson, J. 1984. Manpower strategies for flexible organisations. *Personnel Management*, **16**(8), 28–31.

Lepak, D.P. and Snell, S.A. 2002. Examining the human resource architecture: the relationships among human capital, employment, and human resource configurations. *Journal of Management*, **28**(4), 517–43.

Johnstone, S. 2019. Employment practices, labour flexibility and the Great Recession: an automotive case study. *Economic and Industrial Democracy*, **40**(3), 537–59.

Wright, P.M. and Snell, S.A. 1998. Toward a unifying framework for exploring fit and flexibility in strategic human resource management. *Academy of Management Review*, **23**(4), 756–72.

SECTION II
HR STRATEGY, REWARDS AND PERFORMANCE

6
Determinants of human resource management strategy in a franchise

Ashlea Kellner

INTRODUCTION

There are some different – and interesting – characteristics about HRM in franchises that make for a unique case study. Franchises straddle contrasting business types, and hence, their approach to managing people is distinctive. Franchises systems are managed by a 'franchisor' (the owner of the brand, business systems and intellectual property), and supported by a Corporate Office that generally operates like a large business. The Corporate Office maintains functions like marketing, finance, IT, operations, site development, and – sometimes – HRM. Often, the franchisor also owns and manages corporate 'units' (stores) whose employees are legally employed by the franchisor. Other units are owned and managed by 'franchisees', essentially independent business people who purchase the rights to use the franchisor's trademarked name and business model to sell a product or service in their own unit. Typically, these franchised units are small businesses operating in the framework of a large business system.

In a fully corporate-owned business with multiple sites, HRM policy can be dictated to employed frontline managers who implement it. In franchises, however, there are restrictions, and drawbacks, of being overly invested and involved in how franchisees manage HR in their units. Conversely, there are also risks involved with completely disassociating from franchisees' HRM activities. In this chapter, we consider the factors that complicate the franchisor's decisions about appropriate HRM strategy in franchise systems. Drawing on a well-established Australian café chain – which we will call The Coffee Chain – this chapter will demonstrate the key factors that determine this franchisor's approach to managing HR in their business.

BUSINESS OVERVIEW

The Coffee Chain is an Australian café brand, owned by a larger entity that also owns two other food brands. With around 400 stores (300 in Australia, the remainder overseas), The Coffee Chain is one of the largest food franchises in the country. There are a number of store variations, from counter service kiosks to fully-licensed table service restaurants serving prepared meals. The system is almost fully franchised, retaining only a small number of corporate stores.

Since its inception three decades ago, The Coffee Chain has experienced significant expansion, particularly in recent years. While the organisation has long considered itself to be a young, small, family-style business, ongoing expansion has forced them to reconsider this image. In the last decade the brand has opened stores in New Zealand, the Middle East, the Maldives and South East Asia. This expansion has required a shift from an ad hoc small business style of management to a more formalised and professional approach.

Prior to 2007, The Coffee Chain did not operate an HR department, and HR support provided to its Australian franchisees was minimal. As they grew in size, a need arose for someone to manage the initial and ongoing franchisee training more formally – at least in respect to its Australian franchise operation. In 2007, the Corporate Office recruited a Learning and Development (L&D) Manager, with an established HRM background in non-franchised organisations. The L&D Manager recognised an opportunity to provide a higher level of support to the Australian franchisees in the broader area of HRM, while raising general matters of consideration for its franchisees.

> Because my experience was providing information and advice to line managers, when I came here I saw a gap and corresponding potential risk - we're not providing information nor supporting our franchisees in this area. My philosophy, stemming from an L&D background, is that 'people can only do what they know'. If our franchisees don't know, they can't act accordingly. I could see a possible risk to The Coffee Chain brand. The more I think about it retrospectively, the more I realise it's my corporate background that has influenced my actions. Having not come from the franchising sector, I had no preconceived ideas nor paradigms about what the franchisor should or should not be doing (L&D Manager, 2009).

This quote highlights the understanding in the franchise sector that there are HR practices that the Corporate Office typically would not involve themselves in. In a non-franchised business, however, such practices *would* have corporate involvement. There are many factors that influence the strategic decisions that businesses make about HRM strategy. In franchises, two particularly pertinent factors are the compliance environment and brand protection.

THE COMPLIANCE ENVIRONMENT

The L&D Manager hired in 2007 progressed over the next couple of years to become the HR Manager. This was a time of prolonged labour market reform in Australia, which saw significant changes to employment conditions. In the 2007 federal election, the Australian Labour Party came into power and the existing legislation governing employment (the *Workplace Relations Act 1996*) was soon repealed. As the government began designing a new workplace relations system (that would later be governed by the *Fair Work Act 2009*) it appeared the employment relations environment in Australia was going to become even more complex and difficult for franchisees to interpret. The HR Manager identified a need at this time to create a level of HRM and particularly employment-related support for franchisees.

The Coffee Chain moved on to provide support in all key HR functions such as employee recruitment, induction and training, employment templates, HR policies and regular assessments to ensure fair and compliant franchisee behaviour. Although comfortable advising franchisees on general HRM, the HR Manager was less familiar with complex employment matters such as unfair dismissal claims or determining correct rates of pay. Any advice given to franchisees could potentially place the Corporate Office at risk of liability for providing misinformation. For example, if the L&D Manager advised franchisees to use a pay rate subsequently proved incorrect, staff could be underpaid, and the Corporate Office – rather than the franchisee – could have been legally responsible. So, over the next decade, a key factor influencing the HR strategy of The Coffee Chain was how to avoid the risk of liability posed by providing advice to franchisees.

The HR Department went to great lengths to protect the franchisor from liability. Legal notices, including disclaimers, were included in all materials or communications provided to franchisees. This reconfirmed amongst other points that information provided by the team was of a general nature and franchisees should seek specialist advice. Notes of all verbal conversations with franchisees and Corporate Office staff were documented. Even the basic methods of communicating and phrasing of advice had to be considered, as the HR Manager explained:

> You have to be so careful with what you tell franchisees. I structure all of my emails as employer–employee… So I say, 'if the employer has a situation like this then the employer must do this'. I'm not telling them what they should be doing… They take that information away and think – is that my situation? Should I do that? So I'm not giving specific advice. I am very, very careful. (2009)

Around one decade later, the compliance environment dramatically shifted again, following the introduction of an amendment to the *Fair Work Act (2009)*, known as the *Protecting Vulnerable Workers Bill (2017)*. This amendment appeared to be largely in response to a high-profile case against convenience store franchise 7-Eleven, where rampant and systematic employment violations were publicly exposed. The legislation enabled a shift of responsibility for ensuring compliance with employment obligations from the franchisee to the franchisor, with penalties in the order of up to $630 000. Franchisors (or holding companies) could now be liable for franchisees' employment violations if it were deemed the franchisor knew (or could have reasonably known) the franchisee wasn't following workplace laws, or if they didn't take reasonable steps to prevent it. This placed a new responsibility on franchisors, particularly corporate managers responsible for HRM or wage compliance, to ensure processes were in place to prevent franchisee non-compliance and to monitor their behaviour.

Comparative to similar franchises, The Coffee Chain had already demonstrated a well-developed and robust HRM system. However, this change to the compliance environment required a reconsideration of strategy and HRM support available to franchisees. As the new HR Manager stated after the introduction of the amendment:

> We reviewed all of our internal processes to make sure that they were robust enough against the legislation. We have engaged another fulltime employee that has a focus on the compliance side of things. We have implemented the employee assistance line as I mentioned. We have developed the information kit for the franchisees that we distributed. We also wrote [what is] effectively a Complaints Handling Procedure, internal, for us. (2018)

The HR team increased in size significantly from two employees in 2007, to nine employees in 2018, with more of a focus on employment relations specialisation. The franchisor now actively encourages franchisees to approach the HR team with employment queries, given they can potentially be found responsible for non-compliant behaviour. There is of course still concern about liability for provision of misinformation, although this is a less prominent factor in their decision-making process, given the increase in employment specialists in the team: 'Yes, there is that concern that providing advice could be potentially making us liable. But on the other end of things, who better to provide advice than people who work in this particular business, in this particular industry.' (HR Manager, 2018).

Changes to the legislative and compliance environment have had a strong effect on the overall HR strategy and practices adopted by The Coffee Chain. Another significant, if not equally important, factor that has over time influenced the way HR is managed is the effect of non-compliance on the brand and reputation of the system.

PROTECTING THE BRAND

Success of franchise units is heavily dependent on customers recognising the brand. Both positive and negative actions of the franchisee and franchisor equally affect all those associated with the brand. Accordingly, when one franchisee is exposed publicly for a negative incident or behaviour, this impact is equally shared by all members of the brand. Protection of the brand from opportunistic franchisee behaviours is thus a driver for franchisors to become more involved in the operation of the unit (Paik and Choi, 2007).

Franchisees and franchisors have different core interests, which can lead to franchisees engaging in behaviours that benefit them but that are injurious to the franchisor and the brand. Franchisees are most likely to engage in opportunistic behaviours to increase profit or reduce costs (Felstead, 1993). This can be manifested in behaviours that directly or indirectly damage the brand, such as overcharging customers, offering a substandard product, underpaying staff or paying 'cash in hand'. Monitoring and controlling franchisees is therefore imperative to minimising the risk of engagement in brand-damaging behaviours (Pizanti and Lerner, 2003).

Even as early as 2008, the HR Manager was very clear that brand protection was the foremost objective of the role at The Coffee Chain:

> When we have an issue, like a parent calling about their daughter who was on an unpaid trial, I conduct an investigation… The franchisee may say – no, we had a verbal agreement that I wouldn't pay her. What are we going to do for the sake of $19? The answer is obvious – we will pay her. We could ignore the complaint, it's only $19. But if the parents take her to the media it looks really bad for us. (2008)

At this time, media coverage of employment law contraventions by organisations such as this in fact received almost no attention. An analysis by Clibborn and Wright (2018) showed that in 2008 there were less than 20 reports in major Australian newspapers mentioning the term 'underpayment'.

Fast forward past 2015 and the scandalous coverage of the 7-Eleven non-compliance story, media reporting on underpayments increased more than tenfold from 2008 to 2018. There is heightened public interest in stories of employment violations, and this appears particularly the case for well-known franchises. Staying out of the news is now a more pressing role for the franchisor.

If the franchisor does not involve itself in franchisees' HRM activity, it faces the risk of franchisees damaging the brand through non-compliance with employment laws. As early as 2008, The Coffee Chain was aware of other Australian operated franchise groups that had received negative media attention in relation to handling employment issues. The organisation found itself in a no-win situation: if they provided support they risked liability; if they did not provide support they risked damage to the brand. Eventually, it was agreed protection of the brand was paramount, and all steps would be taken to minimise the risk of liability. By 2018, their level of involvement and monitoring of employment and HRM activities was high in comparison to other franchises. In the following section we summarise the HR strategy and practices adopted by The Coffee Chain.

DETERMINING THE BEST APPROACH TO HRM

From 2008, the HR Manager began building a robust system based on underlying philosophies of brand protection and fostering a supportive and sustainable relationship with franchisees. The team developed an HR strategy and formalised a number of practices including: an HRM component of the franchisee induction; an ongoing franchisee leadership programme; an audit of some HRM behaviours; full recruitment and selection for new stores; employee online training; and assistance with employment relations (ER) issues. In the early days, The Coffee Chain had a capable HR team but was reluctant to get too involved (as they saw it) in complex employment matters:

> In the majority of cases we leave it up to the franchisee to address specific issues and take the appropriate action. However, there are a few occasions when we do get actively involved in a situation. This might take the form of a facilitated discussion between a franchisee and an employee, making them both aware of their respective obligations. (2008)

As time has passed, with the changes to the compliance environment and increased risk of brand damage through media reporting, many aspects of the HR system have been 'ramped up'. The franchisor entered into a voluntary agreement with the statutory body of the Australian Government known as the 'Fair Work Ombudsman'. This collaborative relationship publicly demonstrates business commitment to creating a compliant workplace and places requirements on the franchisor to meet conditions around training, communication, reporting and monitoring of employment activity.

By 2018, The Coffee Chain was undertaking regular auditing of franchisees' employment processes through two forms of audit, as the HR Manager explains:

> In response to the amendment of the legislation, we have implemented what we call an express HR audit. So, what I suppose that is, is a shortened version of our usual full audit, and

the express audit is about gathering key pieces of information from a franchisee as a temperature check to see how they are tracking generally against legislation. We also have an option for what we call a full audit… we're looking for a roster, payslips, superannuation receipts, and contracts of employment, position descriptions. The full audit goes a bit deeper, potentially for a longer period of time. It might be interviewing employees as part of that process.

The franchisor conducts a full audit of at least 25 per cent of units in the system annually. They have also increased the ER content delivered to franchisees in their induction, and the breadth and depth of ER information communicated to franchisees through other forms of media (such as newsletters, emails and conferences). The HR Manager maintains it is not only the compliance environment and brand protection that are drivers of their high involvement in HRM. They believe maintenance of a strong franchise relationship where franchisees feel supported is beneficial to both parties:

For the franchisees [offering support] provides them another opportunity to build rapport and a relationship with the support office because – I'm not sure what your experience shows, but I would have thought that typically with the more hands-off franchisors that there would be a perception that it's an ivory tower and really they don't care about us, they just want their franchise fees. (2018)

In all, it seems the philosophy and approach to HRM in this case has followed the same trajectory for ten years. The case has settled into a strategy that acknowledges the importance of the franchise relationship, responds actively to changes in the compliance environment, and seeks to avoid negative publicity and damage to the brand.

SUMMARY

Determination of the most appropriate HRM strategy for a business is complex and there are many internal and external influencing factors. Typically, large and small organisations adopt distinct approaches to HRM, but franchises are a kind of combination of both organisational types. Hence, their approach to HRM tends to represent a unique hybrid.

Franchises are subject to changing environmental conditions just like other business forms. In this case we examined the determinants of a franchisor's approach to HRM, specifically the changes to the compliance environment, and risk of brand damage. We identified how these determinants influenced changes over time in The Coffee Chain, and why this organisation made the strategic decision to pursue a position of high franchisor involvement and support in HRM.

There are costs and risks associated with their strategy that many franchisors in the same industry choose to avoid and hence decide to adopt a lower involvement approach to HRM. It is important to note that two organisations can operate in exactly the same external conditions and still weigh up risks differently, thus making different choices about their own HR philosophy and strategy.

QUESTIONS

1 What are the costs and risks associated with offering a high degree of HRM support to franchisees, such as The Coffee Chain?

2 If you were starting your own professional services franchise, hiring 'white collar' franchisees and employees, do you think franchisee non-compliance with employment legislation would pose the same level of concern as in a café franchise? Explain.

3 Considering Porter's (1985) strategies for competitive advantage, The Coffee Chain could be classified as pursuing a 'quality enhancement strategy'. If The Coffee Chain were pursuing a 'cost reduction strategy', how might the HR approach be different?

REFERENCES

Clibborn, S. and Wright, C.F. (2018). Employer theft of temporary migrant workers' wages in Australia: Why has the state failed to act? *The Economic and Labour Relations Review*, **29**(2), 207–27.

Felstead, A. (1993). *The Corporate Paradox: Power and Control in the Business Franchise*. London: Routledge.

Kellner, A., Townsend, K., Wilkinson, A. and Peetz, D. (2014). Decaf or double shot? The strength of franchisor control over HRM in coffee franchises. *Human Resource Management Journal*, **24**(3), 323–38.

Paik, Y. and Choi, D.Y. (2007). Control, autonomy and collaboration in the fast food industry: A comparative study between domestic and international franchising. *International Small Business Journal*, **25**(5), 539–62.

Pizanti, I. and Lerner, M. (2003). Examining control and autonomy in the franchisor–franchisee relationship. *International Small Business Journal*, **21**(2), 131–59.

Porter, M. (1985). *Competitive Advantage*. New York: Free Press.

7
Contribution based pay in local government

Mathew Johnson

BACKGROUND AND CONTEXT

County Council is located in the South East of England, serving a population of over half a million residents in mostly rural locations with a number of small towns (where council offices are typically concentrated). It is a high wage area with high property prices owing to the relatively short commuting distance to central London by rail and road.

The council itself employs nearly 4000 workers covering a wide range of occupations including professionals such as social workers, town planners, and solicitors, as well as operational roles such as cleaners, catering staff and waste operatives. The council has a board of corporate directors that reports to the Chief Executive of the council, who in turn is accountable to democratically elected political leaders (currently the Conservative political group that holds more than 80 per cent of ward seats across the area).

The council is organised into four 'business units': services for adults; services for children; resources and staffing; and transport, economy and environment. Around half of all services are provided directly by the council and half are outsourced to the private, voluntary and independent sector. HR at County Council is highly centralised, with strategy and policies developed corporately for the whole council, supported by a 'business partner' model offering dedicated support to individual business units. Along with the rest of the council HR has faced significant reductions in resources and staffing levels, and some transactional HR services such as payroll and recruitment are now outsourced to a third party private sector firm that also manages the online cafeteria benefits system of staff discounts and salary sacrifice schemes for travel passes and bicycles.

At around 25 per cent, trade union membership density is comparatively low for the local government sector (which is over 40 per cent nationally), but County Council recognises two main local government unions (UNISON and GMB) and one teachers' union (AUT) for the purposes of 'consultation'. County Council withdrew from national collective bargaining in the early 1990s in order to strengthen direct control over workforce spending, and this local flexibility was crucial to create the scope for managers to overhaul pay systems.

The danger for County Council is that it would be repeating the mistakes of the past. Performance related pay (PRP) in the public sector has been criticised for encouraging instrumental behaviour and weakening collective professional identities (e.g. Marsden, 2004), and a number of local authorities that experimented with PRP in the 1980s and 1990s either abandoned it owing to the bureaucratic burden of administering individualised pay, or managers diluted it to such an extent (in order to maintain worker cooperation) that it became almost meaningless (Bryson et al., 1993; Heery, 1998). Furthermore there were concerns about using performance pay to recruit and retain as labour markets slackened in the recession of the early 1990s. Given these challenges, around 85 per cent of local authorities remain within the national collective bargaining agreement – the NJC Green Book of terms and conditions (Grimshaw et al., 2017). Under this agreement, local authorities follow a national pay spine (that runs from around £17 500 per annum to £46 000) but they are free to decide where to position individual jobs on this pay spine in accordance with established job evaluation procedures. The harmonisation of blue and white collar jobs onto a single pay spine along with the removal of locally administered bonus payments was designed to tackle long-standing issues of gender pay inequality (Oliver et al., 2014).

AUSTERITY AND PRESSURES FOR REFORM

After 2010, in common with most local authorities in England and Wales, County Council found itself faced with severe cuts in central government grants at the same time as demand for services (particularly older people's care) was steadily increasing. This initially triggered a wave of downsizing and internal restructuring as the council looked to rationalise services and reduce staffing costs. Sustained year on year cuts, however, exhausted what could be achieved through incremental 'salami slicing' and managers within the council began looking at more fundamental and transformational changes to cut costs and improve performance.

This coincided with the election of a new Conservative group leader with a background in the private sector who sought to implement more radical reforms of both service delivery and workforce management. This period of change allowed the council to 'break with the past' in respect of dealing with the trade unions, while also renegotiating relationships with workers about their individual contribution to the successful performance of the organisation. For example the council sought to replace costly and 'rigid' job-related enhancements such as overtime rates, weekend/bank holiday supplements and unsocial working premiums, with 'cafeteria benefits' such as discounted rates on utilities and mobile phone contracts, as well as salary sacrifice schemes for bicycles and public transport. Direct communications became increasingly important to set out the new 'vision' for the council, which was strongly oriented toward business efficiency and performance, with greater personal accountability for results. This 'new deal' with the workforce was most clearly articulated in the adoption of Contribution Based Pay (CBP) in 2014.

TIGHTENING THE LINK BETWEEN PAY AND PERFORMANCE

The new Contribution Based Pay system at County Council was designed to signal the modernisation of pay and rewards at the council, bringing it much closer in line with what was perceived by politicians and senior managers to be 'best practice' in the private sector. There were also potential cost savings to be made by decoupling pay rises from workers' length of service, which managers argued resulted in 'unearned' increases for some low performing workers. The key elements of CBP are summarised in Table 7.1.

Table 7.1 Summary of CBP at County Council

Principles	Assessment	Reward mix
Contribution to organisational success	6-monthly appraisal	Total budget for pay awards set by politicians annually
Demonstrating desired attitudes and behaviours	Line-manager judgements overseen by senior management	Mixture of consolidated increase and cash bonus
Incentivise improvement and excellence	Rigorous appeals procedure	Average uplift 2.5%

The CBP system appraises all staff from entry level positions all the way up to corporate directors on a four-step performance ranking (unsatisfactory, satisfactory, good, outstanding), based on the line manager's judgement of individual contribution to organisational success as well as evidence of positive attitudes and behaviours such as 'organisational citizenship' and a 'can-do attitude'. Performance objectives are defined at the start of the appraisal period with a clear link between the tasks, duties and performance goals within individual roles and the overarching corporate objectives. Managers argued that there had to be clear incentives to drive up performance standards and to embed a culture of 'continuous improvement', and variable pay was seen as an instrumental means to achieve this.

Pay increases under the CBP scheme are a combination of consolidated increases in basic pay as staff move through competency stages for three years (entry, competent and advanced), supplemented by non-consolidated cash bonuses for those workers reaching a 'good' or 'outstanding' level of performance. Workers who only reach a satisfactory level of performance would remain on the competent point with no cash bonus (designed to reduce the costs attached with those workers who are 'coasting') and workers who returned an unsatisfactory level of performance would remain on the entry point with no cash bonus. In both of these cases training and development goals would be identified in order to facilitate an improvement in performance.

In order to embed the new performance culture at County Council, CBP is anchored to a new performance management framework that seeks to increase the frequency of appraisal meetings, and to standardise the broad principles of setting and reviewing targets while also allowing some discretion around the specific targets and training needs for individual workers. Setting and reviewing performance targets is designed to be a collaborative process between line managers and workers, and performance judgements are moderated by senior managers to promote consistency and transparency. A formal appeals process has also been introduced to allow an independent review of performance judgements where workers dispute the outcome (but this has only been activated in a small number of cases).

Whether performance pay does increase individual productivity over the long run is debatable (e.g. Marsden, 2004) but certainly the CBP scheme at County Council could be regarded as somewhat 'marginal' in the magnitude of the incentives on offer: staff receiving the top performance judgement could receive a 5 per cent increase but the average uplift across all performance levels was only 2.5 per cent.

THE UNION VIEW

UNISON vociferously opposed the move to CBP, and along with one of the teachers' unions refused to recommend it to their local members during the consultation process. In order to work around the trade unions the council shared the details of the new scheme directly with the wider workforce through individual communications, a dedicated intranet page and open meetings led by directors and senior politicians. Furthermore, the council offered staff a one-off payment of £750 to switch from collectively agreed pay, and around 95 per cent of staff opted into contribution based pay. This was seen by management as a 'vindication' of the new pay system and also reflective of the success of direct staff engagement (rather than the £750 cash payment).

The chief concern within the UNISON branch was that while senior managers and professional staff may derive benefit from an accelerated performance pay system, it would be difficult for those in low-paid jobs with little autonomy and clearly defined outputs to exceed their performance targets and get a bonus. In this sense CBP was seen potentially as a way to justify pay gaps between different levels of seniority, whether or not the levels of effort, performance or success were objectively higher. At the same time, the ambiguous scope and definition of 'expected behaviours' within the performance management framework was potentially a way of creating a cultural expectation of 'over-work': 'They [staff] are taking work home they are doing this that and the other because it's part of the [expected] "behaviour", they feel that [it] will count against them if they don't' (Union rep.).

In broad terms UNISON argued that the real motive for the introduction of CBP was the determination of increasingly hard-line managers and new political leadership (since 2011) to sweep away notions of 'custom and practice' or 'felt fair' comparisons when setting pay awards, and replace them with highly individualised pay modelled on the private sector with little or no input from the trade unions. The new process for setting pay combined with a management sponsored network of 'employee-representatives' was expected to further marginalise the unions and effectively end collective negotiations at a local level.

To try and protect against potential biases in the way in which performance judgements were made, the council introduced the new appraisal system a year ahead of CBP 'going live'. During this period changes were made to the appraisal matrix for management roles as it appeared that they were much more likely than practitioner roles or support roles to receive 'successful' or 'outstanding' judgements (which validated the concerns raised by UNISON that performance pay was skewed towards rewarding managers).

One of the explicit aims of CBP was to strengthen the appraisal process which had in the past been used in an inconsistent way by line managers, resulting in a weak system of staff development with limited goal-setting and feedback. Viewed in this way, contribution based pay was as much a means to correct for poor management as it was poor worker performance.

Furthermore, the specific effects of performance pay on productivity were difficult to disentangle from the wider processes of downsizing and restructuring since 2010. A UNISON shop steward who had been through the appraisal process argued that as a result of staffing reductions since 2010 most staff were already working 'flat out', so the lever of variable pay would be unlikely to realise any significant productivity gains in operational roles.

The council claimed that following the introduction of CBP there had been a 1 per cent productivity increase that was 'worth' around £3m in terms of the increased volume and quality of work performed by individual workers, and reductions in waste and duplication. This figure is hard to verify and HR managers recognised there was no straightforward relationship between pay and productivity, noting that any additional worker effort was likely to be as much a result of the increased attention to feedback and performance management as the motivating effect of bonus payments per se. Further cost reductions were achieved by moving the appraisal system online (saving an estimated £1.4m) and reducing the number of discrete job descriptions from over 1000 to 120 organised into ten broad 'job families'. This saved around £50k by reducing the time taken to undertake detailed job evaluation procedures either when creating new roles or restructuring existing roles.

At the same time, spending on agency staff at the council increased by £500 000 per annum from 2010 as the council faced ongoing difficulties in recruiting and retaining key staff such as social workers and IT technicians. Despite criticism from the trade unions the council turned to temporary staffing solutions at a cost of up to £300 per day for some specialist roles. The council was also paying additional 'market supplements' to attract staff for senior management roles as base salaries and the offer of performance bonuses were not enough to lure skilled and experienced workers away from London. Although this may have been a necessary short-term solution it potentially cuts across the council's efforts to make a stronger link between pay and individual performance (rather than external labour market conditions). In respect of overall organisational performance, external auditors downgraded the rating of the council's social care services, citing high levels of turnover as a key problem.

SUMMARY

As this case demonstrates, the adoption of performance related pay often creates a number of positive and negative outcomes. At County Council the adoption of contribution based pay reflected the desire of politicians to introduce a private sector style approach, but the implementation process raised a number of important tensions. There was resistance from the trade unions and some staff members, and there were concerns about the change in the tone of local HRM and employment relations. More broadly, as has been shown in a number of studies, PRP struggles to address more fundamental staffing issues such as high turnover.

QUESTIONS

1 What do you think management wanted to achieve by adopting contribution based pay? How likely is it that they will succeed?

2 Can individualised reward systems such as performance related pay co-exist with collective forms of employee representation such as through trade unions? How can these competing dynamics be reconciled?

3 What does the case study reveal about the practical problems associated with adopting new reward strategies? What contextual factors can undermine or counteract new systems?

REFERENCES

Bryson, C., Gallagher, J., Jackson, M., Leopold, J. and Tuck, K. (1993). Decentralisation of collective bargaining: local authority opt outs. *Local Government Studies*, **19**(4), 558–83.

Grimshaw, D., Johnson, M., Marino, S. and Rubery, J. (2017). Towards more disorganised decentralisation? Collective bargaining in the public sector under pay restraint. *Industrial Relations Journal*, **48**(1), 22–41.

Heery, E. (1998). A return to contract? Performance related pay in a public service. *Work, Employment and Society*, **12**(1), 73–95.

Marsden, D. (2004). The role of performance-related pay in renegotiating the 'effort bargain': the case of the British public service. *ILR review*, **57**(3), 350–70.

Oliver, L., Stuart, M. and Tomlinson, J. (2014). Equal pay bargaining in the UK local government sector. *Journal of Industrial Relations*, **56**(2), 228–45.

8
A high performance work system in a multi-stakeholder context

Eva Knies, Peter Leisink and Paul Boselie

INTRODUCTION

The focus of this chapter is on the renewal of HR policies and practices that resulted in a High Performance Work System (HPWS) at the Dutch insurance company Achmea. As the majority of publications on HPWSs are based on studies of Fortune 500 companies, mainly from an Anglo-Saxon perspective (Keegan and Boselie 2006), the case of Achmea is appealing for various reasons: a range of stakeholders were involved in the creation of the HPWS (a characteristic of the Rhineland model of capitalism); Achmea is not quoted on the stock exchange; and the role of healthcare insurance providers such as Achmea is subject to major reforms resulting from economic and political developments. By studying the HPWS presented in this case study, one will gain insights into the impact of various contextual factors on the shaping of HPWSs, the relevant characteristics of an HPWS design, the different actors involved, and their interests and the outcomes related to the implementation of HPWSs.

SETTING THE STAGE

Achmea is a large insurance company located in the Netherlands. At the time of the renewal of its HR policies and practices (2007–2010), it employed over 20 000 people. The corporation had seven divisions which provide services to both corporate and individual client customers. The organisation is the market leader in the field of health insurance. The organisation has a long tradition of innovative HR policies, such as introducing a 'cafeteria reward system' (flexible employee benefit scheme) in the 1980s and 'teleworking' in the 1990s, and stakeholder value management. These stakeholders include customers, 'shareholders', distribution partners and employees. The term 'shareholder' is put between quotation marks because Achmea is not publicly listed and has only two institutional shareholders, namely the cooperative Rabobank and the foundation Achmea. Achmea adopts a partnership approach, meaning that the organisation places considerable value on its relationship with employees through their trade unions and the works council.

SENSE OF URGENCY

The healthcare sector in the Netherlands has been subject to many reforms, including the gradual introduction of market mechanisms. These developments have resulted in increased competition which challenges health insurance companies to deliver better service at less cost than their direct competitors. Such reforms affect organisations and their employees and raise new challenges for human resource management (HRM) policies and practices.

In addition to these changes in the market, organisations in the Netherlands are confronted with an increasing number of challenges as a result of demographic changes in the workforce. Western countries see an ageing population and, moreover, the workforce is becoming increasingly diverse, partly as a result of women and immigrants having a larger share of the labour market. Facing a tight future labour market and a growing diversity within the workforce, organisations face the challenge of recruiting and retaining highly motivated and competent employees if they are to maintain a high level of service delivery. Achmea took up this challenge by the introduction of a HPWS involving multiple stakeholders with an underlying approach that could be characterised as adopting a Rhineland perspective, incorporating multiple goals (individual, organisational and societal) (Beer et al., 2015).

RENEWAL OF HR POLICIES AND PRACTICES

Achmea's decision to create a HPWS was also inspired by the merger of Achmea with Interpolis, another insurance company. Achmea did not want simply to harmonise employment policies, it wanted more fundamentally to innovate its HR policies. Therefore, Achmea negotiated an agreement with the trade unions and the works council to design a HPWS. Such an agreement, which is part of a collective labour agreement, is legally binding under the Dutch labour law framework.

At the start of the design process at Achmea, there was no blueprint available for a HPWS design. A bottom-up approach was adopted to determine the main focus of the HR policy and practices. Various stakeholders were interviewed to explore the challenges they were facing and their perspectives on the aims of the innovation process and any preconditions to achieve these aims. Based on interviews with members of the executive board, top managers, HR managers, employees, and representatives of the works council and the trade unions, the HR department phrased the main focus of the new HR policy as follows:

> Employment in Achmea is aimed at developing, using and rewarding your talents as an employee. We believe in the strength of the individual. Every employee is different. Think of differences with regard to gender, ethnic background, life stage, knowledge and experience, and the way in which you see life. Achmea wants to use the strength of these differences. We want to use your talents at the right moment for activities that fit with your talents, your wishes, and your life stage.

FROM POLICY TO PRACTICES

Then the translation of this umbrella view into concrete action plans followed. This process began with a conference with all stakeholders involved to discuss the interview findings. To assure the link between HR outcomes and the business goals of each division, divisions were able to prioritise some practices over others. During the process of designing and implementing the HR practices, two deliberative bodies played an important role: the HR staff at corporate and division levels on the one hand, and the tripartite talks between Achmea as the employer, trade unions, and the works council on the other. On a regular basis, the translation of the vision into various HR practices and the overall progress were discussed. After three years, the result was a mix of practices laid down in HR policies as well as in the collective agreement (see Box 8.1).

> **BOX 8.1**
> **ACHMEA'S HIGH PERFORMANCE WORK PRACTICES**
>
> ABILITY PRACTICES
> - team budgets for training and development (including extra budgets for teams/departments facing reorganisation)
> - special attention to the recruitment of minorities (including refugees, immigrants, and disabled people)
> - encouragement of employees and supervisors to make personal development plans
> - introduction of 'My Career' (virtual career centre on the intranet)
> - health checks.
>
> MOTIVATION PRACTICES
> - continuous dialogue between employees and their supervisors (evaluation and feedback)
> - information about and support for internal promotion
> - flexible working hours and distribution of hours over the year (collective labour agreement)
> - opportunities to work from home.
>
> OPPORTUNITY PRACTICES
> - possibilities for job rotation
> - networking opportunities (for example through networks for women, young professionals and lesbian, gay, transgender and bisexual employees)
> - encouragement of employees to reflect upon their daily work practices and to come up with changes in work processes to improve the quality of service to customers (kaizen principle)
> - possibilities for voluntary community aid (collective labour agreement)
> - maternity coaching to support women pursuing their career after return from maternity leave.

RESULTS

The results of implementing these new HR practices are monitored using an annual survey. The results show that an increasing number of employees report that their talents are recognised and used by the organisation. Moreover, employees are more positive about their opportunities to achieve a good work–life balance. The level of perceived work pressures has remained the same. These results indicate that employees are positive about the implemented HR practices. However, the survey results also show some downsides of these new practices, with approximately 40 per cent of all employees reporting that the same amount of work has to be done with fewer people than a year earlier. The question is how these changes have affected employee and organisational outcomes.

Employees report that they are more satisfied with various aspects of their job (challenging work, pay, work pleasure, opportunities for development and promotion) than before the introduction of the new HR practices. Further, employees report that they are more willing to exert effort at work. Both employees and supervisors indicate that team performance has improved, meaning that customers get better value for money. These results indicate that both employees and Achmea have benefited (in terms of wellbeing and performance) from the implementation of these HR practices.

Overall, the works council and trade unions assess these changes positively. They continue to evaluate the progress and negotiate on measures in the collective agreement that guarantee and facilitate employees' employability.

TOP MANAGERS AND FRONTLINE SUPERVISORS

Two groups of internal stakeholders proved to be very important in the implementation of the renewed HR practices: frontline supervisors and top managers. Frontline supervisors are responsible for the enactment of HR practices. The results of the above-mentioned survey indicated that supervisors provided more support for their employees when they themselves were supported by their superiors. This finding encouraged the HR department and the executive board to introduce employee-related targets. Supervisors are now not only evaluated on the financial targets they achieve, but also on their people management performance. This performance is measured by asking employees in the annual survey to assess the leadership behaviour of their supervisor. To improve the support provided to their employees, all supervisors received training in improving people management skills.

Achmea's top management showed their support not only by introducing employee-related targets but also in other ways. When Achmea was facing the economic recession, the chairman of the executive board announced that Achmea would continue to renew its HR practices because this was a prerequisite for growth and stakeholder-value management. Through this, he acted as a role model: in showing leadership support he demonstrated that he practised what Achmea preaches.

SUMMARY AND OVERVIEW

HPWS

The Achmea case study is a clear example of the development of a HPWS that is aimed at achieving a sustained competitive advantage in a changing, highly competitive market. Appelbaum et al. (2000) define a HPWS as a bundle of HR practices aimed at creating employee abilities (A), motivation (M), and opportunities to participate (O). All three types of practice can be found in Achmea's HR system (see Box 8.1). The notion of 'internal fit' is an important feature of a HPWS. The alignment of individual HR practices, within a bundle or system of practices, is thought to create synergy (Delery, 1998). In other words, a fit between individual HR practices will strengthen the impact of HRM on performance outcomes. An internal fit between the individual HR practices in a coherent and consistent human resource system is assumed to lead to a higher performance than the sum of the individual HR practices (Kepes and Delery, 2007). In the case of Achmea, the alignment of individual practices is effectively guaranteed because all practices are in line with the main vision. An example of a fit between individual HR practices that strengthens the impact on performance is the encouragement to make personal development plans in combination with budgets for training and development, opportunities for job rotation, and internal promotion. As such, the system assures that all practices contribute to developing, using and rewarding the talents of all employees, regardless of their gender, ethnic background, life stage, knowledge and experience, and the way in which they see life.

Comparing Achmea's HPWS to the list of possible HR practices provided by Boselie (2010, p. 134), it is noteworthy that Achmea did not include all possible HR practices. Nevertheless, their approach still delivered positive outcomes. This observation is in line with the idea of so-called 'mini-bundles'. Based on extensive research, Guest et al. (2004) concluded that a limited set of HR practices can also result in heightened performance. The example of Achmea shows that creating a HPWS is not simply a matter of going through a checklist – it is important to align specific practices that fit with the overall HR strategy.

Contextual factors

Overall, the implementation of this HPWS resulted in positive employee and organisational outcomes. This success is partly rooted in the adoption of a partnership approach – a characteristic of the Rhineland model of capitalism which aims to create value for a range of diverse stakeholders (for example, shareholders, employees, trade unions, and society) (Beer et al., 2015; Paauwe and Boselie, 2003). Achmea decided, inspired by its cooperative roots, to involve representatives of the trade unions and the works council in the process, and to aim not only for high performance but also for employee wellbeing. Survey results confirm the working of the mutual gains principle: employees who are more satisfied with their jobs – and are therefore more willing to exert effort in their job – report that their teams perform better. Further, this is a mutually reinforcing mechanism: employees working in high performing teams report greater satisfaction. Having a customer-oriented focus contributed to these outcomes.

Taking a partnership approach has resulted in a HPWS that is firmly embedded in Achmea's HR strategy. HR practices are not only laid down in the organisation's HR policies, but also in the collective agreement. Achmea's innovation process shows that, contrary to what is often assumed, adopting a partnership approach not only involves dealing with constraints, it also requires sufficient leeway to make strategic choices (Boxall and Purcell, 2016).

Process

About one year prior to the change process, Achmea agreed with the trade unions and the works council to renew their HR policies and practices, although a detailed blueprint that mapped out the changes was not yet available. This was because the HR department decided not to take a top-down approach but, rather, to involve various stakeholders in the process. This bottom-up approach included interviewing employees, employees' representatives, and HR and other managers, installing a tripartite steering committee and allowing teams and departments to differentiate in their implementation of the HR practices. These elements all contributed to a sense of ownership by the different stakeholders, making them more willing to invest in the process. The HR department put a lot of effort into managing the relationship with the various stakeholders. For example, when some managers felt that the changes were more about employees than about the business, the HR team emphasised the consistency within the multiple goals. Moreover, they were committed to sending out a survey on the implementation to all employees and supervisors to demonstrate the win–win situation.

Actors in the implementation

Apart from the HR department, two other actors were critical in the implementation process: frontline managers and top managers. Line managers are responsible for implementing the HR policies and practices and, as such, employees' perceptions of the HPWS are heavily dependent on their supervisors' actions. Achmea has established conditions that contribute to an effective translation from HR rhetoric into reality. For example, all supervisors were trained to improve their people management skills, and employee-related targets were introduced to stimulate people management activities. Achmea's top management not only approved the introduction of employee-related targets, they also continued to show their support for the innovation process when Achmea was facing the economic recession. All these aspects continue to contribute to Achmea's high performance, a fact demonstrated by Achmea's place in the ranking of best employers in the Netherlands.

To conclude, our study of Achmea shows that a HPWS's contribution to superior organisational performance is not only about the HR practices included but also about the process and the context. According to Kirby (2005), High Performance Organisations (HPOs) share some important features. Many of these are also characteristic of Achmea's approach to renewing its HR policy and practices. By taking a partnership approach and involving a range of stakeholders from the start of the process, a sense of ownership was created, as well as a collective state of mindfulness. By formulating an overarching HR philosophy, a shared mission was created. By acknowledging the crucial role of line managers in the implementation, it was recognised that leadership at all levels is important. These elements are all linked by the underlying ambition to create value for customers, employees, shareholders and society, and thereby contributed to the unique nature of Achmea's renewal of its HR policy and practices.

> **QUESTIONS**
>
> 1 Identify specific human resource practices within Achmea that serve multiple stakeholders' interests (mutual gains). Further, name at least two practices that have potential downsides for one or more stakeholders.
>
> 2 In what ways did the works council and trade unions assist in the design and introduction of the HPWS? What is your opinion about this type of employee representative participation in decision making?
>
> 3 What factors contributed to the support from Achmea's top management for the organisational change process described?
>
> 4 Did any barriers exist that could have prevented the implementation of the HPWS by frontline managers? If so, what were these, and how could these be overcome?

REFERENCES

Appelbaum, E., Bailey, T., Berg, P. and Kalleberg, A. 2000, *Manufacturing advantage: why high-performance work systems pay off*, Ithaca, NY: Cornell University Press.

Beer, M., Boselie, P. and Brewster, C. 2015, 'Back to the future: Implications for the field of HRM of the multistakeholder perspective proposed 30 years ago', *Human Resource Management*, **54** (3): 427–38.

Boselie, P. 2010, *Strategic human resource management: a balanced approach*, Maidenhead: McGraw-Hill.

Boxall, P. and Purcell, J. 2016, *Strategy and human resource management*, 4th edn, New York: Palgrave Macmillan.

Delery, J.E. 1998, 'Issues of fit in strategic human resource management: Implications for research', *Human Resource Management Review*, **8** (3): 289–309.

Guest, D., Conway, N. and Dewe, P. 2004, 'Using sequential tree analysis to search for "bundles" of HR practices', *Human Resource Management Journal*, **14** (1): 79–96.

Keegan, A. and Boselie, P. 2006, 'The lack of impact of dissensus inspired analysis on developments in the field of human resource management', *Journal of Management Studies*, **43** (7): 1492–511.

Kepes, S. and Delery, J. 2007, 'HRM systems and the problem of internal fit', in P. Boxall, J. Purcell and P.M. Wright (eds), *The Oxford handbook of human resource management*, Oxford: Oxford University Press, pp. 385–404.

Kirby, J. 2005, 'Toward a theory of high performance', *Harvard Business Review*, **83** (7): 30–39.

Paauwe, J. and Boselie, P. 2003, 'Challenging "strategic HRM" and the relevance of the institutional setting', *Human Resource Management Journal*, **13** (3): 56–70.

9
Performance management: Rewarding for performance at Sprooker Inc.

Ryan B. Gould and Wayne O'Donohue

Sprooker Inc. is an Australian owned and based telemarketing firm employing approximately 50 people across two offices, one in Sydney and one in Perth. Founded by Serena Waterford in February 2015, Sprooker launched as an outsourced sales partner for Russell Media with a vision of 'delivering success and sustainability to our partners by implementing disruptive and innovative strategies in the always-challenging sales environment'.

While Sprooker presents an innovative and fresh approach to the market, Serena admits that success in the telecommunication space ultimately boils down to operational excellence as the basis for delivering the business customer an attractive return on investment:

> Media organisations around the world are saying that they would never, ever outsource any part of their business, including their customer service or sales contact centres. We really have to show the results to win their business. Ultimately, we have to show them that our model makes them money … we have to be that well-oiled machine. Cheaper than running it themselves, with no risk to their reputation.

When the company opened in 2015, each state office had a similar structure: a State Sales Manager, reporting to a National Sales Director (NSD), who oversees the day-to-day operations; a receptionist who provides administrative support to the sales team; a graphic designer who liaises with Russell Media journalists; and a sales team with an appointed team leader. The organisation had

Table 9.1 Structure of Sprooker Perth

Sprooker Perth (March 2017) State Sales Manager: Olivia Maiolo Receptionist: Burt Macklin Graphic Designer: Harrison O'Neil	Metro Sales team Team Leader: Leevi Abdi Business Development Managers (BDM): 3 full-time staff, 9 casual staff
Regional Sales Team Team Leader: Audrey Barnes Business Development Managers (BDM): 1 full-time staff, 7 casual staff	Subscriptions team Team Leader: Zavier Mohan Account Managers: 2 full-time staff

a clear formal chain of command with a strong centralised decision-making process. Head office was co-located with the Sydney team. Espousing a 'work hard, play hard' ethos, the executive team promoted and led an aggressive results orientated culture.

In 2017, Sprooker expanded their role with Russell Media on a national basis to cover selling for Russell Media's regional papers. The new Regional Sales Team was established within the Perth office (see Table 9.1). As a reward for her exceptional performance in the Sydney sales team, Audrey Barnes was appointed Team Leader for the new regional sales team.

WE HIRE PEOPLE, NOT RÉSUMÉS

When communicating with potential employees, Sprooker's external messaging remains consistent. As explained by Serena, 'we [Sprooker] can train anyone to do this job, they just need the right attitude. We provide an autonomous work environment with unlimited earning potential.'

To prepare for the role, all new recruits undergo one week (5 days) of induction training. Induction is completed in teams as Sprooker never appoints fewer than three people at a time. Days one and two are dedicated to introducing employees to the company; the product and the incentive plan. Job-specific training begins on day three with an introduction to the proprietary customer relationship management (CRM) database, followed by a half day of phone etiquette training and two days of phone shadowing.

Sprooker presents the role of the BDM as having three core tasks:

- identify and contact businesses by telephone to solicit sales for feature series;
- deliver prepared sales talks, reading from scripts that describe the product and persuade potential customers to purchase a feature series;
- explain the product and pricing structures.

As part of the lead identification process, BDMs are warned of the importance of two Do Not Call Registers (the DNCs):

- National Do Not Call Register (DNCR) – a government-regulated register for which telemarketing firms can purchase a subscription service. However, Sprooker does not have a general subscription. As individual BDMs are required to check their 'leads', there are two fee-for-service options: a BDM can do a 'single number' search of the DNCR just before calling; or, a 'batch number' search (max. 500 numbers) can be submitted to the DNCR.
- Russell Media Do Not Call (RDNC) – this registry of DNCs is maintained in-house by Russell Media using a CRM database. It includes a list of clients currently managed or being pursued by Russell Media's sales teams. BDMs can download the latest copy of the RDNC but must manually update the register with any more recent CRM data of their own.

BDMs are told that attempting to call or finalise a sale with a client who appears on either of these DNCs is grounds for instant dismissal. While to date, no one has been fired for breaches of this rule, there is an unwritten policy of Russell Media first. There have been numerous instances where a Sprooker employee has made a sale, only to have it disqualified with revenue transferred over to the Russell Media team. With little control over the quality of the RDNC, BDMs at Sprooker need to be particularly cautious when approaching new clients. Once vetted, the BDM may then approach the client and deliver the pitch.

The pitch delivered by BDMs represents a Feature Series (Features). Using the scripts provided, features are explained as a newspaper advertisement with a strong link to editorial content. During the pitch, BDMs need to explore how a representative of the client's firm might contribute to a feature article prepared by the Russell Media journalist. Typically, the articles name the client as a relevant expert. This feature article is then accompanied by a half page advertisement presenting the client as a potential solution to whichever problem is addressed within the feature.

Table 9.2 Unit prices of Features

	Floor price (per feature)	Max price (per feature)
Metro	$4,500	$10,000
Regional	$1,500	$3,000

Features are priced within a range set by Russell Media based on market conditions, including the costs of employing journalists in the relevant regions, and represent the minimum and maximum price points for metropolitan and regional sales within which BDMs may negotiate (see Table 9.2). The State sales manager, however, must still approve the final price.

As part of their CRM data entry, BDMs are expected to record whom they called, the date and time of the call, the duration of the call, and the nature of the business and whether the client expressed interest in the product. However, despite the range of data collected, only one measure becomes relevant in the incentive plan.

INCENTIVES AT SPROOKER

In line with the Contract Call Centres Award, all Sprooker employees work a standard 37.5-hour workweek, Monday to Friday. Shifts begin at 8am, finish at 4pm, with a paid 15-minute break at 10.15am and an unpaid 30-minute lunch break at 12.30pm. Full-time continuing employees receive a base salary of $794.70 per week and standard associated benefits including superannuation (9.5 per cent); 4 weeks of annual leave with a loading of 17.5 per cent; and 10 days of personal/carer's leave. In lieu of leave, casual employees are paid an hourly rate of $26.14 (which includes the standard casual loading of 25 per cent).

New BDM recruits, whether their role is in metropolitan or regional sales, typically start as casual employees with the potential of converting to continuing appointments. Serena believes that such an approach pushes new recruits towards meeting their sales targets sooner. In addition to a base salary and benefits, all BDMs also have access to significant financial incentives.

Sales incentives are calculated and paid at the end of each month. While BDMs must log their sales within the CRM database, the chasing of invoice payment and the collection of data for the distribution of commissions are the responsibility of the state office receptionist. Each week, the receptionist identifies which invoices have been paid to determine the qualifying sales. At the end of each month, a list of qualifying sales is provided to the sales managers who review the data before submitting the final commission recommendations to the NSD for approval and payment.

INCENTIVES FOR BDMS (METROPOLITAN)

From start-up in 2015, Sprooker's approach has been to use financial incentives to stimulate sales performance. BDMs in the Metro team have the following tiered commission structure:

- reach your weekly $30 000 sales target, and we will pay you a sales bonus of $3000;
- for each additional Feature you sell after receiving a sales bonus for the week, we will pay you $750;
- reach $60 000 in sales for the week, and we will increase the additional Feature sales bonus to $1500; and,
- once you reach $100 000 in sales in a week, you will receive all profits from additional Feature sales in that week (this could be as high as $3800 per feature).

Although Sprooker's commission structure has seemingly led to today's aggressive sales culture, Serena was mindful of the need to find the right balance between rewarding individual and team performance. As such, a team sales incentive is also available to encourage BDMs to share leads with their sales team colleagues. This incentive, which applies only to the Metro sales team, takes the form of a *Taste of victory* lunch, which happens when the BDMs collectively log $100 000 in metropolitan sales as recorded in the CRM database. Other members of staff (e.g. the receptionist, graphic designer, subscription team and regional sales team) are invited but are often asked to cover their own costs.

From start-up in 2015 to 2017, Sprooker saw phenomenal sales growth, a large measure of which is attributed to its incentive arrangements for individual and team performance. Indeed, Sprooker's impressive ability to generate advertising revenue in metropolitan print media helped it win the contract in 2017 to sell feature advertisements into Russell Media's regional papers.

INCENTIVES FOR BDMS (REGIONAL)

With the expansion and appointment of the regional BDM sales team in 2017, Sprooker saw an opportunity to review its incentive plan. While the senior executive team still wanted to retain an 'unlimited earning potential' mantra, the following non-tiered incentive system based on a profit sharing model was implemented for the regional BDM sales team in Perth:

- reach your $30 000 sales target in a week and we will give you a sales bonus of $3000 plus a bonus of 10 per cent of all additional Feature revenue you generate in the week; and a discount voucher booklet (valid for 12 months) which entitles you to discounts on food, movie tickets and other experiences.

On her own initiative, the State Sales Manager in the Perth office also offered a $30 grocery voucher, as an 'on the right track bonus', to the first regional BDM to sell three Features in a month. There were no team incentives for the regional BDM sales team.

The implementation of a simplified, non-tiered incentive arrangement for members of the regional BDM sales team reflected senior executive concerns about the cost-effectiveness of the existing incentive structure. While the metropolitan and regional BDMs appeared to be exceeding expectations, it had become apparent that some were playing a little harder than they were working.

RATIONALE FOR THE COMPETING INCENTIVE PLANS

In early 2017, prior to the expansion of Sprooker's role with Russell Media to include regional media sales, a senior executive review of CRM sales performance data raised two concerns. First, there were only two star performers in the 12-strong BDM (Metro) sales team who generated approximately 80 per cent of the team's revenue. Second, the data showed a fall-off in performance as the week went by, that is, while sales were strong on Monday and Tuesday, by Wednesday afternoon the number of sales calls fell significantly. Moreover, quality checks on recorded sales calls revealed a significant amount of inappropriate chatter leading, on a number of occasions, to potential business customers questioning the legitimacy of the sales activity.

At the same time, doubts had been growing over the cost-effectiveness of the *Tastes of victory* lunch incentive. Most importantly, they were no longer operating as a mechanism to encourage lead sharing. Additionally, while intended to occur within the standard 30-minute lunch break, State Sales Managers reported some BDMs did not return promptly to work following the lunch, and there was increased dissatisfaction expressed by other office staff over what they felt was an obligation to attend at a not insignificant personal financial cost. For these reasons, a lunch was not offered as an incentive to regional sales team members.

In the light of these concerns about processes in place for BDMs in the metropolitan sales teams, it was decided by the executive team that BDMs should make at least 60 calls a day and State Sales Managers were asked to communicate this requirement to their BDMs. However, even though this requirement was duly raised every Monday during the office meeting, State Sales Managers reported BDMs generally resisted, and in fact became increasingly critical of such requests from head office.

In this context, and with the creation of the regional sales team in the Perth office in 2017, the senior executives took advantage of the opportunity to implement a different incentive structure (outlined above) for the regional sales BDMs. However, not all proceeded according to plan.

PERFORMANCE MANAGEMENT: REWARDING FOR PERFORMANCE

TROUBLE ON THE HORIZON

From implementation in 2017, the differences between their incentive arrangements were a constant point of contention and dissatisfaction for regional BDMs whose concerns were characterised by head office as sour grapes. The consistent message back from senior executives in Sydney was 'the money is there, you just need to work for it. Make the calls, and you'll get the results.'

Within six months of the creation of the regional sales team, all but one of the initial BDM recruits had been dismissed for failing to meet performance targets, and the performance of the BDM metropolitan sales teams continued to decline. Senior executives, frustrated at the lack of motivation exhibited by BDMs, began to double down on performance expectations. Monday sales meetings became more formal and sales targets regularly increased. State Sales Managers were instructed to monitor work performance actively, and prevent deviant behaviour. However, the harder senior executives pushed, it seemed the poorer the teams did.

In early 2018, rumours began to spread that Pukka Entertainment was in takeover talks with Russell Media. In the event that a takeover were to proceed, it was speculated that all print media related sales activities were likely to be brought back in house under the Pukka Entertainment business model.

During this period of takeover speculation, metropolitan sales performance (between September and November 2018) declined to such an extent that only three *Tastes of victory* lunches occurred. Voluntary turnover of BDMs within the two metropolitan sales teams also increased significantly. For instance, eight people commenced work in the Perth metropolitan sales team on 15 October, and all had resigned within two weeks. At this time, Sprooker also began to attract negative reviews on employer rating websites such as 'Seek' and 'Glassdoor'. Disgruntled former employees cited the results-obsessed culture, failure to pay superannuation benefits, and limited earning potential as reasons to avoid the company; one review simply described the company as 'toxic'.

In December, the executive team at Sprooker met with the State Sales Managers to discuss the diminishing performance and poor attitudes of their BDMs. It was decided that the best way to start 2019 would be with a grim warning about the future of the company. As such, the following email was drafted and sent to all employees' private email addresses two days before work was to resume after the holiday period:

> Hi team,
> I hope you have enjoyed your Christmas break and are ready to kick some goals in 2019. Before we get started next week, I just wanted to update you on the Pukka Entertainment/Russell Media takeover talks.
>
> As you know, it has now been confirmed that as of January 2019 Pukka will be managing the papers that we sell into. I know some of you are concerned about the future of Sprooker as Russell Media was formerly our main client. I think we can all agree that there would be less concern if you hadn't failed to meet your sales targets over the last 3 months.
>
> As you know from the Monday meetings, performance thus far has been unacceptable. You are clearly not doing all you can as most of you are failing to meet KPIs on call rates and not utilising all your opportunities.

Pukka has agreed to offer us a 3-month trial, extending the contract with us through until March 2019. However, the target they have set is $1.2 a month – almost 4 times what we have been achieving. This is currently looking like a pipedream.

Your team leaders are now going to pay more attention to your call rates. We have always said that you need to make at least 60 calls per day and it is more important than ever. I will be increasing the number of quality checks as well, so the background noise needs to be kept down! This also suggests you are not utilising your time correctly.

Just to be clear, this is probably our last chance so, come ready on Monday!

Kind regards
Serena

QUESTIONS

Serena has approached your HR consulting firm, and asked you to investigate the poor performance of the metropolitan and regional sales teams. You have been asked for your recommendation as to how poor performance and poor attitudes might be improved.

1. Does Sprooker Inc. have a performance management system in place? (Why/Why not?) Explain the potential value of performance management in small organisations such as Sprooker Inc.

2. What do you consider to be the most appropriate way that Sprooker might measure the performance of Business Development Managers?

3. In what ways might Sprooker's current approach to PM help or hinder the performance of Business Development Managers?

4. What does this case reveal about the role of leadership in managing performance?

10
Gender pay gaps at Southside University Hospital Trust

Carol Woodhams, Sheila Wild and Carol Atkinson

CASE STUDY

Southside University Hospital Trust (SUHT) is a world-renowned centre of clinical excellence and one of the largest NHS teaching trusts in the UK. In 2014 it became a Foundation Trust, giving it a greater degree of managerial and financial freedom. The Trust is made up of three hospitals and provides a wide range of clinical and specialist services. The Trust's collaboration with the town's internationally renowned university delivers world-class research and delivers high-quality education and training for doctors.

The Trust is governed by a Board of Directors, with the Trust Management Executive being the senior managerial decision-making body for the Trust. It is chaired by the Chief Executive, and consists of the Trust's Executive Directors and its Divisional Directors, who are responsible for the day-to-day running of the hospitals. While the leadership groups bring a wide range of skills to the Trust, there is little expertise in reward management or in diversity and inclusion. Moreover, the fact that throughout the NHS the various components of the pay packet tend to be determined at a national level means that pay systems expertise is not as widely spread as it is in other sectors. The Trust has over 11 369 staff, 1601 of whom are doctors.

GENDER PAY GAPS

The term 'pay gap' should not be confused with 'equal pay'. Equal pay is a like-for-like pay comparison between men and women doing equal work. Since the Equal Pay Act 1970 came into force, pay inequality for like work, work rated as equivalent under a job evaluation scheme, or work of equal value has been unlawful in the UK. The provisions of the Equal Pay Act 1970 were carried over into the Equality Act 2010.

A pay gap is the difference in the average mean or median earnings between a privileged and a disadvantaged employee group as a percentage of the higher pay rate (Advisory, Conciliation and Arbitration Service [ACAS]/Government Equalities Office [GEO], 2017). The basis of this comparison may differ, but typically it adopts a per-hour, full-time equivalent mean or median wage, excluding overtime and other enhancements. Usually, this means that men's average wages are compared with women's. The gap is the percentage reduction for women. The current UK pay gap according to the Office of National Statistics (2018) is 17.9 per cent and this has not significantly altered for many years.

A pay gap statistic leaves many questions unanswered because it encompasses differences both in the labour market, for example, the type of industry, and in individual career factors, such as seniority, experience, length of service and occupation. All of these have an impact on pay and typically are unequally distributed between men and women.

THE GENDER PAY GAP REPORTING REGULATIONS

Since April 2018, public, private and third sector bodies employing 250 or more employees have been required to publish a report about their gender pay gap. For private or third sector bodies the reporting regulations form part of the Equality Act 2010; for public sector bodies such as SUHT, the regulations are part of that same Act's public sector duty.

SUHT must report on a prescribed set of measures, and may, if it wishes, include a short narrative explaining the figures. The Regulations require each organisation to report the following:

- Mean gender pay gap: the difference between the mean hourly rate of pay of male employees and that of female employees.
- Median gender pay gap: the difference between the median hourly rate of pay of male employees and that of female employees.
- Mean bonus gap: the difference between the mean bonus pay paid to male employees and that paid to female employees.
- Median bonus gap: the difference between the median bonus pay paid to male employees and that paid to female employees.
- Bonus proportions: the proportions of male and female employees who were paid bonus pay during the relevant period.
- Quartile pay bands:[1] The proportions of male and female full-pay employees in the lower, lower-middle, upper-middle and upper quartile pay bands.

PAY DETERMINATION WITHIN THE NHS

Different methods of pay determination are applied to different groups of staff in the NHS, but, on the whole, the pay of people working within or for the NHS is determined nationally, which may reduce the scope that SUHT has to address any gender pay gaps revealed by the reporting process.

Agenda for Change (AfC)

Agenda for Change (AfC) is the current pay and grading system for non-medical NHS staff. AfC has been in effect since 2004; it is grounded in a gender-neutral job evaluation process, and was designed and implemented with a view to achieving gender equality in pay. AfC is kept under review and updated by agreement between the parties involved, including the recognised trades unions. Its relevance to SUHT is that it creates two clearly identifiable groups, one for whom the pay system has been 'gender proofed', and one for whom it has not.

The Doctors' and Dentists' Review Body (DDRB)[2]

The majority of doctors work in the NHS. The pay of those on national agreements, like at SUHT, is reviewed annually by the independent Doctors' and Dentists' Review Body (DDRB). The DDRB makes recommendations on the levels of pay for doctors, but it is for government to accept or reject these. The salary levels are mapped onto a skills framework, but this does not amount to a job evaluation exercise, and was not designed with gender neutrality in mind.

Pay progression

Although technically progression is driven by length of service, there is no clearly defined system for moving through the bands. In the two-year phase of foundation training, most trainees pass through at a similar pace, but if trainees take time out, perhaps for health or maternity reasons, or work on a less than full-time basis, pay rates can start to vary.

Speciality training can take a number of years and again, while many trainees will progress at similar rates and receive the same pay, health, maternity and caring responsibilities can delay progress, and if this happens it is unclear how pay progression occurs (or indeed does not occur). More women trainees than men step off their training programmes, and pay in these non-training associate roles tends to be by individual negotiation within quite limited ranges, which suggests a possible contribution to the gender pay gap.

For those who complete training and become consultants, pay progression within the specified band is again technically dependent on length of service. Pay rates for consultants can vary widely, however, even where there are similar lengths of service. Shortages in particular specialisms also mean that individual pay negotiations can occur when recruiting or to support retention, and pay progression is then divorced from length of service.

Banding supplements

Junior hospital doctors are currently paid a banding supplement according to the terms specified in their contract. Banding supplements are determined in accordance with national guidelines by the BMA and NHS employers.[3] As banding is associated with hours worked, SUHT will have some control over the supplements paid.

Clinical excellence awards and discretionary points

Throughout the UK, as an addition to basic pay, there is a system of clinical awards for which consultants may be eligible. In England, these are known as Clinical Excellence Awards (CEAs).[4] The value of these awards is subject to review by the DDRB.

There are 12 levels of award. Levels 1 to 8 are awarded by local awards committees (LACs) and SUHT will have some control over these. Levels 10 to 12 are awarded by the National Advisory Committee on Clinical Excellence Awards (ACCEA). Level 9 may be awarded by either the ACCEA or LACs and this depends on the type of achievement being recognised. The system for awarding CEAs has the potential to impact on SUHT's gender pay gap at three different points in the process: first, the decision about who gets the award; second, the decision about the level of the award (1–12); and third, the decision about the monetary value of the award. Each of these involves a different decision-making body.

CEAs are worth from £1000s to many £10 000s, creating the potential for substantial variations in salary between one consultant and another, and have been identified as contributing to gender pay gaps. For example, while women who apply have similar success rates to men, far fewer women than men apply for CEAs. They are also not open to those in associate doctor grades, the majority of whom are female.

Medical academics

SUHT's collaboration with the university means that it will also have to examine the pay of its clinical academics, that is, doctors employed by the university but also doing clinical work for the Trust, which is paid for by SUHT.

Other elements

There are also other elements to pay, including undertaking additional programmed activities and overtime that may also contribute to pay differences. In order for SUHT to determine whether these do in fact contribute to the gender pay gap it will be necessary to drill down into them.

PAY DETERMINATION AT SUHT

Taking all the above together, it can be seen that the gender pay gap at the Trust is influenced by a number of factors, some unique to the Trust itself, some common to the NHS, and others part of the national picture. The combination of clinical and specialist services with medical education, training and research is likely to be a complicating factor, calling for a more nuanced examination of pay and personnel data. The division across the NHS as a whole between staff on AfC terms and conditions and those whose pay is determined by the Doctors and Dentists Review Body is key both to understanding the gender pay gap and to taking action to reduce it. With only 1601 out of 11 369 staff being doctors, the majority of employees at SUHT are on AfC terms and conditions.

The Trust has a new CEO who is keen to reduce pay inequalities, not only by gender but also by ethnicity, and in order to do so she is setting up an interdisciplinary team, adding staff with skills in data analysis, diversity and inclusion, and reward management to the existing team of clinical directors. The Trust's recognised trade unions, with whom there is a constructive relationship, are also involved.

This move has met with some resistance, which the CEO puts down to a lack of appreciation of the reality of the gender pay gap. Many of the existing senior staff and some union reps see the gap as due to the impact of motherhood on women's earnings, and therefore inevitable. The CEO recognises that this is a problem she has to deal with, but is not sure how. Ideally, she would like to reduce the gender pay gap to zero within five years, but wonders if this is a realistic target, particularly in those areas where the pay gap is widest. The CEO releases the figures to the workforce in advance of publishing the report, but has not worked out a communications plan. In consequence, she is wrong-footed both by the negative reaction from some sections of the workforce, dismayed by the gap, and from the considerable number of questions posed by the Board.

GENDER PAY GAP REPORT

The Diversity and Inclusion Advisor and the Workforce Intelligence Manager at SUHT, Sam and Charlie, are responsible for creating the Gender Pay Gap Report to upload to the Government website (https://gender-pay-gap.service.gov.uk/).

Both are members of a regional collaboration of NHS Trusts for the purpose of sharing and benchmarking gender pay gap reporting data.

They have written a report on the gender pay gap using a measure of total pay including bonuses. They have worked out an hourly rate of pay for each member of staff by dividing their monthly salary by hours worked. In their report on the gender pay gap at SUHT, the following information is presented:

The trust has 11 369 staff, most of whom (68.5 per cent) are women (see Figure 10.1). From their benchmarking activity, Sam and Charlie know that this is typical of many NHS trusts.

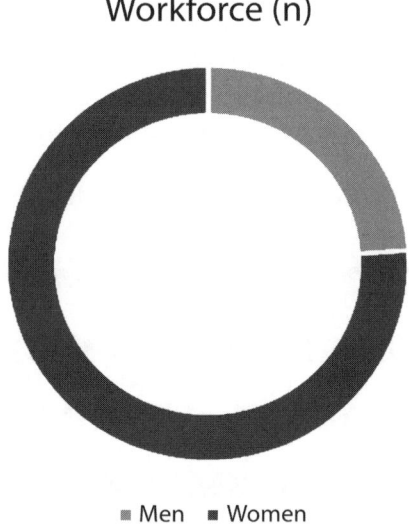

Figure 10.1 SUHT workforce gender split

The mean gender pay gap measured at an hourly rate is 24.19 per cent in favour of male employees. This is much higher than trusts in the benchmarking group, but unlike others in the group, SUHT has not distinguished between the contribution to the pay gap made by non-AfC as compared to AfC employees.

Figure 10.2 Comparison of men's and women's mean hourly pay (£)

Figure 10.2 shows that the mean hourly pay for male employees in SUHT is £5.28 higher than that of women.

They also, as required, split the pay distribution into quartiles (blocks of 25 per cent; quartile 1 being the lowest-paid, quartile 4 the highest-paid) and showed the proportion of men and women in each quartile. The result of this analysis is shown in Figure 10.3. In broad terms this shows that although there aren't as many men in the workforce as a whole (31.5 per cent), they are over-represented in the highest-paid quartile (67 per cent of that quartile) and relatively under-represented in the other three.

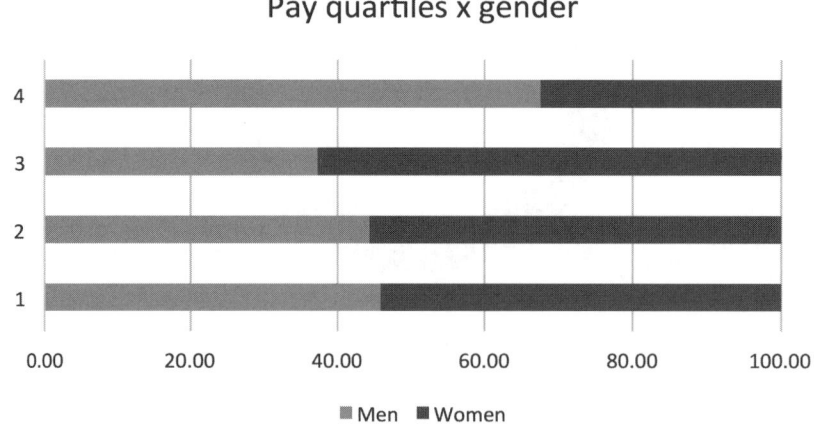

Figure 10.3 Distribution of men and women in pay quartiles (%)

On the back of the uproar, the HR Director commissioned further work and Charlie and Sam produced a table from the same data (Table 10.1).

Table 10.1 Agenda for change plus medical pay grades and workforce segregation

Band	n	Mean hourly rate (£)	Gender pay gap (%)	Proportion men (%)	Indicative job roles
2	27	8.61	+0.24	25.9	Catering Assistant, Cleaner, Admin Assistant, Health Care Support Worker, Porter
3	1422	9.33	0.89	22.92	Secretary, Occupational Therapy Assistant, Physiotherapy Assistant, Speech Therapy Assistant
4	1065	10.22	+1.53	15.58	Office Supervisor/ Team Leader, Medical Secretary, Personal Assistant, Finance Officer, Assistant Nurse Practitioner, Nursery Nurse, Pharmacy Technician
5	972	11.67	+2.91	17.48	Office Manager, Staff Nurse, Midwife (Newly Qualified), Diagnostic/Therapeutic Radiographer, Dietician, Senior Pharmacy Technician, Occupational Therapist, Physiotherapist, Clinical Physiologist, Speech & Language Therapist (Newly Qualified), Biomedical Scientist (Entry Level)
6	2527	13.94	+3.08	19.23	Management Accountant, Junior Sister, Senior Radiographer, Emergency Nurse Practitioner, Health Visitor, Senior Physiotherapist, Senior Occupational Therapist, Biomedical Scientists, Chaplains, Trainee Clinical Scientist
7	1962	17.46	+2.79	15.95	Department Manager, Senior Sister, Advanced Nurse Practitioner, Senior Radiographer, Qualified Psychologist, Senior Paramedic, Senior Physiotherapist, Senior Occupational Therapist, Physician Associate, Biomedical Scientist (Senior Level), Clinical Scientist
8a	1217	21.32	+2.15	17.58	Assistant Director, Senior Nurse Manager/ Matron, Advanced Pharmacist, Superintendent Radiographer, Senior Chief Clinical Physiologist, Senior Physician Assistant, Chief Biomedical Scientist, Consultant Paramedic
8b	336	25.49	0.81	30.05	
8c	142	30.91	6.83	26.76	
8d	70	36.75	+0.82	32.85	
9	27	45.08	+3.39	37.03	Very Senior Clinicians, Deputy Board Directors and Very Senior Managers just below Board level responsibility
Medical	1601	34.03	11.26	54.09	Foundation Doctors, Speciality Registrar, Staff Grade Doctor, Consultant
Total/Mean	11,369	17.80	24.19	31.5	

QUESTIONS

1. What does the table show, and why might this be?

2. What additional information would be useful to Sam and Charlie to help them to diagnose reasons for SUHT's gender pay gap?

3. What are the challenges in reducing the 24.19 per cent gender pay gap to zero? How quickly is the reduction likely to take effect?

4. What purpose has gender pay gap reporting served?

END NOTES

1. Quartiles describe each of the four equal groups that a population is divided up into.
2. Information obtained from the BMA website.
3. https://www.nhsemployers.org/-/media/Employers/Documents/Pay-and-reward/Banding-questionnaire.pdf?la=en&hash=D3AC5AF568064C9673539DB050439D544C85F893.
4. CEAs were previously known as discretionary points and distinction awards.

11
The campaign for a 'real Living Wage'

Peter Prowse, Tony Dobbins and Ray Fells

BACKGROUND AND CONCEPT

While the concept of a Living Wage is not new, the modern Living Wage movement is viewed as having developed in America in the municipal government sector. In 1994, seeing full-time employees coming to their soup kitchens, Baltimoreans United in Leadership Development (a coalition of churches, trade unions and neighbourhood groups) started campaigning for a Living Wage (Luce, 2017). Their campaign spread and Lammam (2014) reported that more than 140 American municipalities have Living Wage laws. In contrast, the modern campaign for a Living Wage in the UK emerged in the commercial district of London's Canary Wharf. The East London branch (TELCO) of the community organisation Citizens UK launched the campaign in 2001, staging protest actions which led to payment of the Living Wage at prominent city banks. The campaign became national and is coordinated by the Living Wage Foundation, established in 2011 by Citizens UK. As a direct result of these campaigns, wage increases have been secured in universities, banking and financial services, healthcare, cleaning, hospitality, catering and retail (Wills and Sims, 2004; Lopes and Hall, 2015). A Living Wage campaign has also developed in New Zealand where the legislative framework for collective bargaining was essentially dismantled (Parker et al., 2016). Campaigns to achieve a Living Wage increasingly feature in developing countries such as Indonesia and Myanmar (Ford and Gillan, 2017), often as part of grassroots political campaigns in elections (Anker and Anker, 2017). The development of the UK living wage is similar to the US. In 2001 TELCO (The East London Citizens Organisation, which later developed into London Citizens) developed a campaign to influence employers to pay a rate known as 'Living Wage' to their employees. TELCO was an alliance of local community groups, faith organisations, schools and trade union branches. Their campaign involved a number of different elements including demonstrations, parliamentary lobbies, press and publicity to direct action including occupying a major branch of HSBC to highlight the poor pay and conditions of cleaners working in the bank's Canary Wharf office. Campaigners also bought HSBC shares, allowing them to raise the issue at the HSBC AGM. This was developed from the idea that the National Minimum Wage set by the Low Pay Commission was not sufficient, especially in London where living costs are significantly higher than the rest of the United Kingdom. This developed and established a voluntary organisation known as the Living Wage Foundation which campaigned to increase pay for the lowest paid workers in the UK (see Heery et al., 2017).

CAMPAIGNING FOR THE LIVING WAGE

This campaigning developed into an institution working with major employers in London, and particularly financial institutions, to pay the Living Wage. The campaign has also developed nationally under the auspices of Citizens UK and there are over 5500 accredited Living Wage Employers across the UK, including KPMG, Nationwide, Burberry, National Grid, Oliver Bonas and both Houses of Parliament. The UK voluntary (known as 'Real') Living Wage is currently £9 per hour in regions outside London, in 2019. The London Living Wage is currently £10.55 per hour (see Table 11.1).

In July 2015 the then Chancellor of the Exchequer George Osborne announced mandatory increases in the National Minimum Wage (NMW) set by the Low Pay Commission to increase pay rates. However, the decision was to extend the £6.70 hourly rate for over 25-year-olds to £8.25 per hour and to plan to raise it to £10 per hour from 2020. They also renamed this mandatory increase, changing it from the National Minimum Wage set by the Low Pay Commission to 'The National Living Wage'. This actually interfered with and challenged the independence of the Low Pay Commission to set and recommend wage rates for employers (Brown, 2017).

Establishing what is a 'real' Living Wage and exploring what this means for workers in a rapidly changing world of work is important. Equally important is how this Living Wage might actually be achieved. The market-driven approach to low pay that underpins much of public policy has led to an unintended consequence – a rapidly growing social welfare budget as governments try to address issues of poverty and the working poor through transfer payments. The prospect of continuing budget deficits is encouraging governments to adopt a more munificent approach to minimum wage levels, as shown in the UK. The interplay between economic and social implications of low pay and the politics of addressing them is an area for further research. As Sellers (2017) and other observers suggest, the trade union movement has traditionally sought to use its political influence on behalf of the low paid, but as union movements around the world face the challenges of declining membership, other

Table 11.1 Rates for national minimum wage and real living wage

Time periods	Referred to as	National Minimum Wage (NMW)/National Living Wage (NLW)	Real Living Wage – UK/London (announced each November)
Oct 11 to Sep 12	2011 NMW	£6.08 (NMW)	£7.20 / £8.30
Oct 12 to Sep 13	2012 NMW	£6.19	£7.45 / £8.55
Oct 13 to Sep 14	2013 NMW	£6.31	£7.65 / £8.80
Oct 14 to Sep 15	2014 NMW	£6.50	£7.85 / £9.15
Oct 15 to Mar 16	2015 NMW	£6.70	£8.25 / £9.40
Apr 16 to Mar 17*	2016 NLW	£7.20 (NLW introduced)	£8.45 / £9.75
Apr 17 to Mar 18*	2017 NLW	£7.50 (over 25 years)	£8.75 / £10.20
Apr 18 to Mar 19*	2018 NLW	£7.83 (over 25 years)	£9.00 / £10.55

Note: *National Minimum Wage for over 25 years now changed by government and known as 'National Living Wage'.

actors have also become engaged on workers' behalf. This again reflects that low pay and the Living Wage is more than a purely economic issue. Both Heery et al. (2017) and Werner and Lim (2017) highlight the important contribution of employers in promoting a Living Wage, and further research is needed, for example on the policies and practices of the more established employer groups.

These differing pay rates and terms based on changes affecting adults over 25 years of age are now confusing employers, unions and employees (see Table 11.1). However, there have been campaigns by both unions and community-based organisations led by the Living Wage Foundation. The campaigns have been related to the nature of union and community campaigning over workplace issues, typically over issues of low pay and the payment of the real living wage to address poor working conditions.

The Living Wage issue has also been pursued through more traditional union-led rather than community-led campaigns, raising questions about the nature of the respective campaigns. A community-led campaign over the Living Wage in London has been compared below with a union-led campaign in the local government sector. Both campaigns provide insights into the importance of collective action, in whatever form, to achieve improved pay and conditions for workers in some of the most challenging sectors of the economy.

Community-led Living Wage campaigns have originated from an American-style strategy of community organising (Luce, 2017). Having a clear local focus, these campaigns place great emphasis on the training of local volunteers and potential leaders to act collectively on their own behalf (Whitman, 2006). Training and education are seen as crucial as they are the main vehicle used to inculcate a deeper understanding about the nature, culture and ideology of broad-based organising (Holgate, 2014). Moreover, community organisations aim to develop a base of organised people and this is achieved through relational meetings.

Community-led Living Wage campaigns have typically involved some form of direct or public action. Classic examples include asking questions in companies' Annual General Meetings, public marches, carol singing and events such as 'flashmops', where community alliance members suddenly congregated in supermarkets with mopping and other cleaning instruments and called on the employers to consider the Living Wage, in a song (Parsons, 2011).

COMMUNITY-LED CAMPAIGN AT UNIVERSITY OF EAST LONDON (UEL)

The community-led case reported here is the campaign to implement the London Living Wage at a university in London's East End (UEL). (For a fuller account of the campaign, see Lopes and Hall, 2015.) The campaign was instigated in 2010 when, in a presentation to the students, a TELCO speaker drew attention to the fact that the sub-contracted cleaning employees were not paid the Living Wage Foundation rate. As awareness began to translate into action TELCO took the lead, and this leadership continued through the campaign.

The initial campaign team included academics, students and cleaning workers. Unison's UEL branch had not recruited among the cleaning staff because the cleaners were employed by contractors, not the university. Initially the union office was unable to offer direct organising support but did find a way to do so under the umbrella of its Hidden Workforce project (www.unison.org.uk/tag/hidden-workforce/). This project was an initiative to give support to marginalised workgroups and was able to provide encouragement and practical support through workshops to help the workgroup develop and manage their campaign.

Phase 1 of the campaign was kick-started by a letter requesting a meeting with the university's vice-chancellor to discuss the Living Wage. The aim was to build a relationship with senior management and gain recognition, a strategy that was in part successful as it resulted in the vice-chancellor announcing that the university would sign up to be a Living Wage employer and that it would be introduced as contracts came up for re-tendering in 2011. The campaign then entered a new phase, aiming at speeding up the tendering process and implementation of the Living Wage. The main campaign tool used was the performance of a 'complaints choir' in which the cleaning staff put their 'complaints' in a song, such as that by a 58-year-old female Dominican worker: 'Mucho trabajo, Y poca plata, [Lots of work, Not enough money]'. The campaign team produced a three-minute film containing footage of the choir practices and interviews with cleaning staff. This was posted on YouTube and caught the attention of the vice-chancellor, succeeding in its aim of focusing attention on the tendering process and getting the ethical track record of the company pushed up the agenda.

Supportive members of community groups attended the workgroup's activities and in doing so helped the employees feel less vulnerable to potential retaliatory action by the employer. UEL's cleaning workers received the Living Wage in August 2011 and in 2013 the university became an accredited Living Wage employer. In the same year, UEL students and staff launched a campaign to introduce the Living Wage at London City Airport, following requests from cleaning staff for assistance. Unlike other unions, Unison's involvement with Citizens UK has been continuous and sustained (Holgate, 2015).

BRITAIN NEEDS A PAY RISE: THE GMB, UNISON AND UNITE NATIONAL LIVING WAGE CAMPAIGN

Pay and conditions in the local government sector are established through negotiations in a National Joint Committee (NJC); in 2013 approximately 22 per cent of 446,300 local government workers were paid below the Living Wage Foundation rate. In October of that year the GMB Union, Unison and Unite established a national campaign to increase the pay of their members in the local government sector to the then Living Wage Foundation rate of £7.45 and a London rate of £8.80. By 2015, 175 of 375 local councils in England, Northern Ireland and Wales had adopted this rate (GMB, 2015).

The unions' campaign for an increase first took the form of a claim for an additional £1 per hour above the minimum NJC rate (i.e. to just above the Living Wage rate – a £1 increase being much easier to campaign for than one for 92 pence). However, the eventual settlement fell short of this. The GMB then campaigned at the local level, and extended the issue to the rates for sub-contractors (who were not covered by the NJC Agreement).

The GMB has concentrated its recruitment and organisation of members on catering, cleaning, environmental services and other sub-contracting areas (including schools). Consequently, the union has a greater proportion of members in these occupations than Unison and Unite and so was a major driver in the local government campaign. (For further information about this campaign see Prowse and Fells, 2016a.) The local pressure was exerted through worksite meetings, keeping to contract, overtime bans and local newspaper publicity, community campaigns and lobbying local councillors (GMB, national officer and regional secretaries). The election of local councillors in local government offered unions an alternative route through Labour councillors, especially in Labour controlled or marginal councils where Labour had the potential to secure an electoral majority Council control. This was used directly by petitions, letters and lobby meetings with Labour councillors, and indirectly through the National Labour Party lobbying. The GMB turned to the media where it did not have political influence. The numbers of direct and indirect employees that benefited from the union's campaign and the estimated costs to the local authorities are shown in Table 11.2. The data show a significant flow-on to employees of contract service providers. There was no evidence of community and faith group involvement in this campaign but there was evidence of clear lobbying of local Labour councillors and national lobbying.

All the local governments in these cases eventually paid the Living Wage (i.e. a rate above the NJC rate), which applied not only to direct employees but also to sub-contractors. From the union's perspective the campaign was a success in terms of membership but also coverage as the campaign led to wage increases not only for employees of the targeted employers, the local authorities, but also for two-thirds as many again of employees of private sector companies providing contracted services (see Table 11.2).

Table 11.2 Local councils in GMB national living wage campaign

Local Authority	Employees Affected		Total Cost (£)
	Direct Employees	Employed by Subcontractors	
London (Hounslow)	283	811	109,375
London (Barnet)	390 (341+49 casuals)	497	424,106
London (Islington)	20	500	123,000
London (Barking)	286	497	106,000
North West Liverpool	600	600	52,920
North West Knowsley	900	0	1,267,200 (est.)
Lancashire Wigan	235	0	330,880
Wales Cardiff	2,000	0	1,000,000
Yorkshire Sheffield	257	3,257	908,000
Yorkshire Bradford	2,265	2,000	1,600,000
South-West Exeter	56	0	25,000
Total	13,292	8,162	5,946,481

Source: Prowse et al. (2017, Table 1, p. 829).

DISCUSSION

How effective were the respective campaigns? The specific aim of both campaigns was to achieve the Living Wage rate for employees and by this measure both were a success. In both campaigns this success extended to sub-contracted employees, a problematic area for unions. This success was not immediate in the case of three of the councils surveyed that did not award the Living Wage until 2015. These councils (Bradford, Cardiff and Knowsley) had not previously contracted work out and so the impact of paying the Living Wage had a more direct impact on their labour costs. In contrast, one council (Islington) benefited financially from their decision to bring sub-contracted services back in-house. Cardiff Council cited support from Labour councillors after the GMB members assisted in the 2014 local elections campaign in Cardiff. The Labour Council made a commitment, if re-elected, to pay the Living Wage Foundation rate.

The achievement of the Living Wage at UEL was also not clear-cut. The commitment was to achieve it through the tendering process but this process was not straightforward and so led to the second phase of the community campaign to ensure the proper outcome. However, although the workers are now paid the Living Wage they have been offset by other terms and conditions. This, however, points to another measure by which the campaigns can be judged, namely, the extent of ongoing activism and connections with community groups. In this respect, the community-led campaign at UEL has been a success. The relationship between workers at UEL and the community groups has been maintained. Even more, UEL students and staff launched a campaign to introduce the Living Wage at London City Airport, following requests from cleaning staff for assistance.

In both cases, the respective unions (GMB Unison and Unite) report an increase in membership which, by their criteria, would be a measure of success. The local Unison branch at UEL was energised by the recruitment of a number of active members; this activism continued at the university through the broad coalition of staff, students and the union branch. There is less evidence of ongoing activism in the national campaign by the GMB where the picture seems to be more of local activity on a 'care and maintenance' basis in anticipation of the emergence of the next workplace issue that needs to be negotiated and a longer-term campaign for £10 per hour in the future.

QUESTIONS

1. To what extent does the UK Living Wage campaign offer a model for union organising in the UK?

2. What is the potential of community organising for increasing the influence of trade unions?

3. What do you think the barriers might be to trade unions developing coalitions with community and other groups?

4. How can you differentiate between the 'National Living Wage' set by the Low Pay Commission and the higher Living Wage set by the Living Wage Foundation?

5. The National Minimum Wage now includes specific increases under the 'National Living Wage' for those age 25 and older. How does this appear to be a challenge for employers who previously paid rates for over 21-year-olds? Can this be challenged by employees and does this present issues for employers?

6. Advise employers on the advantages and disadvantages of setting the voluntary Living Wage for employees for (a) direct employees; (b) sub-contractors; (c) self-employed.

REFERENCES

Anker, R. and Anker, M. (2017), *Living Wages around the World*, Cheltenham, UK and Northampton, MA, USA: Edward Elgar Publishing.

Bales, K., Bogg, A. and Novitz, T. (2018), '"Voice" and "choice" in modern working practices: Problems with the Taylor Review', *Industrial Law Journal*, **47**(1): 46–75.

Brown, W. (2017), 'The toxic politicising of the National Minimum Wage', *Employee Relations*, **39**(6): 785–9.

Employee Relations (2017), Special Issue: 'Low pay and the living wage: An international perspective', **39**(6), available at: http://www.emeraldinsight.com/toc/er/39/6.

Ford, M. and Gillan, M. (2017), 'In search of a living wage in Southeast Asia', *Employee Relations*, **39**(6): 903–14.

GMB (2015), List of 184 Councils on Living Wage, accessed 12 November 2015 at: www.gmb.org.uk/newsroom/list-ofcouncils-on-living-wage.

Heery, E., Hann, D. and Nash, D. (2017), 'The Living Wage campaign in the UK', *Employee Relations*, **39**(6): 800–814.

Holgate, J. (2015), 'An international study of trade union involvement in community organizing: Same model, different outcomes', *British Journal of Industrial Relations*, **53**(2): 431–55.

Labour and Industry (2016), Special Issue: 'The living wage: Concepts, contexts and future concerns', *Labour and Industry*, **26**(1), March, available at: http://www.tandfonline.com/toc/rlab20/26/1.

Lammam, C. (2014), *The Economic Effects of Living Wage Laws*, Fraser Institute, January, Vancouver, BC, available at: www.fraserinstitute.org/sites/default/files/economic-effects-of-living-wage-laws.pdf.

Lopes, A. and Hall, T. (2015), 'Organising migrant workers: The living wage campaign at the University of East London', *Industrial Relations Journal*, **46**(3): 208–21.

Luce, S. (2017), 'Living wages: A US perspective', *Employee Relations*, **39**(6): 863–74.

Parker, J., Arrowsmith, J., Fells, R. and Prowse, P. (2016), 'The living wage: Contexts, concepts and future concerns', Editorial, *Labour & Industry*. Special Issue 'Low pay and the living wage – comparing concepts, practice and evidence', **26**(1): 1–7.

Parsons, R. (2011), '"Flashmop" protest over Tesco cleaners' pay', *Evening Standard*, 21 June, available at: www.standard.co.uk/news/flashmop-protest-over-tesco-cleaners-pay-6413480.html.

Prowse, P. and Fells, R. (2016a), 'The Living Wage: Policy and practice', *Industrial Relations Journal*, **47**(2): 144–62.

Prowse, P. and Fells, R. (2016b), 'The Living Wage in the UK: An analysis of the GMB campaign in local government', *Labour & Industry*, **26**(1): 58–73.

Prowse, P., Lopes, A. and Fells, R. (2017), 'Community and union led living wage campaigns: A comparative analysis', *Employee Relations*, **39**(6): 825–39.

Sellers, P. (2017), 'The UK Living Wage: A trade union perspective', *Employee Relations*, **39**(6): 790–99.

Werner, A. and Lim, M. (2017), 'A new living contract: Cases in the implementation of the Living Wage by British SME retailers', *Employee Relations*, **39**(6): 850–62.

Whitman, G. (2006), 'Beyond advocacy: The history and vision of the PICO network', *Social Policy*, **37**(2): 50–59.

Wills, J. and Simms, M. (2004), 'Building reciprocal community unionism in the UK', *Capital & Class*, **28**(1): 59–84.

SECTION III
WORKPLACE RELATIONS AND VOICE

12
Employee voice and transnational regulation: Double-breasting at BritCo

Niall Cullinane, Tony Dundon, Jimmy Donaghey, Eugene Hickland and Tony Dobbins

CONTEXT AND BACKGROUND

BritCo is a British-owned multinational corporation operating in more than 170 countries. It is a former utility which was privatised in the UK in the 1980s. Since the early 1990s, BritCo has expanded into international markets. In 1990 for example, BritCo entered the Republic of Ireland (RoI) market through a joint commercial venture with an Irish semi-state company. While it recognises unions in its UK (including Northern Ireland) bases, in non-UK sites, including the RoI, it operates on a non-union basis.

BritCo management claim they exhibit many elements of what is called diffused 'best practice' HRM across its sites with a leading hand from the corporate HQ. Diffused arrangements include selective hiring, semi-autonomous teams, performance-related pay, culture management, harmonisation, and training opportunities.

DOUBLE-BREASTING VOICE

But there is not so much of a diffusion when it comes to employee voice. There is a marked distinction in differential practices and culture in different multinational sites. Northern Ireland (NI) has a very different and much longer history in contrast to the company's operations in the RoI. BritCo operated in NI for many decades and there is a long tradition of heavy unionisation and collective bargaining, with two trade unions who are fully recognised with a membership density of over 90 per cent. In contrast, BritCo operations in the RoI are entirely non-union and the practice of employee voice is very much shaped by a non-union culture and greater emphasis on individualistic and informal communication channels.

BritCo thus represents a classic case of a 'double-breasting voice' arrangement, whereby the corporation actively decided to operate one plant, in one location, on a non-union basis (e.g. in the RoI), and in another location the workforce enjoy union bargaining and representation (e.g. in NI).

In NI, BritCo utilises a wide range of both indirect and direct employee voice methods:

- bi-monthly meetings with representatives of the two recognised trade unions;
- twice-yearly Joint Consultative Committees (JCCs);

- a weekly newspaper;
- monthly team level briefing;
- a staff email/intranet;
- an annual company-wide survey.

In other BritCo sites similar 'direct' voice schemes to those in NI also existed (e.g. company newsletters, surveys, emails, team-briefing). In addition, in the RoI acquired plants, substantially different non-union employee representation (NER) channels existed, namely:

- BritCo Vocal, a non-union employee representation forum covering the whole Republic;
- the Southern Works Committee (SWC), a non-union employee representation forum designed exclusively for the BritCo Dublin engineering site to deal with issues specific to this site (any Republic company-wide issues being treated through BritCo Vocal NER Forum).

VOICE AND TRANSNATIONAL REGULATION

The strategies for double-breasting at BritCo are set against a changing and evolving regulation context of European regulation for employee information and consultation (see Box 12.1).

BOX 12.1
KEY FEATURES OF I&C DIRECTIVE

The Directive, entitled General Framework for Informing and Consulting Employees (2002/14/EC), was introduced in 2002 and obligated member states to have regulations that conformed to its key principles, including structures for 'employee representatives' to access information and consultation under three general areas, as follows:

1 **Information** pertaining to the economic situation of the organisation;
2 **Information *and* consultation** on the structure and probable development of employment (including any threats to employment); and
3 **Information *and* consultation, *with* a view to reaching agreement**, on decisions likely to lead to changes in work organisation or contractual relations.

In Ireland, the ICD was transposed with the *'Employee Provision of Information and Consultation Act (EPICA) 2006'. In the UK it was transposed with the 'Information and Consultation of Employees (ICE) Regulation 2004'*.

THE PRACTICE AND CHALLENGES OF DOUBLE-BREASTING VOICE

In the years before the Directive, employer–employee communications at BritCo RoI were characterised by informality, adhocracy and individualism. Information disclosure by the employer on terms and conditions of employment was limited to provision of individual contractual details at the start of employment. Further operational matters were addressed on a one-to-one basis, typically when raised by an individual employee either via their line manager or through the individual grievance procedure. Such arrangements were conducive to a situation where it was not clear to staff if a standard pay grade existed in the organisation. There was no formal structure for collective employee voice, and employee representatives reported widespread dissatisfaction over the lack of clarity on pay awards across the organisation.

In the mid-2000s, growing organisational size required greater coherency and the HR function was expanded. A corollary of this was that the newly expanded HR department drew senior management attention to the regulatory requirements of the Directive. However, the intent and response of BritCo was, as one HR Department manager described, a 'tick box exercise'. An 'Information and Consultation Forum' was established to fulfil the criteria of a Pre-Existing Agreement in 2005, although the structure was not formally agreed with workforce representatives (either union or non-union). While formal provisions for elected employee representatives were provided in the Forum's constitution, actual representative selection was informal and haphazard. Typically, line managers would select employees and then ask them to sit on the Forum. In terms of process, meetings of the Forum were initially once a quarter as per the constitution but within a year such scheduling fell by the wayside, with meetings becoming irregular and eventually petering out altogether. The HR Director and employee representatives assessed Forum meetings as disorganised, with no set agenda about intended points of discussion. In terms of content, there was a shift to some information disclosure where it had not been present: a report was presented by the Finance Director on the organisation's financial situation, although HR representatives noted that this was presented in a complex way and not conducive to including the employee representatives, who made requests for information on salary scales, which were ignored. Notably, the creation of the Forum dovetailed with a period of operational restructuring and relocations that created uncertainty over future job security. Operational changes were rolled out with minimal notice, with communication, according to employer representatives, tending to be on a 'need to know' individual basis. The Forum was not utilised for genuine representative employee voice, as the regulations intended. Indeed, the Forum soon lapsed and eventually became defunct and stopped meeting altogether.

A minority of the workforce, comprising approximately 30 per cent, sought recourse to trade union recognition over the lack of employee voice concerning restructuring, redundancy threats and salary changes. In the non-union plant, union organisers were keen to stress (and management acknowledged) that the union recognition campaign prompted a shift in BritCo's strategy for voice. The Forum was rebranded with a new name, 'Vocal', and promoted across the whole organisation. Both process and content improved. Agendas were pre-agreed and employee representatives were elected and offered an opportunity to contribute to agenda items. Information disclosure and communications improved: redundancy action plans became the subject of active consultation and agreements made with employee reps in the new Forum, resulting in a revised handbook on terms and conditions. A means to achieve greater clarity on salary scales and job categories/bands was the subject of consultation at the Forum.

However, the union organiser assessed the body as 'a union avoidance mechanism' and the union was excluded from its meetings. Campaigning for union recognition proved unproductive and organising waned. So too, however, did the momentum of improved employee voice. Two years after the recognition dispute and new Vocal Forum, very few substantive employment matters were discussed at the Forum; management issues appeared to dominate Forum agendas. Several employee representatives expressed frustration with this development and resigned as the employee rep. The Forum nonetheless persisted but did little more than act as a vehicle for organising staff social events and support for external charities. While all respondents indicated that information flows had improved under the re-branded Vocal Forum, the assessment of employee representatives was that their capacity to influence issues and contribute to decisions was weak to non-existent.

QUESTIONS

1. From the case, can you identify how employee voice might have different and conflicting meanings?

2. What features of MNC 'power, politics and HR diffusion' does double-breasting voice at BritCo highlight?

3. After studying the BritCo case, how would you evaluate the impact of EU laws and regulations in promoting effective employee voice at the workplace level of a MNC subsidiary plant?

4. Is double-breasting voice, as reported in BritCo, a euphemism for MNCs to avoid union representation and/or regulation for employee voice rights?

REFERENCES

Cullinane, N., Donaghey, J., Dundon, T. and Dobbins, T. (2012), 'Different rooms, different voices: Double-breasting, multi-channel representation and the managerial agenda', *International Journal of Human Resource Management*, **23**(2): 368–84.

Dundon, T., Cullinane, N., Donaghey, J., Dobbins, T., Wilkinson, A. and Hickland, E. (2015), 'Double-breasting voice systems: An assessment of motive, strategy and sustainability', *Human Relations*, **68**(3): 489–513.

13
Is Ryanair the Southwest Airlines of Europe?

Geraint Harvey and Peter Turnbull

On both sides of the Atlantic, the emergence of low fares airlines (LFAs) was contingent on the liberalisation of air transport services. Prior to the late-1970s in the USA and the mid-1990s in Europe the civil aviation sector was governed by strict rules on market access in the domestic market and bilateral air service agreements (BASAs) between countries that regulated international routes. BASAs typically specified the destinations (city pairs), carriers (typically the national 'flag' airline of the respective countries), flight frequency, capacity, and prices. Some BASAs even included revenue sharing. As a result, an airline only had to be as efficient as the other airline on an international route and there was little or no incentive to drive down costs or drive up productivity. After all, prices were predetermined, capacity was agreed (reducing any scope for economies of scale), and any additional revenue generated might ultimately be shared with the rival airline/state.

SOUTHWEST AIRLINES

In the USA, the domestic market was deregulated in one fell swoop in 1978, opening access to routes (city pairs) to new entrants who were free to set their own prices and offer whatever

Table 13.1 Airline business models

Low Fares Airlines (LFAs)	Traditional Legacy Airlines
Point-to-point	Network/hub-and-spoke
Secondary/regional airports	Primary airports
Multi-European bases	Home country hub
No interlining	Interlining and code sharing
High aircraft utilisation/quick turnaround	Lower aircraft utilisation on short-haul flights
Single aircraft type (e.g. B737-800 or A319)	Mixed fleet
Higher seat density	Mixed class cabin
Pay for service items (e.g. checked baggage)	Inclusive service/price
One-way fares	Round trip price discrimination
Direct selling (telesales/internet)	Travel agents

capacity the market would bear. The low-cost business model pioneered by Southwest Airlines (SWA), which is contrasted with the traditional legacy airlines model in Table 13.1, has been emulated by airlines across the globe, at least in terms of the technical and operational features of the model (Alamdari and Fagan, 2005). The well-known 'Southwest effect' is achieved by dramatically reducing fares (on average by 65 per cent on a route) which then stimulates traffic (typically in excess of 30 per cent) (Gittell, 2005: 7–9). This enables the airline to establish a 'dense' route with high frequency between major cities that will sustain a high load factor (in excess of 80 per cent) and low fares.

In 2018, SWA:

- reported its 46th consecutive year of profitability;
- was ranked top of the US Department for Transportation Customer Satisfaction ranking (2017) and named one of Corporate Responsibility Magazine's 100 Best Corporate Citizens;
- was placed 8th in FORTUNE's list of World's Most Admired Companies (the only airline to make the top ten);
- was recognized as a Best Employer in Forbes' 2018 list and Best Place to Work in 2018 by Glassdoor;
- rewarded employees with $544 million in profit sharing.[1]

Corporate publications highlight the company's strong corporate culture and the desire for all employees to 'live the Southwest Way' (i.e. display 'a Warrior's Spirit, Servant's Heart, and Fun LUVing Attitude') and 'work the Southwest Way' ('to focus on safety and reliability, friendly customer service, and low costs').[2] SWA is a high employment security, high wage, high skill, high productivity airline, a textbook model of 'best practice' (soft) HRM.

Security: The airline has deliberately pursued a conservative but consistent growth strategy of around 10–15 per cent per annum in order to deliver on its commitment to employment and job security. The company avoids layoffs at all costs because, in the words of Herb Kelleher, co-founder and former CEO, 'Nothing kills your culture like layoffs … We could have furloughed at various times and been more profitable but I always thought that was short-sighted' (quoted by Bamber et al., 2009: 92). A defining characteristic of the SWA Way is 'its willingness to forgo quick solutions to invest long-term in the maintenance of relationships among managers, employees and business partners' (Gittell, 2005: 12).

Wages: SWA is one of the highest paying airlines in America and is frequently recognised for progressive employee relations (Bamber et al., 2009: 4–5; Freiberg and Freiberg, 1996; Gittell et al., 2004; Southwest One Report, 2018). Wage negotiations are typically concluded in a timely manner with trade unions (Gittell et al., 2004). This is not to suggest that negotiations always run smoothly, as the recent (long-running) negotiations between the Airline and the Aircraft Mechanics Fraternal Association serve to demonstrate, with SWA even threatening litigation at one point (February 2019) in the negotiations. As always, contract negotiations must be settled, and the parties finally agreed a 5-year contract (March 2019) with the mechanics awarded a 20 per cent raise and $160 million in bonuses throughout the duration of the new contract.

Skills: In 2018, SWA recorded over 2 million hours of health and safety training (over 34 hours per employee), with around 820 000 hours on safety and security. The airline's 'University for People' provides training and career development to help employees 'learn and grow'.

Productivity: High performance at SWA is achieved through the relational coordination of activities during aircraft turnaround at the gate, which maximises the utilisation of the company's most costly assets. This involves different employee groups – flight and cabin crew, mechanics, ramp, gate, baggage handlers, fuelling, cleaning, ticketing – working together, sharing information, and solving problems in a socially complex work environment that is interdependent, uncertain and time constrained (the target aircraft turnaround is typically 20–30 minutes) (Gittell, 2005). Employees work 'as' a team and not simply 'in' a team, which is critical for SWA's system of relational coordination and rapid aircraft turnaround. Whenever problems arise (e.g. a flight delay or technical problems with ground handling equipment) resolution is sought within the team (bottom up) rather than via managerial fiat (top down). SWA regards employee wellbeing as an important driver of high productivity and outstanding customer service standards:

> Southwest is dedicated to providing the highest quality Customer Service, delivered with a sense of warmth, friendliness, individual pride, and Company Spirit. We believe that this commitment begins with our treatment of our Employees—when you treat your Employees well, your Customers feel the difference. We're committed to providing our Employees with a nurturing work environment where they can learn and develop, creating an inclusive Culture that honors each Employee's unique point of view, and sharing our continued success with the People we rely on. (Southwest One Report, 2018).[3]

Underpinning the airline's HR policies is an employee relations strategy built on cooperative collectivism. SWA is the most highly unionised airline in America – union density currently stands at around 83 per cent (Southwest One Report, 2018)[4] – and unions are treated as 'business partners', not 'third parties'. Opportunities for employees to participate in decision-making (e.g. on pay and benefits) have directly enhanced the performance of the organisation as SWA leads the way in timely contract negotiations (efficient collective bargaining) and the airline has only ever experienced one strike in its 40-year history (Gittell et al., 2004: 171–3). Data from other US airlines indicate that efforts to avoid unions are not likely to produce a sustained improvement in either service quality or airline financial performance (ibid: 177; see also Bamber et al., 2009).

RYANAIR

In Europe, the process of liberalisation was more gradual, with three reform packages (December 1987, July 1990 and July 1992) that changed licensing from national to EU criteria, opened access to the market, and removed capacity restrictions (Kassim, 1996: 116). By April 1997 the Single European Aviation Market (SEAM) permitted full cabotage rights (i.e. the right of an airline from one Member State to offer services in another State, such that Ryanair, for example, can now offer flights from Madrid to Ibiza and Parma to Cagliari). A simple calculation based on just some of the variables listed in Table 13.1 serves to illustrate the cost advantages of the low-cost model. In Europe, LFAs pay lower airport charges at secondary/regional airports, while their maintenance costs will be lower for a single aircraft type. Depreciation costs per block hour will be lower with higher utilisation (which is more easily achieved on a point-to-point route using less congested airports), and their distribution costs will be lower due to direct sales via call centres and internet sales (bypassing travel agents and thereby avoiding commission). Taken together, the combined cost savings can amount to 20–30 per cent per trip for a LFA using an Airbus A319 or Boeing 737-800 on an intra-European route. LFAs are able to operate aircraft with around 160 seats with a single class cabin configuration, shorter seat pitch and narrower width, and the removal of hot galleys. In contrast, most legacy airlines operate the same aircraft with 130 seats or less. Therefore, with a higher seat density and higher load factors (around 80 per cent compared to 65–75 per cent), costs can be reduced even further to anywhere between 30 and 50 per cent for most European short-haul operations.

Although not all low fares airlines that entered the European civil aviation industry have survived, the market leaders such as easyJet and Ryanair have thrived. According to passengers carried, Ryanair is now Europe's largest airline and the 5th largest airline in the world (with easyJet placing 8th) behind SWA at third place.[5] The low-cost business model pioneered by SWA and summarised in Table 13.1 was the inspiration for the very different Ryanair that was relaunched in 1990. Michael O'Leary, Ryanair's CEO, stated of the SWA model: 'We thought, you can do this in Europe, in fact Europe is ripe because Europe has been ripped off by the airlines for 50 years' (quoted in Roberts, 2010). Ryanair, which is arguably in a class of its own when it comes to low(er) costs, enjoys a cost advantage of 60 per cent (Harvey and Turnbull, 2014: 14–15).

Contrary to Ryanair's claims to be the 'the Southwest Airlines of Europe',[6] the Irish airline falls well short of the service standards provided by its trans-Atlantic counterpart. In fact, Ryanair was named the 'worst short haul airline' flying from the UK in 2019, for the 6th consecutive year, according to the magazine *Which*.[7] A continuous stream of adverse publicity has dogged the airline over the past few years, ranging from diversions due to a fist fight (Coffey, 2019) and a highly publicised case of racism on board (Jacobson, 2019). The airline has also faced accusations of using a dynamic currency conversion to 'rip-off' customers booking flights to the UK from overseas and faced a substantial fine for 'controversial baggage charges' (Harris, 2019). Consistent with its service philosophy – basic at best and seemingly never getting better – the airline has refused to pay compensation for flight delays (Colbey, 2018). CEO Michael O'Leary referred to the EU261 law as a 'ridiculous' piece of legislation and famously responded to one passenger's request for a refund with, 'you're not getting a refund so f*** off' (The Economist, 2018).[8] Despite this performance record, Michael O'Leary is eligible for a bonus package of £90 million – labelled 'wholly inappropriate' and 'ludicrous' – should the airline simply meet projected growth targets (Williams, 2019). For these reasons, among others, UK Channel 5 aired a programme on 7 February 2019 that posed the question as to whether Ryanair is: 'Britain's most hated airline' (Mangan, 2019).

Union avoidance has been central to Ryanair's unfolding business strategy and industry-leading profitability. Until very recently, the airline vigorously and effectively resisted organising campaigns by pilots in particular (O'Sullivan and Gunnigle, 2009; Harvey and Turnbull, 2015). The company's reasoning for this approach is twofold: 'first that it makes it impossible for the pilot unions to have any influence over the Ryanair contract pilots, and second, that it gives Ryanair far more workforce flexibility than a settled, unionised labour force would ever allow in practice' (Michael O'Leary, quoted by Learmont, 2013: 55). Despite stating that he would rather cut off his own hands than sign a deal recognizing trade unions (Topham, 2018), Michael O'Leary has been forced to do so due to a pilot shortage precipitated by changes to the accounting period for pilot hours and periods of leave. Under the Irish Aviation Authority's (IAA) jurisdiction, Ryanair was able to calculate pilots' maximum flying hours (set at 900 per annum) for the financial year (end of March to 1 April) whereas the European Aviation Safety Agency works on a calendar year (end of December to 1 January). Ryanair pilots must take one month of unpaid leave during the low winter season between November and March. When the IAA brought its regulations into line with the rest of Europe in the autumn of 2017, pilots had only two months (November and December) to take their annual leave. Even substantial bonuses proved insufficient to dissuade pilots from taking leave. In fact quite the contrary, as pilots and their national pilots' associations used the shortage to put pressure on the airline and enforce union recognition. This change exacerbated the shortage caused by a 'haemorrhage' of pilots, leaving to joining rival airlines, most notably Norwegian,[9] due to widespread and longstanding discontent with working conditions at the airline. And so the enforced change to the calendar year might be seen as the flame to ignite a bonfire that had been built over a much longer period.

Ryanair conceded recognition to the British Airline Pilots' Association in January 2018, followed by Unite to represent cabin crew in June 2018. The airline has been bullish about the impact

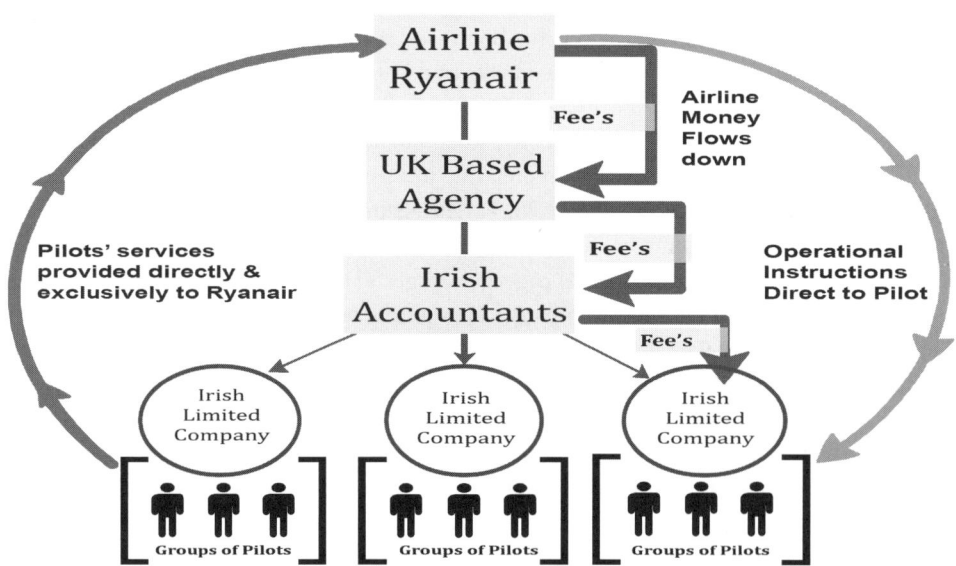

Source: Ryanair Pilots' Group, press conference, Berlin (22 May 2014).

Figure 13.1 'Self-employed' pilots working for Ryanair

of trade union recognition, claiming that it will add no more than €100 million per year (Curran, 2017). Indeed, the airline has maintained its traditional (hard) approach to HRM based on low security, low wages, minimum skill, but high productivity.

Insecurity: Ryanair directly employs only management and a minority of aircrew (over 70 per cent of pilots and more than 60 per cent of cabin crew are hired via agencies on temporary contracts). All ground operations – check-in, baggage handling, aircraft fuelling, and so on – are sub-contracted to third parties. Cabin crew are initially employed on a short-term contract with one of two agencies (Crewlink offers 3-year contracts and Workforce International only 2 years) while flight crew are hired via two different agencies (Brookfield Aviation International and Storm McGinley) but are required to supply their services to Ryanair via a (limited) 'Employment Company', as illustrated in Figure 13.1. For all aircrew, therefore, there is very limited security. While there are opportunities for promotion within the company, especially for First Officers who aspire to be Captain (job security), there is very high turnover (employment insecurity). Flight and cabin crew are paid only for flying hours (income insecurity). Pilot contracts with Brookfield, for example, state that 'the services of the pilot are provided on an as required and/or casual basis', but 'there is no obligation upon Brookfield to locate or offer work' (i.e. a 'zero hours' contract). Work insecurity is indicated by the reluctance of staff to report safety concerns. For example, a recent survey of almost 1100 pilots of the (now defunct) Ryanair Pilot Group revealed that:

- over 78 per cent did not 'have confidence in the confidentiality of the Ryanair safety reporting channels';
- almost 90 per cent were not 'satisfied that the Ryanair safety system provides appropriate feedback on previous incidents that have occurred in Ryanair';
- almost 89 per cent did not 'consider Ryanair to have an open and transparent safety culture'.[10]

Employment insecurity is also felt by staff as a consequence of the airline's limited commitment to specific routes and bases. In 2018, for example, the airline applied for 'collective dismissal' of its 50 pilots and 150 cabin crew based in the Netherlands because it was cutting its Eindhoven base and staff employed there refused to relocate overseas (Adams, 2018). In this instance, the Dutch Employee Insurance Agency has ruled that Ryanair cannot lay off its staff at the Eindhoven base.[11]

Low wages: Cabin crew hired via an agency can expect to earn around €1100 per month, including commission from in-flight sales of food and drinks. However, their contract stipulates three months' unpaid leave (compulsory furlough) in every 12-month period between the months of November and March (Ryanair experiences much greater variation in its schedule – summer peak *vs.* winter trough – than legacy airlines and other LFAs). Over a two-year period, therefore, their earnings are less than €20 000, but they must also pay for their own initial training (€500 to register, €1649 for the actual training, €700 for accommodation – bed only – at the training school, and a €600 administration fee, deducted from their monthly salary during the first six months of employment, if the candidate cannot afford to pay the training costs in advance) as well as hire of uniform (€30 per month). Earnings minus training costs and uniform hire leaves the cabin crew with less than €16 000 (less than €900 per month), which is less than the UK National Minimum Wage for a worker aged 18–20 years. Most pilots have accumulated debts of between €80 000 and €100 000 to obtain a commercial pilot's licence and must then pay around €29 000 (in advance) for their 'type-rate' training at Ryanair (to fly Boeing 737-800 aircraft) and a further €2400 for initial line training. The Ryanair Pilot Group survey found than 45 per cent earned between €30 000 and €60 000 per annum, the majority of whom are First Officers (new recruits) who struggle to pay off interest on their debts after living expenses away from home. Both cabin and flight crew can be assigned to any of Ryanair's 80-plus bases around Europe and they must cover all their own travel and accommodation costs.

Minimum skill: Whereas Ryanair recruits pilots with only 200 flying hours, most airlines demand anywhere in the region of 500 to 1500 hours[12] and the latter is now the minimum requirement set by the Federal Aviation Authority in the USA. Interviews for potential cabin crew at recruitment days run by employment agencies are rather perfunctory – lasting only 10–15 minutes – with most attention on the candidate's appearance, financial situation and willingness to be flexible. Training is 'compliant with regulations' rather than 'comprehensive', with emphasis on sales skills as well as safety. Shortcomings in the company's training of cabin crew were exposed in a Channel 4 Dispatches documentary, *Ryanair caught napping*.[13]

High productivity: The most significant contribution to Ryanair's low-cost base comes from high labour productivity (Barrett, 2004: 93). The airline has claimed that its staff costs per passenger are half that of even its low-cost rivals (Topham, 2017). Indeed, Ryanair's cost per passenger has been estimated at €27 including staff costs, some 50 per cent of that of easyJet (Curran, 2017). Ryanair's costs per employee were less than €50 000 in 2011–12 compared to well over €106 000 at Scandinavian Airlines (SAS), Europe's highest cost legacy airline.[14] With lower wages than its rivals and an intensive working schedule concentrated over a nine-month (summer peak) period when the majority of (temporary) staff work the maximum number of hours allowed under the European flight and duty time limitations (900 hours of flying), Ryanair has very low unit labour costs (labour productivity × labour costs). The company's profit per employee was over €81 000 in 2011–12 compared to €49 000 at easyJet, less than €20 000 at Aer Lingus, and less than €1000 at the International Airlines Group (incorporating British Airways and Iberia).

Although Ryanair's workforce is dispersed across Europe, everyone is employed on an Irish contract, as the 'place of work' is an aircraft that is registered in Ireland. Thus, a Bulgarian worker hired to work in the cabin might be based in Spain and fly predominantly to Italy and Greece, but Irish law governs her terms and conditions of employment. As in the shipping industry, the flag of registration is 'more convenient' (a more permissive common law system in Ireland) and crew can be hired from whichever countries are likewise 'more convenient'. 'Rule shopping' leads to 'social dumping', a situation described by the European Commission as: 'where foreign service providers can undercut local service providers because their labour standards are lower'.[15] Clearly, this would be more difficult, and certainly less profitable, if Ryanair recognised trade unions in Ireland.

Thus, while Ryanair might claim to be the 'Southwest Airlines of Europe',[16] its HR strategy and employment relations could hardly be more different, epitomised in the words of the respective CEOs:

> When I started out, business school professors liked to pose a conundrum: Which do you put first, your employees, your customers, or your shareholders? As if that were an unanswerable

question. My answer was very easy: You put your employees first. If you truly treat your employees that way, they will treat your customers well, your customers will come back, and that's what makes your shareholders happy. (Herb Kelleher, co-founder and Chairman of Southwest Airlines)[17]

MBA students come out with: 'My staff is my most important asset.' Bull****. Staff is usually your biggest cost. We all employ some lazy ******* who needs a kick up the backside, but no one can bring themselves to admit it. (Michael O'Leary, CEO Ryanair)[18]

QUESTIONS

1. What is the basis of cooperation between management and labour at (a) SWA and (b) Ryanair?

2. Are Ryanair pilots genuinely or falsely 'self-employed'?

3. How would you characterise the soul and scope of trade unionism at (a) SWA and (b) Ryanair?

4. What is the nature of employer authority and management's attitude towards trade unionism at (a) SWA and (b) Ryanair?

5. To what extent will trade union recognition at Ryanair make a difference to the employment and industrial relations policies at Ryanair?

6. Critically evaluate whether the business strategy at Ryanair dictates the HRM strategy.

END NOTES

1. http://www.southwestairlinesinvestorrelations.com/news-and-events/news-releases/2019/01-24-2019-113106440; Southwest One Report 2018 (https://southwestonereport.com/about-the-one-report/).
2. http://www.southwestairlinesinvestorrelations.com/our-company/purpose-vision-values-and-mission.
3. http://southwestonereport.com/2017/people/#Customers.
4. http://southwestonereport.com/2017/people/.
5. *Flight Global*'s World Airline Rankings 2017.
6. https://www.cnbc.com/id/100839583.
7. https://www.bbc.co.uk/news/business-46761330.
8. https://www.economist.com/gulliver/2018/02/14/how-to-ensure-ryanair-foots-the-bill-for-flight-delays.
9. https://www.aviation24.be/airlines/ryanair/heavy-turbulence-ryanair-belgian-pilots-many-others-considering-actions/; https://www.thejournal.ie/ryanair-cancellations-3602946-Sep2017/.
10. https://www.ryanairpilotgroup.com/sites/default/files/press-releases/RPG%20Press%20Releases%20-%20Independent%20Safety%20Regulation%2013%20August%202013.pdf.
11. https://www.irishtimes.com/business/transport-and-tourism/ryanair-likely-to-appeal-ruling-on-eindhoven-base-1.3835223.
12. http://www.flightdeckfriend.com/#!latest-pilot-jobs/c1mba.

13 https://www.youtube.com/watch?v=zi-x_UgTTOQ.
14 http://www.centreforaviation.com.
15 http://www.eurofound.europa.eu/observatories/eurwork/industrial-relations-dictionary/social-dumping.
16 http://www.cnbc.com/id/100839583.
17 http://www.strategy-business.com/media/file/sb35_04212.pdf.
18 http://www.telegraph.co.uk/travel/travelnews/9522319/Michael-OLearys-most-memorable-quotes.html.

REFERENCES

Adams, C. (2018). 'Ryanair wants to fire its cabin crew and pilots in the Netherlands', *The Independent*, 20 December.

Alamdari, F. and Fagan, S. (2005). 'Impact of the adherence to the original low-cost model on the profitability of low-cost airlines', *Transport Reviews*, **25**(3): 377–92.

Bamber, G.J., Gittell, J.H., Kochan, T.A. and von Nordenflycht, A. (2009). *Up in the Air: How Airlines can Improve Performance by Engaging their Employees*, Ithaca, NY: Cornell University Press.

Barrett, S.D. (2004). 'The sustainability of the Ryanair model', *International Journal of Transport Management*, **2**(2): 89–98.

Coffey, H. (2019). 'Ryanair flight diverted to Madrid after fist fight causes "chaos" on board', *The Independent*, 15 February.

Colbey, R. (2018). 'Compensation: don't let Ryanair fob you off', *The Guardian*, 4 August.

Curran, R. (2017). 'Real challenge for Ryanair is not cost of union U-turn – it's management culture', *The Independent*, 21 December.

Freiberg, K. and Freiberg, J. (1996). *NUTS! Southwest Airlines Crazy Recipe for Business and Personal Success*, New York: Broadway Books.

Gittell, J.H. (2005). *The Southwest Airlines Way: Using the Power of Relationships to Achieve High Performance*, New York: McGraw-Hill.

Gittell, J.H., Von Nordenflycht, A. and Kochan, T.A. (2004). 'Mutual gains or zero sum? Labor relations and firm performance in the airline industry', *ILR Review*, **57**(2): 163–80.

Harris, C. (2019). 'Ryanair to appeal after being fined millions for controversial cabin baggage charges', euronews.com, available at: https://www.euronews.com/2019/02/22/ryanair-and-wizzair-fined-millions-for-controversial-cabin-baggage-charges-in-italy.

Harvey, G. and Turnbull, P. (2014). 'Evolution of the labour market in the airline industry due to the development of the Low Fares Airlines (LFAs)', Brussels: European Transport Workers' Federation ETF, available at: http://www.etf-europe.org/files/extranet/-75/44106/LFA%20final%20report%20221014.pdf.

Harvey, G. and Peter Turnbull, P. (2015). 'Can labor arrest the "sky pirates"? International trade unionism in the European civil aviation industry', *Labor History*, **56**(3): 308–26.

Jacobson, S. (2019). 'Ryanair racist tirade: Man avoids UK charges as plane was in Spain', *The Guardian*, 25 February.

Kassim, H. (1996). 'Air transport', in H. Kassim and A. Menon (eds), *The European Union and National Industrial Policy*, London: Routledge, pp. 106–31.

Learmont, D. (2013). 'Pilot schemes', *Airline Business*, **29**(5): 54–7.

Mangan, L. (2019). '"Ryanair: Britain's most hated airline?" Review – tales of horror and stinginess', *The Guardian*, 7 February.

O'Sullivan, M. and Gunnigle, P. (2009). '"Bearing all the hallmarks of oppression": union avoidance in Europe's largest low-cost airline', *Labor Studies Journal*, **34**(2): 252–70.

Roberts, L. (2010). 'Ryanair: How Michael O'Leary perfected budget flying', *The Telegraph*, 2 July.

Topham, G. (2017). 'Ryanair's crisis shows the true price of the low-cost revolution', *The Guardian*, 30 September.

Topham, G. (2018). 'Ryanair reaches "historic" deal with UK pilots' union', *The Guardian*, 30 January.

Williams, C. (2019). 'Ryanair boss Michael O'Leary in line for €100m pay bonanza', *The Telegraph*, 8 February.

14
Uber and the problem of regulatory arbitrage

Michael Walker

An underlying assumption of employment law, indeed law in general, is that it is enacted in a milieu in which actors want to follow the law or, if they don't, that the state has adequate means of enforcement. Increasingly this assumption is proving untrue, resulting in organisations paring back employment conditions and states seemingly impotent to prevent it.

There are well-documented problems in supply chains in which lead companies meet all their legal obligations but the companies to whom they subcontract work are less scrupulous about it. This happens both with respect to global supply chains, where production is outsourced to countries that do not enforce labour standards, and even in domestic supply chains. Industries such as horticulture and cleaning have been found to have horrendous working conditions far below minimum legal standards yet fixing the problem has proven notoriously difficult as these workers are not unionised and labour inspectors do not have the resources to investigate their way through multiple layers of subcontractors to find the right person to prosecute.

BACKGROUND AND CONTEXT

Uber presents a new iteration of this problem: in this case the lead company itself has shown it is happy to be a rogue actor, indeed this is an essential aspect of its strategy for growth.

Uber's early corporate culture was that it is too innovative and fast-moving to be bound by regulations that were designed for another era. Rather than waiting for local authorities to grant it permission to operate in their jurisdiction, its approach was to set up and then deal with any fallout as it comes. Uber's early founders gambled they could disrupt the transport economy in a particular market so rapidly that regulators, by the time they took notice, wouldn't be bold enough to shut them down and would instead negotiate to allow them to carry on business. The company has scaled up as fast as it has by acting outside the law at first and reaching critical mass, after which dislodging it would cause more harm than good to a city's transportation networks. The losers in this equation are the legacy taxi drivers and to some extent public transport operators whose market share Uber cuts into. However, as local officials can quickly calculate, Uber's customers greatly outnumber taxi drivers so it is more politically expedient to turn a blind eye to Uber's regulatory non-compliance than to ban it.

A second important element of Uber's growth strategy is to keep prices low, and to do this by keeping drivers' share of earnings as low as possible. Even then, the service actually runs at a loss nearly everywhere, burning through over a billion dollars in venture capital funding every year, while it continues its price war with local taxi operators. Driver pay fluctuates based on demand but averages out to roughly the minimum wage or a little more before taking into account overheads such as vehicle depreciation, repairs and taxes. It can be below minimum wage when these are accounted for. Some drivers receive slightly higher pay by flouting tax and insurance obligations either out of choice or ignorance. Uber's users get to enjoy cheap access to the service for as long as taxis remain a viable source of competition but the company cannot carry such steep losses indefinitely; prices will have to go up eventually if investors are ever to see a return on their money. Uber doesn't want to increase driver pay as that would neutralise the benefit of price increases and, in the short term, result in even steeper losses.

Uber's growth strategy hasn't worked everywhere. A number of jurisdictions as varied as Taiwan and Greece had the resolve to kick them out for not following the law. In others there have been strong local competitors that have forced Uber to retreat: Didi Chuxing in China and Grab in South-East Asia. Still, Uber's strategy has worked in many countries, including all the major common law jurisdictions of the USA, UK, Canada and Australia where it now has hundreds of thousands of drivers offering millions of rides a day and has become a part of popular culture.

Union membership in Uber is negligible apart from two small unions in New York and London: the Independent Drivers Guild (IDG) and United Private Hire Drivers (UPHD) respectively. Drivers have, however, devised their own means of worker voice in the form of online forums, social media groups and group chats where they share information, build a sense of collective identity and from where, occasionally, wildcat strikes have been organised to protest against low pay or changes in company policies.

In each of the common law jurisdictions Uber has been a target of litigation, usually designed to force the company to accept that its drivers are employees and thus covered by employment laws. The cases tend to be brought by unions or city councils trying to force Uber to be bound by regulations applicable to taxis, including employment and safety standards. Uber has fought against these lawsuits, particularly with respect to employment standards. Whenever jurisdictions have threatened to make an enforceable ruling that Uber drivers will be entitled to all the benefits of employment status, Uber has threatened to withdraw from that market. The reason is fairly clear: after investor subsidies end and prices increase, the company will be no more profitable than a taxi firm. The technology behind the Uber app does not create economic efficiencies or make it a superior operating model to taxis; in the end it is still just a vehicle with a driver. Local governments, however, don't want to push Uber so hard that it leaves, because they fear the public backlash, so Uber plays the threat for political leverage.

TWO SUCCESSFUL REGULATORY REIN-INS

Uber's founding CEO was forced out of the role in mid-2017 and since then the company has adopted a slightly less belligerent ethos. Two milestones have been achieved:

- In London, the regulator Transport for London (TfL) sidestepped the employment status question and went after Uber over non-compliance with safety issues, sparked by a number of cases where passengers were sexually assaulted by drivers. TfL briefly stripped Uber of its licence to operate in the city. Supporting the ruling was the GMB union who represent London's traditional black taxi drivers. Uber's drivers, however, were opposed to the ruling on the grounds that it would deprive them of their livelihood. Uber organised a petition amongst its 3.5 million London-based users, putting pressure on London Mayor Sadiq Khan to overturn the ban. After negotiations, a compromise was reached in which Uber agreed to implement additional safety measures including disclosing drivers' private hire licence numbers to passengers and allowing passengers to share their real-time whereabouts with a third party. It also required drivers to take a break of at least six hours after being logged on for ten hours continuously.

- In New York, the regulator the New York Taxi and Limousine Commission (NYC TLC) decreed that all private hire drivers, including Uber drivers, must be paid a minimum wage of $27.86 per hour (resulting in net pay of $17.22 per hour after expenses) irrespective of whether they are employees or contractors. This gave a large boost to drivers' income, which was estimated to be $11.90 per hour net before the ruling. In this case the change was supported by both the taxi workers union *and* the Uber drivers' union, the IDG. Importantly, rather than leaving, Uber agreed to pay the minimum wage and responded by increasing prices. This is the very outcome the company has sought to avoid: something close to a level playing field with taxis.

  New York also has legislation pending that would cap the number of ridesharing vehicles on its streets. This will also help Uber absorb its increased wage cost in New York by ensuring that drivers have less down-time; however, fewer vehicles also means less profit.

These two jurisdictions are examples where regulators have taken a more creative approach to Uber, rather than trying to force them to comply with the existing legal framework. It's also helped that the company itself has been more willing to negotiate. At the time of these rulings London and New York were mature markets where Uber had reached an equilibrium with taxis. In New York that meant Uber is in a position to ameliorate the wage impost by increasing its prices. It's also notable that the New York ruling fell short of bestowing full employment status on drivers as it did not include paid leave and pension contributions. Neither side got entirely what they wanted.

ARE THE DRIVERS EMPLOYEES?

A central argument in the debate over Uber and other companies in the so-called 'gig economy' is whether on-demand workers are employees. Uber's position is that drivers are not employees but rather independent contractors. The reasoning for this is that drivers can choose when they want to drive, or whether they want to drive at all; they are not under any obligation to present themselves for work. Uber says it is not a transportation company but a technology company, merely providing software. Courts have found this argument to be far-fetched. Uber exercises very close control over the way drivers do their work, more than would be expected in a contract for service and far more than would be expected of someone simply making use of an app to do his or her job. Uber designs the environment, monitors behaviour and collects vast amounts of data which it uses to adjust environmental conditions (Howcroft and Bergvall-Kåreborn, 2019). Uber determines who drivers may give a ride to. It determines the route that should be taken. It does not permit drivers to subcontract their task to someone else. It has rules about the appearance of vehicles (they may not, for example, feature advertisements for other businesses). Additionally, despite its official rhetoric about drivers choosing their own work time, Uber pressurises them to get on the road when demand is high and punishes them for refusing jobs by preventing them from accepting another ride. It also has the right to fire drivers at will by 'deactivating' them. The weight of the evidence supports employment status: it is really only the company's unwillingness to cooperate that is preventing it.

There has been some discussion that the way to get out of this dilemma is to establish a third category of employment that is somewhere between that of an employee and an independent contractor, with different rights. So far, no jurisdiction has done this. The main objection is that many employers who currently pay their workforce as regular employees would seize on the opportunity to move workers into this third category and thus downgrade their workplace entitlements, so lawmakers are reluctant to codify it. However, failing to regulate gig work is not making it go away so the issue remains unresolved. The authorities in New York and London decided to ignore the doctrinal question altogether and to focus directly on the substantive issues: regardless of the employment status of its drivers, New York now requires Uber to pay them the minimum wage and London requires them to put better safety procedures in place.

If the operating model followed by Uber and other similar platforms is here to stay, it remains an issue for employment relations to address: how to regulate gig work that is designed to avoid employment regulations? Gig employment arrangements are attractive to organisations who want to lower costs not just on wages but also on sick leave, holiday pay, pension contributions and even payroll taxes. The only trade-off is that gig employment does not lead to the kind of 'buy-in' or brand ambassadorship that most employers want from their workforce. Notwithstanding that, new companies are increasingly adopting Uber's arm's-length employment model, not just in industries where workers have little bargaining power, such as food delivery and home care, but even in highly paid fields such as accounting, law and medicine. Further complicating matters, a majority of Uber drivers, when asked, say they prefer the status of being a freelancer or independent contractor. It is an issue that regulators will have to grapple with sooner or later.

SUMMARY

Uber provides convenient and affordable transport to millions of people around the world and employment to hundreds of thousands. It only achieved the scale it has by acting outside of regulatory frameworks. If its founding CEO had been more scrupulous, it might still be a novelty operating in a handful of cities. However, the company cannot continue to operate this way indefinitely when its competitors have to play by rules. Bringing such a company into the scope of regulation has proven to be a delicate matter as, by the time it has achieved scale, Uber has substantial stakeholders in its drivers and customers. Legislators have mostly proven reluctant to defend the existing regulatory framework if it means refusing Uber permission to do business. As long as the status of these workers is left unresolved, a small but growing number of workers will find themselves excluded from employment law protections.

QUESTIONS

1. Do you think Uber's strategy of acting first and talking to regulators later is ethically acceptable? What will happen if it becomes more commonplace?

2. What do you think of the idea of a third employment category covering the gig economy?

3. Two examples have been discussed here. Can you think of other ways regulators might compel a company like Uber to follow rules?

REFERENCES

Howcroft, D. and Bergvall-Kåreborn, B. 2019. A Typology of Crowdwork Platforms. *Work, Employment and Society*, **33**(1), 21–38.

15
Public sector employee engagement initiatives and employee voice results

Russell Robinson

BACKGROUND AND CONTEXT

Since William Kahn's seminal research on employee engagement, researchers and practitioners have determined and argued the benefits to organizations of having a more engaged workforce. An employee's engagement state has been found to be driven by his/her feelings of value and affect, relationships with leadership, and feelings of working in an open and safe culture. Additionally, this state has been found to have impact on a myriad of individual and organizational outcomes. As research on employee engagement evolves, its relationships with employee voice have become more prominent.

Specific to the United States, Gallup has found that approximately one-third of employees are positively engaged. However, public sector employees have lower engagement scores than their private sector colleagues. The Office of Personnel Management (OPM) administers the Federal Employee Viewpoint Survey (FEVS), an annual survey to measure employees' perceptions of whether, and to what extent, conditions characterizing successful organizations are present in their agencies. One agency, the Department of Public Service,[1] has implemented a new initiative focusing on improving workforce experience and employee engagement. Two of the outcomes of this initiative should be improvement in employee engagement and an increase in FEVS scores. The foundation of this initiative is based on making employee voice the driver of determined solutions.

THE DEPARTMENT OF PUBLIC SERVICE

The Department of Public Service (DPS) is a shared-service provider within federal government. DPS provides a myriad of goods and services to other public sector agencies. In the past, the DPS has had a customer-centric focus with an annual goal of increasing the quantity of goods and services provided to customers. Every year, DPS leaders were tasks to increase its "sales" by 15 percent, and over time the amount of goods and services provided to its public sector customers more than quadrupled. DPS rarely focused on FEVS. During the survey period, DPS would host pizza parties as incentives for employee participation. However, by neglecting its employees, DPS' FEVS participation was sporadic and it constantly scored low on its FEVS engagement scores. These low scores were solidified by other outcomes of low employee engagement, such as low morale, high turnover, customer service challenges and an increase in employee grievances.

Recently, DPS hired a new director who made workforce development through an employee-centric focus the priority. The belief shifted to the theory that if DPS took care of its employees, they would, in turn, take care of customers. This would lead to even more increased sales of goods and services to current and new customers. To foster this change successfully, DPS took steps to improve its employee training by shifting the focus on helping its employees to take control and manage their federal careers. Further, DPS has overhauled its internal newsletter from being a top-down communication from its director to a vehicle that focuses on individual employees.

Last year, DPS decided to further explore the FEVS results and improve its culture by fostering a culture of employee voice—the ideas, thoughts and concerns—to improve the agency. This perspective is aligned to the organizational behavior definition of employee voice. From this perspective, employee voice is a more direct and discretionary form of communication, with the goal of some form of organizational result or change. This perspective is different from the employee relations definition of employee voice, which is more indirect and normally involves employee representation through some form of union structure. The goal of this employee voice perspective is the protection of the workforce. Surprisingly, DPS's organizational behavior-based voice efforts resulted in employee relations-based outcomes on its workforce and leadership. This relationship between DPS's employee voice actions and their results is the subject of this case study because of the impact the actions had on DPS's voice agents, workforce and leadership. The DPS Training and Engagement Center (Training) would be the facilitators of this change.

EMPLOYEE VOICE MECHANISMS

Using FEVS as the starting point for capturing the voice of their employees, DPS established three voice initiatives to interact directly with employees to hear their ideas, thoughts and concerns about their work experience:

- *DPS Director's Brown Bag Lunches*. Once a month, the DPS Director had lunch with a small group of employees to talk about the DPS culture and hear their thoughts and ideas. These lunches help employees get to know one another, while getting face-to-face interaction with the DPS Director.
- *Pulse Surveys*. Sent on a quarterly basis, DPS sent mixed-method, seven-question pulse surveys to employees asking questions about loyalty to the agency, FEVS indices, and one question providing space for employees to identify potential improvements. The survey and its corresponding results were anonymous and confidential.
- *Focus Groups*. DPS hosted about 15 focus group sessions with employees. These focus groups asked questions about FEVS and Pulse Survey results and resulted in a report identifying themes and recommendations. This focus group report was anonymous and confidential by not including names of participants or their direct quotes.

EFFECTS OF VOICE MECHANISMS

The DPS Director Brown Bag Lunches were deemed to be successful by the DPS-Director and the participating employees. The DPS Director appreciated opportunities to interact with employees he normally would not encounter. In addition, this provided a forum for him to hear directly from employees about the strengths and weaknesses of the DPS workforce experience. Employees felt the DPS Director created an open and safe environment where they felt comfortable sharing their positive and negative experiences.

The pulse surveys were also deemed to be successful. These surveys began with a loyalty question, "Would you recommend DPS as a place to work to the talented people to your network?" Research has found that this type of question is one of the truest measures of an employee's engagement state. Results from this question indicated that most DPS employees would not recommend DPS as a place to work. Additionally, the pulse survey asked five questions that gauged employees' feelings about the five FEVS indices: (1) employee engagement; (2) global satisfaction; (3) effective communication; (4) belief-in-action; and (5) new inclusiveness quotient. Those indices represent employees' feelings toward their work experience, job satisfaction, leadership communication, belief that leadership cares about work experience and inclusiveness culture, respectively. The last question was an open-ended question asking employees what they would recommend might improve their work experience. All pulse survey results were shared with DPS staff and remained available on DPS's intranet.

The 15 focus group sessions were conducted with various employees at three of DPS' locations. Focus group sessions were conducted separating front-line employees, managers and supervisors, and directors. In total, approximately 25 percent of DPS employees participated in these sessions. The overarching questions were based on the pulse survey's loyalty question and FEVS indices data. Probe questions were asked based on responses to the overarching questions. Each focus group lasted between 90 minutes and 120 minutes. In addition to the facilitator, there was an additional person responsible for taking notes from employee responses. Afterwards, data was analyzed to determine common themes and develop recommendations. The themes and recommendations were the foundation of a Focus Group Report, which was presented to the DPS Director. To ensure anonymity, the focus group report did not include names of employees, and, to ensure confidentiality, the Focus Group paraphrased actual employee quotations.

EMPLOYEE VOICE MECHANISM IMPACT

The employee voice mechanisms, from an organizational behavior standpoint, met some of the anticipated goals. Overall, employees appreciated DPS taking the time to bring their ideas and feedback into the open. Based on the Brown Bag Lunches, DPS took steps to improve its employee on-boarding process, which was determined to be a weakness. Additionally, based on employee suggestions, DPS created and implemented a mentoring program throughout the agency. The pulse survey data resulted in new processes to recognize employees, including an employee awards program. Additionally, employee feedback was utilized in the development of DPS employee training programs. Last, themes from the focus group identified that staff had positive feelings toward the DPS Director, and that a recently implemented telework program was a rousing success.

However, this journey to fostering and nurturing employee voice resulted in unanticipated employee relations outcomes. Data from the pulse survey identified that employees expressed that some DPS leaders practiced unfair labor practices and created cultures that were driven by fear of retribution on employees daring to buck the status quo. Employee turnover was addressed by increasing the workload on existing employees instead of backfilling the vacant position. The focus group report themes identified specific DPS leaders as fostering a culture of bullying and intimidation. Additionally, specific DPS leaders were identified as being vindictive and creating a hostile work environment. In more detail, leaders were accused of unfair labor practices and creating physical security concerns. This data had an adverse impact on the workforce's morale, psychological safety, work/life balance and health and wellness.

Separately, two hostile work environment grievances were filed against two DPS divisions claiming that employees were working in a hostile and intimidating work environment. As DPS employee relations (ER) employees investigated these claims, they requested the names of the employees participating and commenting in the focus group sessions. ER queried whether the pulse survey questions and data were pre-approved and shared with the DPS union personnel. Additionally, ER investigators attempted to determine if the names of pulse survey participants could be identified. DPS Training staff, the facilitators of the employee voice mechanisms, correctly stated that the pulse survey software was 100 percent anonymous and refused to divulge the names of focus group participants. Further, Training staff argued that since its work was from the organizational behavior prism, pulse survey and focus group data should not be used for employee relations purposes. However, ER and some DPS leaders posited that since data, such as a bullying culture, physical safety concerns and a hostile work environment were in the focus group report, employee relations actions were warranted.

SUMMARY

The results from all voice mechanism reports were shared with DPS employees. Additionally, some DPS leaders were reassigned to other roles, and agency-wide training was implemented. All stakeholders agreed that better preparations are warranted for future use of employee voice mechanisms because data could have an impact on employee relations going forward. While DPS is responsible for ensuring that its leaders are treated fairly, employee protection must, also, be a major priority. DPS continues using the same employee voice mechanisms to improve its workforce experience but has added to its rubric by adding processes should organizational behavior data have employee relations impact(s).

QUESTIONS

1. What does this case study tell you about the relationships between employee engagement and employee voice?

2. What concerns do you think the DPS Training and Development staff were weighing in their original intentions? And, as the data started to have an employee relations impact?

3. What are the impacts to DPS leaders if names are not disclosed? What are the impacts to DPS Training if employee names are disclosed?

4. What could DPS Training and Development have done differently, if anything?

END NOTES

1. Department of Public Service is a fictitious agency.

16
Resistance, mischief and misbehavior @ The Jad-Gin Co. (JGC)

Caroline Murphy, Lorraine Ryan and Tony Dundon

INTRODUCTION AND CONTEXT

JGC is based in Brisbane, Australia, producing artisan small batch gins for several pub chains and wine bars globally. Starting out as a small, family-run micro-distillery with fewer than five staff, it grew rapidly to 120 employees, and more than trebled its overseas exports. JGC would be classified as a *dominated* SME, as it has to compete with more sophisticated and larger corporations. Nonetheless, JGC punches far above its weight for its market share.

At the Brisbane site the Australian Manufacturing Workers Union (AMWU) holds a formal recognition agreement with JGC. Around 100 of the staff, mainly process operatives, are union members. The nature of work on the production floor is reminiscent of a Tayloristic division of labor, with a concentration of multi-skilled production cells, each working on several lines simultaneously. The distillery's most popular item is its caraway-flavored Genever gin, followed by its high-end priced Jade Juniper, while its Old Tom Double Strength is a very niche production of only a few hundred casks per year (due to the limited supply of locally grown herbs). While the pace of work would not be viewed as intense, it is physically demanding, at times monotonous, but demands strict precision in relation to timing of actions on the production floor. The fermentation zone is the least comfortable area to work in owing to the humidity levels so staff regularly rotate the time spent in that section amongst themselves. The site operates a two-cycle rotation shift from 6am to 2pm and 2pm to 10pm, across five days with a skeleton staff at weekends, operated on an overtime basis. Also on site there are five highly skilled chemists and laboratory technicians who design new flavoring compounds from botanicals for gin flavors, as well as a production manager and quality supervisor.

Two years ago the founder of JGC decided to put the distillery up for sale. Many of the employees had been with JGC since its inception, including the production manager and quality supervisor. Together, they sought and secured finance to purchase the distillery from the original owner, and the sale was agreed in principle. However, a few weeks later the owner, known for his carefree attitude to business and employment rights, changed his mind. He announced that he had been approached by a major large-scale distiller, WeKnowGin (WKG), who own multiple maturation warehouses across the Asia-Pacific. The founding owner of JGC accepted the higher offer from WKG, which effectively meant he reneged on former promises to protect jobs and quality standards he made to JGC employees. As a result, several different types of resistance and relationship (mis)behaviors developed as the new ownership structure played out.

NEW OWNERSHIP STRUCTURE AND MANAGEMENT CONTROL

The ownership and change-over of JGC went through very quickly, leaving employees with little time to prepare for the changes. There was no information forthcoming from management during this period, despite worker representatives requesting a meeting with them to discuss employee concerns regarding rumored redundancies and changes in working conditions.

Shortly after WKG officially took over JGC, a new vice-president was appointed, Mr Jeremy Kunz. He began his first week on site by gathering all 120 JGC staff to inform them that it was a "great pleasure to take the helm of a *fledgling* entity like JGC in order to turn it into a *real* brand of substance". He announced a number of senior managerial staff were being seconded from WeKnow-Gin's Kuala Lumpur's head office to "professionalize" the informal and ad hoc manner of JGC.

In contrast to JGC, all WKG sites are non-union. A much greater proportion of staff are in administration, sales and marketing, while the numbers of manufacturing staff have been slimmed to a minimum through lean production techniques and automated processes. It is probably accurate to say that Mr Kunz and WKG are in fact quite hostile to the idea of unionization.

Within months the new management made significant changes at JGC. The first action taken by the management team appointed by Mr Kunz was to formalize things. New techniques including employee involvement (EI) became much more formal and also based around individualist type mechanism (briefings, suggestion schemes, newsletters etc.). Previously, at JGC, such voice arrangements had always been informal, typically the owner speaking to staff on a random or casual basis when on site. Now with the new cadre of professional managers, more formal structures had been created. A new "e-ticketing service" was implemented, where employees could request interaction with an HR business partner and monthly plant-wide meetings run by Mr Kunz were scheduled. Further, WKG used employee communication methods as a way to marginalize collective bargaining and weaken union influence. Representative participation has taken a lower order to newer, more individualistic forms of EI. Collective negotiations regarding pay and conditions remain with the AMWU for manufacturing employees, although a former bi-monthly joint consultative committee (JCC) now meets quarterly and only deals with health and safety matters, whereas previously it dealt with all terms and conditions.

WORK INTENSIFICATION AND THE ONSLAUGHT OF MISBEHAVIOR

At shop floor level, team leaders and production supervisors now have new responsibilities for staff appraisal, objective-setting and disciplinary action short of dismissal. Production levels have been ramped up significantly as JGC gins were launched in new markets. The quality manager and chemists expressed concern that the gin recipes had been amended on the instructions of WKG's Master Distillers and that much of the ingredients, once locally sourced, were now being imported. Artisan craft gin was being replaced with low-cost, high-volume sales. Staff concerns about quality were ignored by WKG management, who pushed new and higher production targets. One consequence has been an increase in the reported level of breakages and spillages by workers on the production line.

The increased growth has delivered little in the way of returns for staff, as even weekend overtime has been replaced with the use of temporary agency staff. As feared by the workers, automation used by WKG at other sites has started to be introduced. Staff were informed that "redundancies would only be required should growth fail to keep pace with projected forecasts". The union sought clarification on how any selection process would work if that were to occur. They were informed that redundancies would be a "managerial decision based on skills and value to the organization".

Management also introduced a new automated clock-in system for all (non-managerial) staff replacing the old manual sign-out sheets. Previously all workers simply "signed out" on a timesheet each day at the end of their shift. Following some brief compulsory training sessions the new system was rolled out and all workers must now log-in on site by scanning a barcode on their ID card via an online system.

However, with the old system workers had over the years devised a way for one person on each shift (taking it in turns) to go home twenty minutes early before the end of the shift. Others on the shift would claim that the person was on a toilet break or a cigarette break if supervisors asked (which they rarely did). The "early bird" would then "sign-out" the previous day's timesheet when "signing-in" for the next day's shift. Now the online system makes all that impossible as the clock automatically voids hours for the entire day at midnight if no "clock out" has been registered for an individual employee. The system can only be amended if authorized by management.

Nonetheless, workers have learnt to circumvent and/or counter managements' systems of surveillance and control. One of the tech-savvy younger workers has discovered it is possible to download the same time monitoring system via an app on his mobile phone, and sign in remotely using his personnel ID number and password. By simply changing the time of the clock on his phone he can clock in and out through the app, as if on site in the factory. He has shared this information with his friends on the shift. Workers have even discovered it is possible to clock in before they arrive on site at work.

Another change that workers find irksome is the introduction of a dress code and uniform. Workers were invited to vote in an online poll to determine the color of the new shirts that form part of the uniform, but had no other input. The new policy stated that shorts and t-shirts were not appropriate attire and were no longer permitted. Given the hot weather conditions, this means staff now have to change into "appropriate attire" on arrival at work. In rebellion against the change, a cohort of long tenured male staff arrived at work in skirts, which the policy made no reference to!

The work intensification of many of management's unilateral changes has been met with different forms of challenge and resistance by workers. In one production unit a series of sabotage attacks were carried out shortly after the system of devolved management was introduced. The production line in question manufactured a unique gin for the European market and a prestigious exclusive boutique hotel in the Burren, Co Clare, Ireland. JGC lost this exclusive contract. The sabotage in question took a variety of forms. Gin bottles were incorrectly labelled, so the hotel name was mis-spelt. Other acts included innuendoes and graffiti written inside cartons. In commercial terms, these acts had a significant impact. They not only led to the loss of a contract with the specific hotel, but also wider reputational damage spread by word of mouth among a craft gin niche market.

MANAGEMENT'S SUBSEQUENT RESPONSES: RESTRUCTURING AND REDUNDANCY

Management's explanation for the sabotage was variable. One manager felt it arose because several employees in the particular unit were young and immature. Mr Kunz also commented that "some long service staff" were just "unable to keep pace with new demands of their roles". Another supervisor put the sabotage down to the use of agency staff brought in to help meet sudden demand. In contrast, the union shop steward explained the sabotage as a form of resistance to inferior employment conditions under WKG; for example increased supervisory powers (i.e. devolved management responsibilities), increased production targets, and fewer opportunities to voice concerns alongside a newer and more macho management style. Interestingly, management failed to pinpoint the culprits because of multi-skilled production cells. It was common for employees to work on several flavoring (botanicals) lines simultaneously, and switch to packaging duties periodically during the same shift.

Due to the loss of the exclusive hotel contract, management announced that there would be "a review of structures, positions and number of posts". The AMWU immediately expressed outrage at the decision, claiming that the contract loss was not significant enough to warrant any redundancies, particularly given the levels of growth in other markets. The targeted redundancies resulted in job losses for three of the five on-site chemists (who had not been union members originally, but who quickly sought membership after the WKG takeover) and up to 12 percent of production staff (around 15 of the 120 workers). The company insisted that given the level of broader expertise in the wider organization there was no longer a need for their skills. Having seen the experience of their co-workers with the recent redundancies, many staff, particularly senior staff, worry that they will be next and have started talking about protecting their jobs and their rights to know what's going on in their company. In fact someone has set up a webpage 'haditwithjade.com' where workers have started to post online about their dissatisfaction with the job, their fears for the future, and most importantly what they can do about it.

The AMWU requested a meeting with management with four items on the agenda: an enhanced severance package for the three chemists and 15 production staff; discussion of the dress code, negotiation of a technology agreement governing automation and skills retraining in the future; and the reintroduction of overtime pay. They claim that some of the changes introduced border on breaching the enterprise agreement (EA) at JGC. Management declined the request, indicating that these items were outside the remit of the union agreement. The AMWU's real concern is that WKG will use the temporary staff employed on the weekend shift to undermine the existing EA. The union was involved in a similar case a number of years ago that was brought before the Fair Work Commission but still resulted in significant industrial action which was difficult for the workers involved.

The AMWU local organizer and a number of worker activists organized a meeting over the weekend to discuss a potential ballot for strike action. Knowing how important image and marketing is to WKG, the union decided to do something to capture media attention and create a sense of solidarity in challenging management and the changes led by Mr Kunz. The workers were all asked to bring to the meeting empty bottles of JGC and were provided with t-shirts with a likeness of

Jeremy Kunz printed on the front (some of the group continued to wear their skirts!), thus directing their attention to Mr Kunz himself as failing to deliver on promises previously made to the workers of JGC. The workers then recorded themselves (and posted on YouTube) singing the working class ballad, "The Man that Waters the Workers' Beer":[1]

> I am the man, the very fat man that waters the workers' beer.
> And what do I care if it makes them ill, if it makes them terribly queer.
> I've a car, a yacht, and an aeroplane, and I waters the workers' beer.

The following week, the local management team, including Mr Kunz, contacted the AMWU indicating that they would like to bring forward the date of their next meeting with the union group. They stated that they were prepared to discuss the union concerns on the issues raised but that in order for talks to be productive it was critical that all members of the "JGC *family*" refrain from behaviors that "damage the brand and reputation" of WKG (and JGC products).

A condition of management meeting the union is the discussion of a revised disciplinary policy, sent to the union for review, in advance of the upcoming meeting. The revised policy includes a new paragraph which specifically notes that any employee who is found to engage in behavior (either on or off site) which "in any way ridicules, derides or disparages any member of management (or staff) of WKG or jeopardizes the name or reputation of the company in any way shall be considered as having engaged in gross misconduct" and shall be liable to be dismissed.

The meeting is due to take place next week.

QUESTIONS

1 Expressions of conflict and resistance can be both latent and manifest. Identify what you believe are examples of each in this case.

2 Trade unions are often portrayed as trouble-makers who stir up conflict. Do you think this is the case in JGC/WKG?

3 Do you think it's wrong that workers are cheating the clock-in system or is it simply their way of regaining some control over their workday?

4 Do you think the union's action with regard to the Twitter/media campaign directed at Mr Kunz will be effective or ineffective? Give reasons for your answer.

5 What is your view of management's proposal to change the disciplinary policy? How should the union respond to management?

END NOTES

1 The lyrics of the original song (Paddy Ryan, 1939) depicting capitalist strategies to control the working class can be found here (https://www.youtube.com/watch?v=SybZrbeBQ3I).

17
The divided workforce: Zero hours work at Sports Direct

Michelle O'Sullivan

BACKGROUND AND CONTEXT

Sports Direct plc was founded in 1982 by Mike Ashley who was the sole owner until the company went public in 2007. He remains as the company's controlling shareholder and Chief Executive. The company is a large and expanding retailer as shown by revenue which increased from £1.35bn to £3.3bn between 2007 and 2018.[1] It operates in over 20 countries with the majority of revenue coming from its UK operations, followed by its European stores, and it has expanded operations into the USA and Malaysia. Its core business involves selling sportswear and equipment through stores and online sales but it has also branched out into luxury clothing stores. A significant part of its expansion strategy has involved acquiring interests in whole or part in other retail brands such as McGurks, Lilywhites, Heatons, Flannels and House of Fraser, as well as in sports equipment manufacturing, and in buying sports brands like Dunlop, Slazenger and Lonsdale. In conjunction with its transition to a public company, it moved its head office, support functions and 24-hour warehousing and distribution centre to Shirebrook, UK. Sports Direct's business strategy has centred on providing a comprehensive product range, ensuring stock availability, closely controlling costs and making efficiencies, and a key part of the strategy is selling clothing at cheap prices.[2] The company's objective in managing its business is to increase long-term shareholder value.[3] The employment practices used to support this objective have been subject to public scrutiny in recent years because of revelations of their negative effects on workers.

THE DIVIDED WORKFORCE

Three identifiable groups work in Sports Direct: executive directors, permanent employees, and workers in non-permanent employment. The first group is made up of two executive directors and most of their remuneration is paid in bonuses and shares rather than basic salary. For example, a performance share plan was introduced to provide "a direct link between executive director's remuneration and the return to shareholders".[4] The awarding of shares under the plan is based on performance targets relating to the company's earnings per share growth and total shareholder return. Performance-related schemes account for between 66 per cent and 81 per cent of the total remuneration of executive directors but the company stated its confidence in 2009 that the packages did not "inadvertently encourage irresponsible behaviour".[5]

A key performance indicator for the company is employee retention and the company reports employee turnover rates annually though it is not clear to which group of workers the rates refer (Table 17.1). The rates are higher than estimates of national turnover. A survey by the HR professional body, the CIPD, found that the UK national median turnover rate fell from 17 per cent in 2007 to 10 per cent in 2013 before rising to 16.5 per cent in 2016.[6] Sports Direct's employee turnover was particularly high in the years following flotation and the move to Shirebook, and the company sought to improve retention by introducing a bonus share scheme in 2009. The scheme though only applied to the second group of workers: permanent employees with not less than one year's service based in the UK. Other objectives of the bonus share scheme were "to drive performance in the short to medium term … and align the interests of employees and shareholders" and this was achieved by basing awards under the scheme on earnings per share growth.[7] The bonus share scheme also applied to executive directors. Only a relative minority of staff benefited from the share scheme as directly employed permanent employees account for a limited proportion of all staff. In 2016 permanent employees accounted for only 19 per cent of the entire workforce but the scheme actually only applied to 2500 employees or 9 per cent of the workforce.[8]

The third group of workers – in non-standard jobs – account for the vast majority of staff. Almost 68 per cent of the workforce are direct employees in retail stores and are employed on zero hours contracts. Zero hours contracts are contracts in which employers do not guarantee to give any hours of work to individuals. Employers only offer hours of work when they need workers. Other countries use a variety of terms to describe contracts with no guaranteed hours such as "if and when" work, on-demand work, on-call work, intermittent work, casual work and "gig" work. A Sports Direct zero hours contract states: "Your work with us will be on a casual, hourly paid basis.

Table 17.1 Employee turnover rates

Year	Turnover rate
2007	48%
2008	38%
2009	29%
2010	17%
2011	17%
2012	17%
2013	15%
2014	19%
2015	19%
2016	22%
2017	17%
2018	23%

Source: Sports Direct International plc Annual Reports 2007–2018.

As such, there are no guaranteed hours of work, your hours of work can vary from week to week, and, as a result, there may be weeks when no hours of work are offered."[9]

Also part of the third group of workers are the remaining 15 per cent of the workforce hired through employment agencies to work in the warehousing and distribution centre in Shirebrook. These workers are mostly Eastern European and two agencies are responsible for their recruitment and pay rates, which are determined by Sports Direct. Almost all of the agency workers are employed on so-called "336 contracts" whereby the employer guarantees to give 336 hours of work to employees in a year but any additional hours of work are only offered to an employee on an "if and when" basis. Such contracts are also known as "low hours contracts", "short hours contracts" or "hybrid if and when contracts". While in theory someone on such a contract should be able to work somewhere else outside of their guaranteed hours, the 336 contracts provided by the agencies stipulated that workers had to accept any assignment offered by Sports Direct unless they had a good cause. Employers use zero hours contracts and agency workers because they allow employers to match labour supply with business need through numerical and time-based flexibility and at a low cost. The Chairman of Sports Direct noted that the use of zero hours contracts "gives us the flexibility of the work force. We have available the staff we need at the times we need them and for the number of hours that we need them."[10]

Even if workers have a reasonable expectation of future work, this does not mean they have an entitlement to hours. In Sports Direct, the agency workers had average working hours of 32 to 39 hours per week[11] but the nature of their contracts means employers can reduce or vary their hours at any time. Generally, there is a significant legal difference between someone on a 336 contract with at least some guaranteed hours and someone on a zero hours contract with no hours. By having some guaranteed hours, 336 workers are classified by the UK, and many other legal systems, as employees, so they have rights under employment law. In this case the workers are employed though agencies, which creates a disconnect between the workers and Sports Direct, which can argue that in many circumstances it is not the agency workers' employer. Someone on a zero hours contract with no guaranteed hours can be in a grey area legally, and often not classified as an employee, so they may have no or limited employment rights. In practice though, there can be little difference between zero hours contracts and agency workers on 336 contracts in terms of the everyday experiences of workers. Both types of employment arrangement provide little certainty as to the number of hours workers get week to week so their income is insecure.

In addition to insecurity of income, investigations into the company revealed reports that the agency workers in Shirebrook in particular were subject to a litany of punitive employment practices including:

- being paid below the national minimum wage;
- a strict "six strikes and out" policy over a six-month period;
- a "strike" resulting from staff taking short breaks and being absent due to sickness;
- staff being criticised about their performance in a public manner such as through a Tannoy (loudspeaker for public announcements);
- one of the agencies providing workers with pre-paid debit cards to access their wages but workers being charged fees for the issuance and maintenance of the cards.

PRESSURE FOR CHANGE

Human resource management best practice suggests that organisations should institute voice mechanisms which give workers the opportunity to provide feedback on issues such as job design and grievances. Prior to revelations about its employment practices, Sports Direct noted that it enabled communication with workers through:

- head office briefings;
- line management communication;
- an "open management style";
- a staff forum in the Shirebrook warehouse;
- periodical staff surveys.

In addition to the above communication channels, the company had recognised the trade union Unite in 2008 but only in relation to its directly employed staff and excluding the agency workers in Shirebrook. The union later stated in 2016 it had no meaningful negotiations with the company since 2012 and claimed the company's staff forum had rarely met. Despite the presence of communication mechanisms in the company, it was investigations by media outlets, trade unions, parliamentary committees and HM Revenue and Customs that exposed the scale of insecure employment and harsh HR practices. The investigations presented a picture of pressure on workers to perform and fear amongst workers to challenge managerial practices. Unite argued that the type of employment contracts used allowed the employer to have absolute control over workers such as denying someone work if they raised a grievance or concern.[12] In a move reflective of a growing trend of shareholder activism, a number of the company's shareholders supported a Unite resolution requesting the company's Board to commission an independent review of the organisation's human capital management strategy. The company opposed the resolution, noting that it had commissioned its own legal advisors to undertake a review.

The company's review examined the allegations against it. In regard to zero hours contracts, the review acknowledged that zero hours contracts mean workers can face difficulties accessing credit such as bank loans and that they can result in inequality in bargaining power but it argued that "the issue is more nuanced than sometimes suggested" and noted that zero hours contracts are commonly used by other retailers.[13] In relation to the union's claims that it had made attempts to meet management previously, the review accepted this and found that management did not perceive "that the problems that have since been identified actually existed".[14] As a result of the review, the company committed to introducing a range of measures including:

- offering directly employed workers the option to elect between a "zero hours" term of engagement or a permanent contract which will guarantee them at least 12 hours' work a week;
- increasing pay of staff on the national minimum wage by at least 15 pence per hour to avoid underpayment;
- correcting pay deductions for lateness;
- back-paying warehouse employees for underpayment of the minimum wage;

- appointment of a full-time nurse and a welfare officer;
- using the company training centre to allow English lessons for agency workers;
- introducing a Tannoy policy so that Tannoys/loudspeakers in the warehouse will be for logistical or health and safety purposes and not used to criticise staff performance;
- improving communications through regular feedback from managers, regular weekly meetings with the agencies and developing dialogue with Unite.

In relation to agency workers, Sports Direct said it could not "dictate the terms and conditions of the agencies that are used across their large workforce with many other customers but it will engage with the agencies"[15] and it indicated that:

- it was recommending that the agencies suspend the six strikes policy and use Sports Direct's own grievance and disciplinary procedure;
- it would engage with the agencies regarding the back-payment of unpaid national minimum wages though it was a matter for the agencies;
- it would consider a test scheme aiming to transfer ten staff a month from the agencies to work as directly employed staff.

Since the review, the company has also introduced a "your company, your voice initiative" involving the use of suggestion boxes, a "listening group" involving warehouse staff, and it allowed a workers' representative onto the company Board.

SUMMARY

Sports Direct is a large organisation in a competitive environment which has sought to achieve its objectives through a largely non-standard workforce. Bodies external to the company have revealed and criticised its approach to its workers, forcing the company to promise changes. Questions remain as to the extent to which the changes will improve the impact of its human resources and employment relations strategy on workers.

QUESTIONS

1 What linkages do you think there were between the company's business strategy, the remuneration packages of senior management and the quality of jobs highlighted in the company?

2 Why do you think the company's communication channels did not result in improved conditions for workers?

3 What do you think the case study tells you about regulating poor job quality in organisations?

4 Evaluate the likely impact of the company's new measures on (a) its business model; and (b) working conditions for staff.

END NOTES

1 Sports Direct International plc. *Annual Report and Accounts 2007*; *Annual Report and Accounts 2018*.
2 Sports Direct International plc. *Annual Report and Accounts 2009*; House of Commons Business Innovation and Skills Committee. (2016) *Employment Practices at Sports Direct. Third Report of Session 2016–17*, p. 12.
3 Sports Direct International plc. *Annual Report and Accounts 2007*.
4 Sports Direct International plc. *Annual Report and Accounts 2009*, p. 23.
5 Sports Direct International plc. *Annual Report and Accounts 2009*, p. 22.
6 CIPD (2017) *Resourcing and Talent Planning Survey 2017*. London: CIPD.
7 Sports Direct International plc. *Annual Report and Accounts 2009*, p. 24.
8 RPC (2016) *Working Practices Report. Prepared for the Board of Sports Direct International Plc*, p. 15.
9 RPC (2016) *Working Practices report. Prepared for the Board of Sports Direct International Plc*, Appendix 4.
10 House of Commons Business Innovation and Skills Committee (2016) *Employment Practices at Sports Direct. Third Report of Session 2016–17*, p. 9.
11 House of Commons Business Innovation and Skills Committee (2016) *Oral Evidence: Working Practices at Sports Direct*, HC 219 Tuesday 7 June.
12 House of Commons Business Innovation and Skills Committee (2016) *Employment Practices at Sports Direct. Third Report of Session 2016–17*, p. 7.
13 RPC (2016) *Working practices report. Prepared for the Board of Sports Direct International Plc*, p. 12.
14 RPC (2016) *Working practices report. Prepared for the Board of Sports Direct International Plc*, p. 37.
15 RPC (2016) *Working practices report. Prepared for the Board of Sports Direct International Plc*, p. 16.

SECTION IV
HUMAN RESOURCE DEVELOPMENT, DIVERSITY, SKILLS AND TRAINING

18
Learning from doing and telling at work

James Brooks, Irena Grugulis and Hugh Cook

BACKGROUND

According to official figures the last 15 years has seen a 57 per cent reduction in the number of fires attended by firefighters (Home Office 2016). This is welcome in many respects, but it represents a fundamental change in the working practice of firefighters, with greater emphasis now placed on fire protection and prevention as opposed to actual firefighting. It has also radically reshaped how firefighters learn and share knowledge. Being a front line firefighter is an occupation characterised by considerable risk, danger and uncertainty. A significant proportion of firefighters' daily lives revolves around prosaic and mundane tasks, with much time spent checking equipment, conducting fire safety visits or cleaning out the training yard. Yet this is not the whole story, because quiet and uneventful shifts can be transformed. Within a heartbeat firefighters can face raging infernos in tower blocks or be required to undertake complex search and rescues.

This means that the ways firefighters learn and the mechanisms by which they share knowledge are important. It is axiomatic that well trained and capable firefighters protect and safeguard society as well as themselves. Conversely, poorly trained firefighters face considerable risk. If their training is not up to date or there are gaps in their core skills and competencies, firefighters could die or suffer serious injury. This case study explores how firefighters learn together and the different types of knowledge that they draw upon using data from a nine-month ethnographic study of Northern Fire (a pseudonym to preserve confidentiality). Northern Fire is one of the UK's largest fire and rescue services, operating within a geographical area of some 800 miles and with a total population of 2 million. Northern Fire has 43 fire stations divided into five districts. The Case Study focuses upon a group of firefighters called Red Watch, exploring how they share knowledge and learn together. Key to this case study is that the reduction in real incidents attended reduced the opportunity to learn from experience and places a far greater emphasis on sharing experiential knowledge.

Firefighters operate in groups called watches that typically comprise between four and ten individuals. Watches are cohesive and tight professional groups with close bonds of loyalty, trust and respect. Many firefighters have worked previously in skilled trades such as joinery, carpentry or construction; these skills are valuable to watches and members will often use them to unlock doors and cut through metal or wire in road traffic collisions. Watches are established entities that have been together for many years, with members working and learning together by sharing common experiences.

Up until the late 1980s firefighting techniques were fairly basic and extinguishing fires was often summarised as 'putting cold over hot.' Essentially blazes were tackled with water dispensed from hoses in a fairly rudimentary fashion. Modern firefighting has become a much more technical craft because knowledge around containing and fighting fire has become much more scientific. Equally, technological developments have digitised many core functions of firefighting praxis. These are wide ranging and include the use of breathing apparatus equipment to electronic learning, training and development. The expectations of the knowledge firefighters must possess and deploy in their everyday working lives are significant. Firefighters need to be up to speed on a broad and eclectic range of subjects. These include dealing with hazardous or toxic materials, casualty care, complex road traffic collisions and responding to acts of terrorism. Knowledge and understanding in these areas is fluid and subject to frequent technical updates. By way of example, medical advancements change how best to deal with victims of trauma or serious injury. Firefighters therefore need to be aware of these changes and be able to implement them on the fire ground.

BREATHING APPARATUS TRAINING

The most important element of firefighter training relates to the use of breathing apparatus (BA) equipment, which is worn by firefighters when tackling fires. The kit comprises an oxygen tank containing compressed air, a BA mask and protective fireproof clothing. A BA set is worn on top of the usual uniform worn by firefighters. BA equipment allows firefighters to breathe and provides respiratory protection in toxic and hazardous atmospheres. Entering burning buildings wearing BA equipment is demanding, both physically and psychologically. In this environment, firefighters are at their most vulnerable and face significant danger. The UK Fire and Rescue Service operates a 'buddy system' whereby firefighters wearing BA are deployed in pairs. They will help each other by undergoing standard BA checks to make sure the equipment is working, that they are fully covered up with their protective clothing and communicate with each other at all times.

The Fire Brigades Union (FBU) has fought tirelessly over many years to improve firefighter safety when using BA equipment. On 23 January 1958 there was a serious fire at Smithfield Market in London. Tragically, firefighters Jack Fourt-Wells and Richard Stockings lost their lives in tackling the blaze. The reason for their deaths was the inadequate BA equipment they wore and the standard of training they had received. At the time, BA was a 'proto set' that was made out of leather, canvas and steel, weighing some 34 pounds. Remarkably some of these old sets were still in operational use in the 1970s. In 2018 on the 60th anniversary of the tragic events at Smithfield Market the FBU noted:

> Unfortunately, one of the sad lessons of history is that it takes lives to save lives. So it took the deaths of the two brave firefighters at Smithfield for authorities to finally wake up and fund the improvements today that have undoubtedly helped prevent many more firefighters from dying in the line of duty. The FBU was at the forefront of the fight for change.

Given the inherent risks in tackling fires whilst wearing BA equipment, training for its use is rigorous. It involves a substantive study of the theoretical aspects of tackling fires together with very practical 'hands on' training on correct BA procedures and techniques.

Knowledge and understanding of BA equipment derives from two primary sources. First, firefighters are given didactic textbook training on how to use BA equipment. This comprises an essential part of the compulsory 13-week training course that all UK firefighters must successfully complete. Only personnel who have successfully passed an initial BA training course are allowed to wear a BA set. In addition, annual tests must be passed to prove continuing competence. Secondly, correct operational use of BA equipment is set out in standard operating procedures (SOP). The SOP for BA is incredibly detailed spanning over a hundred pages and is rich with technical information. It sets out how to use BA competently, and how BA wearers can be supported, with an overarching emphasis on the health and safety of individual firefighters. These SOP emphasise the importance of Incident Commanders and Sector Commanders assessing the initial risk of an incident and demonstrating good leadership. Northern Fire's SOP for BA states:

> The Incident Commander/Sector Commander will need to consider carefully the size and make up of BA teams and ensure that the team leaders are fully briefed on what is required of the teams. The Incident Commander should have a plan to meet the demands of the incident and this should be communicated to crews. Effective leadership is required and the Incident Commander/Sector Commander should ensure, so far as possible, that teams are led by experienced BA wearers. Where possible, BA wearers should be personnel who are familiar with each other.

Accordingly teamwork, learning together and only deploying BA wearers who have worked together are very important guiding BA principles. Equally, the individual safety of BA wearers is of paramount importance. Northern Fire's SOP for BA states: 'A BA wearer should not enter a risk area alone, nor be left alone in the risk area, either to work or withdraw. All BA incidents should take into account the welfare of wearers. Crews should be fully briefed and de-briefed in order to review performance and procedure.'

So the SOP promotes and encourages BA wearers to work together as a team, never leaving colleagues alone. When working together to tackle a blaze or withdrawing from a dangerous incident the safety and welfare of BA wearers is the overriding objective of Northern Fire's SOP. Running alongside the SOP is the National Operational Guidance (NOG). The NOG represents industry best practice developed by a consortium of the London Fire Brigade, The National Fire Chiefs Council and Local Government Associations. It is optional as opposed to mandatory, with the NOG regularly issuing briefs and guidance on the use and deployment of BA equipment.

TALKING, TELLING AND DOING

Frequently, learning is perceived and validated through the acquisition of formal qualifications taught in traditional classroom environments. Here knowledge is didactic and based upon normative 'textbook' learning. There is another way of learning that uses stories and narrative to pass on experiential knowledge. Firefighting is a practical craft and many of the watch at Northern Fire had worked previously in skilled trades, for example, working as joiners or car mechanics. Typically, firefighters would use narrative and storytelling to convey and disseminate knowledge, which opened the opportunity to enrich and broaden knowledge. Stories would be swapped and re-told about how to unpick difficult door locks or the best way to cut through the wreckage of a car to rescue passengers. Often learning occurs through this medium rather than through the more formal mechanisms of textbooks or classroom-based teaching. Firefighters therefore learn vicariously through the shared experiences and stories of their colleagues, which might be told in the back of a fire engine on the way to a job, around the fire station kitchen table and during training exercises. This shared narrative is crucial to the dissemination of valuable experiential knowledge and often fills the gaps and spaces contained within both the SOP and NOG referred to above. These discussions encourage exploration of the 'textbook' techniques discussed above, and serve to reinforce and corroborate learned practice, while at the same time allowing space to critique and develop learned practice through sharing of lived experience. So firefighters at Northern Fire would use stories and narrative to critically reflect upon their working praxis and discuss ways of improving their technical skills. During downtime around the fire station kitchen table previous serious fires or complex search and rescues would be discussed and analysed. Firefighters would discuss how they might have improved their performance, approached things differently or responded with greater or less caution. They would also share amongst their watch practical information on technical aspects of firefighting as well as specific or unique 'one off' experiences such as major fires in warehouses or tower blocks. Stories and narrative can be a powerful learning tool that encourages knowledge sharing and critical reflection.

FIREFIGHTERS IN PRACTICE

Longworth Fire Station is a relatively new fire station of medium size, constructed in 1956. The station is unprepossessing and non-descript, with red paint flaking on the outside walls and doorbells that do not work. Longworth is situated opposite a housing estate and nestled into the side of a large row of shops. The crew consists of 18 firefighters comprising three watches made up of six firefighters in each watch. Each watch is denoted a colour and the watch described here is Red Watch.

Ian is the Station Manager who, due to budgetary cuts, also assumed responsibility for managing a neighbouring station. Ian was assisted by Ryan, who had a peripatetic role, filling in for Station Managers who were sick or on annual leave. Red Watch is the most experienced watch at Longworth, with each firefighter having over ten years' experience. Red Watch comprised Aaron, James, David, Nick, Brian and Louise. Louise was the only female firefighter at Longworth and the newest member of the group, having transferred there nine months before the fieldwork for this research. She was also the most experienced firefighter there, with 13 years' service in a fire brigade in a large city.

THE TRAINING SESSION

The training session in question was to focus on door entry, a specific breathing apparatus technique, which comprised part of the formal BA assessment. Door entry is a compulsory element of probationary firefighters' training, which deals with a specific practice and procedure to check and assess the safety of a building before entry. The explicit element of knowledge has a scientific basis; when spraying a door with water before entry produces steam, it is a reasonable indicator of internal temperature and location of the fire. This process is known to firefighters as 'painting'. The tacit element of knowledge derives from experience of fighting real fires. Often, firefighters will look at a building, its location, where smoke is escaping from and the smoke's colour before deciding to enter, without following the specific procedure. Ryan, the peripatetic Station Manager, was keen to follow the door entry procedure promulgated by Northern Fire. He was very aware that strictly following procedure is something firefighters are judged on and need to satisfy to demonstrate competency.

Ryan: There's a specific way of entering a building, it's down in the operating procedures… they're assessed on it and it has to be right.

Researcher: You mean painting? Seeing if there is excess steam coming off?

Ryan: Yes, looking for signs and seeing if you need to vent the building…I'd rather they back off than jump right in.

Louise: I don't always check … because you can't and sometimes we would go in at my previous station.

The firefighters went on to discuss the tension and dissonance that can sometimes exist between knowledge contained in manuals and experience gained from the craft of firefighting and 'doing the job'. Louise felt strongly that BA knowledge was sometimes more useful as guidance rather than something to be strictly followed. She would not necessarily follow the SOP and check if excess steam needed to be let out of a building before entering it. Louise felt that in some fast-moving situations the need to locate a missing person or quickly extinguish a fire took precedent. Strictly following the SOP could slow her down and limit her ability to exercise professional judgement. Whilst best practice contained in the SOP directed otherwise, Louise felt that her experience and knowledge were key. Sometimes, experience from doing the job for many years meant she could make a decision not to follow the SOP for BA strictly. Louise explained that in some circumstances the SOP was a little too restrictive. Other firefighters in her watch agreed with this and stressed the importance of learning collectively about BA techniques.

The use of storytelling and narrative was viewed as being very important; all the firefighters recognised how they shared and learnt BA techniques through swapping stories of their experiences in using the equipment. The watch would share stories of tackling serious blazes in tyre factories, industrial mills and blocks of flats. Through these stories they would share technical knowledge of using equipment such as cutters, hoses and erecting ladders in confined spaces. Firefighters would also recount specific stories of tackling 'once in a lifetime' experiences like football stadium fires or responding to large-scale emergencies such as flooding. Some of the members of Red Watch had been firefighters since the late 1980s. They would tell stories of facing ferocious blazes with the most basic of equipment. A true and authentic firefighter was one who had experienced 'singed' ears. This was a colloquialism for experiencing exceptionally high temperatures that penetrated firefighters' tunics and burnt their ears. A fire in the basement of a tanning salon had been particularly problematic for Red Watch. The salon had many dangerous chemicals stored in it, which increased significantly the risk of explosion and toxic fumes. The location of the fire made it difficult to gain access and deploy BA wearers to tackle the blaze. The fire took several hours to extinguish and the watch swapped stories on how to tackle the blaze and the best means of containing it. These stories helped pass on knowledge, skills and experiences amongst the watch and from which they could all learn and benefit from each other's experiential knowledge.

QUESTIONS

1. What are the advantages and limitations of learning only from textbooks and/or classroom teaching? Can practical skills be successfully conveyed and learnt in this manner?

2. What are the advantages of learning from the experiential knowledge of colleagues? Are there dangers to this approach and if so, what are they?

3. Do you agree with Louise's decision to deviate from standard BA operational policy and procedure based upon her own professional experience as a firefighter? Do you think this was a reasonable decision?

4. What are the benefits of using narrative and storytelling as a means of learning in the workplace?

REFERENCES

Home Office. 2016. 'Fire Statistics'.

19
For some or all? Debating the value of inclusive and exclusive approaches to talent management

Sharna Wiblen

BACKGROUND AND CONTEXT

ProfessionalCo (an assumed name) operates within the professional services industry and delivers knowledge-based services and is structured as a member firm of a larger private listed company, headquartered in the United Kingdom, and operating in over 150 countries. ProfessionalCo is responsible for the Asia-Pacific region, with this part of the multinational business self-described as one of the largest management consultancy firms operating within the region. Clients engage ProfessionalCo's services via a distinct Business Unit (BU), which offers deep expertise in various areas of speciality including consulting, accounting, finance, taxation, digital transformation and strategy. While able to operate independently, the firm maintains a partnership business structure with two levels of seniority – equity partner and non-equity partner – creating a situation whereby equity partners are simultaneous "employers" and "employees" as revenue and equity are distributed amongst these stakeholders. The senior executive team comprising the Chief Executive Officer (CEO), Chief Strategy Officer (CSO), Chief Operating Officer (COO) and Chief Financial Officer (CFO), are responsible for setting the firm's strategic direction.

Boasting over 44 000 staff, its workforce is separated into either a Corporate-based role, which focuses on the provision of services delivered subsidiary-wide, or within a specific part of the business. That is, employees either work for the organisation in the subsidiary headquarters (referred to as Corporate Executives) or in a distinct Business Unit (referred to as a Business Unit Executive). Each BU differs in relation to the services and knowledge provided to clients, workforce size, number of partners, and the skills and capabilities desired in "talent". The firm's Human Resource function is also separated into three teams: recruitment; policies and practices to be implemented organisation-wide; or the management of talent within a specific BU.

IMPORTANCE OF TALENT MANAGEMENT

In stark contrast to many of their competitors, ProfessionalCo did not seek to downsize the organisation dramatically during the 2007–2009 period of economic uncertainty (otherwise referred to as the Global Financial Crisis in some parts of the world). Instead of making a large part of the workforce redundant, ProfessionalCo implemented a new remuneration policy severely restricting pay increases, bonus and equity distributions. The CEO was particularly proud of the ability to "keep its workforce intact" during the wider Global Financial Crisis and frequently referred to this action (or lack of action) as the firm's unbridled commitment to talent management.

References to the importance of talent and talent management feature prominently in both internal and external talk and texts. The firm publicly declares that talent and talent management is imperative to its operational and strategic ambitions. The importance of talent management stems not only from the inherent connection between the quality of its internal workforce and organisational success but also the desire to compete in and win the widely heralded "War for Talent". Asserting the presence of a talent shortage, ProfessionalCo deliberately invested in enhancing the firm's external reputation in order to "win its unfair share of talent". Being recognised as an Employer of Choice operated as a further mechanism to pull potential talent towards the organisation and to widen the external talent pool.

Operating within a knowledge-based industry presents a unique set of challenges for talent management because, without talent, there would be no ProfessionalCo. The fixed relationship between talent management and the firm's operations further compounds the imperative need to manage "talent" effectively. Professional services are different from production or manufacturing organisations which provide stakeholders with physical goods and/or services, as the value proposition and "talents" of its workforce represent the sole source of competitive advantage. That is, knowledge-based firms such as ProfessionalCo sell services to clients. These services are founded on the skills, capabilities and knowledge of the people within. While many organisations adopt the adage that "Our people are our most important asset", this sentiment is factually correct for ProfessionalCo, as the people-based assets underpin all assets within the organisation.

Driven by a formalised talent management strategy to "grow" concerning size and revenue, the subsidiary proactively invested in talent management policies and practices to enhance the organisation's competitive positioning domestically. Employing discourse by strategy approaches which recognise the power of words and talk in shaping actions, the firm's senior executive team explicitly encourage everyone to "take action and invest in their talent" to achieve the subsidiary's strategic ambitions and goals. The charismatic CEO acted as a salient stakeholder in all talent management and strategy interactions and was frequently observed conversing with employees about their experiences working at ProfessionalCo, instigating opportunities to garner real-time data about the organisation's progress and the ability to balance client and workforce needs.

FACTORS INFLUENCING TALENT MANAGEMENT

The ability to enact an integrated approach to talent management – whereby all Business Units and Senior stakeholders were "doing the same thing" – and realise formalised strategic ambitions, however, is encased in complexity for the following reasons.

Talent management practices were not founded upon a pre-established definition of talent. There is no single agreed-upon understanding of "who" (individuals or everyone) and "what" (skills and capabilities or pivotal roles and positions) is talent across the organisation. Senior partners and HR managers within each BU can define talent in a way that they see fit, without intervention from the Firm's Asia-Pacific or global headquarters. This creates a situation whereby understandings of the defining characteristics of a "talented" employee may be vastly different within the firm. The potential for diversity in talent conceptualisations results in ambiguity and confusion within the workforce as employees are unaware of specific promotion requirements beyond the ability to present a convincing business case and demonstrate the ability to contribute to the firm through revenue generation.

Although talk about talent permeates throughout the organisation, with the term "talent" used frequently to describe certain policies and practices, Corporate HR executives acknowledge that there are vastly different perceptions of what "talent" looks like in an idealised sense. While there was the widespread agreement of the crucial importance of "talent" to the organisation (for the reasons noted above), Senior HR and non-HR executives held different opinions about whether there should be "one" talent conceptualisation. Questions about whether there was one-way or a best-way to define the defining characteristics required in order for a certain individual to be classified as "talent" was frequently debated.

Assertions about the value of a consistent and one-size-fits-all approach resulted in a few of the BUs establishing set talent parameters about the defining characteristics of talent. Via a formalised "talent definition", these BUs articulated the specific criteria used to evaluate an individual's "performance" and their "potential". This also created a situation where individuals are privy to the same evaluation methods within the context of these BUs. Other BUs, however, elected not to instigate one specific idea about the composition and defining attributes of a talented individual and elected to enact talent management founded upon fluid and agile conceptualisations, whereby the definition of talent could change if and when needed.

Another challenge arises from the absence of a talent management "system". The firm does not utilise technologically-enabled processes to guide talent evaluations and subsequent talent identification. The firm uses a software-as-a-service vendor created technology to evaluate individual and team performance as part of the organisation-wide performance management process. However, the use of HR technology stops at performance management, and although data captured during this process informs remuneration allocation, there is no mandate to use, or guidelines of how to use, this information to quantify an individual's value and distinguish between higher and lower performing employees. As a result of this, BUs and senior partners within each separate division can self-determine the criteria for and processes of talent identification without any input from Corporate executives.

The absence of a talent management system and talent definition resulted in divergent perceptions about how talented individuals are best identified. While debate rages about the value of either intuitive (unstructured and informal processes based on gut feel), individualised (informal processes that focus on a single individual) or strategic (integrated, and proactive processes applied consistently) talent identification processes within industry and academia, ProfessionalCo executives debated whether talent was best identified by "measuring" or "observing". BUs adopting the measuring perspective believed that talent is a construct that is quantifiable and that stakeholders can capture and represent employee value via statistical measures and "scores". This talent identification process relied heavily on Business Unit Line managers. Line managers were tasked with evaluating the performance and potential of team employees annually via the organisation-wide performance management practice. Line managers, during this process, would allocate scores (out of five) to each employee following defined criteria and then would input these numerical scores into the relevant HR technology module. These processes relied heavily on HR technology to capture line manager determinations and used the embedded algorithms to force-rank employees from highest to lowest performing employees. Line managers could also use HR technology to rank employees with the highest levels of potential and generate a list of individuals with the highest evaluations of both performance and potential. Individuals included in this latter list were subsequently classified as "talent".

The alternative observational-based approaches sought not to measure an employee's value quantitatively but instead emphasised subjective evaluations and observations. While individuals were subject to the organisation-wide performance management and allocated scores for performance and potential, senior stakeholders in these Business Units didn't want to rely on these scores or technology-based algorithms to decide which individuals could be identified as "talent". Line managers, in combination with senior HR managers, would meet face-to-face to share opinions and then debate and discuss which individuals had the characteristics of future leaders of the specific Business Unit and/or the wider organisation. From this perspective, humans, rather than technology, were responsible for making talent decisions.

There are also divergent opinions about whether the subsidiary should adopt and enact an inclusive or exclusive approach to talent management. Corporate HR executives tasked with providing talent development activities across the organisation would like the organisation to adopt an exclusive approach whereby only some individuals are invited to participate in the organisation-wide talent development programme. While some Units within ProfessionalCo agree with their Corporate HR counterparts, others, including the Taxation-based Unit, assert that all employees are valuable, therefore advocating for an inclusive understanding of "who" is "talent" and arguing that all employees should have equal access to talent development opportunities.

SUMMARY AND OVERVIEW

Overall, while there is an unbridled acceptance of the inherent importance of talent to both the wider organisation and its Asia-Pacific subsidiary, the ability to manage talent effectively in an integrated and consistent manner is complex. Business Units, via the senior stakeholders within these Units, have differing opinions about whether there should be a pre-determined definition of what talent is (or is not). There are also different ideas about whether the organisation should identify talented individuals consistently and systematically. These differing perceptions have implications for the role of HR technology in determining which individuals are talent, the role of HR and line managers and whether talent management applies to some or all (employees).

QUESTIONS

1. The case study implies that people-based resources and "talent" are more important to professional services' firms than other types of firms, including manufacturing companies. Do you agree? Give reasons and evidence to support your opinion.

2. ProfessionalCo is a subsidiary of a larger multinational organisation based in the United Kingdom. What challenges and opportunities does this present?

3. Given that ProfessionalCo currently operates without a definition of the defining characteristics of a talented employee, is there any merit in seeking to establish one definition of "talent" within the organisation? Why or why not?

4. Assume that you work in the Corporate HR function and the CEO has asked you to create a ProfessionalCo definition of talent. List 10 skills, capabilities and attributes that you think an individual requires in order to be classified as "talent". Give reasons for each criterion.

5. Articulate potential problems associated with both "inclusive" (all employees) or "exclusive" (some) approaches to talent management. Give reasons to support your position.

20
What is competence? Theory, policy and practice

Jonathan Winterton and Travis Turnbow

The following account describes the evolution of competence theory, its influence in recent European policy and an example of how it has been used in practice by the European transnational company Airbus.

Competence, like skill, is a contested and sometime controversial concept, but there is broad consensus that it encapsulates the skills, knowledge and behaviours necessary to perform to the standards of employment in a work context. How such competence is developed, assessed and deployed inevitably varies substantially between sectors and occupations, but there are also profound theoretical differences between countries. Therefore, when the European Commission was seeking to create a credit transfer system for vocational education and training, and ultimately the European Qualifications Framework (EQF), it was necessary to find the best fit with existing approaches to competence. The team that developed the competence typology for the European Credit transfer system for Vocational Education and Training (ECVET) analysed the three dominant approaches in Europe and proposed a unifying framework based on the common factors.

The UK was the first to adopt a competence-based approach to vocational education and training (VET) with the system of National Vocational Qualifications, which was focused mainly on functional competence, skills required to undertake specific work tasks, and the underpinning knowledge associated with those tasks. France adopted a more comprehensive '*triptyque*', a word borrowed from art, to describe a painting in three panels, like *The Garden of Earthly Delights* by Hieronymus Bosch that now hangs in Madrid's Prado museum. The French *triptyque* involves knowledge (*savoir*), skills (*savoir faire*) and behaviours (*savoir être*), implying that individuals need to know things, be able to do things, and to behave appropriately, to be effective members of a work team. The German approach is more complicated and involves in the knowledge domain (*Sachkompetenz*) both specific domain knowledge (*Fachkompetenz*) and work process knowledge (*Methodenkompetenz*), the latter straddling skills, along with social competence (*Sozialkompetenz*), which also straddles the behavioural domain, shared with personal competence (*Personalkompetenz*).

Since most European countries had adopted systems that are largely based on one of these three dominant approaches, it was possible to propose a best-fit typology of competence with which all countries could align to enable credit transfer and mutual recognition of qualifications to support labour mobility. The French approach offered a framework that had most in common with the others and which corresponded most closely with Bloom's taxonomy globally used in training, often summarised as 'knowledge, skills and attitudes', but where 'attitudes' underpin behaviours, the meaningful outcome measure. In terms of competence *theory*, those component dimensions of cognitive, functional and behavioural competence remain the fundamental building blocks of competence and appear in most qualification frameworks.

Whilst the analysis of European approaches to competence led to a best-fit solution for the competence typology proposed for ECVET, its adoption proved more problematic. Rather than adopting our recommendations, the Technical Working Group charged by the European Commission with developing ECVET decided to retain the terms 'knowledge, skills and competences' from the original remit, subsuming meta-competences under 'competences', leading to the confusion that competence was an umbrella term, a dimension and, in the sense of meta-competence, a sub-dimension. In parallel, the Expert Group convened by the Commission to develop the EQF retained knowledge and skills in their typology but replaced competence with 'personal and professional competence', which was further subdivided into four categories: autonomy and responsibility; learning competence; communication and social competence; and professional and vocational competence. Including autonomy and responsibility as a competence shows the extent of the conceptual confusion since these are characteristics of work organisation rather than individual attributes, even if responsible autonomy implies a certain level of knowledge and skills. Eventually the EQF competence framework returned to knowledge, skills and competence, but with the addition of 'responsibility and autonomy' in brackets after competence. In subsequent initiatives, competence appeared as an over-arching term, a dimension of that term and even as a sub-dimension of itself, suggesting that confusion has flourished in policy application.

Given the confusion in policy instruments, it is perhaps fortunate that their impact on practice has been relatively limited. Many companies had already been working on developing their own competence frameworks in isolation or in collaboration with other employers in the same sector and continued to do so. Companies such as Daimler, Ericsson and Metso were among the first to develop corporate competence frameworks. Progress had also been made on European-wide occupational competence frameworks, notably for nursing and welding, and in sectors such as chemical processing. The case study below describes comparable contemporaneous developments in Airbus at Toulouse, where the first author had supervised managers studying on the Aerospace MBA at Toulouse Business School and was *directeur de thèse* of the second author, then a doctoral student at the Université de Toulouse with a CIFRE scholarship and working for the company.

Airbus, at that time part of EADS (European Aeronautic Defence and Space Company), is a European trans-national aerospace corporation headquartered in Toulouse. One of the world's leading manufacturers of commercial aircraft, Airbus is also a major producer of helicopters and military aircraft as well as having divisions dedicated to satellites and navigation systems. Airbus currently has some 134 000 employees worldwide, compared with its major US competitor Boeing, which has 153 000 employees. At the time the competence management project was undertaken, the A380, the world's largest passenger airliner, was in the final stages of test flights and while orders for the Airbus A320 were lagging behind those for Boeing's 737, that situation has since reversed. For several decades the commercial aircraft industry has been a de facto duopoly of these two dominant manufacturers.

The aerospace sector, particularly in relation to commercial aircraft, is quite cyclical in nature, with production lagging behind air transport demand and a permanent disequilibrium between demand and supply. The traditional human capital management response was to lay off employees during a market down-turn and bring them back in during the next up-turn. That traditional approach failed Boeing when laid-off employees were picked up by the IT boom in Silicon Valley, so aerospace companies began to think more strategically about forecasting future jobs and skills, and about managing human capital to retain core competence. The human resources team at Airbus recognised the need for a system that would help managers make more informed decisions in relation to future competence needs and to put in place mechanisms to forecast more accurately future competence gaps and to secure or develop these in the medium term. In the process, there was explicit recognition of the need to identify and retain core competence underpinning competitive advantage and avoid a situation where most of the higher skills resided in older employees who could soon be retiring.

Airbus already had in place a sophisticated tool, Optimise Skills, which involved employees and managers together comparing the required competences defined by the line manager and the acquired competences currently possessed by the individual in post. The process compares self-appraisal of existing competence with the line managers' assessment in the Optimise Skills interview, leading to an update of any identified competence gap and subsequent training needs. The company was not, however, practising a technique developed in France for predicting future jobs and skills needs known as GPEC (*Gestion Prévisionnelle de l'Emploi et des Compétences*), which was considered too challenging in such a complex high-tech operation.

The Airbus Operating Plan covering a five-year period was the starting point for the company's Resource Planning Model, which compared the workload calculation against workforce capacity (headcount). At the end of that process occupations were added to give a qualitative estimate of the workload/workforce conversion. Whilst Airbus already had one of the most comprehensive competence management frameworks, it was largely focused on current competence needs and the introduction of the qualitative dimension came too late in the process. The aim was to introduce competence scenario development and simulation linked with the appropriate business drivers at the outset of the process, and in consultation with internal stakeholders, six essential needs were identified for the competence scenario and simulation tool.

For each profession or occupational group, expert stakeholders were asked about qualitative changes in the key competencies involved as well as quantitative changes through internal mobility (in and out) as well as externally through recruitment and attrition. Users of the scenario analyses made hypotheses about the rate of quantitative changes while training hypotheses were added concerning the rate at which competence proficiency would be acquired. In six divisions of Airbus involved in the project, there was a positive correlation between the maturity of competence management and forecasting. Forecasting appeared to be the impetus to competence management, driving the improvement of tools and processes while raising perceptions of competence gaps to be addressed.

The practical part of the project was concerned to enhance the existing Optimise Skills competence management tool, designing and implementing a tool and associated processes for competence forecasting and management across Airbus and EADS. Known as EADS Competence Management (ECM), the objective was to ensure uniform competence management across all EADS divisions. The system developed compared the status quo with future needs based on simulation of different scenarios interpreting the EADS Operating Plan (EOP). The competence planning and simulation process developed is shown in Figure 20.1. There was extensive piloting of this planning and simulation process to test the utility of the 'HR mix' options in capturing the key 'make or buy' options for sourcing human capital. With each iteration, the processes were refined based on user feedback, which was actively solicited. Most users found the tool to be user-friendly and institutive. In general, users appreciated the 'look and feel' of the tool, although there were some bugs concerning clarity of the graphics. The tool was piloted in English, then the refined version was translated into the other four EADS languages (French, German, Italian and Spanish).

The final version of the competence forecasting and planning process is shown in Figure 20.2, which shows the five elements of establishing the 'as is' and 'to be' situations, the latter driven by the operating plan, comparing these to identify future gaps, then developing a competence action plan to meet staffing needs through identifying the most appropriate HR mix. Ultimately, a customised software solution was built to embed the system in EADS and all competence management in Airbus was integrated into the EADS Competence Management Project. The competence forecasting tool was then reviewed by all EADS divisions, which led to changes in the competence catalogue and the

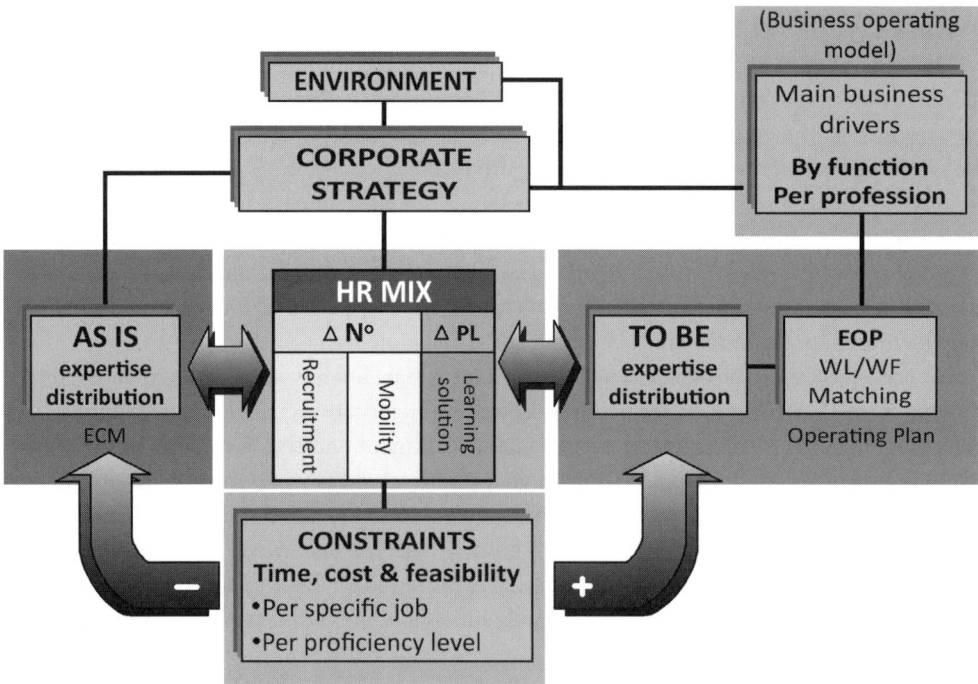

Source: T. Turnbow (2012), *Forecasting and Competence Management Maturity: Their relationship, measurement, and practical implementation. A study at EADS Airbus*. Thèse du Doctorat de l'Université de Toulouse 1 Capitole, p. 245.

Figure 20.1 Competence planning and simulation process

redefinition of some of its core components. However, the fundamental competence forecasting tool and process was not significantly altered and the technological solution developed within the study represented a forerunner in the field of competence management and an industry benchmark.

For HR professionals, the project holds many lessons, both substantive and procedural. In substantive terms, perhaps the key issue is the need to establish mechanisms to link business strategies with competence needs and to enable assessment of the competences people possess and those they will need to acquire. The most important procedural lessons are the need for top management strategic support and key stakeholder engagement, including line managers in different functions. At the time the project was undertaken, a survey of HR leaders in French organisations showed almost two-thirds acknowledged the importance of retaining key competences and expressed a desire to improve their systems for forecasting competence needs. Even today, relatively few organisations have developed such sophisticated integrated systems for managing human capital, although this will certainly change as human capital analytics becomes more commonplace. At the time, Airbus was clearly at the frontier of competence management and their example has inspired other organisations.

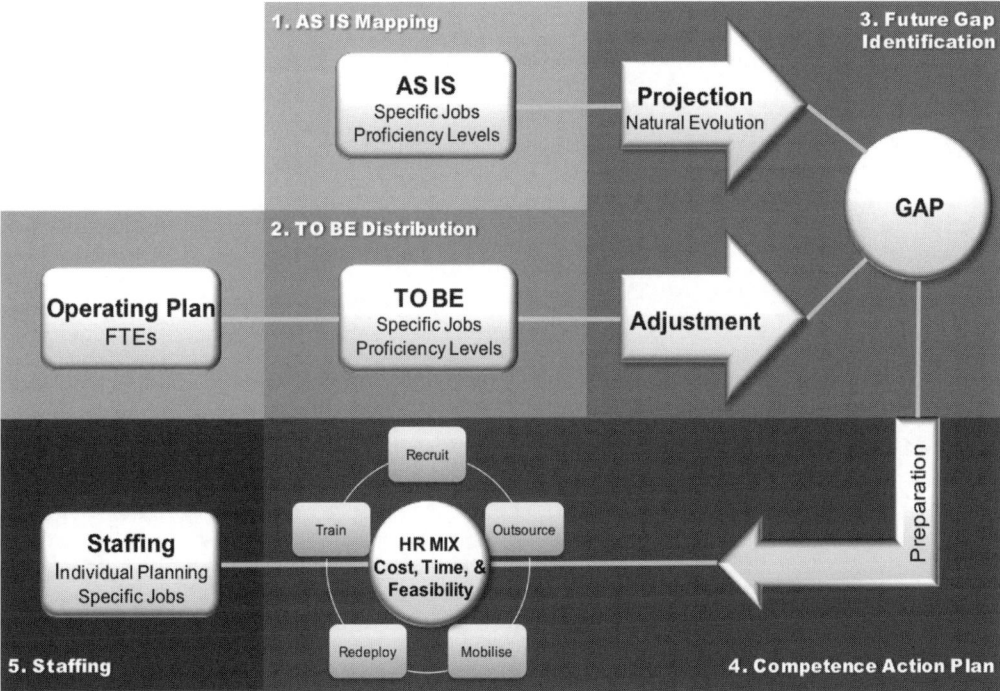

Source: T. Turnbow (2012), *Forecasting and Competence Management Maturity: Their relationship, measurement, and practical implementation. A study at EADS Airbus.* Thèse du Doctorat de l'Université de Toulouse 1 Capitole, p. 292.

Figure 20.2 Final competence forecasting and planning process

QUESTIONS

1. Why is it necessary to start from a business or operational plan to forecast future human capital needs, in terms of the quantity and quality of labour?

2. How should managers assess the competencies individuals possess and help them acquire what they will need in the future?

3. What must managers consider in ensuring core competence is retained and future needs are met?

4. Are such approaches to competence management only relevant to high-value, knowledge-based sectors like aerospace or biotechnology?

5. What would be appropriate for relatively low-skilled work like aged care, which is crucially important in societal terms?

6. What difficulties are posed in developing a human capital management system in a transnational enterprise given that countries have diverse cultural approaches to skill and different institutional arrangements for skill formation?

21
Gender at Victoria Police: A long way travelled

Georgina Caillard and Julie Wolfram Cox

In 2017 Victoria Police celebrated 100 years of women in policing. The Victoria Police Museum mounted an exhibition entitled *Agents of Change*, celebrating how women had contributed to the shaping of policing in Victoria, Australia. The Police website also contained a section celebrating the milestone with timelines and stories of significant women in policing. In its promotion of the museum exhibition, the website stated that, 'The overall aim of the exhibition is a celebration of women's contributions to policing in Victoria over a century. It aims to acknowledge the historical struggles and discrimination women faced, in order to highlight the equality and diversity of Victoria Police today' (Victoria Police 2017). There is no denying that Victoria Police has transformed in just over a century. However, while women are much better represented now than in 2017, Victoria Police acknowledges that it has not yet achieved gender equality. In 2014, the Chief Commissioner of Police, Graham Ashton, recognised that there was a need to address discrimination and sexual harassment in Victoria Police. Seeking to take a leadership position in gender equality, he called upon the Victoria Equal Opportunity and Human Rights Commission (VEOHRC) to review, report and make recommendations upon sex discrimination and sexual harassment in Victoria Police. The Report was delivered in 2015. It included twenty recommendations that covered issues from governance structures and leadership training to cultural change, recruitment and promotion targets for women in Victoria Police and the establishment of independent oversight, all of which Victoria Police committed to act upon.

A BRIEF INTRODUCTION TO POLICING IN VICTORIA

In order to understand the history of women in Victoria Police and to appreciate the complexity of the organisation reviewed by the VEOHRC it is helpful to have some background in how policing operates in Victoria. According to the Victoria Police Act 2013, '[t]he role of Victoria Police is to serve the Victorian community and uphold the law so as to promote a safe, secure and orderly society' (Section 8). Evolved at common law (that is, through the decisions of the courts), police officers have powers reasonably necessary to perform their duties, balancing the general good against the rights and liberties of the individual. The rights and powers evolved through the courts have been both supplemented and qualified by statute.

Under the Victoria Police Act 2013, Victoria Police comprises the Chief Commissioner, Deputy Commissioners, Assistant Commissioners, other police officers, protective services officers, police recruits, police reservists and Victoria Police employees. In its report, the VEOHRC simplified the categories to those of police, protective service officers or public servants. Each of these groups is distinct in relation to its recruitment, training, duties and powers. Police officers, for example, undergo a rigorous recruitment process that involves physical, intellectual, psychological and character assessments. Recruits then undertake two years of training commencing with 12 weeks full time at Victoria Police Academy, after which they are sworn in. Only sworn officers may exercise the full powers of a police officer. Protective Service Officers (PSOs) provide protective services (as the name suggests) for persons holding certain public offices, or in relation to specific places such as train stations. While having more restricted powers than police, PSOs also undergo 12 weeks' training at the Academy. They then undertake a further three months' training under the supervision of an experienced PSO. Public servants employed by Victoria Police support the police officers to fulfil their duties but are not sworn officers. They therefore have no greater powers than any general member of the public.

HOW FAR HAS VICTORIA POLICE COME?

While some women had worked with Victoria Police in earlier undercover operations, the first two female 'agents' were appointed in 1917. Their roles were limited; they were not sworn officers so had no power of arrest and they received half the pay of their male colleagues. A Police Women's Division was established in 1922, largely running parallel to the male ranks (but still subject to male management) and seven years after she joined, Madge Connor, the remaining original agent, was finally sworn in, along with the three other female members of Victoria Police at that time. They now had the power to arrest and were paid the same base salary as their male counterparts but, unlike their male counterparts, they did not receive overtime payments and had no uniform. The distinction was further reinforced by their title, police *woman* (PW). By 1929 the number of police women had only risen to eight.

In 1939, when Grace Brebner applied to join Victoria Police, there were still only eight women serving. Brebner went on to become Victoria Police's first female detective in 1951 and in 1971 became the first woman to achieve the rank of Inspector. The year she joined the police, 1939, WWII began. Through necessity, as men went to war, women joined the labour force, entering into jobs that in peacetime were closed to them. As many male members of the police joined the armed forces, there was a need to fill the gap and a female auxiliary was established. This female auxiliary force, which had at its peak over 200 members, was unsworn. However, unlike the sworn female police officers at the time, they had a uniform. Police women did not get a uniform until 1947.

While the number of women in Victoria Police was steadily growing, the duties they were considered suitable to perform were still quite restricted, typically involving welfare or domestic issues. Kath Mackay, who had joined the force in 1922, passed the sergeants' exam and applied for promotion to sergeant in 1953. However, her superiors were reluctant to promote a woman into a position of authority over men, and her later appeal was dismissed on the basis that a sergeant in charge of a station might need to perform duties for which she was unsuited (implicitly by virtue of her sex). By 1956 women were still not permitted to drive police vehicles. A prohibition against married female recruits was not lifted until 1972.

Women continued to advocate for greater equality from within Victoria Police and to demonstrate their aptitude. In 1960 the first three places amongst graduating recruits had been taken by women and in 1975 Bernice Masterson became the first woman to come top in Detective Training school. Their efforts received a boost when, in 1977, the Equal Opportunity Act 1977 (Vic) was enacted, which prohibited discrimination in employment, education, accommodation or the provision of goods or services on the basis of marital status or gender. Subsequent legislation has extended the categories protected to include disability (1982), race, religion, ethnic origin, political belief and de facto spouse status (1984) and age, carer status, disability, industrial activity, lawful sexual activity, marital status, parental status, physical features, pregnancy, race, religious belief/activity, sex and personal association with someone else perceived to have one or more of the listed attributes (1995). Sexual harassment also became unlawful in 1984 (VEOHRC, n.d.).

Change was swift and varied. Women could wear trousers as part of their uniform from 1981. Police women began to transfer to general duties policing and in 1982 the Police Women's Division was abolished. That same year the first woman was appointed as the officer in charge of a station. Tragically, this decade also saw Angela Taylor become the first female police officer murdered on duty when the Police Headquarters in Russell Street, Melbourne was car bombed. One of the clearest indicators that times had changed, and also a harbinger of change to come, was the appointment in Victoria of Australia's first (and to date, only) female Chief Commissioner of Police, Christine Nixon in 2001.

CHRISTINE NIXON: CHIEF COMMISSIONER OF VICTORIA POLICE

Nixon was born in 1953 in New South Wales, the daughter of a New South Wales policeman. After completing high school, she was told that she would not be considered as a management trainee by the supermarket for which she had worked part time because she was a woman. Instead, she joined the New South Wales Police. At that time police women were on limited duties, which included working with the victims of sexual assaults and domestic violence. In the wider world the first wave of feminism was in full swing and, not without struggle and opposition, wider roles were opening up for women everywhere, including in the New South Wales police.

Nixon was ambitious but found her upward path often blocked by entrenched (male) power structures and on at least one occasion, by a (male) politician. These road blocks prompted Nixon to take up non-traditional career pathways including opportunities to study overseas. She achieved a Master's Degree in administration from Harvard University and also undertook some research with the Metropolitan Police in London. While establishing a point of difference in her career and equipping her with ideas and insights to which she was unlikely to be exposed from within police practice, this pathway also saw her criticised as 'an academic' as opposed to an operational police officer (Nixon with Chandler, 2011).

Towards the end of her time at New South Wales Police, Nixon applied for the job of Chief Commissioner in New South Wales, and put in an initial application for the role of Police Commissioner in South Australia. She subsequently withdrew the South Australian application when the new Commissioner in New South Wales, Peter Ryan, offered her a five-year contract involving interesting and challenging work with a significant pay rise to persuade her to stay. In early 2001 the role of Chief Commissioner of Police in Victoria was advertised. She applied and was successful.

When Nixon took over as Chief Commissioner, Victoria Police was an organisation of about 12,000 people. Only 15 per cent of sworn members at that time were female and of the 193 inspector positions only three were held by women. The gender balance among the public service members of Victoria Police was skewed towards more women, yet the dominant culture was masculine. It was common to hear sworn police referred to as 'the brotherhood' of police, a term Nixon uses herself in her autobiography. Less positively, Victoria Police was sometimes referred to as 'a boys' club'.

Nixon came in with an agenda to change the culture of Victoria Police. She wanted it to be more inclusive, reflecting the diversity of the community it served, to diminish the emphasis on hierarchy and be more consultative and democratic in management style. She set about changing the command structure. A number of people who could not or would not get behind her ideas and vision left the organisation. Reporting layers were removed and in the flatter structure Nixon had over 30 direct reports. She established a Corporate Committee comprised of senior sworn and public service members as a decision-making body for Victoria Police, which met regularly in locations around the state. In order to give greater voice to all police irrespective of rank or location, members, from recruits upwards, were invited to email Nixon directly with suggestions, problems or complaints and she undertook to respond in person to each one.

Other changes were brought in that in more subtle ways impacted on the hierarchy and traditions of Victoria Police. Nixon instigated uniform reforms, which saw the introduction of baseball caps and bomber jackets, and relaxed the rules around hair and tattoos. Targets were set for the recruitment of women and the height, weight and fitness requirements for admission as a police officer were reviewed to be more realistic reflections of requirements and not unfairly discriminatory against women. For example, if you review the entrance requirements today, there is no mention of a minimum height (Victoria Police, 2019). Nixon herself was declined at first instance by New South Wales Police for being a half inch too short.

Several reforms during Nixon's tenure were specifically directed toward issues of sexuality and gender. As a sign of support for members of Victoria Police who were gay or lesbian, she agreed in 2002 to march in the St Kilda Gay Pride parade and authorised other members of the force to do so, in uniform. This outraged many members who saw allowing officers to march in uniform as degrading the office. Yet, despite this evidence of support from the Chief Commissioner, few police felt confident to 'come out' (Nixon with Chandler, 2011, p. 134). Wider social concern related to family violence saw reforms in this area too. Victoria Police and the government had both been looking into ways to improve prevention and responses in family violence situations. In 2008 the new Family Violence Protection Act came into force requiring the police to reform their customary practices, which too often found such violence dismissed as 'just a domestic' (Nixon with Chandler, 2011, p. 251).

Nixon was Police Commissioner in Victoria for eight years. She faced many difficult scenarios, which required determination, perseverance, conviction and emotional control. Faced with the death of several serving officers from diverse causes, she visited grieving colleagues and family to express sympathy on behalf of the force. In her autobiography, she recounts how she snapped a response to insensitive questioning during a press conference after one such death, and speculates how this spontaneous reaction seemed to give other members tacit permission to admit to their own emotions in the situation. Yet, she was aware that showing too much emotion in her role was inappropriate. She had a strategy of gritting her back teeth so as not to shed tears.

The defining event at the twilight of Nixon's term as Chief Commissioner was Black Saturday. On 7 February 2009 a series of bushfires were burning around Victoria. The fires were preceded by unprecedented hot weather with many days in late January above 43 degrees Celsius. The state was tinder dry and on Saturday, 7 February, the winds were ferocious and the temperature in Melbourne, Victoria's capital city, exceeded 46 degrees Celsius (115.5 degrees Fahrenheit). These were the worst fire conditions ever seen in Victoria. Over 400 individual fires were recorded on that day, resulting in 180 deaths. At the time, responsibility for emergency response was shared by the Department of Sustainability and Environment (DSE), the Country Fire Authority (CFA) and Victoria Police and for the first time the DSE and CFA control centres were co-located. At 6 o'clock that night, Nixon left the control centre to have dinner. While she states in her autobiography that she genuinely believed that suitable delegations were in place and her role was covered, there was in fact a gap in police responsibility between 6 pm and 9 pm. The subsequent Royal Commission found 'that Ms Nixon's approach to emergency coordination was inadequate. Ms Nixon herself acknowledged that leaving the integrated Emergency Coordination Centre and going home at about 6.00 pm on 7 February was an error of judgment. The Commission shares this view' (2009 Victorian Bushfires Royal Commission, 2010, p. 8).

On 10 February, 2009, three days after the fires devastated the state, the Premier of Victoria announced the formation of the Victorian Bushfire Reconstruction and Recovery Authority and that Christine Nixon would be retiring early from her position as Police Commissioner to head the Authority. She suffered extensive and lengthy criticism in the media for her actions on Black Saturday. In contrast, Moira Rayner, who had been Commissioner for Equal Opportunity in Victoria between 1990 and 1994, wrote a piece entitled *The Crucifixion of Christine Nixon* (Rayner, 2010), which asserted that her treatment at the hand of the press would have been different had she been a man. First, Rayner argued, a man would be less likely to admit, as Nixon had, that they could have done better. Second, the flames of criticism were fuelled by those Nixon had run up against during her tenure.

THE VICTORIAN EQUAL OPPORTUNITY AND HUMAN RIGHTS COMMISSION (VEOHRC) AND VICTORIA POLICE

Since Nixon's term as Chief Commissioner, Victoria has had three Police Commissioners; Simon Overland, Ken Lay and Graham Ashton. In 2014, recognising the need within Victoria Police to change the culture in relation to sexual harassment and discrimination and seeking to be a social leader in gender equality, Chief Commissioner Graham Ashton asked the VEOHRC to study the problem and make recommendations. At the time of the Commission's investigation Victoria Police numbered around 17,000 people, of whom approximately 13,200 were sworn members (approximately 31 per cent of these were women). The Commission found that there was 'a highly gendered breakdown of the workforce in terms of rank/level, nature of role performed and place of work, as well as between public servants, PSOs and police' (VEOHRC, 2015, p. 16). Over 5,000 people participated in the survey and interviews were conducted with current and former members (VEOHRC, 2015). The key findings of the Report, delivered in 2015, included that:

- Almost one in five women and one in twenty men had experienced sexual harassment in a Victoria Police workplace in the past five years.
- The prevalence of sexual harassment in Victoria Police workplaces was higher for women than in the general community but for men it was lower than in the general community.
- Women were more likely to be targeted by someone of higher grade/rank, while men were more likely to be targeted by someone of the same or lower grade/rank.
- The level of understanding and identification of sex discrimination and sexual harassment by supervisors and management was inconsistent.
- Incidents of sexual harassment often occurred in front of others. Such harassment was widely accepted; victims were encouraged to 'deal with it' and move on.
- Women experienced discrimination at all points in the process from recruitment, to retention and promotion. This was especially noted in relation to women who become pregnant, take parental leave and on their return from leave. Discrimination was faced by both men and women who sought access to flexible work arrangements or part-time work.
- Sex discrimination and sexual harassment were chronically under-reported in Victoria Police. Reasons given included the perceived damage to reputation that might arise from reporting the behaviour. Women also named the negative effect such reporting might have on their careers, while men named that they felt a report would make no difference.

In sum, 14 years after the appointment of Christine Nixon as Chief Commissioner the power structures of Victoria Police were still seen as male dominated and the 'brotherhood' or 'boys' club' remained strong. There was a widespread attitude that the men did the 'real' police work, while women did 'soft' policing. A contributing factor here was the gender difference in specialist branches. For example, men dominated in crime and homicide work but the mounted branch and sexual assault were seen as the domain of women. On a slightly more positive note the report stated that many did agree that the gendered culture was not as bad as it used to be.

The VEOHRC identified violence against women as having the same causes as other forms of gender discrimination: unequal power between men and women and rigid adherence to gender stereotypes (VEOHRC, 2015, p. 13). The Commission also identified that Victoria Police did not exist in a vacuum, but that gender inequality was 'reflected and supported in multiple ways including through commonly held community assumptions and implicit and explicit rules or expectations about "the way we do things" (norms)' (VEOHRC, 2015, p. 53).

The action plan provided by the Commission in its Report laid out a whole-of-organisation approach, addressing structures, norms and practices. The Review proposed that Victoria Police's leadership needed to be united around a vision of gender equality and strategies and policies aligned with the vision needed to be developed and communicated. Advisory bodies with external expert membership should be established to assist in implementation to overcome the propensity for gendered practices to be reproduced generationally. Training and development needed to be addressed, from the Academy to senior management. Resources needed to be committed in alignment with the vision and organisation-wide measures and benchmarks established. Notably, the Review action plan included explicit targets of at least 50 per cent for recruitment, promotion and representation of women across policing, PSO and public service cohorts.

Chief Commissioner Graham Ashton undertook on behalf of Victoria Police that all the recommendations of the Review would be implemented. However, the Commission had noted evidence of hostility towards the Review itself and 'a significant number' (VEOHRC, 2015, p. 101) of employees who identified any attempt to address inequality as unfair to men. Both these facts suggested a difficult road ahead for Victoria Police in achieving real and ongoing change in gender equality.

A Phase 2 Review, to be conducted 18 months after the original report, was anticipated in the original reference to the VEOHRC. This review has been completed and the Report handed down in 2017, the same year as Victoria Police celebrated 100 years of women in policing in Victoria. It found that:

> Victoria Police has invested significant effort and resources into the implementation of recommendations to date. In order to ensure the reforms have the necessary impact and enable Victoria Police to realise its necessary state, a robust approach to evaluation is required. To date, there has been a limited evaluation of new structures, programs or pilots. (VEOHRC, 2017, p. 23)

The *Agents of Change* exhibition promoted in 2017 stated that its aim was to highlight the equality and diversity of Victoria Police today. Undoubtedly, Victoria Police is a vastly different workplace for women than it was 100 years ago, but the equality and diversity afforded by this organisation now and into the future remain to be seen.

QUESTIONS

1. Chief Commissioner Graham Ashton stated that, in instigating the VEOHRC Review, he wished Victoria Police to be a leader in gender equality. To what extent do organisations influence society or society influence organisations? Support your response with examples from the case study and wider reading.

2. How might the persistence of gender discrimination at Victoria Police be explained? Be explicit about the theoretical frame or frames that you are using.

3. What are some reasons that might explain the negative reactions of many police towards those who take parental leave or seek to access flexible work hours? To what extent are these reasons gendered?

4. Why is the proportion of full-time female staff and recruits of importance to the achievement of gender equality at Victoria Police?

5. It is easy to fall into the error of seeing gender discrimination and sexual harassment in terms of 'men versus women'. However, both gender and sex are broader than these two categories. What examples of broader issues emerge from the case?

6. It has been suggested that Victoria Police has a strongly masculine culture. In what ways did Christine Nixon challenge this?

REFERENCES AND ADDITIONAL READINGS

Acker, J. (2012), Gendered organizations and intersectionality: Problems and possibilities, *Equality, Diversity & Inclusion*, **31**(3): 214–24.

Equal Opportunity Act 1977 (Vic).

Janssens, M. and Steyaert, C. (2019), A practice-based theory of diversity: Respecifying (in)equality in organizations, *Academy of Management Review*, **44**(3): 518–37.

Melgoza, A.R. and Wolfram Cox, J. (2009), Subtle sexism: Re-informing intergroup bias and regulating emotion in an Australian police organization, *Journal of Management and Organization*, **15**(5): 652–66.

Nixon, C. with Chandler, J. (2011), *Fair Cop*, Carlton, Victoria: Victory Books.

Rayner, M. (2010), The crucifixion of Christine Nixon, *Eureka Street*. Accessed at https://www.eurekastreet.com.au/article/the-crucifixion-of-christine-nixon.

VEOHRC (2015), *Independent Review into sex discrimination and sexual harassment, including predatory behaviour, in Victoria Police: Phase one report*, Carlton, Victoria: VEOHRC.

VEOHRC (2017), *Independent Review into sex discrimination and sexual harassment, including predatory behaviour, in Victoria Police: Phase 2 audit*, Carlton, Victoria: VEOHRC.

VEOHRC (n.d.), *How Victoria's Equal Opportunity Act has changed over time*. Accessed at https://www.humanrightscommission.vic.gov.au/index.php/about-us/item/572-howvictorias-equal-opportunity-act-has-changed-over-time.

Victoria Police (2017), *100 Years of women in policing*. Accessed at https://www.police.vic.gov.au/content.asp?Document_ID=48462.

Victoria Police (2019), *Careers*. Accessed at https://www.police.vic.gov.au/careers.

Victoria Police Act 2013 (Vic).

Yates, S., Riach, K. and Johansson M. (2018), Stress at work, gendered dys-appearance and the broken body in policing, *Gender, Work & Organization*, **25**(1): 91–105.

2009 Victorian Bushfires Royal Commission (2010), Accessed at http://royalcommission.vic.gov.au/finaldocuments/summary/PF/VBRC_Summary_PF.pdf.

22
Workplace bullying at Neptune Plc

Ria Deakin and Helge Hoel

BACKGROUND AND CONTEXT

Neptune Plc is a British facilities management and infrastructure company. It works with public authorities and utility companies to deliver repair and maintenance services across a range of areas including water, sewage, electricity and refuse collection. Neptune Plc operates across the UK through a number of regional sites, employing over 13 000 people in total. Most sites are divided into departments dealing with particular services and contracts. Each of these departments has a customer service team, a service delivery team, and a commercial team. Each team has a manager who reports to the departmental manager. Managers are appointed on the basis of their technical skill, knowledge and experience, rather than on their management capabilities. They are required to undertake some management training but this is minimal and the requirement is not strictly enforced.

Neptune Plc has a central HR department, based on one of the sites in the North West, but there is no onsite HR representation in the other regional branches. Neptune Plc has a well-populated company intranet that provides access to their grievance procedure and their Dignity at Work policy. All policies and procedures have been developed in line with good practice guidelines from the UK Advisory, Conciliation and Arbitration Service (Acas) and the Chartered Institute of Personnel and Development (CIPD), and recommend that concerns and problems should, as far as possible, always be raised with the line managers in the first instance. The grievance procedure mentions the possible use of mediation but there is no internal company mediation scheme in place. The company also has stated corporate values around the importance of working together with respect and dignity.

The terms and conditions of employment are consistent with competitors and are generally considered to be good. However, the standard hours are relatively long, at 42.5 hours a week, and the work can, at times, be stressful, especially during busy periods and when large contracts are up for review. There are systems for the close monitoring of performance to help ensure targets are achieved.

Overall, job satisfaction and employee retention at Neptune Plc is good, but there are examples of problematic relationships across the sites. The commercial team at one of the West Midlands sites is a particular cause for concern.

THE PROBLEMATIC TEAM

The cause for concern lies in the significance of the utilities contract that the commercial team is currently working on. The contract is a lucrative one that is due for renegotiation and review within the next six months. However, there is currently a problem of a large backlog of work which is having an impact on the amount of income being generated. There is a concern that not only will this backlog lead to short-term financial problems, but that it will also have a negative impact on the reputation of Neptune Plc and on perceptions of its ability to deliver to contract in the future. The team is, therefore, under pressure to deliver.

There are eight people working in the team: Habib, the team leader and line manager, Colin, a Quantity Surveyor, and six commercial assistants (Beth, Lucy, Nick, Anne, Zoe and Sarah) responsible for processing orders and payments. Although Colin is not a manager, he is more senior than the assistants. The majority of the team are employed on full-time permanent contracts and have been with the company for at least five years, but three of the assistants (Anne, Lucy and Sarah) have been brought in as agency workers to help clear the backlog and have only been there for about three months. Due to the importance of the contract, Dave, the regional manager for the department, has also been working at the same site to oversee the work.

The team work in a large open plan office. The commercial assistants work the basic 42.5 hours a week on a 7.30 am–4 pm basis, but have also frequently been working overtime in evenings and on weekends too to help clear the backlog, meaning a 60-hour week is not an unusual occurrence. Habib and Dave are based in the same office but tend to work 9 am–6 pm. Colin often works off-site but sits with the assistants when he is in the office.

MANAGEMENT STYLE

In line with company practice, both Habib and Dave were promoted on the basis of their technical knowledge and experience, rather than their management experience. Both have attended a basic management course where they were taught about the importance of communication with their team and were introduced to the company performance and appraisal system. Neither, however, rated the training, and feel that managing people is "just common sense". The relationship between Habib and Dave is generally good and they get along well, frequently joking and laughing with each other. They also adopt a "banter" attitude with the team members, often making sarcastic or teasing comments.

Habib said he would hold weekly team briefings on a Monday to "touch base" and provide updates on the status of the contract but these are frequently cancelled so he can attend "more important" operational meetings. When they are held, the agency workers are not always invited, despite the fact they are completing necessary work; the meetings are also held in the open plan office so those not invited are, nevertheless, present. They have said that this behaviour leaves them feeling disrespected and isolated. Habib has frequent one-to-one meetings with the assistants at their desks to allocate tasks, although these are conducted on an ad hoc basis. At times, these result in the assistants being pulled off uncompleted work they have previously been told is of the highest priority to work on something else that is now more important. This has led to confusion, as well as duplication of work across team members, causing disruptions to productivity and arguments between team members. This sense of confusion is made worse when Dave also steps in to allocate work or readjust priorities, without necessarily first consulting with Habib. This has led to some heated arguments – involving raised voices and bad language – in the open plan office between Habib and Dave in front of the team.

A number of the assistants have noticed that when Dave and Habib allocate work seen as important, they tend to give it to certain members of the team – particularly Lucy and Nick. When working late, Anne and Zoe have overheard Dave and Habib openly rating the capabilities of the team and mocking other team members. For example making fun of Sarah for being an "uptight killjoy" for questioning whether comments made by Dave that the reason a female colleague in a different team was only on her way to promotion because she dressed in a way that "showcased her assets" and because she was "very friendly and accommodating" with her male boss were really appropriate. Dave and Habib were also openly discussing what a push over and how slow at her work Beth was – with Habib laughing and saying she was "a stupid little useless girl who is always cocking up and needs some sense knocking into her". They also commented that one of the reasons they liked Lucy was because "she could handle herself and give as good as she gets" as she pushes back against their comments and demands. Anne and Zoe felt like they were not able to challenge the comments and instead decided to tell the rest of the team the next day at work. While Lucy, Nick, Sarah – and especially Beth – were angry and upset, they were not terribly surprised as they had had their suspicions that Dave and Habib felt this way but this was the first explicit confirmation they had had. The team collectively decided not to raise the issue further as they had heard from colleagues in other teams across the contract that their managers were the same and therefore the team felt that though they weren't happy with it, it seemed to be the way things were done there and to try and change it would be too challenging. As agency workers, Anne, Lucy and Sarah were also not sure if it was their place to raise this with Neptune Plc.

The conditions, however, have started to have an impact on productivity and retention, with Sarah choosing to leave and Lucy, the second highest performer, contemplating leaving. Lucy feels a sense of frustration over a lack of respect and tension between being wanted when there was important work to be done and not being invited to team meetings and otherwise being ignored to the extent she feels she is being treated "like productive furniture". Additionally, for some time, Beth had been feeling insecure in her position and had felt as if the quality and speed of her work was being unfairly criticised by Dave and Habib in the one-to-ones in front of everyone; the comments reported by Anne and Zoe had reinforced this feeling and led to her being increasingly absent from work. She feels that the criticisms are unwarranted but that if conversations about her work are going to happen, they should happen in private and to have them in public was embarrassing and humiliating. Although Beth feels that the comments were incorrect, her productivity measures did indicate a relative decline over time and a lower completion rate than the rest of the team. As a result of this decline, in her recent annual appraisal Habib decided to monitor Beth and her activities more closely. Beth responded to this development by bursting into tears and leaving the meeting feeling as though she was being "picked on". She requested a meeting with HR to talk about the situation but never received a response to her request. Rather than chase HR, she decided she did not want to risk making the situation any worse by following up so carried on working as before.

TEAM DYNAMICS

On the whole, despite the occasional tensions over the allocation of work, the relationship between the assistants in the team is good. The workload is high but the work itself is monotonous and repetitive and easy to complete while chatting. The team work long hours together and often talk and joke about things like films and television, food and hobbies to help pass the time. Although based off-site at times, Colin often also comes and works in the office.

Colin is good friends with Habib and Dave and joins in with their jokes – although not any jokes about fellow team member performance or capability. When he is in the office, Colin likes to be the centre of attention and his presence changes the team dynamic as the usual conversations become easily side-tracked to what Colin likes to talk about. He is competitive in nature and likes to quiz people on general knowledge. Lucy finds Colin to be too arrogant and therefore won't play his games. Zoe is fond of general knowledge so initially played along. However, when she was able to answer his questions, Colin got annoyed and started to accuse Zoe of cheating. The first time it happened, Zoe laughed it off but on more than one occasion conversations ended with Colin becoming loud and dismissive over disagreements. At times when it appeared Colin was becoming angry, Lucy and Anne would intervene but this did not seem to make much of a difference – with Colin responding by saying "it's all just a bit of fun". When the issue was raised with Habib, he just said it was a "personality clash" and that Zoe and Colin need to "find a way to work together as there's a lot of work to do to make sure that the contract is renewed and they can keep their jobs".

Although initially participating, Zoe began to withdraw from conversations with Colin and her mood has become noticeably different. However, the variance in her mood now occurs not just when Colin is present but also occasionally when he is not. This is causing some tensions in the wider team since the other assistants feel that when Zoe is "in a mood" they are not able to chat and joke as usual. They try and engage Zoe but she does not respond. Lucy and Anne have tried to talk to Zoe about what's going on but she has said she doesn't want to talk about it as she has spoken to Habib and he hasn't done anything, and she doesn't see the point in going to HR as "they don't care". She has said she would rather just keep her head down and concentrate on her work.

Although he would join in with the group conversations, during the interactions between Zoe and Colin, Nick would remain quiet. Nick is the youngest team member and this is his first job. He is ambitious and would like to be a manager one day so feels that he can learn a lot from Colin, Habib and Dave and doesn't want to risk falling out with them. In the past Colin has made jokes to Nick about his age and his ambitions for "when he grows up". Colin, Habib and Dave socialise outside of work and Nick has been hinting that he would like an invite but this is either ignored or dismissed, often by Colin, on the grounds that Nick is "not one of the big boys". At the time, Nick laughs these comments off and doesn't challenge Colin, Habib or Dave, but he does get annoyed and vents to the rest of the team about it when Colin, Habib and Dave are not around.

One day, after a particularly stressful week, Colin raised a query about Nick's work but did so in an aggressive and confrontational manner, calling Nick an "infant who should go back to school to learn how to read", asking "how can you be this shit?", and if he was "thick because only an idiot could mess up work this bloody simple". Nick initially tried to respond in a measured and calm way but Colin continued to shout at him and began to physically square up to him. In response, Nick lost his temper and started to shout back, calling Colin "an arrogant prick" and a "show-off who thinks he's smarter than he really is" and arguing that his work was "perfectly fine" and Colin was "just picking a fight to make himself feel better by making someone else feel like shit". Out of fear of harm or aggression being directed at them, the rest of the team felt that they weren't able to intervene; eventually Dave stepped in to break it up. Colin was sent outside to calm down and Nick was immediately sent home. Nick has now found out he (but not Colin) is facing a disciplinary process and is upset about this, as he feels it wasn't his fault. As far as he is concerned he was just "standing up to a bully". The team suspect that the reason Colin has been "let off" is because he is worth more to the company than Nick. Nick was thinking about submitting a complaint because he feels there is a "massive problem with bullying in the team". However, in the circumstances, Nick is now thinking of leaving rather than going through the disciplinary process and pursuing a grievance as he thinks leaving will do the least damage to his reputation and future prospects.

QUESTIONS

1. Do you agree with Nick's statement that there is a "massive problem with bullying in the team"? Explain and justify your answer.

2. To what extent do you think the management approach and culture of the team have led to the problems experienced?

3. Critically evaluate the options available to help address any allegations of bullying that may be made in this case. In your answer think about what you would recommend to address the issues in the following relationships: (1) Beth and Habib/Dave; (2) Colin and Zoe; (3) Colin and Nick; (4) the agency workers and Habib/Dave; and (5) the team generally.

23
New forms of worker organising: Sex work in Argentina

Kate Hardy

BACKGROUND AND CONTEXT OF THE ORGANISATION

AMMAR (*Asociación de Mujeres Meretrices de la Argentina*, the Argentinean Female Sex Workers' Union) was established in 1994 in the capital city of Buenos Aires. 'Sex work' can refer to a range of jobs and practices, including stripping, webcam work, escorting or other forms of selling sexual services and labour. In the case of AMMAR, they focus on women directly selling sex, sometimes known as 'prostitution'. AMMAR – and others – adopt the term 'sex work' in order to bring this form of work in line with other forms of work, arguing that it is used as a source of income and because it shares features with other forms of work and employment.

Argentina identifies itself as an abolitionist country, in which it is intended that sex work ('prostitution') be eradicated using legislation. Yet prostitution itself is not illegal. According to Article 19 of the Constitution, 'private actions that in no way offend order and public morals or do damage to a third party are reserved to be judged by God and fall outside the competence of judges'. However, it is illegal to solicit in the streets, to aid or abet a prostitute, live off their earnings or run a brothel (Mariño et al. 2003). Due to Argentina's federal constitution, however, it is provincial laws that govern sex work through *Códigos Contravencionales* and *Códigos de Faltas*, which also frequently regulate and manage social issues outside the penal code, such as groups of young people on the street, disturbances on the street, 'causing a scandal' (solicitation) and drunken behaviour. This means that working conditions for sex workers on the street vary geographically, from city to city depending on provincial codes and ordinances.

Spaces of solicitation exist across both indoor and outdoor places such as casinos, bars and hotels. Most outdoor prostitution occurs either in bars or in *plazas* (squares in towns and cities), parks and around transport hubs. This sector generally caters for both domestic and tourist demand for commercial sex and for both heterosexual and homosexual clients. Police practices discouraged large numbers of women working together. Instead women worked alone or in pairs, in spatially dispersed areas, hoping to fall under the radar of the state, embodied in the police. Despite this, informal districts and areas emerged, often located around transport hubs such as train and coach stations. Dispersal was intensified in periods of police repression, as sex workers spread out and worked alone in order to avoid attracting attention. This meant there was no defined and shared workplace, but instead a more loosely defined and unbounded workspace, with constantly shifting boundaries and inhabitants. In addition to work in cities and large towns, a number of women also worked on the *rutas* (arterial roads) leading into and out of towns.

It is from this context that AMMAR emerged in 1994 in order to defend the interests of women engaging in sex work in these conditions. Over time, AMMAR has developed from a small handful of women distributing condoms in working areas to a formally recognised non-governmental organisation, with over 6000 members across nine cities in Argentina. Essential to this expansion has been their inclusion in the trade union umbrella organisation, the Argentine Workers' Centre (*Central de Trabajadores Argentinos*, CTA).

VIOLENCE AND REPRESSION AGAINST SEX WORKERS

Sex workers all over the world face high levels of violence and repression. While workers' clients are often seen as the key source of this violence, sex workers themselves tend to report the police as the central actors responsible for committing violence against them.

Specifically, in Argentina, the military regime between 1976 and 1983 increased repression against sex workers. However, with the fall of the junta in 1983, the state ended its regime of terror against those it saw as political threats and ended the period of intense state violence. Women working in this industry, however, continued to face strong police repression throughout the 1990s and to the present time. In a study by AMMAR in 2018, 90 per cent of sex workers stated that they had experienced violence from police or other security forces during the last year, with violence increasing dramatically since 2016.

It was in response to this repression and police brutality that AMMAR was formed in 1994. Their initial demand was that sex workers should not be re-arrested within 24 hours of leaving a police station. Over the longer term, AMMAR view decriminalisation (that is, the lifting of specific laws against sex work) as key to reducing the power of the police over their working lives. The federal nature of Argentina means that sex work is regulated locally. In order, therefore, to decriminalise sex work, AMMAR have focused on attempting to repeal the *Códigos de Faltas* and *Códigos Contravencionales* (provincial codes that they see as enabling abuse of sex workers by transferring power to the police to regulate them).

As a result of AMMAR's work with local social movements and legislators, laws which enabled police to detain and charge sex workers have been revoked in the provinces of Entre Rios (2003), Santiago del Estero (2008) and Santa Fe (2010). This has, to some degree, decreased police violence against sex workers in these provinces, although laws remain in place in 17 other provinces in the country. Violence against sex workers from the police has, however, begun to target activists as AMMAR have begun to organise against their mistreatment by police officers, the judiciary and other state officials. For example, Sandra Cabrera, the Branch Secretary of AMMAR-Santa Fé was murdered in 2004 following complaints she made against police involvement in trafficking and the prostitution of minors.

WORKER RECOGNITION

A key argument in favour of decriminalisation of the laws around prostitution is that sex work is work like any other and therefore should be legislated as such and should not be repressed. The phrase 'sex work is work' has become ubiquitous across the world for women, men and trans people working in the sex industry as a basis for demanding better rights. In identifying as workers AMMAR are able to demand the equal protection of the law afforded to other workers and citizens. This discourse of labour is highly contested, however, and has often been opposed by groups including religious organisations and some feminist groups in Argentina.

AMMAR have developed a strong identity as workers and as themselves as part of the working class, through their membership with the CTA. The CTA emerged from the turbulent years of the 1990s in which, following economic crisis, growing numbers of workers in Argentina found themselves working in the informal sector or without pay in the public sector. In this context, the CTA broke away from the *Confederación General del Trabajo de la República Argentina* (CGT) to form a new umbrella union concerned with growing casualisation and privatisation-led insecurity and unemployment across all sections of the economy. By 2010, the CTA included over 1.2 million affiliated members from 240 organisations, ranging from traditional unions to indigenous groups, pensioners and the unemployed and it has a presence in every province across Argentina. As well as traditionally unionised sectors, it also comprises 'picketer' organisations such as *Unión de Trabajadores Desocupados* (UTD, Unemployed Workers Union) who emerged in the 1990s to protest against unemployment, pensioners' organisations including the *Centro de Jubilados de La Matanza* (Retirees Centre of La Matanza) and *Jubilados del Banco Provincia* (Retirees of the Provincial Bank), and organisations committed to broader issues of social justice, including *Federación de Tierra, Vivienda y Hábitat* (FTV, Federation of Land, Housing, and Environment) and *Movimiento Nacional de los Chicos del Pueblo* (Children's National Movement).

In 1994, when a small number of women began organizing in Buenos Aires, the local head of the CTA offered them a small office in their building. By 2001, they formally integrated into the union and in the present day, AMMAR is integrated with the CTA in provinces across the country. This is important in several ways. First, it embeds AMMAR in a wider labour movement; second, it has provided an important political education for sex workers understanding themselves as workers; and third, because recognition of sex work as work also has specific, material significance in the case of Argentina, since trade unions have the ability to administer high quality services such as pensions and healthcare.

While integration in the CTA offers symbolic status as a trade union, in order to access the right to distribute services AMMAR needs to achieve status as '*Personería Gremial*' through which the state recognizes them as a formal trade union. As such, in seeking formal legal recognition, AMMAR's main strategy was seeking this status through the Ministry of Work. It is only through recognition from the Ministry of Work that AMMAR would be able to act in similar ways to other unions and 'be able to discuss all areas: health, pensions, education, housing'. Despite recommendations that AMMAR should be awarded this status from other state agencies including the Ministry of Health, Justice and Education and officials from provincial HIV/AIDS programmes, AMMAR faced a number of problems in dealing with the Ministry of Work. Primarily, the

Ministry was not willing to engage seriously with the conditions and relations of work that occurred in street sex work. The Ministry of Work requested receipts and documents in order to recognize sex work, but due to working informally, this documentation did not exist. As such, sex workers have remained outside the formal trade union system, because informal and autonomous labour relations could not be recognised within industrial relations that were institutionally embedded in the state.

ACCESS TO HEALTHCARE, PENSIONS AND WELFARE

As a result of the misrecognition of sex work as work, AMMAR has been given *Personería Jurídica* (NGO) status, but has not been awarded recognized trade union status (*Personería Gremial*), meaning that they are unable to distribute benefits such as healthcare and pensions. In Argentina, formally recognized unions are licensed to provide such services for their members, meaning that their members can enjoy higher quality healthcare and pensions than those offered to the general public by the state. In light of this, AMMAR have generated alternative methods for providing these essential benefits to their members and to sex workers more widely.

Low levels of literacy amongst sex workers necessitate access to education as a key component for improving both their lives and working conditions. In some places, provision has been somewhat piecemeal and made up of night classes, provided by the city government. Attending alongside other pupils, however, many women reported feeling unconfident and ashamed, as their classmates were ten to twenty years younger than them. In 2001, the CENPA school opened in Córdoba. The school was attended by sex workers, their children and some other women with low levels of education. The hours of the school, which began at 2 pm, were designed to suit women who have been working all night. CENPA allowed women to undertake classes and receive a certificate which was recognised by the state and more importantly, by employers.

In relation to healthcare, sex workers have taken on important roles as '*multiplicadoras*', or health multipliers. Essentially, this involves distributing condoms and health advice, both in working areas and also more generally in the community. In addition, AMMAR activists have worked with medical workers to arrange appointments and testing for the women. In Buenos Aires, AMMAR won funding from the Global Fund Against Aids, tuberculosis and malaria to offer testing with the NGO NEXO, as many of the women would not go to hospitals, but were willing to attend independent clinics. In Córdoba, the organization arranged appointments at hours suitable for the women in the afternoon at the Hospital Rawson, through contact with the Director of Infectology.

Perhaps the biggest achievement is the establishment of the 'Sandra Cabrera' Health Centre in La Plata. This is a joint initiative with the CTA and the Buenos Aires Province Ministry for Health. It has created a space for sex workers in which all their healthcare requirements can be addressed directly alongside other personal needs. Supported by money from The Global Fund, the centre attends to a thousand sex workers a month and is also open to members of the public. As well as sexual health services, women can see a psychologist and get advice about other medical issues. While all of these efforts at the municipal and provincial scale significantly increased women's access to healthcare, full systematic access to healthcare depended on full recognition of sex work as work and AMMAR as a union at the national scale.

SUMMARY AND OVERVIEW

AMMAR offers an example of organising in one of the 'hardest to reach' sectors, amongst informal, female workers operating in labour conditions in which there is no obvious third party against whom to organise and in conditions of legal liminality. Since women in street sex work work independently, they have largely directed their demands against the state, rather than vis-à-vis an employer.

The violence faced by sex workers, largely from the police and other security forces, complicates the organising process. Repression leads to women avoiding contact with each other and orientating away from visibility as sex workers. Despite this, AMMAR have thousands of official members and have reached many more thousands with their health and education outreach work.

The gains that AMMAR have achieved run counter to claims that it is not possible to organise workers operating in these conditions – informally self-employed in a semi-legal industry. AMMAR remains limited, however, by the refusal of state institutions to recognise sex work as work and therefore to confer the full rights enjoyed by other trade unions. Moreover, police harassment of sex workers appears to have been increasing in recent years, indicating that there is significantly more work to be done in terms of institutionalising sex workers' rights as workers in the Southern Cone country.

QUESTIONS

1 In what ways can sex work be considered work?

2 What challenges do sex workers face that are: (a) similar to other workers? (b) different from other workers?

3 What does the case study show you about the ways in which workers are able to mobilise even in complex and difficult conditions?

4 How would you evaluate the degree of success that sex workers have achieved?

REFERENCES

Mariño, R., Minichiello, V. and Disogra, C. (2003). Male sex workers in Cordoba, Argentina. *Pan American Journal of Public Health*, **5** (13), 311–19.

SECTION V
CULTURE AND JOB QUALITY

24
System error, restart? Allegations of sex discrimination at Microsoft Corp.

Anthony Rafferty

In October 2015, Katherine Moussouris and Holly Muenchow[1] filed as named plaintiffs for certification for a class action to the United States District Court, Washington, to cover 8600 female engineers and IT professionals who had worked at Microsoft Corporation since 2012.[2] Their allegations concerned a purported "continuing policy, pattern and practice of sex discrimination against female employees in technical and engineering roles, including technical sales and services positions, with respect to performance evaluations, pay, promotions, and other terms and conditions of employment". The human resource management practices of Microsoft, as implemented through its performance and reward management system, the "Calibration Process" (since 2014 "People Discussions") were central to these claims. This system in both forms was alleged to systematically produce bias through a *disparate impact*[3] on female employees, with further allegations that Microsoft negatively engages in *disparate treatment*[4] through a general policy of intentional discrimination (Box 24.1). Further allegations were raised regarding the handling of sexual harassment cases and an "unchecked gender bias that pervades its corporate culture."[5]

BOX 24.1
DISPARATE IMPACT, DISPARATE TREATMENT AND COMMONALITY

Disparate impact refers to where people are treated equally in relation to a set of rules but the rules are constructed to favour one group over another (e.g. men over women). In this sense even where a person acts without personal prejudice, a discriminatory outcome can result from applying a biased set of rules (e.g. a biased performance evaluation and reward system) (see Pager and Shepherd, 2008).
Disparate treatment in contrast requires proof of *intentional* discrimination. Unlike disparate impact claims, disparate treatment claims generally do not require the identification of specific companywide policies that cause discrimination. In the current case, according to Microsoft's opposition, to further meet the notion of *commonality*, disparate treatment would need to establish corporate leaders operated under a "general policy of discrimination", nonetheless. **Commonality** for both disparate impact and treatment refers to different instances of discrimination sharing the same underlying causes rather than being independent.

THE CASES OF MS MOUSSOURIS AND MS MUENCHOW

Ms Moussouris was employed at Microsoft between 2007 and 2014 in a senior role. During this time she alleges she was given poorer performance rankings than she deserved based upon her contribution, was paid less than male peers, and was overlooked for promotion in her last four years at the company.[6] She had also complained about the director of her team, The Trustworthy Computing Group, lodging allegations concerning the sexual harassment of other women. This director had since been moved to another group but Moussouris asserts that in retaliation for raising the claims the director had awarded her a lower bonus.

Ms Muenchow in contrast was still employed at Microsoft, where she had worked since 2002. During this time, she alleged she was passed over for promotions in favour of male colleagues and only progressed four levels in the company's technical career track. She also claims she was criticised for being too assertive whereas such behaviours were evaluated more positively among men. Microsoft's opposition team in contrast argued that both Moussouris and Muenchow had been promoted on several occasions and were paid well. Moussouris in particular was among the highest paid in her cost centre, making more than her male manager, but her communication skills were suggested to require development, something she had mentioned in her own evaluations.[7]

> … I see male colleagues doing the same behaviour I do, of assertiveness, and getting promoted and/or positive feedback for that.[8]

SYSTEMATIC BIAS? THE CALIBRATION PROCESS AND PEOPLE CONVERSATIONS

Between 2010 and 2016, women at Microsoft filed 238 complaints with the company's HR department. These comprised of 108 complaints about sexual harassment and 119 about gender

Table 24.1 Distribution of men and women by stock level at Microsoft Corp.

Level	% Male	% Female
81+ (Vice Presidents & CEO)	100	0
80 (Vice Presidents)	93.3	6.7
68–70 (Partners)	93.0	7.0
65–67	89.9	10.1
63–34	85.8	15.2
61–62	79.7	20.3
59–60	79.6	20.4

Source: Submitted evidence in Case 2:15-cv-01483-JLR Document 381 Filed 03/12/18 Page 11 of 51.

discrimination. There were also eight complaints regarding retaliation and three concerning pregnancy discrimination.[9] A central requirement for class action certification was to establish *commonality*; that different instances of discrimination shared the same underlying reasons. Pivotal to the plaintiffs' argument was the claim that the pay and promotion systems in Microsoft systematically produced discriminatory outcomes, rather than such outcomes being attributable solely to the discretion and biases of individual managers in isolated and exceptional instances. The Microsoft defence team in contrast saw the extent of line manager discretion afforded by the performance evaluation and rewards system as evidence for a lack of commonality, meaning any claims for discrimination covered by the class should instead be pursued on an individual case-by-case basis.

The Calibration Process (from 2011 to May 2014) was designed by the Microsoft Corps Human Resources team. This involved the evaluation of employee performance relative to their "peer groups", consisting of employees at similar "career stages", categorised between stages 2 to 9 based on common sets of competencies and key results, who were performing similar work although they could be in different pay bands ("stock levels") or have different rates of pay within bands. Stock levels ranged from 58 to 98, with the CEO, Satya Nadella, holding level 98. For many years the review system "Calibration Process" involved what the plaintiffs referred to as a "stack ranking" approach, where twice a year employees were ranked from best to worst (1 = best to 5 = worst), with only 20 per cent of employees assigned the top ranking.[10] The process began with direct line manager evaluations that are discussed in manager "calibration meetings". This procedure was alleged to result in women being paid less than their male peers, regardless of their performance, given that women were disproportionately represented in lower pay band stock levels than men (see Table 24.1), and because women were given lower scores than their male peers, despite having equal or better performance.

The award of promotion in contrast utilised the same policy but involved movement between pay band stock levels to a higher level. Microsoft required managers to discuss candidates for promotion as part of the Calibration Process, and sets out criteria that must be met in order to make recommendations; these being business need, demonstrated employee readiness and available budget. To establish employee readiness, managers must confirm that: (1) employees have successfully delivered results at a level in their current role that indicates readiness for greater scope; (2) the manner in which results were achieved demonstrates their ability to be successful at a higher level; and (3) an employee has a demonstrated history of taking increasingly challenging work whilst continuing to deliver results. Pay and promotion recommendations made by lower-level managers are approved, rejected or modified by each higher-level manager in the reporting chain, meaning such decisions are not at the sole discretion of immediate line managers.

Microsoft abandoned the Calibration Meetings in favour of "People Conversations" in 2014, partly in an effort to seek a more collaborative culture and greater developmental focus to which the level of employee competition created from the prior system was viewed as unconducive.[11] Much of the underlying criteria (e.g. employee readiness), however, was purported by the plaintiffs to have remained the same, as was the alleged systematic bias against women. Microsoft in their opposition in contrast asserted that these two procedures were different and the new system afforded new forms of discretion and flexibility to managers in structuring reward decisions. One main difference was the abandonment of an explicit forced ranking component, freeing up greater discretion on distributing rewards. Both processes were also asserted by Microsoft to involve input from a wide range of sources, including peers, supervisors and high-level managers, whilst allowing reviewers to exercise their judgement. Consequently, given this flexibility, a common mode of exercising discretion was claimed by Microsoft to not be identifiable to establish commonality.

THE COMPETENCY MODEL AND CAREER STAGE PROFILES

A key claim made in the Plaintiffs' application was that the Calibration Process's structural features precluded consistent decision-making in evaluation judgements about comparable people and relied on invalid criteria. Dr Ann Ryan, an Organizational Psychologist at Michigan State University, submitted evidence in support of this claim. This centred on the "Competency Model" at the company underpinning "career stage profiles" designed to reflect the scope, impact and complexity of different disciplines and professions. The purpose of these frameworks was to connect pay and promotion decisions to job requirements based on companywide criteria. Dr Ryan asserted that although there was a common competency model for assessing work performance, there was a failure to tie criteria for compensations and promotions to this model. The implication made was that this produced a system-wide defect failing to ensure employees were evaluated based on common competencies. Dr Ryan further suggested a lack of standardisation in the calibration process in terms of what information served as inputs to the process, who attended the meetings (e.g. whether direct supervisors attended), and the process used to arrive at decisions. This was deemed to undermine the reliability and validity of pay decisions. Further claims were made that Microsoft does not adequately train managers or, importantly, monitor the process to ensure its reliability and validity.

ALLEGED STATISTICAL EVIDENCE ON GENDER PAY AND PROMOTION GAPS

Dr Henry Farber, a Professor of Economics at Princeton University, submitted statistical evidence on behalf of the Plaintiffs purported to provide evidence of sex discrimination resulting from Microsoft's common pay and promotion process. The interpretation of the data asserted was that sex differences in pay were not explicable in terms of productivity-related characteristics such as work experience or differences in the type of work undertaken – that women were paid less than men in the same job title with the same level of performance. Dr Farber's regression model for pay controlled statistically for relevant individual characteristics, these being year, age (used as a proxy for work experience), length of tenure at Microsoft, job location, performance rating, and also the class of specific work (profession, discipline, and standard title of job). This found a statistically significant gender pay gap estimated to produce a combined shortfall in pay for affected women of approximately $100 million. Using a similar methodology, Dr Farber further estimated that between 2011 and 2016 women in Engineering and IT operations received 518 fewer promotions than would be expected given their characteristics other than gender.

Microsoft had received employee reactions to two equal pay announcements during the period of the class action, and broader pressure from activist shareholders who wished to see greater action on gender equality within the tech sector more broadly.[12] Employee concern revolved around a comment made by CEO Satya Nadella who made the news for statements made at the 2014 Grace Hopper Institute (women in technology conference) about equal pay being a function of "karma," when asked a question regarding whether women should ask for a raise. Subsequent corporate communications claiming overall pay differences between men and women and by "race" were within 0.5 per cent further attracted employee attention. Unlike Dr Farber's analysis, Microsoft statistically accounted for stock level to produce these figures, with a similar methodology also being implemented in its 2016 Equal Pay Study. In light of the communications, employees responded to Microsoft's leadership and HR teams, arguing that analysing pay within stock levels was erroneous because stock level was nothing more than pay bands and women in the same jobs were consistently paid less than men through their greater representation in lower bands: "If I'm doing the exact same job [as a man] but I'm at a different [stock] level, that's not pay equality" (Microsoft Employee).[13] "There is an important distinction between equal pay for equal level, and equal pay for equal work. The latter presupposes women are appropriately levelled [stock level], and numbers suggest this is not the case at Microsoft" (Microsoft Employee).[14]

Dr Farber similarly submitted comments to this effect as the reason for omitting stock level from his regression controls, suggesting such a method would effectively be tautological, "accepting pay as an explanation for pay".[15] This partly explained the disparities between Dr Farber's and Microsoft's estimates. Criticism of the comparisons within stock levels suggested the focus overlooked the "real issues", which were gender biases in representation between stock levels (rather than in pay within levels) and the related lower promotion velocity of women.

DEVALUING WOMEN? AN ALLEGED CULTURE OF DISCRIMINATION

The class action further made claims regarding evidence for an alleged culture that systematically devalues women's contributions at Microsoft. In addition to presenting figures regarding the over 230 incidences of complaints regarding discrimination and harassment against female technical employees, this argument drew on details of more informal complaints. These included dissatisfaction expressed in female employees' emails pertaining to a "boys' club" atmosphere or "bro culture" that was perceived to hinder female progression in the organisation. Relatedly, the tone of language viewed as permitted in communications, such as referring to employees as "pussies" and CEO Steve Ballmer (2000–2014) as the "limp dick CEO", was further viewed to contribute to an adverse cultural environment against women.[16] Other declarations suggested that men's contributions to projects were valued more highly than similar projects managed by women, women had difficulties participating in male-dominated meetings, and men were helped more with development and career progression than women. The communications submitted were also purported to show that Microsoft was aware of the adverse impact of the Calibration Process on women but did not seek to fix it.

A further alleged manifestation of a negative culture against women concerned the handling of discrimination and sexual harassment claims. Microsoft's Employment Relations Investigations Team (ERIT) was responsible for investigating claims of discrimination and sexual harassment. Rhona Young, a legal expert in human resource management, was called on by the defendants to provide a view on such activities at Microsoft. Ms Young concluded that the steps used by Microsoft in its investigations are based on being thorough, timely, accurate, objective, well-documented, and focused on thoughtful and reasoned conclusions.

Dr Caren Goldberg, an Associate Professor in Management at Bowie State University, was called on by the Plaintiffs to respond to evidence submitted by Ms Young. Dr Goldberg questioned whether Microsoft had clear anti-discrimination and anti-harassment policies that were communicated effectively. Microsoft Standards of Business Conduct Training was the only mandatory programme. The content of this programme varied from year to year and in one year (2017) did not include content on gender discrimination. Whilst noting that what constitutes an effective level of training remains an open question subject to academic research, Goldberg drew on a meta-analytic review (Kalinoski et al., 2013) of 65 studies that suggested that diversity training of less than two hours, in passive formats (not including engagement in role play, discussions or simulations), or delivered in computer format was unlikely to be effective. Microsoft training was stated to be 45 minutes and computer based.

Dr Goldberg produced further evidence to suggest some people with complaints did not trust that HR would uphold their confidentiality. A further issue raised was that the complaint system did not flag up if an individual had been named in multiple or prior complaints. Ms DeLanoy (ERIT, Microsoft) submitted that it would not be proper to apply or hold prior investigations against a new allegation. Dr Goldberg in contrast disagreed, suggesting this practice prevents the electronic system from providing a practical and realistic context to understanding complaints. This was also seen to constrain the ability for the organisation to increase the severity of action taken for serial offenders in order to escalate disciplinary action. Testimonies presented suggested some staff also felt that their discrimination complaints were not sufficiently followed up. Some members of the ERIT team, Dr Goldberg noted, also had no employment law or investigations background, calling into question their capacity to undertake investigations of this nature.

Despite allegations regarding its culture, Microsoft at the same time had made considerable strides in seeking to improve diversity and promote greater work–life balance, particularly under the leadership of Nadella, who took over the position of CEO in 2014. In its opposition to the class action it further noted how it goes beyond legal requirements in order to challenge broader societal issues such as gender inequalities that are pervasive in the industry more broadly. The senior leadership team also had made broader statements and tried to implement initiatives focused on issues of equal pay, diversity and inclusion at Microsoft. The company at the time had a 25-person team working on diversity issues and a budget of more than $55 million a year through to 2020 for new initiatives.

DENIAL OF THE CLASS ACTION AND MOVEMENT TO APPEAL

District Court judge, the Honourable James Robart, rejected the application for class certification, ruling that the lawsuit would not be expanded to cover more than 8600 women in technical roles who have worked at the company since 2012. A central argument put forward for the rejection was that the appellants had failed to establish that a uniform pay and promotion policy was in place to support the disparate impact claim. This ruling thus concurred with the view of Microsoft's opposition who argued that evidence put forward on the lack of standardisation such as by Dr Ryan actually precluded the notion of systematic bias. Although the court acknowledged that the Calibration Process created a common structure creating common requirements and direction to pay and promotion decisions, the procedures were seen as too subjective and insufficiently defined to meet the criteria for commonality.

The notion of flexibility also concerned discretion regarding how managers engaged in the process. For example, the District Court noted that whereas some managers used PowerPoint presentations to communicate information in Calibration Meetings, other managers did not use visual aids at all. One argument for commonality rested on the fact that senior managers approved all pay and promotion decisions. However, the fact that these were generally approved was seen to still place the power in the process at the discretion of line managers. The District Judge further rejected that there was sufficient evidence to assert there was "a culture of evasion and refusal to acknowledge the problem". Differences in the characterisation of claims between the reports of different class members were also seen as evidence of a lack of typicality, required for class action. Following rejection by the District Court, the application was moved forward to Court of Appeal.

QUESTIONS

1. To what extent can organisational practices, culture and leadership be held as systematically responsible for the discriminatory behaviour perpetrated by individual employees? Consider the concept of disparate impact versus disparate treatment.

2. Other than differences in the "promotion velocity" of male and female employees, what other factors might account for the lower representation of women at more senior stock levels?

3. What should organisations do to ensure the effective monitoring of gender equality in performance and reward management? Provide a set of recommendations to Microsoft to help bolster their practices.

4. Based on alleged problems identified in this case, how might organisations improve their monitoring and handling of sexual harassment allegations? What do the allegations at Microsoft tell us about the types of problems or tensions human resource departments may face when handling such claims?

END NOTES

1 Ms Moussouris filed the original class action in September 2016. An amended complaint was filed in October 2015 adding Ms Muenchow and Ms Piermarini as named plaintiffs. Moussouris and Muenchow are discussed as the representative plaintiffs.
2 The details of this case study are primarily based upon the redacted public access court proceedings for Case 2:15-cv-01483 for the United States Court for the West District of Washington. See: https://www.wawd.uscourts.gov/ (accessed 20 April 2019).
3 Title VII of the Civil Rights Act of 1964, 42 U.S.C. §§ 2000e *et seq*. ("Title VII").
4 Washington Law Against Discrimination, Rev. Code Wash. § 49.60.010. *et seq*. ("WLAD").
5 Case 2:15-cv-01483-JLR Document 8.
6 See https://microsoftgendercase.com/ (accessed 20 April 2019).
7 See https://www.geekwire.com/2018/judge-denies-former-microsoft-employees-bid-class-action-gender-discrimination-suit-tech-giant/ (accessed 20 April 2019).
8 Case 2:15-cv-01483-JLR Document 381 Filed 03/12/18.
9 First ERIT Log 14 October 2016 Case 2:15-cv-01483-JLR Document 279-3 Filed 12/08/17 page 2.
10 Case 2:15-cv-01483 Document 1 Filed 09/16/15 page 4.
11 See https://www.theguardian.com/technology/blog/2012/aug/13/microsoft-human-resources-culture (accessed 20 April 2019).
12 MSFT_MOUSSOURIS_00017963, also see https://www.washingtonpost.com/news/on-leadership/wp/2016/04/12/microsoft-and-facebook-tout-equal-pay-but-theres-a-more-glaring-problem/?noredirect=on&utm_term=.6d5a-8c9a8a3f (accessed 20 April 2019).
13 Case 2:15-cv-01483-JLR Document 381 Filed 03/12/18 page 20.
14 MSFT_MOUSSOURIS_00705352 page 353.
15 Case 2:15-cv-01483-JLR Document 381 Filed 03/12/18 page 14.
16 ER1076 ER95.

REFERENCES

Kalinoski, Z.T., Steele-Johnson, D., Peyton, E.J., Leas, K.A., Steinke, J. and Bowling, N.A. (2013). A meta-analytic evaluation of diversity training outcomes. *Journal of Organizational Behavior*, **34**(8), 1076–104.

Pager, D. and Shepherd, H. (2008). The sociology of discrimination: Racial discrimination in employment, housing, credit, and consumer markets. *Annual Review of Sociology*, **34**, 181–209.

25
Changing organisational hierarchies: KnowledgeLtd
Rory Donnelly

BACKGROUND AND CONTEXT

KnowledgeLtd is one of the world's largest and most successful professional service firms. Originally established over a century ago, it has enjoyed substantial growth through a combination of mergers, acquisitions and organic expansion. The firm is headquartered in the UK, but has offices in over 150 countries from Australia to Zimbabwe and employs over 200 000 people worldwide. In 2018, its global revenues exceeded US$40 billion. As an organisation, it is held in high esteem and consistently features in the 'top employer' lists of many countries.

The firm engages in the delivery of intangible services rather than the production of physical goods and so can be categorised as 'knowledge-intensive' (for further information on knowledge-intensive firms, please see Ejler et al., 2011). These include assurance, tax advisory, consultancy, legal, actuarial and financial advisory services. Such services are derived from the integration of human and organisational knowledge and most of the work undertaken by its staff requires the use of a high level of expertise to solve complex client problems and generate innovative solutions. Indeed, the firm is a member of the Global MAKE (Most Admired Knowledge Enterprises) Hall of Fame.

The firm adopts a hierarchical partnership structure. At the time the study was carried out, the structure in the UK consisted of six principal levels (see below). Each of these levels reflected seniority-based differences in an individual's status, role and centrality in the firm as well as client and professional networks.

- Partners
- Directors
- Senior Managers
- Managers
- Consultants
- Assistant Consultants

This type of structure continues to be adopted by the firm even though growing evidence suggests that it can inhibit knowledge sharing in knowledge-intensive firms (Dalkir and Beaulieu, 2018; Mabey and Zhao, 2017; Hislop and Bosua, 2018). This case study provides insight into tensions between the removal and retention of the organisational hierarchy in the consulting arm of the business, through the analysis of interviews conducted with individuals at each level of the structure set out above across five of its UK offices.

CHANGES IN THE ORGANISATIONAL HIERARCHY

The interview data revealed that although the organisational hierarchy was firmly embedded across the organisation, there was a desire from some quarters in the firm to gradually move away from the existing structure to suit managerial interests. For example, in newly established and relatively small departments, distinctions between the responsibilities and the nature of the work performed at each level were being progressively dismantled in order to flatten the hierarchical structure and in doing so reduce the pay levels of affected staff. This meant that in such departments, staff at the level of consultant faced demands and performed work that was typically undertaken by managers in other departments, but received consultant-level remuneration.

These developments occurred alongside redundancy programmes at the firm as well as reductions in the relative availability of high-level positions. This served to temper complaints from affected staff. However, it also adversely affected staff morale. Consequently, some senior members of the firm called for the provision of alternative career progression opportunities. This included the creation of a series of role types rather than pay-related grades.

This strategy was, however, merely being pursued on a localised basis due to differences in the relative performance of individual business units and the continuing presence of comparable structures in competitor firms. There was also concern among some senior members of the firm that such a strategy would negatively affect staff motivation and commitment to the firm and profession. Senior positions conferred kudos within and outside the firm and members would be less able to gauge their position in the professional hierarchy, as traditional 'signposts' would begin to lack relevance.

Professionals traditionally expect that with time and personal development, they will progress through most or all of an organisation's ranks (Empson et al., 2017). Where continued career advancement is constrained, it is likely to have a negative impact on motivation, particularly as incentives for going the extra mile become less tangible. In addition, this was likely to have negative spillover effects on the firm's performance and ultimately its profits. The firm's hierarchy therefore motivated staff. However, it also moderated the exchange of knowledge as discussed in the section below.

HIERARCHICAL RELATIONS AND THE EXCHANGE OF KNOWLEDGE

Although flatter organisational structures are believed to be more effective in promoting the communal exchange of knowledge, the firm continued to retain a hierarchical structure, which encouraged a microfoundational perspective on knowledge ownership, which generated tensions between members of the firm. The structure was supported by an up-or-out career progression ethos and so competition between consultants was pronounced.

This competition extended to the exchange and ownership of knowledge, due to the link between the form and degree of knowledge held by individuals and their hierarchical status and corresponding reward levels. Therefore, members of the firm tended to withhold key pieces of information/knowledge in order to preserve and enhance their position within the firm.

> The level of knowledge/expertise is what makes the difference between the different levels … Some people are deliberately obtuse because they don't really want to share their information … it's like in project work; some people like to keep all the work or knowledge to themselves and don't forward information or emails, so that you do a bad job and the client complains, so that they look better. (Consultant)

Many consultants consequently retained elements of their knowledge they perceived to be of importance to their personal and professional advancement. This behaviour can be linked to tensions in the relationships between members of the firm, generated by the hierarchical and competitive nature of the career structure. The exchange of knowledge between levels of the firm was encouraged through team working, networking and mentoring arrangements. However, competition between members of the firm transcended these relations. For example, junior members of the firm reported that mentors and senior colleagues retained much of their knowledge and only shared information that was needed to perform work to the required standard, in order to preserve their competitive advantage relative to colleagues. The hierarchy in place also hindered the exchange of knowledge, because an individual's status influenced the nature of the work that they performed. Junior members of the firm tended to be largely office-based and so were more active in disseminating and exchanging knowledge, whereas senior members of the firm tended to have more client contact and so had less time to spend in the office transferring knowledge, impacting on the degree of knowledge exchanged and the level of professional development achieved.

The tendency to retain elements of personal knowledge also extended to individuals' engagement with the firm's codification systems. Indeed, the accounts provided by the interviewees revealed that individuals only contributed basic information to the firm's databases, in order to retain ownership of the elements of their knowledge that they perceived to be of value to them as individuals. The firm's databases therefore contained only incomplete and dated segments of information that were of little value either to the firm or its staff, particularly due to constant changes in consultancy knowledge. In addition, members of the firm were reluctant to contribute too much information due to concerns that entries into such databases could expose gaps in their knowledge base.

The hierarchical environment in place exacerbated these concerns. Junior members of the firm were reluctant to post questions on database forums, because this could elucidate gaps in their knowledge and influence the perceptions that senior members of the firm held of them and their professional competence. They also tended to exchange knowledge with peers at a similar level rather than with individuals further up the hierarchy, while senior members of the firm did not wish to be seen to draw on the knowledge of their junior colleagues. This all shaped knowledge flows within the firm. If the firm embraced a flatter structure, members might engage in knowledge acquisition and exchange activities more freely and view knowledge as communal, thus improving the efficiency and effectiveness of the firm and its members. However, this would weaken the credibility of the hierarchy and the position of those in more senior grades.

HIERARCHIES AND FLEXIBLE WORKING

Hierarchical divisions between the grades also mapped on to the take-up of flexible working arrangements (FWAs). The firm had recently introduced formalised FWAs. Full-time members of the firm were eligible to participate in the scheme, enabling them to vary their office start and finish times within two-and-a-half-hour margins either side of the core hours of 10.00 until 16.00 defined by the firm, so long as they worked a minimum of 7.5 hours per day. Participation in the scheme was subject to business and management requirements and the agreement of an individual's manager(s) and client(s).

The interview data revealed that it was primarily junior members of staff who had chosen to take up these arrangements. Many senior members instead elected to retain their informal arrangements, due to the demands and nature of the work that they performed and because they believed that informal flexibility offered them greater freedom to structure their work around their own personal needs. They tended to have been with the firm for a considerable amount of time and therefore believed that the firm should have sufficient confidence in their commitment to the firm to trust them and enable them to exercise flexibility over their working time arrangements.

These patterns in the take-up of FWAs at the firm also reflected gender divisions. The majority of those choosing to operate under the FWAs were women, who were concentrated in junior-level roles. The firm recruited equal proportions of male and female consultants. However, senior positions in the firm were overwhelmingly male-dominated. While women's representation has improved at partner level, women still only account for one in five partners in the firm.

The interview data revealed that the adoption of FWAs negatively impacted on an individual's hierarchical progression. Career advancement was directly linked to billable time and those choosing to work shorter hours were at a relative disadvantage when competing for promotion opportunities. The gendered take-up of flexible working consequently hampered the progress of women, as they often remained in junior roles and performed work that could be accommodated more easily into their working patterns and so was typically less demanding and prestigious. In addition, their hierarchical progression was shaped by the presence of old boys' networks and the glass ceilings in operation at the firm.

The hierarchical structure at the firm was therefore marked by vertical gender segregation. The firm has stated objectives to increase the recruitment and retention of women and to enhance women's representation. These aims are underpinned by increasing equality legislation. However, the link between gender, working hours and this structure means that it is unlikely to achieve its goals of enhancing diversity and equality within the firm.

THE INTERNAL AND EXTERNAL FACE OF THE HIERARCHY

The salience of the organisational hierarchy varied according to organisational boundaries and played a direct role in shaping external interaction and engagement with clients. Internally, junior members of staff performed much of the work on client projects and even headed up teams on an informal basis. However, it was normally only senior and experienced members of staff who engaged with clients, in order to meet client expectations and ensure the appropriate management of the relationship. This generated tensions between junior and senior members of staff.

> I have headed up groups that have had more senior people in than me … but in a client situation, you always have the most senior person at the top, because the client expects that

and most senior people always think that they are the ones with the most knowledge, even if they aren't. (Assistant Consultant)

In addition, it was mostly senior members of the firm who engaged in external networking activities. Junior members of the firm tended not to engage in external networking, as they typically had little contact with clients and were not necessarily encouraged to network externally as they could potentially interfere with the social relations that more senior members of the firm had built.

The organisational hierarchy therefore caused tensions over client engagement and ownership as well as networking activities. However, the removal of this structure would run counter to client expectations and undermine the role and legitimacy of senior staff in generating client work.

SUMMARY

KnowledgeLtd is a leading knowledge-intensive firm. It strives to be an agile organisation at the forefront of business developments. However, its hierarchical structures and relations remain deeply embedded. While these hierarchies offer benefits to businesses and those occupying senior positions, they also hamper progress on a number of increasingly important fronts. The organisation and its members must therefore navigate these evolving tensions.

QUESTIONS

1 What countervailing tensions are presented by the potential retention or dissolution of the structural and relational hierarchies operating at KnowledgeLtd?

2 What does this case tell you about the factors likely to influence the nature and degree of change to an organisation's hierarchies?

3 Why are hierarchical structures and relations at the firm so intractable?

4 Given the insight you have gained into the hierarchical nature of the firm, would working for a firm like this appeal to you?

REFERENCES

Dalkir, K. and Beaulieu, M. (2018). *Knowledge management in theory and practice*. Boston, MA: Massachusetts Institute of Technology.

Ejler, N., Poulfelt, F. and Czerniawska, F. (2011). *Managing the knowledge-intensive firm*. Abingdon: Routledge.

Empson, L., Muzio, D., Broschak. J. and Hinings, B. (eds) (2017). *The Oxford handbook of professional service firms*. Oxford: Oxford University Press.

Hislop, D. and Bosua, R. (2018). *Knowledge management in organizations: A critical introduction*. Oxford: Oxford University Press.

Mabey, C. and Zhao, S. (2017). 'Managing five paradoxes of knowledge exchange in networked organizations: New priorities for HRM'. *Human Resource Management Journal*, **27**(1): 39–57.

26
Worker wellbeing at Jacaranda House

Susan Ressia, Adrian Wilkinson and Paula K. Mowbray

BACKGROUND AND CONTEXT

Jacaranda House is a not-for-profit organization and one of the first providers of aged care services in Australia. Jacaranda House is a large employer of professional, community and personal service workers who are employed across a number of sites in a major capital city. Jacaranda House has been in operation for over one hundred years, and the organization prides itself on its history of ingrained caring philosophies, practices and innovations that carry on to this day. Compassion and inclusivity is reflected in the organization's overriding mission, they take pride in striving to be a welcoming and caring community, and have a strong emphasis on patient wellbeing. This requires significant input from staff in order to achieve an environment that provides the best care and attention to its residents. All staff are expected to uphold these organizational values and goals.

Jacaranda House operates with over 2000 staff, and has over 1000 volunteers who work together to provide care and support to over 80 000 people each year. The management consists of a 15-member Board and a 7-member Executive Team. The organization employs staff within a range of occupations, characterized by people originating from a wide range of backgrounds. The organization recently opened a new 'state of the art' aged care facility, housing over 100 residents, and features a mix of indoor and outdoor spaces, well equipped rooms and additional services for patients including an on-site hairdresser.

Staff working at Jacaranda House can expect the following working conditions: to have a job that is clearly defined, challenging and rewarding; to experience relationships based on teamwork, respect and honesty; to work in an environment where there is zero tolerance for discrimination, harassment and bullying or intimidating behaviour; to work in an organization where decisions are made transparently, fairly and applied consistently; and to have a say concerning employee conditions, such as workloads, which can be discussed and resolved fairly and promptly. Jacaranda House states that the opinions of all staff count when it comes to ensuring satisfaction with their working life and so they seek out views and feedback from staff through a number of voice mechanisms. These include a staff survey, improvement logs, performance management systems and exit interviews. The organization keeps policy and best practice approaches for resident care up to date, and seeks to continually improve the working environment. It also has in place a Whistleblower Policy for staff to report 'wrongdoing' or 'reportable conduct' to senior executives. Further, there are opportunities for staff career development and the provision of flexible work arrangements and job security.

ORGANIZATIONAL ISSUES AND THE IMPACT ON WORKER WELLBEING

Jacaranda House is headed up by the Director of Aged Care, who oversees a range of senior and middle management roles, including a clinical care consultant, clinical nurse specialists, administration officers, leisure and lifestyle coordinator, client services coordinator, kitchen supervisor, chaplains, registered nurses, hospitality staff and enrolled nurses and assistants in nursing/caring staff. While the organization espoused having the aforementioned policies and practices, the Director identified a range of issues that were occurring in the new facility and was concerned about the effect these issues were having on worker morale and the overall culture of the workplace. The Director contacted the consultancy firm *WellbeingCo* to look in to why the issues were occurring, with the aim to develop strategies to help the organization get back to being a 'great place to work'.

The Director informed the *WellbeingCo* team that there appeared to be challenges associated with communication and voice within its diverse aged care workforce, and so there was a need to explore the difficulties of workplace communication, particularly in relation to the increasingly culturally diverse workplace environment. The Director advised that they wanted to understand both the positive and negative aspects influencing the employees in the workplace.

WORKFORCE DEMOGRAPHICS

WellbeingCo identified that the workforce's new facility employed 182 staff and was highly gendered, with 154 (82.5 per cent) staff being female. The age of staff ranged from 20 to 61 years, with females more likely to be aged between 51 and 61 years, and males being concentrated in the 26–35 and 46–50 year age groups. Of the 154 females, 150 are employed as permanent part-time staff, two are permanent full-time and a further two are fixed-term part-time. Of the males, 26 are permanent part-time and two are permanent full-time. Staff comprise people from 23 different countries, with over 53 per cent of the workforce born in countries other than Australia. Of the occupations, most staff are employed as assistants in nursing (AiN), a total of 90 employees; hospitality has a total of 38 employees, and registered nurses total 22 employees. Overseas born employees make up approximately 58 per cent of AiN, 43.25 per cent of hospitality, and almost 69 per cent of the registered nurse positions. The largest overseas born groups originate from the Philippines, at 14.3 per cent, followed by India, at almost 7.1 per cent. Australian born totalled approximately 46.2 per cent.

Turnover of staff for the twelve months prior to the investigation totalled 27 (almost 15 per cent), attributed in the majority of cases to resignation.

WELLBEINGCO'S INVESTIGATION

WellbeingCo visited the site and met with staff in the HR department to obtain a broad understanding of how the organization functions in terms of managing its workforce. *WellbeingCo* were also very interested in what the employees of Jacaranda House had to say, and a range of employees within the new facility were interviewed, including carers, hospitality workers, registered nurses and clinical nurse specialists. A range of issues were identified by workers including workloads, resourcing (staff and equipment), and communication issues. While management felt that they provided staff with many formal and informal channels to voice concerns or to raise good ideas, there was an underlying culture of employees feeling that they lacked the support and trust of management. They also felt a lack of trust among fellow workers. *WellbeingCo* identified a range of issues that were voiced by employees as follows:

Trust and safety

Staff who were below the level of middle manager reported that there was a culture of not speaking up. There was anxiety about speaking up, with one employee saying that 'we have to be bold to bring up issues'. Employees also felt there might be repercussions for speaking up: 'it can come back and bite you', or that it would be futile, as they believed that decisions had already been made by management. Others described a reluctance for staff to put anything in writing.

Gossiping

A 'gossip culture' was also evident within the staffroom. Employees said that they no longer take their breaks in the staffroom because they felt that even though they were 'not taking part in it, you're included in things that you have heard'. This meant that they would be implicated in the gossip, even though they were not part of any conversation.

Managing change

Staff were amalgamated from two older facilities into the one new facility five years earlier, but at different times. This created a segmented 'us vs. them' culture of suspicion between the two workforces. As one employee put it: 'We're divided … I felt at that time we are the underdog … we were the last one [group] who transferred [to the new facility] … they should have brought us as one.' This ongoing tension and friction was also highly evident to new staff.

Training

There appeared to be a lack of induction training for new staff, and many staff were uncomfortable with learning a new tablet technology system that enabled staff to record patient notes and receive important information about patient care. Some staff reported that the messages delivered through this technology had a harsh tone and contributed further to the levels of distrust of management.

Workload and continuity

Work pressures impacted the ability of management to communicate effectively and this was exacerbated by a lack of staff continuity, as staff are moved around on a daily basis. This had implications for continuity of care and accountability, particularly when the tablet technology was not being used as intended (e.g. tablets not being powered up, leaving staff unable to check messages).

Financial constraints

Employees spoke about the finances and how money (or the lack of it) appeared to influence a range of behaviours. One participant who worked shifts advised that they no longer got paid for time to attend staff meetings held outside of their shift hours. There was a general sense that budgets were tight and this fed through to workloads. One employee reported that supervisors complained that staff were too slow at their job and, consequently, staff felt there was no time to take a break; they often skipped lunch or burned their mouth as they had to eat their food quickly. Other staff felt that they were given shorter time slots to provide care for specific patients.

Examples of cost-cutting measures included the use of disposable wipes to save on laundry costs and having to rehang towels and use them again on patients without laundering them. One employee reported that this was discussed at a general staff meeting:

> they said that we had to start rehanging towels. ... because they [Management] needed to find a way of cutting down the cost ... It's really, really unhygienic. Not only that, if we hang up a wet towel it's a lot harder the next day. These people's skin is so see-through ... and it causes so much damage [to patient's skin]. ... Nobody speaks up because you just get shot down.

MANAGEMENT PERSPECTIVES

The management felt that overall they provided good opportunities for staff to communicate issues to management. Despite this, employees feel that there may not be adequate and/or appropriate ways to raise issues, and they do not always feel comfortable in doing so. Management had also become aware that the effectiveness of 'top down' communication mechanisms had become a challenge. As one member of the executive management team describes it: 'communication is a big challenge for us. At the executive level we've recognized this ... we recognize that at the executive level it's got a number of challenges around how we get the message out ... there are some key [areas of communication], legal; anti-discrimination, workplace bullying.'

Management recognized that there are key issues that require good communication, but in addition, the concern is how this information is best communicated. This means that the organization needs to be aware of and take into account the diversity of staff and differences in communication skills. Another overarching view was that communication must also link back to the organization's values in the way that they respect their staff members.

SUMMARY

While patient care and wellbeing is important in the context of Aged Care facilities, so is the wellbeing of the organization's employees. The Director of Aged Care was very concerned and wanted the culture of the organization to change. While management felt that they had excellent programmes in place that encouraged effective communication, there were many barriers to achieving this that were identified. The organization therefore needs to take action in order to achieve their aim of being a 'great place to work'. While management singled out the issue of communication as being the greatest difficulty in the organization, *WellbeingCo* found within the broader context of the Aged Care workforce, communication issues did not arise in isolation from other workplace systems and practices. For example, they found that communication was influenced by issues around trust and safety, managing change, workloads and rostering, and the lack of training and financial resources, as described above. As such, the issues to be resolved within this workplace are far more complex than first envisaged. The organization must now consider strategies in which to address and solve the identified issues, as failure to do so could see the continuance of an unhealthy workplace culture and many unhappy employees.

QUESTIONS

1 What are the flow-on effects of low worker morale in organizations?

2 Provide some recommendations for what the organization can do to improve the workplace culture.

3 Define 'worker wellbeing', then discuss what level of responsibility the organization and the individual has in achieving this outcome.

4 What are some of the outcomes for organizations if worker wellbeing is not taken seriously? What are the implications of this for workers?

PRACTICAL EXERCISE

Identify organizations that characterize themselves as a 'good place to work'. Perhaps these organizations have won awards as 'employer of choice' or similar.

1 Perform a search on the World Wide Web to find an organization.

2 How does the organization present itself to the public?

3 How do they attract employees to work for them?

4 Present your organization and findings to the class.

27
What makes a good job for low-waged workers?

Chris Warhurst and Sally Wright

This case study examines what makes a good job for low-waged workers, with Scotland as an example. It raises broader questions about employer choices around job quality and what might make them improve job quality in their organisations.

WHAT IS JOB QUALITY?

Following the 2017 *Taylor Review of Modern Working Practices*, the UK Government has committed itself to improving job quality in the UK and delivering more 'good work'. The UK is not alone in wanting to improve job quality. Other governmental bodies of which the UK is part have also developed policy on job quality. To ensure its future economic growth and competitiveness, the European Union, most obviously, wants to create better, not just more, jobs. The OECD, which is sometime called the rich nations' club and includes Australia and the USA as well as the UK, also wants its members to create more and better jobs. Likewise the G20, which includes governments and central bank governors from 19 developed and developing countries, including the UK and USA, Australia, Japan, India and China, plus the European Union, has committed its members to improving job quality in order to promote inclusive and sustainable growth.

Whilst job quality can be influenced by government – as well as trade unions and, in some countries, community organisations – ultimately it is employers who provide jobs and therefore bear most responsibility for the quality of those jobs (Findlay et al. 2017). What is important to note is that even in the same country, same industry and same market segment, some employers provide better quality jobs than other employers (Metcalf and Dhudwar 2010). There is thus some choice available to employers. Employers can, for example, offer permanent rather than temporary jobs or jobs that provide training and development opportunities.

Job quality comprises both the terms and conditions by which workers are employed, such as their pay and type of contract, and the nature of the work that they are employed to undertake, for example the extent of task autonomy or control. However, deciding what constitutes a good job is difficult. There can be objective criteria in the form of economic and/or non-economic indicators such as pay. This approach involves focusing on the characteristics of the job. Thus, using this indicator, a good job might be one that pays above the national average. However, job quality can also be subjective. This approach tends to focus on the reported attitudes and experiences of the job-holder (i.e. the employee) and the extent to which the job meets the job-holder's needs, for example parent-workers with childcare responsibilities. This second approach also recognises that this subjectivity is affected by workers' characteristics such as sex, age, ethnicity, qualifications and stage in the lifecycle. It also gives employees a voice in what constitutes a good job (Knox and Wright forthcoming).

WHAT MAKES A GOOD JOB?

A good example of this second approach is provided by Sutherland (2011) in his examination of what makes a good job for Scottish workers generally. His analysis is based on there being two kinds of job attributes: extrinsic, such as pay and which relates to material needs, and intrinsic, such as variety in the type of work, which relates to personal preferences. He used questions from the 2006 Employee Skills Survey to create a ranking of what is reported by workers to be important in their jobs. He found that four of the top five attributes were intrinsic: #1 'work you like doing', #3 'opportunity to use your abilities', #4 'friendly people to work with' and #5 'a job where you can use your initiative'. The only extrinsic attribute in the top five came second: 'a secure job'. The headline finding therefore is that intrinsic job attributes top workers' views on what makes a good job. However, Sutherland also noted that rankings varied by the type of worker answering the questions. For example, female workers were more likely than males to favour 'convenient hours' (extrinsic); highly-qualified workers were more likely than workers without such qualifications to favour 'use of initiative' (intrinsic).

Another complication is that whilst the UK Government favours use of the term 'good work' when it refers to job quality, a plethora of other terms or concepts are used, such as 'quality of working life', 'quality of employment', 'work quality', 'meaningful work', 'fulfilling work'. The UN, through its International Labour Organisation (ILO), prefers 'decent work', which tends to focus on poverty reduction in developing countries. To make matters even more complicated, these terms are often used interchangeably. For example, the European Commission and its agencies use 'decent work' and 'fair work', sometimes even in the same policy documents. However 'fair work' is used differently by governments of different countries to emphasise different policy priorities. In Australia, it refers to the provision of minimum standards of employment (National Employment Standards) covering, for example, maximum weekly hours of work and parental leave entitlements, plus a national minimum wage. In Scotland it centres on the promotion of social partnership, including employees having an effective voice, both as a feature of, and to support progressive workplaces.

Warhurst et al. (2017) outline this 'family of concepts' and provide brief explanations for each. They also try to make sense of what each is trying to do through a 'hierarchicalised mosaic'. Referring back to the debate about objective and subjective aspects of job quality and the underpinnings of job quality, moving up the hierarchy there is a shift from basic worker needs that tend to be met by statutory regulation, towards higher-level employee preferences that are provided by progressive human resource policies within organisations (left and right-hand side arrows respectively in Figure 27.1). As Warhurst et al. state, 'employers opting for minimum standards derived from external regulation will offer decent or fair work,[1] attending simply to workers' basic needs – for

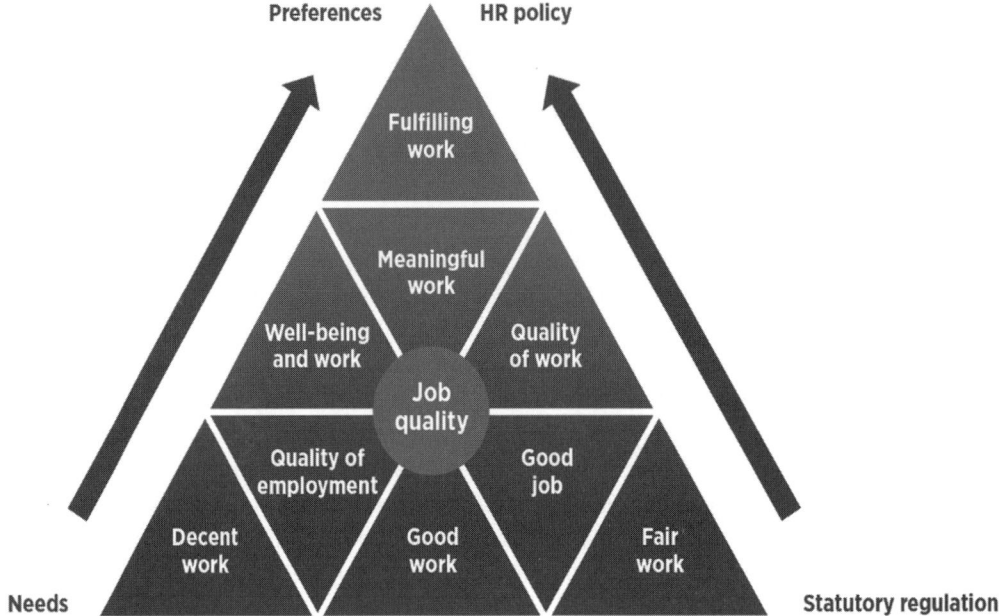

Source: From Warhurst et al. (2017: 27).

Figure 27.1 The family of concepts and options around job quality within organisations

example by paying a statutory minimum or living wage – but only because they are statutorily required to do so'. Conversely, they continue, 'other employers will attend to the needs and preferences of their workers, driven by internally derived HRM, providing, for example, meaningful or fulfilling work. These employers … see merit in mutual gains' (p. 27).

What comes across from this body of research is that, whilst job quality and improving it is important, what constitutes a good job varies by type of worker. In addition, the different terms used to express job quality can have underlying different purposes. These different purposes, however, still relate to employers' provision of job quality, with employers making choices about the quality of jobs they offer. These points coalesce in a recent study into what makes for decent work for low-waged workers in Scotland, as the next section reports.

DECENT WORK FOR LOW-WAGED WORKERS

Oxfam is a charity that works in some of the poorest countries in the world. Headquartered in Oxford in the UK, its origins lie in famine relief in the 1940s. Since then it has grown to be a worldwide confederation of 20 independent charities with a common aim to alleviate global poverty. Although often associated with providing aid and support for developing countries, Oxfam also champions poverty alleviation in the UK, recognising that in-work poverty is an issue – that is, workers who are paid too little to be raised out of poverty.

Oxfam notes that drives to raise the minimum wage and/or establish living wages have tended to dominate debate about job quality. It acknowledges, however, that job quality comprises more than just wages. Because low-waged workers are more exposed to the risk of being in poverty, Oxfam draws on, but has adapted, the ILO's concept of decent work for its study of these workers in Scotland (see Stuart et al. 2016). This adaptation was developed by one of us based on a literature review of job quality and decent work. It comprises five dimensions: pay; terms and conditions of employment; characteristics of work; work–life balance; and health and safety. Each dimension had a series of indicators, of which there were 26 in total. Scotland was a useful location for Oxfam to try to influence policy debate because, with its commitment to fair work, the Scottish Government is leading the way in trying to improve job quality in the UK.

The study involved participatory research asking low-waged workers about their job priorities, concerns and ambitions in relation to what they need to live well. The research had three main methods: 30 focus groups involving 277 people; 11 street stalls engaging 433 people across Scotland targeting low-waged participants; and an online opinion poll of 802 low-waged Scottish workers. Using the 26 indicators, each method resulted in a set of weighted rankings for decent work; see Table 27.1.

The ranking varies slightly by research method, though the key issues recur: the need for decent pay and job security. In terms of pay, one female focus group member explained: 'I'd love to just say it was not about the money … like job satisfaction. I really do want that. But I need the money'. Another spoke about precarious employment: '… a friend in my job was on holiday. [She] called in to ask if she could stay a week longer and was told "yes", came home and she was fired'. Having a safe working environment was also highlighted as important. A call centre worker illustrated why: 'That heavy rain we had last week, the roof was leaking onto four of the computers and they just unplugged them … and left them there … [they] put a bucket next to it to catch the rain'. There was a supplementary set of 18 interviews with low-waged workers from different areas of Scotland.

Table 27.1 What makes jobs decent for low-waged workers

Rank	Focus groups	Street stalls	Opinion poll
1	Decent hourly rate	Decent hourly rate	Decent hourly rate
2	Job security	Job security	Safe environment
3	Paid leave	Safe environment	Fair pay to similar jobs
4	Safe environment	Paid leave	Job security/ paid leave/ no discrimination*
5	Supportive manager	No discrimination	

Note: *jointly ranked. The next indicator therefore was ranked 7th.
Source: From Stuart et al. (2016: 14–15).

These interviews allowed low-waged workers to speak in depth about their personal experiences of bad work and employment practices. It revealed that, despite the law, some had not even received contracts of employment that outlined their rights and entitlements such as pay and holidays.

These findings for Scottish low-waged workers both contrast and align with Sutherland's findings for Scottish workers generally. Whereas the latter favoured intrinsic job attributes, such as 'work you like doing', the low-waged workers focused on extrinsic job attributes: pay. This difference is captured in the distinction between needs and preferences of the hierarchicalised mosaic. However, both workers generally and low-waged workers in Scotland favour having job security. The difference for the low-waged workers is that they appear more vulnerable in this respect, having precarious employment and sometimes not even having a contract.

Oxfam argued that these findings show consistency in what low-waged workers in Scotland need from jobs to make those jobs decent. It also argued that these needs are not being met. It called on the Scottish Government to develop minimum standards for decent work in Scotland and encourage employers to adopt these standards.

SUMMARY AND OVERVIEW

When it comes to job quality, there are undoubtedly good employers as well as bad employers. The Oxfam study affirms the importance of job quality and what aspects of job quality need to be improved for vulnerable workers. Change is needed both to raise standards and to ensure compliance with existing laws. Violation of labour laws by employers in low-wage industries is not confined to Scotland. In the USA, Theodore et al. (2012) note that there is increasing evidence that employers routinely break these laws in a wide range of low-wage industries, from construction to retail, from hospitality to home healthcare.

In this respect, positing a dichotomy between good and bad employers might be too harsh. There are employers who want to improve the quality of jobs that they offer but need a mixture of guidance and direction on how to do so. Related research commissioned by Oxfam (Gibb and Ishaq 2016) revealed that employers and human resource managers in Scotland were not opposed to providing decent work for their employees, viewing it as a potential tool to create an attractive workplace. However, their understanding of what constitutes decent work was limited and they welcomed the idea of having a clear, widely accepted and easily measurable definition.

Having a clear definition of job quality, backed up by agreed dimensions with minimum standards would therefore be useful, both to employees and to employers. For all employees there would be a solid floor of rights supported by employer responsibilities. This floor would be particularly helpful for low-waged workers. It would provide those employers looking for guidance clear indication of what is needed. Moreover, monitored and enforced, the introduction of minimum standards of job quality would also create a level playing field between companies that comply with regulations and those that do not. Bad employers would not be able to compete on non-compliance, that is, through breaking the law.

There are already initiatives to create these minimum standards. Echoing Oxfam's suggestion, following the Taylor Review, a working group set up to create measures of job quality also recommended consideration of a minimum job quality standard in the UK (Job Quality Working Group 2018). The European Union is to introduce a new Directive on Transparent and Predictable Working Conditions that will increase the number of workers in Europe who receive written notification of their working conditions and have more stable employment, and which is intended to push up standards of job quality.[2] Australia already has minimum standards through its National Employment Standards, though their effectiveness in raising job quality has yet to be evaluated. Clearly, as the case of low-waged workers in Scotland demonstrates, there are normative reasons to create more good jobs, most obviously, in the twenty-first century, so that all workers should have jobs that support their wellbeing. A key next step will be developing a business case for good jobs so that more employers recognise the instrumental benefits to their companies of offering these good jobs.

END NOTES

1. Based on Australia's version of 'fair work'.
2. https://ec.europa.eu/social/main.jsp?catId=89&furtherNews=yes&langId=en&newsId=9297.

REFERENCES

Findlay, P., Warhurst, C., Keep, E. and Lloyd, C. (2017) 'Opportunity Knocks? The Possibilities and Levers for Improving Job Quality', *Work and Occupations*, **44**(1): 3–22.

Gibb, S. and Ishaq, M. (2016) Decent Work: The Employers' View, accessed at http://http://uwsoxfampartnership.org.uk/wp-content/uploads/2016/05/Decent-Work-Thematic-Report-2-Employers-View-Web.pdf.

Job Quality Working Group (2018) 'Measuring Good Work', accessed at https://www.carnegieuktrust.org.uk/publications/measuring-good-work-the-final-report-of-the-measuring-job-quality-working-group/.

Knox, A. and Wright, S. (2020 forthcoming) 'Understanding Job Quality Using Qualitative Research', in C. Warhurst, C. Mathieu and R. Dwyer (eds), *Oxford Handbook of Job Quality*, Oxford: Oxford University Press.

Metcalf, A. and Dhudwar, A. (2010) 'Employers' Role in the Low-pay/No-pay Cycle', York: Joseph Rowntree Foundation.

Stuart, F., Pautz, H. and Wright, S. (2016) 'Decent Work for Scotland's Low-paid Workers: A Job to be done', accessed at http://uwsoxfampartnership.org.uk/wp-content/uploads/2014/10/Decent-Work-in-Scotland-Low-Paid-Workers-final-report-.pdf.

Sutherland, J. (2011) 'Job Attribute Preferences in Scotland', *Working Paper 27*, Centre for Public Policy for Regions, University of Glasgow.

Theodore, N., Bernhardt, A. and DeFilippis, J. with Milkman, R., Heckathorn, D., Auer, M., Luz Gonzalez et al. (2012) 'Under the Radar: Tracking the Violation of Labour Standards on Low-wage Industries in the US', in C. Warhurst, P. Findlay, C. Tilly and F. Carré (eds), *Are Bad Jobs Inevitable?* London: Palgrave.

Warhurst, C., Wright, S. and Lyonette, C. (2017) *Understanding and Measuring Job Quality: Part 1 – Thematic Literature Review*, accessed at https://www.cipd.co.uk/Images/understanding-and-measuring-job-quality-1_tcm18-33193.pdf.

28
Organizing project-based work in the games industry: Two contrasting cases*

Wike Been and Noëlle Payton

BACKGROUND AND CONTEXT

The Dutch games industry is young, dynamic and growing fast. There are many start-ups, but at the same time the business failure rate among these companies is high. In comparison to other countries, an important share of the Dutch market is made up of companies that focus on so-called serious games (also referred to as applied games), or combine entertainment games and serious games in their business model. The games industry is a hot industry with an oversupply of labour, which is related to the numerous educational institutes that offer games-related programmes in the Netherlands. The work is generally project-based, regardless of whether it is work-for-hire or developing own games.

CASE 1

SeriousEst is one of the older games development companies in the Netherlands. They employ about forty people. Given that the Dutch games sector is characterized by many small companies (Koops, 2016), SeriousEst can be considered one of the larger ones in the Netherlands. They are not involved in entertainment games but focus solely on the market for serious games, developing products on demand for a broad range of clients in both for-profit and non-profit sectors. Most of the staff today are involved in games development. A few are in managing or supportive roles. The aim of SeriousEst is to develop and deliver high-quality and innovative games. To this end they have made the conscious decision to stay small, as this contributes to a lower burn rate, which allows the company to engage in projects offering less financial security but more possibilities to be innovative. Additionally, staying small facilitates interaction between individual employees and a more informal and personal atmosphere, which are conditions they value.

CASE 2

GameCoal is a small, young games company in the Netherlands made up of two friends who are the founder-directors. They have no permanent employees but scale up when necessary for projects by making use of freelance workers and interns who are recruited through informal networks, thus forming project-based coalitions. Their work-for-hire projects have been in both serious games and entertainment games, while their own 'founding game', the game around which their company was originally established, can be qualified as both: an entertainment game with educational intent. Clients for work-for-hire projects include both for-profit and non-profit organizations, and several are games or IT development companies themselves. They have recently acquired a major project as subcontractor for a larger games company creating an educational game for a large non-profit end client for which they had to upscale. The project's timespan is some eight months, which is considered exceptionally long.

> **BOX 28.1**
> **VARIETY IN THE GAMES INDUSTRY**
>
> SERIOUS VS. ENTERTAINMENT GAMES
> The games industry knows roughly two kinds of games: 'serious' and 'entertainment' games (Dörner et al. 2016; Koops 2016). As implied, the latter are games for fun and entertainment and can range from simple apps for phone or tablet to elaborate productions for consoles (Nintendo, Xbox etc.) or PCs, with budgets spent on graphics, sound, and marketing matching Hollywood blockbusters. Serious games, also referred to as applied games, are games with entertainment as well as practical intent. They can be educational (for both children and adults), for marketing purposes, awareness-raising (e.g. a game simulating the experience of dementia), and there are many applications in healthcare (e.g. games stimulating movement and interaction, games to improve diet, etc.).
>
> PRODUCT-BASED VS. PROJECT-BASED BUSINESS MODELS
> Both cases in this chapter are companies with a predominantly project-based business model. Games companies with a project-based business model generate revenues by carrying out temporary projects for clients who commission them to develop a particular game or application. These are often (but not exclusively) applied games (e.g. developing a game for company training), but could also consist of a certain part of a game. This can be contrasted to a product-based business model. A product-based business model is centred around a finished product: a game, in some cases combined with dedicated hardware. Revenues are generated through the sales of these products, as new games and new versions are continually developed.

PROJECT-BASED BUSINESS MODELS

Both organizations are based on a project-based business model, referring here to a business model in which revenue is generated by executing temporary projects for external clients. As a consequence of the variation in the number of projects running and the intensity and size of the projects, the companies must deal with fluctuations over time in the amount of work and revenues.

For SeriousEst, this means that there are times with internal labour shortage and times of internal labour oversupply. A central strategy of SeriousEst to cope with these fluctuations is to have some long-running but low-paid projects based on subsidies that people can work on during times of labour oversupply, as well as allowing for personal 'pet projects' during work time, which is also seen as a way to promote 'fun' at work and foster creativity and innovation. In times of shortage, freelancers are contracted, but as few as possible because they are expensive and less integrated into SeriousEst's corporate culture. At any given time there may be three or four freelancers working at SeriousEst, and in peak periods this may be upscaled to up to a quarter of the workforce. When there is serious shortage, work is outsourced to another company.

In the past, SeriousEst has considered alternative business models: to attract major investors or to solicit a takeover by a larger company. These options would lessen the financial pressure and potentially allow for major innovations, which were said to be highly capital-intensive. However, these alternatives have been rejected so far for the sake of retaining autonomy. Autonomy is highly valued by the company as well as its workers. They feel that they already have to share their autonomy with paying clients, and adding an investor would add another party to share it with, as well as putting pressure on the company to be profitable. They fear this will lower the intrinsic job quality and joy they experience in their work, although – admittedly – it may provide financial room to improve on wages and secondary benefits.

GameCoal deals with the fluctuating workload by hiring freelance workers according to a project's needs. In a sense, they are the coordinators in a temporary coalition of freelance workers executing a project, which will break up as soon as the project is finished. The recently acquired major project meant that they had to scale up, not only with interns as is their habit, but also with more experienced freelancers and an experienced project manager. These freelancers are often 'indie' game developers (independent game developers) who develop their own games besides the work-for-hire they do to provide for income. They do work-for-hire until they hopefully reach the ultimate goal: achieving success with their own independently developed game to the extent that they can make a living off of it, although there is also a realization that this may never happen. The same can actually be said for GameCoal itself: the ultimate goal is for their own game to sell well enough so that it can sustain them. In the meantime, they engage in work-for-hire projects for external clients to sustain themselves.

HR STRATEGIES

SeriousEst prefers to work with employees rather than a large pool of freelance workers, as they feel employees are generally more engaged with the company and its goals, and will feel more motivated to really make a good product. In the hiring process, candidates are questioned explicitly on their identification with the company and their intrinsic motivation for the work. They are warned that you do not join the company to get rich, and elaborate portfolios are prioritized over formal education as proof of intrinsic motivation and craftsmanship. The company almost exclusively hires highly skilled, preferably multi-disciplinary people. The resulting multi-skilled teams with multidisciplinary backgrounds are considered by SeriousEst to be the most innovative.

Compared to the past, the organization has become more critical in their hiring and retention practices. As a retention strategy to have the best and most motivated people, there are regular reviews of 'who gets picked first/ last' when putting together project teams. These reviews are used as a performance evaluation. Those who consistently get picked last are engaged early on to talk about their place in the company, whereas retention efforts focus on those whose performance is best. SeriousEst tries to retain employees not through wages but through 'just letting them do the attractive projects', based on the assumption expressed by the operational director that true 'craftspeople' are not interested in getting rich, but rather have challenging work. To get the most out of employees, the work environment at SeriousEst has been designed to foster near-exclusive focus on employees' core work by limiting procedures and bureaucratic control so that they can fully express their 'craftsmanship' without interference and distraction. Other means are also adopted to maximize the pleasantness of the workspace, for example through interior design and the provision of lunch. Finally, the operational director emphasizes that the company must feel like a safe place for people to play, try and fail, in order to optimally stimulate creativity.

People are initially hired for one year, then two years, then on a permanent basis. The majority of the workforce works on a permanent contract. An important recent step in professionalizing the employee-centred policies of the organization was the creation of a specific HR position. The appointed manager was not trained as an HR professional, which is seen as an asset as it allows for thinking out of the box. The most important concrete policies that have been introduced are a system of self-reporting workload to improve the use of employees' slack time and a major effort at mapping employee skills and interests in order to better match them to projects and to each other.

In contrast, GameCoal exclusively works with freelance workers and interns. Freelance workers are found through their own personal networks and assessed based on prior experience with them: if they provide good work they will be considered for the next project. Freelance workers are hired based on the skills they possess and the required skills for a specific project. Interns are used frequently in order to get the work done without going over budget. GameCoal has no wish to employ people as employees, citing the short project timespans and the speed at which the games market changes, both necessitating flexibility and making employing people too troublesome. Moreover, as a relatively young company, the successful acquisition of projects is still unpredictable. Furthermore, at least one of the GameCoal founders is a firm believer of individual freedom and autonomy, which could be undermined by an employment relationship. Such a view is in line with the general 'indie' culture of free-spiritedness.

Since GameCoal has no employees, there is no formal HR policy. Nonetheless, they do have practices aimed at optimizing the effectiveness of the workers. Most notably, a project manager was hired for the large project in order to 'shield the rest of the team from the changeable and chaotic external circumstances', to create the 'calm and focus' necessary for the 'rigid' work of software programming; this is somewhat similar to SeriousEst's policy aimed at allowing workers to focus exclusively on their core work. Furthermore, in line with the beliefs valuing individual freedom and autonomy, there are very few rules about working hours. Although a minimum amount of overlap in working hours is deemed necessary for effective collaboration, the freelancers are basically expected to deliver whatever part of the project that has been agreed upon by a certain time. Beyond that, there is little to no control.

ASPECTS OF JOB QUALITY

Wages at SeriousEst are near-competitive, but people could earn more elsewhere with their skills, especially developers. The company deliberately keeps the wages relatively low for several reasons. Workers as well as management state that you don't work at SeriousEst for the money. In other words, accepting lower pay is interpreted as a sign of intrinsic motivation. The lower wages are also partly seen as a consequence of the irregular project-based model with different and riskier products (as opposed to offering routine products and services), which is also reflected in end-of-year bonuses: if the company had a good year, everybody gets some, and if not, nobody does. Wages are therefore traded in a way for more interesting and challenging work, a sacrifice employees are willing to make. Even though wages are relatively low, effort is put into a fair distribution of the wages among colleagues according to experience, for example making sure the lead programmer gets paid more than non-lead programmers. There is also an ongoing effort to make the wage structure more transparent.

At GameCoal hourly wage offers are made to the freelancers depending on their experience and ability to take responsibility over parts of the projects and manage others (for the positions for art lead and tech lead), divided roughly into three wage categories plus a higher category for the project manager, who currently earns more than the founder-director. In most cases it appears the wage offer was accepted. Hourly earnings for workers in work-for-hire projects are said to be some 30 per cent lower than hourly earnings in the IT sector for persons of similar experience and skill. It needs to be kept in mind, however, that these concern wages for temporary projects, not steady employment. Unsurprisingly, even after including work-for-hire in the business model, job and income security remain very low in this part of the games industry. Contracts between client companies and freelancers or interns are temporary, spanning the time period set for a project, a few months at most for a larger project. Late payment by clients, which happens more than occasionally, exacerbates income volatility. The longer one is in the field, however, and the larger the established network, the higher job and income security become. This does require that you 'survive' long enough in the field to build up a convincing portfolio.

As for working time, overtime appears to be a regular occurrence on projects people do for fun or on the side at SeriousEst, for example testing a game someone has developed or brainstorming during 'pizza sessions' after work. This can be seen as a remnant of the indie industry in which people do paid and unpaid own projects alongside each other. Taking part in such sessions occurs on a voluntary basis; 'plenty of employees don't do it and it's fine'. There is no indication of extremes – crunch time (working extremely long hours for several days on end, sometimes with hardly any sleep) – to meet deadlines at the end of projects. Working time can also fluctuate for individual employees because of the project-based set-up. Old projects may need extra attention even after new projects have started. Managers indicate that project flow is not easily regulated, and employees indicate that the sense of ownership and responsibility for projects make it difficult to say 'time is up, I'm going home', when something requires attention, even if it means unpaid overwork. It is experienced as stressful sometimes, but it was said to be better than being bored. Also, seeing the high workload among other employees motivates people to keep working, which is an indication of some peer pressure.

QUESTIONS

1. These cases highlight the very different ways in which companies can deal with the fluctuating workload that accompanies a project-based model of work.
   a Reflect on the relation between a project-based business model and a fluctuating workload.
   b What are the solutions SeriousEst and GameCoal have adopted to cope with the fluctuating workload?
   c What does your analysis mean for the often assumed necessity of flexible work in sectors and companies with a fluctuating workload?

2. Management choices have different kinds of consequences for workers.
   a What are the consequences of each business model for the job quality experienced by the workers?
   b Zooming in on two particular elements of job quality, reflect on autonomy and income security experienced by workers in both companies.

3. Could these companies' HR strategies be applied equally effectively in other segments of the labour market?

END NOTES

* The case studies discussed in this chapter originate from the QuInnE (Quality of jobs and Innovation generated Employment outcomes) project, financed by the European Commission's Horizon 2020 Programme (project reference number: 649497).

REFERENCES

Dörner, R., Göbel, S. and Kickmeier-Rust, M. (2016). Introduction to the GI-Dagstuhl Book on Entertainment Computing and Serious Games. In Dörner, R., Göbel, S., Kickmeier-Rust, M., Masuch, M. and Zweig, K. (eds) *Entertainment Computing and Entertainment Games*. Cham: Springer International Publishing.

Koops, O. (2016). *Games Monitor: The Netherlands 2015*. Utrecht: Dutch Game Garden.

29
Human resource management and relationship marketing: How two organizations leveraged tattoos to build their brand*

Andrew R. Timming

BACKGROUND AND CONTEXT

In recent decades, much of the manufacturing sector in advanced Western market economies has either been automated or relocated to developing countries where the cost of production is comparatively lower. As factories closed down in the West, new forms of employment emerged to fill the vacuum. It is in this context that the interactive services economy rose to prominence. The interactive services sector is defined here as that part of the economy in which companies engage customers face-to-face, offering them a positive consumer experience. Physical products, many of which are manufactured in the East, are still retailed in this sector, but the key to encouraging consumption is for firms to create the right atmosphere for customers to part with their money. To achieve this atmosphere, firms employ a number of marketing techniques that elicit a positive response to the products and/ or services on offer. Increasingly, these same organizations are starting to recognize that the physical appearance of front-line staff can also play an important role in business success (or failure).

The two organizations featured in this chapter[1] operate in such a context. We will call them PubCo and SkateCo to preserve their anonymity. Both companies are based in the United Kingdom and, as we shall see, depend on the patronage of a similar clientele. PubCo is a multinational corporation headquartered in Scotland and founded after the turn of the century. As the pseudonym suggests, it is a brewery/ pub that prides itself on offering high quality beer, among other drinks and nibbles. Its pubs are located across the UK, with recent expansions internationally, especially into Australia. PubCo's brand is largely based on "punk rock" culture, and its identity centers around rebelliousness and non-conformity. The company has strategically located its pubs especially in university towns to take advantage of this young clientele. SkateCo, in contrast, is a small, independent, locally owned and operated skateboard and apparel shop. Its single location is primarily geared towards the alternative skateboarder sub-culture. The shop sells skateboards, clothes and shoes and, very much like PubCo, typically plays punk rock or heavy metal music in the background. Most of the clientele are younger and, generally speaking, male.

The key challenge faced by PubCo and SkateCo is that they offer products that can potentially be purchased at a cheaper price either in a supermarket (in the case of the former) or online (in the case of the latter). For example, a liquor shop can sell cheap beer and lager to consumers in bulk, whereas PubCo offers their drinks at a premium so that customers can enjoy not only the alcohol, but also the atmosphere. Similarly, inasmuch as anyone can order a skateboard from an internet retailer that enjoys lower overhead costs, SkateCo has to offer a positive experience for customers to offset the higher price of buying one in a bricks-and-mortar store. How can management at both companies stay competitive in a free market in which, *ceteris paribus*, consumers are always looking for the best deal?

IDENTIFYING CUSTOMERS: WHO IS THE TARGET DEMOGRAPHIC?

The first step for them is to understand their customer base. Who, exactly, is the target demographic? This involves some strategic thinking about what type of person is most likely to be interested in a product or service. No two persons consume equally. We all have values, tastes and preferences that align with some products or services more than others. Different groups of people also have different resource constraints that play into the equation. Let's look at a few examples. Older consumers are more likely to purchase a luxury car, such as a Jaguar, whilst younger consumers are more likely to go with a more affordable, but reliable, brand of automobile. Women are more likely to purchase cosmetics than men. Aficionados of classical music are more likely to purchase an expensive wagyu steak when eating out, whilst punk rockers are likely to opt for a cheeseburger. People who live in houses are more likely to own the latest iPhone than those who live in trailers. Attractive people are significantly more likely to purchase certain articles of clothing, such as a revealing dress, than less attractive people. The list could go on and on. Certain types of people, with certain looks and personalities, are inclined toward some brands and disinclined toward others.

So, what is the target demographic of consumer for our two case studies? As noted above, both firms are seeking to attract a similar clientele. Those most likely to frequent trendy pubs and skateboard shops, for starters, tend to be a young demographic. They may also possess a concomitant rebellious personality, one that actively resists conformity and mainstream pop culture. They may listen to punk rock or heavy metal music when hanging out with their friends. They may identify with counter-cultural celebrities and seek to emulate their distaste for authority and rules. They may be ardent individualists, with a penchant for anarchy and mayhem. Crucially, for the purposes of this chapter, they are also likely to have visible tattoos and body piercings. Body art has long been seen as an important cue to these, let's call them, "anti-establishment" traits.

ALIGNING HUMAN RESOURCES WITH RELATIONSHIP MARKETING

If a company aims to target a particular demographic of customer successfully, it needs to pay close attention to the environment and design of the workplace. This is where relationship marketing comes into play. The logic underlying relationship marketing is that firms, especially those in the interactive services sector, stand to benefit insofar as they can establish a close and intimate relationship with customers. Ideally, successful marketing converts a brand into a trusted friend or a role model. In order to project this image to the consumer, management must take care to structure the workplace environment according to the norms and mores (i.e., the culture) of the targeted consumer.

The design and physical layout of the retail space is crucial in establishing a close relationship with the consumer. Marketing scholars often refer to these environmental considerations as "atmospherics". Of course, a retail space should be clean and tidy, but it should also utilize appropriate lighting, colors, music, art, décor, and even smell. From the placement of furniture and the temperature of the retail space to genre of music playing in the background and location of products, sales can be optimized by ensuring that these features are properly aligned with the expectations of the target demographic of customer. Where the customer's expectations are met, the experience is perceived as positive, resulting in an increased probability of consumption. On the other hand, failure to ensure that the design and physical layout of the store are aligned with customers' expectations can, and often does, manufacture a negative experience.

The inquisitive student may be wondering, at this point, what this all has to do with human resource management (HRM). The link between relationship marketing and HRM is based on the assumption that front-line, customer-facing employees are a crucial element of a retail space's physical design, layout and overall atmosphere. Employees with the right "look" can have an important positive impact on the consumer experience. This is especially true in the interactive services sector, where employees represent the brand, or image, of the company. The opposite is also true. In other words, employees with the "wrong" look can have a negative effect on the consumer experience. The crucial question at this point is: what is the "right" look and the "wrong" look? The answer to this question depends on the unique brand, or image, that a company is trying to project, which, in turn, is closely related to the target demographic of customer, discussed above.

Let's look at PubCo as an example. Its clientele is typically young, into punk culture, and, as described by the regional manager, "edgy". She continued, "you know, we're a little bit out there on the edge of perhaps what some employers would feel is acceptable". Many of those who frequent their establishments for a pint of lager also, perhaps unsurprisingly, display visible tattoos. Body art is traditionally associated with punk rock, non-conformity, and individualism. With this in mind, PubCo's recruitment and selection strategy for front-line staff factors in the "look" of job candidates. Specifically, they're looking for younger employees with visible tattoos because they signal a connection between the company and its clientele. A frequent visitor to PubCo even noted that many of the bartenders there have the PubCo logo tattooed on their body. She recounted a story of a friend who applied for a job at PubCo and was successful at least in part because he had a PubCo logo tattoo that he could show off during the job interview. Visibly tattooed job applicants may struggle to attain gainful employment in industries where the target demographic of customer is older and more conservative (e.g., a fine dining restaurant), but in the context of PubCo and its punk rock image, having a tattoo is, in fact, an asset for job applicants.

A similar story unfolded at SkateCo. The manager explained, "We have the kind of culture that's associated with tattoos … we've got a skate vibe … At the end of the day, it's a lifestyle for us … It's just, basically, be yourself, you know?" When asked to explain why he prioritizes the employment of front-line staff with visible tattoos, he responded that many of his customers have "tattoos, so they like looking at tattoos every day, and then they're coming in here, and looking at us with tattoos, *because that's who they want to be* [emphasis mine]." A potential customer at SkateCo corroborated this point. When I showed him some photographs of the SkateCo manager's tattoos, he responded, "he probably knows what he's talking about when it comes to skateboards". When probed further on this assertion, he explained,

> A lot of people in the industry are tattooed, meaning a lot of the pro-skaters have a lot of tattoos … It's also a lot like the art on the back of the boards … If the community behind your job involves a lot of body art, it's just one more thing to draw you closer to your customers. Your customers are also going to have some body art.

Thus, employee selection and assessment at SkateCo was based, at least in part, on the perceived cultural "fit" between its customer base and front-line employees. The latter are selected into employment on the basis of the fact that they represent the former. Herein lies the essence of the link between human resource management and relationship marketing.

SUMMARY

The decline of factory work in the West has resulted in a marked increase in service sector jobs, where front-line staff and customers meet face-to-face, and the experience (as perceived by the customer) is central to promoting consumption. Many service sector firms, especially those in bricks-and-mortar retailing, struggle to compete with lower-cost rivals. In order to gain a competitive advantage in the market, such businesses must ensure that their customers are not simply buying a product, but also enjoying a positive experience.

Traditionally, a firm's marketing function has been a key player in the manufacturing of a positive consumer experience. Many companies, especially in the interactive services, invest heavily in the physical design, layout and appearance of the retail space. The physical appearance of a retail space must always align with the expectations of the target customers. But it is increasingly recognized that the physical space only partially contributes positively to the "aesthetic" sensibilities of consumers. It is also important to ensure that the appearance of front-line staff is closely aligned with customers' expectations. Ideally, human resources managers, in the recruitment, selection and development of customer-facing staff, should pay attention to the aesthetic "fit" of employees, all of whom present as the face of the company. Often, only employees with the "right" look are selected into employment. The "right" look, in this context, means that the employees must appeal favorably to the customers' preferences.

In this chapter, we looked at two case study organizations, PubCo and SkateCo, to illustrate the link between relationship marketing and human resource management decision-making. We demonstrated that visible tattoos, which may present as a liability for many job seekers, are, in fact, an asset in these two organizations. That is to say, job applicants with tattoos are viewed favorably in recruitment and selection. The main reason for this positive assessment of body art is that many of the customers at both organizations are themselves adorned with tattoos. Thus, it would appear that employers are keen to make sure that the appearance of front-line staff corresponds with the appearance of their customer base. One of the key implications of these case studies is that human resource managers, to be effective in their jobs, must possess a well-rounded knowledge of the business, including the areas of relationship marketing and branding.

QUESTIONS

1 In what kinds of organization do you think visible tattoos might prevent someone from getting a job? Why do you think this is the case?

2 What are the ethical and moral implications of hiring an employee based on how he or she looks? Should hiring always be based on an individual's knowledge, skills and abilities? Why or why not?

3 These two case studies have shown that visible tattoos can potentially be an asset for a job seeker, but are there also certain types, or genres, of tattoos that will always be a liability? If so, what specific tattoos will reduce your employability, even in companies like PubCo and SkateCo?

4 Do you think tattoos will become increasingly acceptable in all workplaces in the future? Why or why not?

END NOTES

* I want to thank the many respondents who volunteered their valuable time to talk with me about body art (theirs and others') in the two case study organizations.

1 It should be noted that this chapter is adapted from the following article: Timming, Andrew R. (2017) Body art as branded labour: At the intersection of employee selection and relationship marketing. *Human Relations* **70**(9): 1041–63.

SECTION VI
LEADERSHIP AND CHANGE

30
Meaningless leadership

Leo McCann

BACKGROUND AND CONTEXT

Being in charge of anything is rarely easy. Leading an organization or a team is a demanding, often thankless, task. People in senior management positions have wide responsibility and are compelled to make tough decisions. They are responsible not just for their own behaviour, performance and conduct, but also for those who report to them. Senior leaders in large organizations typically work very long hours, confront heavy workloads and face intense pressure and stress. Front-line supervisors who have been promoted into middle or senior management positions fret about whether they can handle the transition from worker to manager and whether subordinates will respect their newfound authority. Entrepreneurs who have grown their own business suddenly have to oversee a hierarchy of management and supervisory roles. A police sergeant promoted to inspector will have to get used to being called 'Boss' by fellow cops who until recently were close, trusted companions at police stations, in patrol cars and out on the streets.

Leadership can be a tough and lonely job. But there is no need to panic. Fortunately, the stressed and uncertain manager – newly-minted or highly-experienced – has some important places to turn for advice. Enter the multi-million-selling leadership guru book, something that instantly offers a ready-made psychological crutch. There's no need to blunder through a leadership position making a string of naive and costly errors. Instead, a wise manager can learn from the cutting-edge analysis of world-leading leadership gurus.

'Leadership' has developed into one of the hottest sub-categories of the business book. Leadership texts have several genres of their own: psychological self-help, memoirs of courage under fire, reflections on 'winning' by retired sports stars, historical studies of major political leaders, commercial advice from innovative entrepreneurs who dropped out of university to develop cutting-edge tech companies, and tales of 'turnaround champions' who went into 'basket-case' companies and transformed them into world-beaters through their 'vision' and 'excellence'. These leadership stories often employ narratives of heroism, danger, machismo and excitement (Farber, 2004; Larson, 2010; and, for a critique of the 'extreme leadership' genre, Burrow, 2015).

But what is 'leadership', exactly? It is a concept marked by ambiguity yet also imbued with a high degree of rhetorical power. In some sense great leadership is a timeless idea calling to mind ancient Greek generals or radical political figures such as Mahatma Gandhi or Emmeline Pankhurst. In another sense, 'leadership' is a contemporary and cutting-edge concept, having replaced 'management' as the most up-to-date, effective, inspiring and ethical way of running an organization. If the 20th century was characterized by 'managers' who 'managed', 'administered' or 'coordinated' workers and workplaces through hierarchical command structures, technical manuals, double-entry book-keeping and standard operating procedures, then the 21st, by contrast, is characterized by 'leaders' who 'lead' their organizations by their vision, passion and charisma and by abandoning control and micro-management. This trope – that 'management' is outmoded, failing and boring whereas leadership is new, dynamic and exciting – is a simple hook many leadership texts employ (McCann, 2016). Leadership rhetoric encourages the rookie or experienced manager to throw off their anxieties and embrace the dynamism and energy of the exciting world of leadership. Being in charge is not something to be anxious about. Rather, being a leader is an exciting 'stretch goal' for dynamic individuals who can accomplish anything. Old-style management texts instruct the manager to set up rules, establish procedures, and measure people and processes against objectives. Newer leadership texts encourage leaders to ditch the policy manuals and explore the greatness and resilience of a sporting champion, a renegade colonel, or a 'steely-eyed missile man' (Hill, 2018: 1).

Some of these books are so famous they warrant case studies all of their own. This chapter is a case study of *Good to Great*, a blockbuster text written by Jim Collins, one of the USA's most prominent business, strategy and leadership gurus. First published in 2001, the book has sold over 4 million copies and its leadership lessons have been promoted globally. This chapter tells a story of how this book developed into a major cultural product, including the release of sequels, companion volumes, websites and what amounts to a *Good to Great* concept or brand. It goes on to describe how this brand has also struggled and faced a need to re-invent itself, for example where some of its prophecies failed and where criticisms have emerged. Ultimately it will suggest that the insights provided by leadership books such as *Good to Great* are pretty limited. Sometimes leadership texts are thought-provoking. Sometimes they contain small kernels of truth. Sometimes they are fun to read. But they also contain serious weaknesses and contradictions that terminally weaken the value of the advice they profess to supply (Rosenzweig, 2007). Worst of all, their superficial advice and stories can be used as legitimating devices for management aggression, arrogance and authoritarianism, usually with devastating results for organizations, their employees and their clients.

JIM COLLINS AND HIS GOOD TO GREAT WRITINGS

Collins' work is hugely influential, having been read and studied by students, managers and leaders from across a wide array of sectors, including all kinds of public sector organizations, such as schools, universities, hospitals, government ministries and even military units. His books have been internationally successful, leading to consulting invitations and speaking engagements the world over. His bombastic, emphatic approach is in many ways typical of the 'guru' genre. But beyond this, *Good to Great* includes some interesting and eye-catching ideas that differentiate it from the crowd. Collins' style is often to approach his questions from contrarian directions, looking to overturn conventional wisdom and promising surprising revelations that challenge his readers' preconceptions.

The central claim of the book is that organizations the world over tend to be poorly run, providing mediocre performance well below what they are capable of. Most are good, rather than great, and 'good is the enemy of great' (2001: 16). Companies, their leaders and staff are capable of much more. But they get stuck in a cycle of weak performance followed by repeated attempts at restructuring that achieve little, leading to further (failed) change efforts. Organizations seem to have lost contact with the essence of their core business and identity. It is the duty of great leaders to discover and eliminate the root causes of mediocrity and to move beyond tolerating just 'good' performance so that their companies can become 'great'. Collins and his research team claim that their comprehensive and data-driven research has highlighted just 11 truly 'great' companies out of 'an initial universe of companies that appeared on the Fortune 500 in the years 1965–1995' (Collins, 2001: 6). These companies showed a pattern of 'good' performance up until a 'transition point' whereupon they shifted into 'great' performance, as defined as a cumulative total stock return of at last three times the general market for 15 years dating from the transition point (Collins, 2001: 219).

Collins claims to be surprised by the companies that cleared this high bar. The 11 companies he and his team isolated seem to be unremarkable, even boring. None of them is involved in especially dynamic or revolutionary sectors such as high-end technology. Indeed 'a dowdier group would be hard to find' (Collins, 2001: 6). Some are unheard-of outside the US, such as Abbott Laboratories, Kroger or Pitney Bowes (the latter a manufacturer of dull and practical office equipment). More recognisable are the retailers Circuit City and Walgreens, the government-backed mortgage-lender Fannie Mae, Wells Fargo bank, Gillette, Kimberly-Clark, the steel manufacturer Nucor, and tobacco company Philip Morris. Weirdly there is no Walmart or Microsoft, and the book mostly predates the meteoric rise of Google, Amazon or Facebook. Collins cleverly amplifies and broadens his leadership lessons by constructing them out of very prosaic material. The implication is that any organization, however unremarkable, can move from 'good' to 'great' if it is led properly.

LEVEL 5 LEADERSHIP

Good to Great and its various companion editions and follow-ups (Collins, 2001; 2006; 2009; 2019; Collins and Hansen, 2011) cover many substantive areas such as strategy, finance, marketing and business history. It would be wrong to suggest they are all straightforwardly and solely leadership texts. A significant part of the *Good to Great* brand concerns how companies can enjoy success by 'getting the right people on the bus', installing 'a culture of discipline' and developing momentum via a construct called 'the flywheel'. But, in keeping with broader publishing trends, leadership is a central animating idea at the heart of Collins' work. Collins' most famous leadership construct is presented early on in *Good to Great*: the notion of 'Level 5 Leadership.'

What is this? Level 5 Leadership is probably the most memorable and potentially the most valuable contribution of the book. It is the supposedly fundamental ingredient in stimulating and then sustaining a company's transition to greatness. Collins has an interesting take on what makes 'great' as opposed to just 'good' (or simply bad) leadership. A figure on page 20 shows a hierarchy of leadership greatness, from Level 1 'highly capable individual' at the bottom, to 'contributing team member' at Level 2, to 'competent manager' at Level 3, and 'effective leader' at 4, until we reach the summit of the 'level 5 executive'. Many of us are familiar with heroic stories of dynamic, authoritarian, ambitious, high-profile chief executives such as Jeff Bezos or Jack Welch. But Collins suggests that self-promoting and noisy bosses represent only 'effective' leadership at Level 4. Such an approach can, of course, work for a time, but will never make a company 'Great'.

Level 5 Leadership instead is what will take a company to greatness. It involves quiet, self-effacing, disciplined leaders who don't seek the limelight and only want what is best for the company, not for themselves. Level 5 Leaders have usually worked their way up to the top from within the company, rather than being parachuted in from elsewhere. Collins is especially critical of obnoxious 'turnaround champions' brought in from outside, whose understanding of a company is necessarily limited and whose policies are weak or destructive. This is an important point that many readers will be able to relate to. Toxic, bullying and ill-informed bosses are usually unpopular with workers and Collins shows that their actions tend towards drastic, reckless, showpiece actions that do not deliver value and are actually counterproductive. Nobody 'buys-in' to the leadership style or change programmes of the arrogant and selfish Level 4 leaders. Rather, staff at all levels resent the disruption caused, and outsiders often look on bemused as a company goes through restructuring agonies (painful layoffs, failed attempts at 'culture change', sudden closure of facilities and lines of business). Collins argues that radical change imposed from the top results in (at best) a short-term uplift in performance, followed by a deep slump back into the problems that persisted before (or worse). The Level 5 executive rises above this by focusing on what matters and improving every aspect of their companies via a passion for results and a devotion to detail. In this way, the Level 5 leader is portrayed by Collins as a humble, respected, careful, but very able person. This is a powerful rhetorical move, one that the aspirant manager or leader can surely relate to. A Level 5 Leader is not only a great businessperson, but is also a humane and righteous citizen.

Later, in *Great By Choice* (Collins and Hansen, 2011), the notion of leadership greatness is updated, morphing into something called 10x Leadership. Moves like this are quite typical in follow-up business bestsellers, whereby the core message is recycled, upgraded and repackaged, much like in other consumer products such as pop music, films or software packages. The latest business blockbuster from an established guru offers variations on well-known themes, while being careful not to offer anything too different so as to disturb a core audience accustomed to a certain sound. So we go from Level 5 Leadership to 10x. It's kind of more of the same but it's newer and therefore better. Maybe twice as good.

The weaknesses of this kind of writing tend to surface here. Many critics have described leadership and business guru products as exaggerated, unoriginal and devoid of real insight (Rosenzweig, 2007; Spicer, 2016). Academic researchers have highlighted major problems with the methodology of *Good to Great*, to such an extent that the selection criteria are arbitrary, meaning that many of the 11 companies don't belong on the list and their leaders are anything but special or great (Neindorf and Beck, 2008; Resnick and Smunt, 2008).

There are further problems for Collins. Some 'great' companies subsequently got into trouble or collapsed (Circuit City) and companies and leaders who were once lauded as great, innovative and ethical went on to disgrace themselves by their complicity in the great financial crash of 2008

(Fannie Mae). And can it really be right for a tobacco company (Philip Morris) to be promoted as a 'great' organization? Why do some companies excluded from *Good to Great* such as Microsoft then appear prominently in follow-up texts such as *Great by Choice*? Why does Collins and his team focus only on the USA? Surely, there are leadership lessons to be had from other nations? Or from organizations that are not publicly listed corporations on the Fortune 500? Lastly, why does he use stock performance as his indicator of greatness? The focus on how Wall Street values a company seems to fly in the face of the main leadership argument, that great leaders are selfless, devoted, caring professionals who focus wholeheartedly on the internal processes of their companies.

'Moving from good to great' has become a corporate mantra, so taken for granted as part of the business landscape and lexicon that it is sometimes not even attributed to Collins. Some of the 'takeaways' from *Good to Great* such as Level 5 Leadership, the Flywheel, and the Hedgehog Concept often find their way into corporate presentations, TED talks, other leadership texts, and business school essays, sometimes without Collins being directly referenced (see, for example, a rather suspicious 'healthcare flywheel' as portrayed in Larson (2010: 30)). Books of this kind thrive on asserting, repeating and adapting business fads, especially the master narrative that management is dead and leadership is king (McCann, 2016). While undoubtedly influential, it is difficult to get away from the feeling that the main outcome of these texts is the promotion and recycling of *meaningless leadership*.

SUMMARY AND OVERVIEW

Leadership texts claim to offer basic, universal lessons applicable to any kind of organization in any kind of sector. You don't want to read leadership books just for your own selfish goals – you need to read them to get yourself up to Level 5, and hence increase the general standards of leadership around the world. Very often, leadership texts argue that the standards of leadership are in decline – most companies suffer with weak leaders who are just 'managers' at Level 3; bureaucratic and dull characters lacking vision or dynamism. Others contend with Level 4 Leaders who at least have some charisma, but are aggressive, volatile and don't do detail. In some sense there is nothing inherently wrong with Collins' texts. One can imagine them offering some useful advice, and the critique of leadership aggression and arrogance is refreshing.

But Collins' simplistic analysis and hectic launching and rebranding of concepts are worrying. The straightforward lessons and bombastic confidence of a Collins text can easily be abused by assertive and aggressive executives. In a powerful paper entitled 'Get off my bus!', education researchers Steven Courtney and Helen Gunter argue that the widespread promotion of *Good to Great* and its associated visionary leadership into schools has contributed to a rise of employer aggression and hostility towards teachers. Any professional who questions the 'vision' will be 'thrown off the bus' (Courtney and Gunter, 2015). A controversial staff downsizing at a major British university was justified by senior leadership using the 'good to great' catchphrase (UCU, 2017). There is a very fine line (maybe entirely illusory) between the leadership style of executives praised by Collins as 'zany and flamboyant' (Collins and Hansen, 2011: 32), 'fanatically driven' and 'resolved to do whatever it takes' (Collins, 2001: 39) and styles of leadership involving aggression, bullying, ruthlessness and not listening to subordinates, advisors, or outsiders. Workers, professionals – indeed labour in any form – almost never appear as human actors in Collins' work, and there is barely a mention of trade unions, staff associations, professional bodies, or workplace consultation or democracy of any kind. These leadership texts are extremely CEO-centric. Obviously they are pitched at a senior management audience, but they deliberately screen out and downplay the role of other stakeholders as if their roles are illegitimate or irrelevant. We know from hundreds of research studies that when top management insists on pursuing policies in a top-down fashion without adequate workplace consultation then failure, conflict and resentment are extremely likely. In a strange sense Collins often argues this himself with his idealized notion of Level 5 Leaders. Yet he doesn't seem able to welcome any other possible actors into his domain of leadership – Level 5 remains a place populated only by CEOs and their mysterious visions, cultures and values. Workers just have to leave it to chance that their leaders might have their interests at heart.

The same problem pertains to other contemporary literature on 'compassionate leadership', 'leading quietly' or 'servant leadership'. These ideas aren't necessarily wrong. The issue is more that in the real world, as opposed to the pages of an airport leadership text, 'leaders' rarely correspond to the ideal of the honest, self-deprecating, compassionate professional who listens, cares and is trusted. Sadly, often the motivations and incentives of leaders are actually opposed to those of workers. Leadership texts are pitched at senior managers and nearly always re-enforce a distinctly 'unitarist' conception of work and organization which denies there can be any differences in the interests, aims, goals and worldviews of managers and workers. As we know from countless examples of industrial relations conflict, corporate scandal, bankruptcy and failure (including some that spring from the history of 'Good to Great' companies themselves), there are good reasons to be very sceptical of such a blinkered framing of the realities of employee relations. Leading an organization is not easy. But embracing meaningless leadership texts often means taking an easy option, rather than a constructive one.

QUESTIONS

1 Why has the term 'management' largely been replaced by 'leadership'?

2 Why is it so widely argued that standards of leadership are generally so poor?

3 Think of three examples of poor leadership from any sector: e.g. business, politics, charities, trade unions, public sector organizations. In each case explain what went wrong and who was to blame.

4 Explain what Jim Collins means by 'Level 5 Leadership.'

5 Is it true that the best leaders are humble, self-effacing characters who successfully lead through a 'paradoxical blend of personal humility and professional will'?

REFERENCES

Burrow, R. (2015) 'The Leading Edge: Leadership as extreme work?', *Organization*, **22**(4): 606–10.

Collins, J. (2001) *Good to Great: Why Some Companies Make the Leap ... And Others Don't*. London: Random House Business.

Collins, J. (2006) *Good to Great and the Social Sectors: Why Business Thinking Is Not the Answer*. London: Random House Business.

Collins, J. (2009) *How the Mighty Fall: And Why Some Companies Never Give In*. London: Random House Business.

Collins, J. (2019) *Turning the Flywheel: Why Some Companies Build Momentum ... And Others Don't*. London: Random House Business.

Collins, J. and Hansen, M.T. (2011) *Great By Choice: Uncertainty, Chaos, and Luck – Why Some Thrive Despite Them All*. London: Random House Business.

Courtney, S. and Gunter, H. (2015) 'Get off my bus! School leaders, vision work and the elimination of teachers', *International Journal of Leadership in Education*, **18**(4): 395–417.

Farber, S. (2004) *The Radical Leap: A Personal Lesson in Extreme Leadership*. New York: Kaplan Business.

Hill, P.S. (2018) *Mission Control Management: The Principles of High Performance and Perfect Decision-making Learned from Leading at NASA*. London: Nicholas Brealey.

Larson, K. (2010) *Frontline Heroes: A Story of Saving Lives*. Gulf Breeze, FL: Fire Starter Publishing.

McCann, L. (2016) 'From Management to Leadership', in Edgell, S., Gottfried, H., and Granter, E. eds, *The SAGE Handbook of the Sociology of Work and Employment*. London: Sage, pp. 167–84.

Neindorf, B. and Beck, K. (2008) 'Good to Great or Just Good?', *Academy of Management Perspectives*, **22**(4): 13–20.

Resnick, B.G. and Smunt, T.L. (2008) 'From Good to Great to…' *Academy of Management Perspectives*, **22**(4): 6–12.

Rosenzweig, P. (2007) *The Halo Effect: And the Eight Other Business Delusions that Deceive Managers*. New York: Free Press.

Spicer, A. (2016) *Business Bullshit*. London: Routledge.

UCU (2017) 'Briefing on University of Manchester Dispute', available at http://manchester.web.ucu.org.uk/files/2017/07/Briefing-on-UoM-Dispute.pdf (accessed 22 November 2019).

31
Amazon: HRM and change in the house of neo-liberalism*

Brian Harney and Tony Dundon

BACKGROUND AND CONTEXT

Amazon is one of the world's most recognised organisations. It was the first to leverage on-line platforms for selling and distribution, making its first book sale on-line in 1995 before diversifying into CD, DVDs and electronics and ultimately becoming the 'everything store'.[1] As Google is to internet search, Amazon is to e-commerce, practically inventing this category of shopping. Amazon's overriding goal is 'to be Earth's most customer-centric company, where customers can find and discover anything online'.[2]

Financial results suggest the company and its founder and CEO Jeff Bezos are doing exceptionally well. Amazon's share price has grown exponentially, while the company has been expanding at an impressive rate. Jeff Bezos has been lauded for his achievements, including numerous best CEO awards. Industry adjusted shareholder returns under his stewardship have reached a massive 12 266 per cent.[3] Cementing his leadership status, in 2018 Jeff Bezos overtook Bill Gates as the wealthiest person on the planet.[4]

According to Bezos, Amazon's success to date is attributable to a unique culture and capacity for re-inventing.[5] This is seen in inventions such as customer reviews, the Kindle, and Amazon Web Services. Recent developments include moving to compete with Netflix in streaming, whilst experimenting with drones to achieve 30-minute delivery times.

THE 'COMPETITIVENESS' OF HRM

In human resource and employment relations terms, Amazon has a workforce of over 600 000 employees, surpassing the likes of Microsoft. Employees are known as 'Amazonians', and are managed culturally to be 'ultra-competitive' and achieve 'high performance'. Amazon is renowned for pioneering creative work practices. CEO Jeff Bezos is an outspoken supporter of technological innovations to reconfigure the world of HRM by engendering 'self-management' spaces where Amazonians are encouraged to take ownership of their own career destiny and earnings potential. Bezos is famed, among other things, for coining the mantra that Amazon wants to be 'misunderstood'[6] and that being 'normal just deserves to be messed with'.[7] It is claimed that all employees (Amazonians) are empowered to maximise their potential. These features, combined with a corporate reputation for innovation, re-invention as well as wealth creation, mean that on many readings Amazon is seen as *the* leading-edge company in the creativity and innovation space.

Figure 31.1 (above) Sample public reaction

Source: http://www.nytimes.com/2015/08/16/technology/inside-amazon-wrestling-big-ideas-in-a-bruising-workplace.html?_r=0

Figure 31.2 (above right and right)
Sample public reaction

Yet at the height of its most successful financial year, Amazon encountered its most severe criticism for being a bullying and bruising place to work. A damning *New York Times* (NYT) exposé in August 2015 put Amazon and its CEO Jeff Bezos under intense scrutiny.[8] Allegations included severe work pressure with workers crying at their desks, aggressive and confrontational managerial styles, including inhumane treatment of those suffering personal traumas such as miscarriages and cancer, and a culture of constant 'anytime feedback' encouraging employees to undermine one another. The report prompted Jeff Bezos to make a very rare and public rebuttal. The debate resonated widely across the media (see Figures 31.1 and 31.2), raising public questions that resonate with themes such as what constitutes fair and ethical treatment at work, what are the wider societal and human resource management implications of wealth and success and, in this context, what equates to appropriate ways of managing people?

THE IDEOLOGY OF 'HARD' LEADERSHIP

Amazon's managerial approach is, and always has been, unashamedly one of 'hard work'. In managerial discourse Amazon is evidently unitarist: that is to say the likes of Bezos and other senior figures demand that employees strive to achieve and deliver the Amazon way with no time or space for externalities or undue influence (such as union representation or independent worker voice). In fact, the first two words of the company's motto to new recruits are just that, 'hard work'. Bezos himself defines the company culture as 'friendly and intense', adding that if he had to choose, 'we'll settle for intense'.[9] The work regime and culture are certainly intense and fast-paced, privileging customer needs above all else. In a symbolic act, it is claimed Bezos periodically leaves a seat free at conference meetings informing all attendees that 'they should consider that seat occupied by their customer, the most important person in the room'.[10]

In order to reinforce these ideals Amazon espouses a set of so-called 'Leadership Principles' which guide what every Amazonian (employee) is supposed to do in their daily work (see Box 31.1). According to Amazon:

> Our Leadership Principles aren't just a pretty inspirational wall hanging. These Principles work hard, just like we do. Amazonians use them, every day, whether they're discussing ideas for new projects, deciding on the best solution for a customer's problem, or interviewing candidates. It's just one of the things that makes Amazon peculiar.[11]

The contents of these 14 'principles' are unashamedly about driving a hard working culture that is obsessed with the customer above all else (#1). As can be seen in Box 31.1, the language of macho-leadership is used excessively to try and push workers' effort. Ownership, and by consequence responsibility, is cascaded down the organisation (#2), with activities conducted by only the elite best (#3). The principles boast of 'unreasonably high standards' (#6), 'a bias for action' (#8) and delivering results (#14).

BOX 31.1
AMAZON'S LEADERSHIP PRINCIPLES

1. **Customer Obsession**
   Leadership obsesses about customers. Work vigorously to earn and keep customer trust.
2. **Ownership**
   Leaders are owners and act on behalf of the entire company. Leaders never say 'that's not my job'.
3. **Invent and Simplify**
   A leader will always find ways to simplify and innovate; externally aware; look for new ideas everywhere. Amazon accept that we may be misunderstood for long periods of time.
4. **Are Right, A Lot**
   Leaders are right and have strong judgement and good instincts. They seek diverse perspectives and work to disconfirm their beliefs.
5. **Hire and Develop 'The Best'**
   Leaders raise the bar with every hire and promotion; recognise people with exceptional talent. Leaders develop leaders and coach others.
6. **Insist on the Highest Standards**
   Many people may think our leaders have unreasonably high standards, continually raising the bar and delivering high quality products, services and processes.

7 **Think Big**
   Leaders 'look around corners' and create and communicate a bold direction that inspires results to serve customers.
8 **Bias for Action**
   Speed matters in business. Many decisions and actions are reversible and do not need extensive study. We value calculated risk taking.
9 **Frugality**
   Accomplish more with less. Leaders don't get extra points for growing headcount, budget size or fixed expense.
10 **Learn and Be Curious**
   Leaders are never done, always seek to improve themselves and are curious about new possibilities and act to explore them.
11 **Earn Trust**
   Leaders listen. They don't believe their or their team's body odour smells of perfume. They speak candidly, treat others respectfully, are vocally self-critical (even when it's embarrassing). They benchmark themselves and their teams against the best.
12 **Dive Deep**
   Leaders operate at all levels. No task is beneath them.
13 **Have Backbone; Disagree and Commit**
   Leaders respectfully challenge decisions. They have conviction and are tenacious and do not compromise for the sake of social cohesion. Once a decision is determined, they commit wholly.
14 **Deliver Results**
   Leaders focus on the key inputs. They rise to the occasion and never compromise.
   Source: Adapted from: http://www.amazon.jobs/principles.

The 14 leadership principles make HRM an ideologically-driven goal at Amazon. The undercurrent is to enhance performance, reward those that excel and, equally, highlight those that are not meeting these imposed standards. Work pressure and intensity is manifest through a focus on analytics, metrics and technology, from the use of 15 000 Kiva robots in warehouses to enhance efficiency and workforce effort to real time performance analytics.

Beyond the explicit performance dimensions are hints that such principles could be manipulatively dangerous. For example, one Amazonian, Dina Vaccari, who previously worked on corporate gift cards explained to the NYT: 'I was so addicted to wanting to be successful there. For those of us who went to work there, it was like a drug that we could get self-worth from.'

It is suggested that Amazon even encourages staff to instil similar principles when rearing their children. Critics find the inference that all Amazonians (workers) are somehow leaders to be misguided. Warehouse attendants, pressured to perform with increasing precision and under the watchful eye of monitoring surveillance technology signifies a lack of job autonomy or discretion to make meaningful, engaged employee decisions. Further, the NYT report suggested that the lack of female representation on Amazon's leadership team (relative to the likes of Facebook or Walmart) is probably the result of these hard and ideologically-driven principles, which privilege 'competition' and a 'long hours' culture.

ETHICAL HRM AS A FORM OF CULTURAL CONTROL?

Jeff Bezos is alleged to support immediate action and encourage quick decision making, with a tendency to micro-manage and push boundaries.[12] From the beginning Bezos was attentive to ensuring a good cultural fit when employing new hires: 'I'd rather interview 50 people and not hire anyone than hire the wrong person. Why? ... cultures aren't so much planned as they evolve from that early set of people.'[13]

In spite of Amazon's growth, these lean start-up principles remain. One example of frugality concerns expenditure on office equipment. Bezos holds true to his long-standing two pizza test; if you can't feed a team with two pizzas, the team is too large.[14] Amazon differs from the likes of high-tech contemporaries Google and Facebook, which are renowned for supporting and developing employees through a fun work culture, surrounded by foosball, on-site massages and independent thinking time. Rather than engaging in a battle for employee talent based around perks and benefits, the 'no-frills Bezos is proving the potency of another model: coddling his 164 million customers, not his employees'.[15] In a letter to shareholders Bezos wrote 'You can work long, hard or smart, but at Amazon.com you can't choose two out of three'.[16] These expectations about the nature and intensity of work are made explicit to new hires who are screened for biases and ability to deliver. Glassdoor.com, a platform where current and former employees evaluate their workplace experiences, does not hold Amazon with any great expectations, ranking it 3.1 on a 5-point scale, similar to Burger King (3.0).[17]

Criticism of Amazon's actual day-to-day workplace regimes has publicly surfaced previously with reference to the poor working conditions faced by employees and agency workers in Amazon warehouses. At the warehouse in Allentown in the US it was reported that workers had to walk distances of 5–17 miles a day in conditions that were so intense that emergency ambulances had to wait outside for those that had fainted or fallen ill.[18] In James Bloodworth's book *Hired*,[19] Amazon was one of the companies where he secretly worked as an undercover journalist. Among other things, he found that warehouse employees would have to urinate in plastic bottles and forgo toilet breaks because of work pressure and performance demands. In the *New York Times* piece, criticism extends to numerous HR policies to control professional, lower and middle managerial staff. In no uncertain terms it said Amazon is 'conducting a little-known experiment in how far it can push white-collar workers, redrawing the boundaries of what is acceptable'.

The NYT story reports of brutal work practices that resemble something akin to the Hunger Games peppered with a sprinkling of George Orwell's *1984* Big Brother tactics. Veteran workers use the term 'Amabot', denoting a good worker who has become self-directed, internalising the Amazon mode of working to 'become at one with the system'. Work–life integration is said to be complete as white collar and lower managerial employees are expected to be 'ever-present', including checking in and working during vacation time. Another work practice that has evolved to be culturally normal is sending emails late at night. When a response is not immediate, the unanswered email is often followed up with a phone text message to the person (who is usually lower or junior to the one waiting on a reply). This sense of normality is evidenced in attempts to add humour to this dilemma: 'The joke in the office was that when it came to work/life balance, work came first, life came second, and trying to find the balance came last' (Jason Merkoski, former Amazon employee reported in NYT).

The culture of employee voice, common among many leading firms to help generate ideas, has a somewhat sinister twist at Amazon. Employees are encouraged to criticise (even purposely undermine) co-workers using a HR policy called 'anytime feedback'. Amazon's leadership principles refer to being 'vocally self-critical, even when it's embarrassing' (see Box 31.1, principle 11). The Amazon rationale is that this will engender in-house staff competition. Reports suggest Amazon encourages conflict and debates, particularly over performance metrics so that 'there's an incredible amount of challenging the other person,'[20] with 'feedback that can be blunt to the point of painful'.[21]

The undercurrent of bias for action and results also forms a significant and harrowing part of the critique. The NYT article talks of a woman being told to focus on her work after a miscarriage. Another employee is given a low performance rating because of time out for cancer treatment. The woman, a professional level manager who had breast cancer, was referred to a 'performance improvement plan' which, internally, is known to mean that the person may be at risk of being fired. The cancer treated employee was informed that 'difficulties' in her 'personal life had interfered with fulfilling her work goals'. The performance ethic and fear of retribution is also clearly manifest at the top. A former Amazon employee referred to his former CEO as the 'Dread Pirate Bezos', noting his mandates made workers 'scramble like ants being pounded with a rubber mallet'.[22]

Just as Amazon obsesses over customer analytics, so too it constantly measures employee effort via technological control and surveillance systems. In Amazon warehouses workers carry handheld devices which report their performance (timing and quantity) against specific targets; technologies mean humans interact with robotics at an increasing rate. Many devices can also receive incoming text messages from management telling workers to speed up or to conduct additional tasks.[23]

The same workers are subject to airport security-type scrutiny on exiting the warehouses to prevent theft. Amazon is a metric-driven organisation with professional workers subject to 'anxiety-provoking sessions called business reviews'. These reviews can be based on 50-plus pages of results. The NYT reports that employees can be cold-called and questioned on any one aspect of their performance. Commentators reflect that these are 'burn-out' practices which have become embedded into Amazon's work culture, which can financially penalise recent hires who may exit the company within two years. With such negative media around its work culture, some suggest Amazon may alter the way it does things.[24] Yet with strong financial results, it is questionable whether there is sufficient motive in the upper echelons of managerial control for any improved staff improvement change programmes.

(UN)ETHICAL HR: WHEN THE END JUSTIFIES THE MEANS?

The sinister, manipulative and hard-hitting images reported in the NYT piece along with James Bloodworth's (2017) first-hand accounts are less a new revelation than an observation of the changing contextual changes to global neo-liberal capitalism. Bezos was quick and may be right to counter the commentary of HR practices and work experiences reported in the media and other research, noting that 'they don't describe the Amazon I know.'[25] However, he was equally explicit in reinforcing that Amazon's performance is underpinned by an intensity for pushing a hard-working culture and a focus on enhanced performance using competitive work models and high-tech practices.[26] According to the Amazon way, the logic is that those who complain are simply disgruntled underperformers who just can't do the job and don't fit: thousands of 'Amazonians', claims Mr Bezos, are happy and eager to stay and earn big bucks. Or maybe many just realise there is little choice: leaving Amazon may result in no work or being employed at another high-work intensification job. Defenders of Amazon's culture suggest that the evidence of the NYT exposé is based on 'rounding-up a 100 or so disgruntled employees (past and present) out of a workforce of 150,000'. A current Amazon employee, Nick Ciubotariu, mounted a public defence of Amazon's practices (see Box 31.2).[27]

BOX 31.2
AN AMAZONIAN'S DEFENCE

'During my 18 months at Amazon, I've never worked a single weekend when I didn't want to. No one tells me to work nights.'

'Our sheer size and complexity dwarfs everyone else, and not everyone is qualified to work here, or will rise to the challenge. But that doesn't mean we're Draconian or evil. Not everyone gets into Harvard, either, or graduates from there. Same principles apply.'

'I also think teaching Amazon's Leadership Principles to one's children is kind of funny (my opinion only, if there are indeed Amazonians that do this).'

Source: https://www.linkedin.com/pulse/amazonians-response-inside-amazon-wrestling-big-ideas-nick-ciubotariu.

Defenders of Amazon argue that in contrast to those former employees who bemoan the culture, there are plenty of others who thrive on the Amazon way. One Senior Technical Program Manager, Nimisha, explained 'you either fit here or you don't, you either love it or you don't, there is no middle ground really'.[28] The argument goes that if Amazon's culture was founded on such extreme brutality they simply would not have any employees working for them.[29]

However, the unitarist undertones re-emerge again and again in the discourse espoused by Amazon: 'if we put customers first, other stakeholders will also benefit'.[30] The ideology belies that if the company is doing well, employees will be better off, along with its shareholders. With customer data analytics having proved so successful for the Amazon business model, it may be inferred that the company assumes that a logical corollary is to manipulate employees in the same way, using real-time performance tools and a technologically-pervasive system of monitoring to adapt behaviours. Former HR Executive Robin Andrulevich suggests that 'purposeful Darwinism' filters out underperformers: 'they never could have done what they've accomplished without that'.[31]

Furthermore, Amazon is an avidly anti-union company which has hired the services of anti-union consultants to fend off any attempts at collective employee representations.[32] With respect to opportunities for those who are disgruntled or aggrieved, Amazon points to its regular team briefings and 'all-hands' meetings where pressing issues could be brought to management attention. Bezos finished his public memo advising staff that they could also contact him directly: 'You can also email me directly. Even if it's rare or isolated, our tolerance for any such lack of empathy needs to be zero'.[33]

GOING FORWARD: THE POTENTIAL FOR COUNTER-MOBILISATION?

Amazon is one of the few early internet companies that survived and eventually thrived. The company is renowned for its zeal, track record of change, and for Bezos' grand ambitions. What emerges is a corporate culture that is determined, focused and centred on its own ambitions and wealth. What is more questionable, however, is whether this neatly equates to a 'sustainable' corporate model that values people, human need and justice. It is likely that under the rubric of finance capitalism, even if Bezos wanted to be more people-centric, shareholder expectations for even higher market returns means squeeze will be put on workers to work harder and be subject to even more forms of technological control and surveillance. However, winds of change and opportunities for workforce challenge may yet emerge. Workers are not cultural dopes and know when they being duped. Even though there is an evident power disadvantage, employees are not blind to the potential for collective mobilisation or protest. Underlying challenges in people management issues may also surface as Amazon moves its business from 'clicks to bricks'. Its first physical store opened in Seattle's university shopping mall in November 2015. One suggestion is that a physical store brings different managerial and cultural challenges as workers engage and build relationships directly with customers: direct shopping outlets will enable 'customers to experience the tension between front-of-house and back-of house as a kind of pleasure'.[34] In other environments worker resistance has emerged in the likes of TGI Fridays, Uber Eats, JD Wetherspoon pubs and resultants, McDonald's,[35] and even Google.[36] Such employee protests signal a mood to question unfair treatment and the seemingly taken-for-granted nature of management by stress and discrimination. Employees remain an agent capable of challenge and change, especially if organised and mobilised collectively.

> ### QUESTIONS
>
> 1 Why does Amazon treat its customers better than its employees? Why do we, as customers, accept that?
>
> 2 Can Amazon claim to be a legitimate 'ethical' HR organisation?
>
> 3 In what ways do any of the Amazon leadership principles contradict one another?
>
> 4 Do the HR issues at Amazon lend weight or support to any particular arguments to managing work and employment in more ethical or socially sustainable ways?

END NOTES

* Brian Harney acknowledges funding received from the European Union's Horizon 2020 research and innovation programme under Marie Sklodowska-Curie grant agreement No. 734824 while working on this case.
1. Sone, B. (2014), *The Everything Store: Jeff Bezos and the Age of Amazon*, Back Bay Books.
2. http://www.amazon.jobs/.
3. Hansen, M.T., Herminia, I. and Peyer, U. (2013), 'The best-performing CEOs in the world', *Harvard Business Review*, Jan–Feb, 81–95.
4. https://www.forbes.com/billionaires/#7455673251c7.
5. Economist (2012), 'Taking the long view', *Economist*, 3 March.
6. Hansen, M.T. et al. (2013) see note 3.
7. Amazon 'something new' commercial http://worldwidegadget.blogspot.ie/2012/09/amazon-something-new-commercial.html.
8. Kantor, J. and Streitfeld, D. (2015), 'Inside Amazon: wrestling big ideas in a bruising workplace', *New York Times*, 15 August, accessed at http://www.nytimes.com/2015/08/16/technology/inside-amazon-wrestling-big-ideas-in-a-bruising-workplace.html?_r=0.
9. Streitfeld, D. and Kantor, J. (2015), 'Jeff Bezos and Amazon employees join debate over its culture', *New York Times*, 18 August, accessed at http://www.nytimes.com/2015/08/18/technology/amazon-bezos-workplace-management-practices.html.
10. Anders, G. (2012), 'Inside Amazon's idea machine: how Bezos decodes customers', *Forbes*, 23 April, accessed at http://www.amazon.jobs/principles.
11. http://www.amazon.jobs/principles.
12. Deutschman, A. (2004), 'Inside the mind of Jeff Bezos', *Fast Company*, August, 85: 52–8.
13. Deutschman, A. (2004), ibid.
14. Deutschman, A. (2004), ibid.
15. Anders, G. (2012), see note 10.
16. Kantor, J. and Streitfeld, D. (2015), see note 8.
17. Anders, G. (2012), see note 10.
18. Soper, S. (2011), 'Inside Amazon's warehouse, of the morning call', 18 September, accessed at http://www.mcall.com/news/local/amazon/mc-allentown-amazon-complaints-20110917-story.html#page=1.
19. Bloodworth, J. (2017), *Hired: Six Months Undercover in Low-Wage Britain*, London: Atlantic Books.
20. Manfred Bluemel, a former senior market researcher at Amazon reported in Anders, G. (2012), note 10.
21. Kantor, J. and Streitfeld, D. (2015), see note 8.
22. Anders, G. (2012), see note 10.
23. O'Connor, S. (2013), 'Amazon unpacked', *Financial Times*, 8 February.
24. Liacas, T. (2015), 'What will it take to make Amazon a great place to work?', *The Guardian*, 18 August.
25. Price, R. (2015), 'Jeff Bezos has responded to a report slamming Amazon's working conditions', *Business Insider*, 27 August.
26. Scheiber, N. (2015), 'Work policies may be kinder, but brutal competition isn't', *New York Times*, 17 August.
27. https://www.linkedin.com/pulse/amazonians-response-inside-amazon-wrestling-big-ideas-nick-ciubotariu.
28. 'What is it like to work at Amazon: go beyond the badge with Nimisha', *Inside Amazon*, accessed at https://www.youtube.com/watch?v=lWFxFBD8Qus.
29. Price, R. (2015), 'Jeff Bezos has responded to a report slamming Amazon's working conditions', 27 August.

30 Hansen, M.T. et al. (2013), see note 3.
31 Kantor, J. and Streitfeld, D. (2015), see note 8.
32 http://time.com/956/how-amazon-crushed-the-union-movement/.
33 Geekwire company memo, Nicolaou, A, and Bullock, N. (2015), 'Bumper holiday season sends Amazon soaring', *Financial Times*, 30 December, accessed at http://www.ft.com/intl/cms/s/0/9ec3e288-ae5b-11e5-993b-c425a3d2b65a.html#axzz3vqmXPyzG.
34 De Monchaux, T. (2015), 'How Amazon's bookstore soothes our anxieties about technology', *New Yorker*, 22 December.
35 https://www.business-humanrights.org/en/uk-jd-wetherspoon-mcdonalds-tgi-fridays-uber-eats-workers-strike-over-pay.
36 https://www.theguardian.com/technology/2018/nov/01/google-walkout-global-protests-employees-sexual-harassment-scandals.

32
Leadership and change at Ford Motor Company

Dan H. Langerud and Peter J. Jordan

BACKGROUND AND CONTEXT OF THE ORGANIZATION

The Ford Motor Company has an iconic reputation that all started with Henry Ford and the introduction of the first affordable automobile to the general market, the Model T in 1908. The revolutionary large-scale mechanized mass production system that Henry Ford developed is still apparent in the global automobile industry today across the spectrum of manufacturers. The Ford Motor Company has existed and maintained its position as one of the top three US automakers for over a century, but not without challenges requiring organizational restructuring to address changes in the industry and in society. In 2006, Ford reported a loss of US$12.1 million, with US$5.8 million of that loss happening in the fourth quarter of the year. At this time, Ford's market share had dropped from 25.7 percent in 1997 to 17.5 percent in 2006.

At the turn of the millennium, the entire US car industry and the Ford Motor Company faced difficult times leading up to the climax during the Global Financial Crisis, which started in 2007. The car manufacturer had neglected its overseas markets and focused on American consumers who had a preference for powerful SUVs with large engines. This led to a downturn in profits globally (Legget, 2014; Taylor III, 2009). As gasoline prices recorded soaring record highs, car buyers abruptly changed preference towards more sustainable cars with smaller engines. Other issues also affected Ford, including personnel policies (e.g., generous health care to employees), increased diversification through overseas acquisitions of other car brands, and spiraling production costs (Hoffman, 2012; Taylor III, 2009). With major problems emerging around the structure of the company and operational issues, the value of Ford stocks fell to a new, unprecedented low for the proud automotive manufacturer, with its stock plummeting from $17.34 in 2004 to $1.01 in 2008.

It was clear that the company was in dire need of a new direction.

NEW CEO – MULALLY

In September of 2006, Bill Ford Jr, the chairman of Ford, ignored internal candidates and head-hunted an external CEO from Boeing. Alan Mulally, a former aerospace engineer, who had risen to the role of chief executive of Boeing's jet passenger business was asked to take on the task of turning the tide for the company. This decision did not go without controversy. Within the organization, several senior executives found it difficult to accept that someone with no knowledge of the automotive industry could make successful changes to the practices and strategies of the company (Reed, 2012).

One of the first things that Mulally did when he arrived at Ford was to arrange a line of credit of $23.6 billion in 2006. In the aftermath of the Global Financial Crisis this move was seen as exceptionally astute and clever, as their main American competitors, General Motors Corporation (GM) and Chrysler LLC both had to ask for financial support from the government because they did not have the same financial liquidity as Ford. Both GM and Chrysler filed for bankruptcy protection in 2009 during the Automotive Industry Crisis of 2008–2010. During that time all three automakers testified in front of the Congress to justify why the government had to intervene in order to protect the American automaker industry from collapsing. At those hearings, Mulally advocated that the US government should financially support the rivals, while he refused to accept any financial aid from the government, believing that Ford should work their way out of the hardship. Consequently, this led to a better relationship with American consumers as Ford continued to invest in improving their cars and cementing their reputation domestically as a strong American built company.

MULALLY'S PERSONALITY

Mulally employed the engineering approach to tackling problems, which is to solve them while acknowledging that problems in organizations are complex issues which are not solved by technical expertise alone, but rather by people. His leadership was focused on having a compelling vision, comprehensive plans, a relentless implementation and bringing talented people together in efforts to achieve goals. Mulally explained that people found meaning in their work by working with others to achieve goals that are greater than could be achieved by oneself. He clarified that a vision for a company is not a hope: it is an action plan. He stated that the only way it is possible to achieve this in a company is through growing the company, improving the margins, and making products that people want and value and in a way that is more efficient than one's competitors.

Mulally's method was straightforward. Understand the problem and how it came about, then determine what to do about it. In his words, leaders must "pull everybody together around a compelling vision, a comprehensive strategy and a plan aimed at achieving your goals." His view was that once you have the people and have developed the plan, you stick with it (Kurtzman and Distefano, 2014).

CULTURAL CHANGE

Mulally did not fit the traditional characteristics of a senior executive at Ford. The company was widely known for its toxic culture and an endless number of meetings among executives. The common theme was a focus on short-term achievements and goals, with a cut-throat and careerist culture, where each executive would focus only on their area of responsibility. Consequently, in meetings, everyone would present figures that focused on positive achievements and neglected to present information that indicated poor performance or problems within the company. The result of this practice led to an excessive number of meetings with few decisions being made, as executive self-preservation held a higher priority than finding good solutions (Kaipa and Kriger, 2010).

Toxic workplace practices between its executives had plagued Ford. By prohibiting the practice of ridiculing others and persuading the executives to work together, Mulally started his progress by changing the culture of the company. Executives were required to grade their own progress against targets honestly, and when problems arose, they were told to face this head-on. In meetings, Blackberries were banned, and Mulally acted initially as an active mediator facilitating the process between presenting issues and encouraging others to come up with solutions to problems. In particular, he encouraged his executives to seek solutions from unrelated parts of the company and told his executives from different divisions to take responsibility to solve issues together. This strategy was enhanced by a change in the incentivization process from individual performance target bonuses to overall company performance bonuses. These changes quickly established a foothold within the company and executives saw cooperation being in their best interest. Despite initial reluctance, the executives eventually embraced Mulally's plan for changing the culture at Ford (The Associated Press, 2011). As Bill Ford noted of the company culture since Mulally took over, "At the old Ford, you had heroes and villains, now, it's, 'OK, where do we have issues and how do we solve them?'"

Mulally also made changes to the portfolio of the company. Prior to Mulally joining the company, Ford owned many other car brands. Indeed, when Mulally started at Ford, the first thing that he noticed was that most of the executives were driving Aston Martin, Jaguar and Land Rover cars. His view was that if his executives did not want to drive a Ford vehicle, how could they convince the American public to drive one? A quick decision was made for Ford to sell these other brands, as well as Volvo and other investments, including their partial ownership of Mazda. These assets had been acquired during better times, and Mulally saw the need for Ford to focus on the core of the company's own vehicles, before investing in other places. The sale of these 'non-core' assets had a positive benefit in terms of providing additional capital for the company. Removing these other (often competing) car brands meant less fighting for resources and management time, and an opportunity to establish the central values of Ford. Even though these actions applied a short-term solution to the financial problem at Ford, the organizational culture was the primary target that Mulally wanted to change with this new focus exclusively on Ford.

EVIDENCE-BASED MANAGEMENT: HONESTY AND FACTS

To enhance the efficiency of meetings held within Ford, Mulally established a mandatory weekly meeting for all senior executives. At each meeting, a few individuals would present comprehensive progress updates on their department's backdrop of their turnaround plan. Mulally labeled this meeting a "Business Plan Review". Prior to Mulally arriving at Ford, executives in meetings would cherry-pick what numbers to present and spend significant time presenting these with the focus on explaining their actions. Under the new regime, Mulally allowed no explanations in the executive presentations. The numbers had to speak for themselves, and only the performance itself was important.

Mulally reports that a breakthrough was achieved after a few months of the senior executives constantly presenting positive figures. During one meeting, he addressed the group and asked, "if we are doing so well, how come we are still losing US$1 billion a month?". After that meeting, one executive decided to show numbers that indicated they had a problem with a workflow that was costing Ford money at a specific plant. Rather than berate this executive, Mulally asked if there was someone else at the meeting who could help and praised both parties when an executive from another division was able to provide a solution. At that stage, others started to reveal both positive and negative reports.

The key to this change was a focus on evidence-based management with accurate and honest figures required to understand the performance of the company. Linked to this was an acceptance of risk and potential failure as a part of the business. The key was the acceptance that every company makes good and bad decisions, and the important thing is to understand what decisions work and what decisions do not work and to rectify these before they become a problem. Failure in the old Ford was an opportunity for "sharp elbows" to emerge and for other executives to promote their abilities. Under the new Ford, failure was seen as a learning opportunity for the entire company.

INCREASED FOCUS: MANY IDEAS AND DIRECTIONS BUT NO FOLLOW-THROUGH

The analytical, direct and follow-through approach to his leadership in practice is best described by Mulally himself (Taylor III, 2009):

> I arrive here, and the first day I say, "Let's go look at the product line-up." And they lay it out, and I said, "Where's the Taurus?" They said, "Well, we killed it." I said, "What do you mean, you killed it?" "Well, we made a couple that looked like a football. They didn't sell very well, so we stopped it." "You stopped the Taurus?" I said. "How many billions of dollars does it cost to build brand loyalty around a name?" "Well, we thought it was so damaged that we named it the Five Hundred." I said, "Well, you've got until tomorrow to find a vehicle to put the Taurus name on because that's why I'm here. Then you have two years to make the coolest vehicle that you can possibly make." The 2010 Taurus is arriving on the market this spring, and while it is not as startling as the original 1986 Taurus, it is still pretty cool.

There were several situations at Ford that had similar characteristics. The company was no stranger to changes and developing plans. Every year, there were new strategies and actions implemented to address the shortcoming of the previous year's strategies. The outcome of this was a distinct lack of follow-through to prior commitments and a short-term focus that caused significant financial ramifications. In addressing this, Mulally established an overarching plan that he would talk about in every meeting, town hall session, analyst meeting and press conference. A four-step plan, part of the mission statement he labelled the "One Ford".

The "One Ford" concept was a simple four-step plan. Mulally made sure everyone in the organization understood the ideas which were: Coming together and working as one team, leveraging Ford's global assets, building cars that people want and value, and doing so with the resources available.

Mulally also initiated the process of a structural merger within the company. The motive behind this was to connect all parts of the organization together, to cut down on unnecessary duplication of functions, and to enhance the opportunity to foster cross-regional collaboration and development. With this restructure, he established better communication systems at Ford including lines of communication that were previously non-existent. All of these changes were achieved under the umbrella of the "One Ford" plan.

Within the plan, Mulally established a set of behaviors he expected employees to follow, such as "foster functional and technical excellence", "own working together", and "role model Ford values". The purpose of these changes was to alter the company's culture. Mulally felt the changes were needed to make the company profitable over the long run. The "One Ford" plan created a consistent focus that worked towards what Mulally wanted to achieve with Ford. It enabled investors and business partners to understand what was important at Ford and to use these factors to evaluate the performance and development of the company.

SUMMARY AND OVERVIEW

Leading up to the Global Financial Crisis of 2007, the Ford Motor Company faced significant challenges which would have severe ramifications for the future of the company. These challenges required the company to drastically change its organizational operations and culture. By reducing the diversity of competing brands that the company owned, Mulally freed up resources which enabled Ford to further develop around its core business. The focus was on establishing a culture of cooperation directed at achieving a common goal of building cars and trucks that people wanted and valued. The successful turnaround of Ford during times of uncertainty and intense change can be, in large part, attributed to decisions, practices and strategies implemented under the direction of its CEO, Alan Mulally.

When significant changes are made to the operation of a company it is not uncommon for the leader to encounter resistance. In this case, resistance to change may have been greater as Mulally was an outsider coming in with a radical perspective on how to run the business. Mulally came in with a clear vision to unite and create an organization focused on Ford as a brand, incentivizing and fostering a culture of cooperation of working towards a common goal and by making tough decisions on brands that the organization owned that, although holding prestige, inhibited the growth of the company.

During Alan Mulally's period as CEO of Ford Motor Vehicles, the organization not only managed to turn around immense losses but also did so through a period of uncertainty and change, leading Ford to become one of the most profitable automakers in the world by 2012 (Hoffman, 2012). In 2015, Ford reported a record (for them) US$10.9 billion profit. These figures stand in stark contrast to some of their competitors, who still struggle from the aftermath of the financial crisis.

QUESTIONS

Compare the process of change followed under Mulally's leadership at Ford to an established theoretical change process.

1 Transformational leadership is a style of leadership that facilitates change. Was Alan Mulally a transformational leader? Why/why not?

2 Describe how the change that occurred at Ford relates to one or more specific models of contingent change management/ contingent leadership?

3 What changes in performance management occurred during Mulally's leadership at Ford?

REFERENCES

Hoffman, B.G. (2012). *American icon: Alan Mulally and the fight to save Ford Motor Company*. Three Rivers Press.

Kaipa, P. and Kriger, M. (2010). Empowerment, vision, and positive leadership: An interview with Alan Mulally, former CEO, Boeing Commercial—Current CEO, Ford Motor Company. *Journal of Management Inquiry*, **19**(2), 110–15.

Kurtzman, J. and Distefano, M. (2014). Alan Mulally: The man who saved Ford. *Korn Ferry Institute*. Accessed 24 September 2019 at https://www.kornferry.com/institute/alan-mulally-man-who-saved-ford.

Legget, T. (2014). How Ford's Alan Mulally turned around its fortunes. *BBC News*. Retrieved from https://www.bbc.com/news/business-28087325.

Reed, J. (2012). How Alan Mulally rescued Ford. *Los Angeles Times*. Retrieved from http://articles.latimes.com/2012/apr/15/business/la-fi-books-20120415.

Taylor III, A. (2009). Fixing up FORD. *Fortune Magazine*. Retrieved from http://archive.fortune.com/2009/05/11/news/companies/mulally_ford.fortune/index.htm.

The Associated Press (2011, January). Ford says culture change has led to success. *CTV News*. Retrieved from https://www.ctvnews.ca/ford-says-culture-change-has-led-to-success-1.594439.

33
Implementing performance management in a public sector organisation in a developing country

Thuraya Farhana Haji Said

BACKGROUND

Since New Public Management (NPM) leadership was introduced in developed countries in the 1990s, many developing countries opted for similar reform to modernise and improve their public-sector performance (Pollitt, 2005; Araujo and Branco, 2009; Pollitt and Bouckaert, 2011). This is the same for Brunei Darussalam where the influence of NPM has been noticeable even though the country has very different political and institutional systems from where performance management (PM) was developed (Mohd Jamil, 2008; Rashid and Said, 2018). Brunei public administration represents a dual system of Western-style bureaucracy and a traditional monarchy. In 2003, the Monarch, who is also the Prime Minister and has the highest executive authority in the nation, mandated through his Titah (speech) for performance management practices, such as strategic plans and key performance indicators (KPIs), to be incorporated into public sector organisational activities. As a result, a National Strategic Alignment Program (NSAP) was established that aimed to drive the public sector organisations towards the Brunei national vision and development plans by monitoring and reviewing strategic plans of respective government organisations. Over the years, the importance of strategic planning and cascading it to the level of departmental KPIs and to be understood by the public servants has been repeatedly emphasised.

The intended impact of introducing PM practices was to foster performance or a result-oriented culture within the public sector as there was a need for fundamental shifts in the attitude and behaviour of the public servants towards ensuring greater performance of the public sector (Metussin, n.d.). However, there were no standard guidelines on how to implement PM practices for the NSAP. This could be because the aligning process within the public sector was multi-faceted and non-linear as the organisations had diverse and complex roles and strategic goals, so they had to tailor their strategic plans with the respective goals and objectives. There were also limited structural changes, in terms of budgeting and human resource management (HRM) to accompany the NPM. For example, the performance appraisal (PA) system was not reformed to accommodate the PM implementation. Some argue PA should be closely linked with PM to assess to what extent an individual was able to achieve the agreed targets and what the reason was if targets could not be achieved (PUMA, 2002; Pollitt, 2005; Norhayati and Siti-Nabiha, 2009). In this case, there was a missing link between PM and PA, which means a performance-based reward policy was considered absent. As for the budgeting process, the organisations still followed the traditional line of approach where it was mainly based on the items of the previous budget. It is argued that implementing PM may stimulate demand for performance budgeting in order to ensure strategic plans and budget structures were linked towards results of KPIs (Athmay, 2008). However, our case shows that there was no strong connection between the strategic plans and budgeting.

Nevertheless, in response to the Titah, some organisations had taken the initiative and began formulating their strategic planning. There were variations in terms of timings and initiatives to implementing PM practices and processes within the public sector organisations, which led to different responses in implementing PM (Rashid and Said, 2018). This case study will demonstrate the variation of two organisations, called Agency A and Agency B, when implementing PM and the nature of implementation within them.

ORGANISATIONAL CHANGE AND STABILITY AFTER THE INTRODUCTION OF PM SYSTEM

While Agency A was amongst the first organisations to start formulating their series of strategic plans after the Titah and the NSAP in 2003, Agency B introduced their first strategic plan in 2008. Since 2003, the governmental pressure to introduce PM had gradually increased and to some extent this had influenced other organisations to imitate the ones they deemed successful implementers. According to an officer in Agency B: '[PM] tools were recommended by the Prime Minister's Office … They encouraged all agencies to use the tools … the one that had succeeded in implementing them is [Agency A]. So we are trying to do the same thing.'

It was noticeable that several initiatives were put in place so that PM activities could be carried out effectively, for example, the use of the balance scorecard (BSC) approach for its PM process

Table 33.1 Timing and model of PM implementation and the position of Office of Strategic Management

	Agency A	Agency B
When strategic plan was first introduced	2003	2008
Team that look after PM process	Office of Strategic Management	Ad hoc OSM and Strategic Planning Unit
Its position in the agency	A dedicated department (under the Deputy Minister)	Ad hoc unit under a division (4 levels below the Minister)
Where does the OSM report?	The Deputy Minister	The Deputy Permanent Secretary

and existence of an office of strategic management (OSM) to manage PM process and track the progress of organisational KPIs that were linked to their strategic plans. However, how OSM was established and where the office was put in each agency were not the same. Both agencies adopted a functionalist approach; while a dedicated OSM in Agency A was placed under the control of its Deputy Minister, OSM in Agency B was an ad hoc office that was placed four levels down from the Minister (see Table 33.1). Kaplan and Norton (2005) suggest that OSM will be most effective when it has direct access to the CEO because the executing strategy requires ongoing organisational changes that only the CEO has the power to authorise. The timing and OSM variation could also be a signal of how the key organisational members were keen to act strategically or to comply symbolically with pressure to implement PM and how the different ranks between the organisations drew their understanding of how PM should be implemented (see Currie et al., 2012; Lounsbury, 2008).

Within the Brunei public sector, while PM literature suggests that cultural change is necessary to implement PM principles, the obedience culture remained and was indeed beneficial for implementing PM as compliance with PM depended highly on the hierarchical authority. This could be because of the path-dependent policies, both HR and budgeting, that had no strong link to PM and posed as structural barriers to implementing PM effectively. Thus, leaders played a very important role as a medium of change where their actions could be viewed from a spectrum of 'active' to 'passive' (similar to Oliver, 1991; Rashid and Said, 2018).

As seen from Table 33.1, the chair of the strategic management team in Agency A was the second highest rank in the organisation and was seen to take a more proactive role by keeping the OSM close to him and showed that PM was deemed to be a priority. There was a general alignment between the ministerial and departmental strategy, and the BSC map in the strategy had become an active document and progress of KPIs was being monitored periodically. The OSM in Agency A was close to the CEO and enabled high levels of cooperation from the senior members, including departments for performance to be reviewed or information to be shared rather than hidden. The frequency of meetings also seemed to play a key role in securing commitments from its members in terms of monitoring and reporting KPI results. This has shown that because of the contextual factors, an embedded autocratic style of organisational leadership was rather encouraged to generate and ensure compliance with implementing PM.

For Agency B, managing the PM process involved having to go through bureaucratic red tape and a longer reporting process. The chair of its strategic management team was the third highest rank in the organisation. Because of where OSM was positioned within the organisational structure, its members lacked authority as order givers where there was a low level of compliance from the KPI/Objective owner in carrying out the PM activities in terms of monitoring and reporting the results. The limited buy-in from the objective-owners could be due to low management support and the fact that the involvement of a much higher authority was limited that it did not create enough pressure of every member to comply. This can be seen below:

> Our [Ad Hoc OSM] problem is that we don't have a proper structure to monitor all [PM activities]. When we ask for something … people don't really bother … maybe because we are just normal officer in a division … people do not feel afraid if they do not submit their

data. [Agency A] has a very good stand-alone department ... that looks at the strategic plan and progress ... what we have here are just a few officers who are also doing other things (Agency B).

PM activities only survived for a few months in Agency B after its implementation in contrast to Agency A. At some point, PM in Agency B was being regarded as 'bespoke demand' as these quotations explained that:

Reporting was very ad hoc, say only if there is a strategic review meeting ... the plan was to have it every two months, but when they [chair and management level] got too busy ... [reporting] the plan fall out.

I'm (objective-owner) still measuring the KPIs ... but I don't do the report for BSC anymore. Even if I did, I don't know to whom I should forward the report.

Some argued that goal alignment was important for enabling motivation and commitment to the process; in this case deferral to hierarchical authority had been far more influential than being driven by performance. However, the implication of this top-down approach was that it could incentivise behaviours that simply satisfy requirements rather than optimising the performance. Another reason could be that it was challenging to gain commitment and ownership from the organisational members because of the path-dependent structures in which leaders and members were allowed to resist PM as there were no punitive actions applied for not doing so (see Oliver, 1991; Siti-Nabiha and Scapens, 2005; Rashid and Said, 2018).

THE ROLE OF ORGANISATIONAL MEMBERS IN MAINTAINING THE EXISTING PRACTICE DURING ORGANISATIONAL CHANGE

Although the formal rules concerning the PM process were established in terms of setting, reviewing and reporting KPIs for departments in both agencies, PM was seen to be decoupled from the existing practice of the agencies. Although attempts were made to institutionalise PM this was only realised to a limited extent. PM was rather seen as a diagnostic tool that improved transparency, but was limited to fundamentally addressing organisational performance. At the time, it could be considered that PM enacted as a ceremonial tool. PM was not strategically integrated with the path-dependent management policies of budget and HRM and this resulted in a lack of autonomy and resources to take action towards performance objectives and targets (similar to Bromley and Powell, 2012). The limited link between strategic plans of the agencies and budgets meant there was no strong connection between KPIs and budgeting, which had implications for the practical use of PM such that to some extent it resulted in 'tunnel vision' behaviour at the expense of measuring performance (see Waggoner et al., 1999; Fryer et al., 2009). This was explained by a senior officer in Agency A:

Sometimes when we discuss performance in our meeting, it is easy to identify what the problem is … but it's all come down to budget […] although there are BSC and KPIs … they don't work if they don't give you the right [resources] to give/justify decision or give the money that they [department] need […] What's the point of talking [reviewing results]?

The conflict between the requirements of strategic plans, BSC and KPIs and the budget was reflected in most accounts in the agencies when they spoke about PM. Because budget allocation was determined by an external agency, the limited financial resources had influenced not only how the agencies organised their OSM (as to whether they could afford to have a dedicated or an ad hoc office and personnel), but also how they build competency in applying BSC and KPIs in terms of training and readiness of organisational members. For some people in the agencies, it was less an issue of commitment but more a matter of the limited capability in implementing PM practices. Due to budgetary constraints, lack of priority given to PM training and/or no flexibility in staffing, this resulted in a low level of perceived usefulness of PM as an instrumental tool which undermined its implementation. KPIs owners had difficulty in translating their activities into performance measures and not all KPIs could fully reflect the complexity of their roles and activities. They also had to collect and analyse data, which consumed considerable time and effort and due to the multifaceted nature of the public sector, the outcome measurement was limited by the range of factors beyond the control of both agencies (similar to Fryer et al., 2009; Nakrosis, 2008). As a result, some opted for fixed targets that focus on indicators rather than desired outcomes that could be argued to have led to the implementation of BSC and KPIs as a formality.

In the same vein, another structural barrier in terms of integrating HR policies and strategic plans was that the PM process became an 'addition' to the existing structure of both agencies rather than a core driver to other aspects of the organisation. The absence of rewards within the process resulted from the limited link between the PA system and KPIs, appearing to undermine the notion of meritocracy and in this case, that influenced the legitimacy of PM in the case of agencies and also affected the priorities between PM and existing practices. PM was mainly seen as an additional administrative workload by the KPIs owner and this was evident in both agencies:

This [reporting of KPIs] is not what I'm supposed to do… but if I don't finish [core job] maybe I will die … something like that. What I mean is … I will be in trouble. If I don't finish this [KPI], people might understand because this is not my core job. That mentality … although it is wrong, it is the mentality…. That is making PM not moving forward. (An officer affected by PM process in Agency A)

People 'hate' it … when they see my face, but I need to put on 'thick skin' to ask for monthly performance report … I have to be persistent and phone them and ask if they needed help with their reports … some did their report. But for some, we had to do reports for them … because they were just too busy. It could be true or they just could not be bothered doing it … (An officer in the OSM of Agency B)

Not linking performance to performance appraisal or to bonus or salary resulted in an unintended performance paradox. As there was no reward/ punishment for carrying out the PM the organisational members perceived this as optional rather than a core practice, whereby it became more a matter of habitual reporting in Agency A and rather ignored by Agency B. Rashid and Said (2018) argued that it was difficult for agencies to be able to change the existing routines without the changes in the existing policies and to be able to use PM beyond the habitual. In some cases, it was normal for objective-owners to give reasons, such as they were 'busy' or that there was 'other important work' for not meeting targets when they could not submit their data on time. There were accounts in both cases that PM was sidelined several times, especially in Agency B. This is because the implementation increased workloads and work complexity, but without proper reward, organisational members felt psychologically disconnected and as a result PM activities were given low priority.

CONCLUSION

The case study has shown the difference between the reality of implementing and the rhetoric of PM. Although both agencies showed their acquiescence with PM practice due to higher-level institutional pressure, the implementation of the practice was a complex process and dependent on the agencies' internal dynamics, especially the way members perceived the benefits of PM.

The path-dependent policies had considerable influence upon PM implementation, resulting in the members lacking capabilities and PM practices lacking strategic integration with budgeting and HR policies. Thus, BSC and KPIs that were developed could not fully reflect the complexity of the agencies' modus operandi and they were not strong enough to challenge the existing values and norms of most members and also the existing practice of the agencies. Nevertheless, leadership had played a very important role in the implementation, especially in Agency A. The motivation to use PM as a means to attain organisational objectives was apparent although it generated commitment towards the PM implementation through an obedience culture towards hierarchical authority.

This highlights that one needs to take into account institutional context in order to understand how a practice, in this case PM, is implemented, by looking at how different cultures or structures modify PM in a significant way. In light of this, implementing PM was necessary to achieve legitimacy as a public sector organisation, but PM did not appear legitimate, or core, for the members. Even though not all benefits of implementing PM were realised (as suggested by the literature) due to structural barriers, PM had nevertheless become a diagnostic tool that was useful to improve transparency within the agencies, especially for Agency A. At the point when the research was about to end, both agencies were still in the process of revamping their strategic plan and its PM processes, and also since then, there have been new initiatives introduced by the Brunei government which are within the PM area.

QUESTIONS

1 What is the link between leadership, culture and motivation in this case?

2 Can leadership and organisational incentives be used to balance the competing needs of the organisation when implementing PM or must they be complementary?

3 What other initiatives do you think should be introduced to support and improve the culture and practice of PM within the agencies?

REFERENCES

Araujo, J. and Branco, J. (2009) Implementing performance-based management in the traditional bureaucracy of Portugal, *Public Administration*, **87**(3), 557–73.

Athmay, A. (2008) Performance auditing and public sector management in Brunei Darussalam, *International Journal of Public Sector Management*, **21**(7), 798–811.

Bromley, P. and Powell, W. (2012) From smoke and mirrors to walking the talking: decoupling in the contemporary world, *The Academic of Management Annals*, **6**(1), 483–530.

Currie, G., Lockett, A., Finn, R., Martin, G. and Waring, J. (2012) Institutional work to maintain professional power: recreating the model of medical professionalism, *Organization Studies*, **33**(7), 937–62.

Fryer, K., Antony, J. and Ogden, S. (2009) Performance management in the public sector, *International Journal of Public Sector Management*, **22**(6), 478–98.

Kaplan, R. and Norton, D. (2005) Creating the office of strategy management, working paper 05-071, pp.1–21.

Lounsbury, M. (2008) Institutional rationality and practice variation: new directions in the institutional analysis of practice, *Accounting, Organizations and Society*, **33**(4–5), 349–61.

Metussin, H.A.G. (n.d.), Preparing the Brunei Darussalam's civil service for the 21st century, *Asian Review of Public Administration*, pp. 124–31, available at: http://www.bruneiresources.com/pdf/preparingbruneicivilservice.pdf.

Mohd Jamil, A. (2008) Performance management in the Brunei Civil Service: issues and challenges, *Civil Service Institute Journal*, **18**, 30–46.

Nakrosis, V. (2008) Reforming performance management in Lithuania: towards results-based government, in Peters, B.G. (ed.), *Mixes, Matches and Mistakes: New Public Management in Russia and Former Soviet Republics*, Budapest: Open Society Institute, pp. 53–115.

Norhayati, M.A. and Siti-Nabiha, A.K. (2009) A case study of the performance management system in a Malaysian government linked company, *Journal of Accounting and Organizational Change*, **5**(2), 243–76.

Oliver, C. (1991) Strategic responses to institutional process, *Academy of Management Review*, **16**(1), 145–79.

Pollitt, C. (2005) Performance management in practice: a comparative study of executive agencies, *Journal of Public Administration Research and Theory*, **16**(1), 25–44.

Pollitt, C. and Bouckaert, G. (2011) *Public Management Reform: A Comparative Analysis*, 2nd edn, New York: Oxford University Press.

PUMA (2002) *Focus; the OECD Public Management Newsletter June (24): Holding the executive accountable.*

Organisation for Economic Co-operation and Development. Accessed 2 January 2011 at: http://www.oecd/dataoecd/13/33/1935844.pdf.

Rashid, F.R. and Said, T.F. (2018) Strategic responses towards a performance management and measurement system in the public sector of a developing country, *International Journal of Public Sector Performance Management*, **4**(4), 393–410.

Siti-Nabiha, A. and Scapens, R. (2005) Stability and change: an institutionalist study of management accounting change, *Accounting, Auditing and Accountability Journal*, **18**(1), 44–73.

Waggoner, D., Neely, A. and Kennerley, M. (1999) The forces that shape organisational performance measurement systems: an interdisciplinary review, *International Journal of Production Economics*, **60**(1), 53–60.

SECTION VII
INTERNATIONAL HRM

34
HR function at MNC subsidiary level: Mediating challenges and tensions

Jonathan Lavelle, Patrick Gunnigle and Sinead Monaghan

The focus of this case study is to demonstrate the impact of a multinational corporation's (MNC) rationalisation process on the human resource management (HRM) function at subsidiary level and to explore the role that the HRM function can play in that process.

CONTEXT

GenCo (pseudonym) is a large multinational company (MNC) with operations across the globe. It is a multi-sector MNC with operations spanning a range of sectors including the pharmaceutical, chemical and medical devices sectors. In relation to Ireland, GenCo has had a presence in the country over the last thirty years and currently employs some 5000 people across a number of subsidiaries – both manufacturing and services-based subsidiaries. Ireland is widely viewed as a location of strategic significance, with some of GenCo's leading products and services located there. In the aftermath of the global financial crisis and increasing market pressures on some of its main products, GenCo came under pressure to secure substantial costs savings and efficiencies throughout its global operations. This would mean a significant rationalisation process, with all operations and countries under the spotlight. Senior management across all of the subsidiaries in Ireland were well aware of the potential impact of this rationalisation process on their operations. In addition to pressures relating to economic depression, local Irish senior management in their subsidiaries have always been cognisant of the potential threat of relocation of some operations to countries such as China and India. In the last ten years, countries in Eastern Europe have also become potential threats where some countries are developing a reputation for high quality output at a low cost base. Indeed, internal competition between international subsidiaries represents an important strategic concern for local senior management in Ireland.

In order to achieve cost reductions and greater efficiencies, GenCo has initiated a number of global corporate-level rationalisation strategies in which the subsidiaries in Ireland have also been impacted. Rationalisation in this case refers to the reduction in employment size of the MNC globally through closures, relocation, off-shoring and headcount reduction. In Ireland the number of subsidiaries has been cut by half (from eight to four). The four divested subsidiaries were either sold or closed down and operations relocated to cheaper international locations. In addition to job losses in the closed subsidiaries, employment numbers were reduced in the remaining subsidiaries.

Between closures and headcount reduction it is estimated that roughly a third of the Irish workforce were made redundant in the last two years.

HRM ISSUES

HRM structural changes

Often the focus of rationalisation tends to be on the areas that represent the largest cost for organisations. For example, in a manufacturing company, the focus may often be on reducing headcount among operatives/technical staff as this can often offer the optimal means of quickly reducing the cost base. In this case study the HRM function itself was not immune from such attention. Corporate headquarters took the view that jobs losses should also include what may be described as the enabling functions – HRM, legal, finance – and sought cost reductions in those functions in addition to operational and some other categories of staff. For example corporate headquarters questioned the need for an HRM function in each subsidiary location, as was the practice heretofore. For example each of the subsidiaries operating in Ireland had their own HRM function, which generally included an HRM Manager and a number of HRM personnel and one HRM Director based at one of the subsidiaries largely overseeing HRM for all of the Irish operations. In effect the corporate level were questioning the rationale for having, for example, training and development personnel in each subsidiary location, some of which may be located in close proximity.

Faced with these challenges, local HRM management at each of the subsidiaries decided to be proactive and initiated a number of locally managed changes to the organisation of the HRM function among the Irish subsidiaries. In the wake of corporate desire for HRM rationalisation, the HRM Director and local HRM managers acknowledged that having separate HRM departments in each subsidiary represented something of "overkill". This was most clearly evidenced in the proportionately high levels of employment in the HRM function in Ireland as a proportion of total employment and consequent duplication of services across multiple subsidiaries. "We [initiated structural reform] off our own back because we [HRM] had such a presence in Ireland, it made no sense, duplication of everything, we weren't getting the synergies or we weren't sharing knowledge" (HRM Director).

The major structural change to the HRM function was to move towards a so-called "centres of excellence" model, but at country level. In this context "centres of excellence" are units which specialise in specific aspects of HRM and share that expertise and knowledge across national subsidiaries. In the case of GenCo, the subsidiaries created a centre of excellence for each of the main functions within HRM – namely a *Recruitment and Selection* centre of excellence, *Training and Development* centre of excellence, *HR Administration* centre of excellence and a *Compensation and Benefits* centre of excellence. These four centres of excellence were given responsibility for the design, development and delivery of those specific aspects of HRM in each of these domains and also to build the appropriate electronic tools to allow HRM personnel or line managers to access the required information and expertise. These centres of excellence were centralised in one of the existing subsidiaries in Ireland. Existing HRM personnel from across each of the subsidiaries in Ireland in many cases transitioned from their existing roles into one of these centres of excellence. However, there were also redundancies for HRM personnel, where approximately 30 per cent of the overall headcount in HRM across all of the subsidiaries lost their job.

The impact of this move to an Irish centre of excellence model had a significant influence on the HRM function and on the wider management of operations across the existing four subsidiaries. HRM managers have gone from a situation where they have traditionally had a small team of HRM personnel to support the HRM function at each subsidiary (possibly 8–10 HRM personnel in each subsidiary) to a significant reduction in HRM personnel and the need to link up with these centres of excellence. Senior HRM managers observed that the HRM function has been reduced to the "bare minimum". The remaining HRM presence at subsidiary level is now an HRM manager and generally an employment relations specialist – the HRM Director is still also in place. Another concern for local HRM personnel within subsidiaries was the impact of the substantial reduction or elimination of face-to-face interaction between employees and HRM practitioners and the knock-on effects this may have in terms of HRM's own role and reputation in delivering HRM services.

The impact of this change has also been felt by line managers. Traditionally if a line manager wanted to run a training intervention they would contact the local training and development manager and it would largely be the responsibility of the HRM function to run and coordinate the required training intervention. However, a side-effect of restructuring the HRM function was that the responsibility for training (and many other HRM matters) has now shifted to the line managers themselves. In the new arrangements, line managers have undergone training to provide them with the necessary skillset they need to carry out training interventions themselves and the *Training and Development* centre of excellence will provide the materials and guidance through an online system as necessary. Thus line managers must now become more self-sufficient on aspects of HRM that were previously the responsibility of the HRM function. "The response is the line will and must manage this for themselves, the days of mollycoddling the line is over … and behind this is cost, drop the numbers, push more work back to the line, drive specialization so the knowledge is better" (HRM Director).

The changes also have potentially broader implications for the HRM profession. Traditionally, employees in HRM would get a range of experience across the broad range of issues within HRM when working for a subsidiary of a MNC like GenCo – that is, their role would entail responsibility for the various operational aspects of HRM (e.g. recruitment and selection, training and development, compensation and benefits, employment relations). However, with the move towards the centres of excellence model, it means that HRM personnel will become very specific in their role and lack that breadth in terms of HRM knowledge. Thus an HRM practitioner becomes only skilled within a narrow aspect of HRM.

With all of the changes occurring at subsidiary level it was obvious that there was a real need for employment relations expertise at subsidiary level. This was evident in the restructuring process that the only remaining HRM personnel at subsidiary level were the HRM Manager and an employment relations expert – all of the other functions within HRM had moved to the centre of excellence model. There was a need for expertise in navigating and executing the restructuring process including the need for expert negotiation skills, expertise on redundancies and severance packages at subsidiary level. It was important that this expertise was available for two main reasons. First, issues such as redundancies and layoffs are very important to employees and there is a need to ensure that these processes are managed fairly and efficiently in such situations. It is not easy to deal with such situations, but employment relations practitioners have this expertise – ensuring the redundancy process is fair and equitable, providing career advice and support to the redundant workers. Second, the company does not want to end up in a labour dispute with employees and/or trade unions. And whilst employment relations as an area may not have been as visible when the MNC was in good times, in times of restructuring and retrenchment the issue of employment relations comes back to the fore.

Corporate headquarters picked up on the changes made in Ireland and sought to build on these initiatives. Corporate headquarters are now driving a move towards a global HRM shared services centre model whereby aspects of HRM will be centrally organised, with all other operations having access to the service. For example the HR administration centre of excellence that was located in Ireland has now moved to Asia, with the remit of serving the administration aspects of HRM for all global operations. Thus if an employee in Ireland or any other country in which GenCo have operations wants to find out about their annual leave, for example, they contact the global HRM administration shared service centre. The main rationale for establishing shared service centres is cost saving – that is, it reduces HRM headcount, it avoids replication of services and it also helps in the standardisation of HRM practices. The relocation of the administration centre of excellence did lead to some HRM job losses in Ireland. Other functions have also been restructured, such as training and development, which is now located at a regional level (Europe) whereby a very small number of people are now responsible for training and development across all of the subsidiaries in Europe.

Corporate headquarters relations/communication

The senior managers in the Irish subsidiaries have always been focused on developing excellent relations with those in corporate headquarters. This task has been made easier with some of the senior positions in corporate headquarters being filled by Irish people who previously worked in Irish subsidiaries. The drive for greater rationalisation and the move to shared services centres and centres of excellence models were driven by corporate headquarters. And whilst local HRM managers were aware of the challenges with such a move, they knew that implementing such changes were critical to the survival and development of the Irish subsidiaries. Whilst GenCo have sought to standardise HRM policies and practices across their operations globally, they have traditionally afforded local subsidiary management some autonomy in translating corporate headquarters initiatives into the local environment. Local HRM managers in Ireland are aware of the importance of their relationship with corporate headquarters and the need not only to implement HRM policies and practices driven by corporate headquarters but also to be the source for HRM policies and practices for the wider MNC. Garnering favour with corporate headquarters means putting the Irish subsidiary in a good position to compete for, and win, new investment.

One area that local HRM managers spoke about was the need to explain to corporate headquarters the different employment relations environment that exists in Ireland. Having to negotiate with trade unions and how they may react needed explanation. Being headquartered in the USA, and having no experience of dealing with trade unions in the home country, corporate headquarters had little knowledge of dealing with trade unions within the Irish context. What also complicated the picture for corporate headquarters was the lack of formal regulations and laws guiding employment relations in Ireland. As compared to countries like Germany or France where there is clear legislation around dealing with worker representatives, in Ireland negotiations with trade unions were described as more uncertain – despite a good working relationship between the Irish subsidiaries and the trade unions. Thus local HR management assumed an important role in translating and explaining the local employment relations environment.

> They [corporate headquarters] almost feel safer with this co-determination model which is very slow and rigorous but you kind of know what you are going to get at the end … and then you come to the Anglo-Saxon model … you have got the free independent will of the union and you don't know what you're going to end up with. That scares the[m] … [be]cause they just know anything could happen and it is that uncertainty that is the issue. (HRM Director)

Key role for HRM – strategic and/or operational role?

The above case outlines the challenges and opportunities for the HRM function in such a rationalisation scenario. HRM played a central role in addressing many of the key challenges facing GenCo during the rationalisation phase. For example the responses, such as redundancies, outsourcing, changes to terms and conditions of employment, enacted by GenCo fall within the domain of HRM. This by its very nature brings the HRM function to centre stage in addressing key strategic challenges facing the MNC, most notably pressures to reduce costs and enhance productivity. This arguably provides HRM with greater visibility within the MNC and an opportunity to demonstrate its ability to contribute to the strategic objectives of the organisation.

However, the above case study also illustrates the challenges that such a scenario presents to HRM. As noted above, there was significant restructuring of, and financial pressure on, the HRM function itself, which manifested in major structural changes of the HRM function at subsidiary level and reduction in headcount within HRM. Thus despite being a key player in achieving the strategic goals of the MNC, the HRM function itself was not immune from the impact of rationalisation.

SUMMARY

This case study illustrates the changing role of HRM at subsidiary level within an MNC. With greater pressures for rationalisation and standardisation of HRM practices, such changes are likely to become an issue for the HRM function at subsidiary level. Whilst the case study illustrates the important role that HRM can play in achieving the strategic objectives of an MNC, it also outlines the significant challenges HRM face at subsidiary level.

QUESTIONS

1 What are the challenges the HRM function at subsidiary level faces with a reduction in headcount and how might it respond?

2 What are the opportunities and challenges for both line managers and the HR function with the devolution of HR activities to line management?

3 Why is it important that corporate headquarters understand the host country institutional and cultural environment in relation to the implementation of HRM policies and practices?

4 What role does HRM play in implementing a rationalisation process – strategic or operational?

35
Implementing HRM within multinational corporations: Localisation or global standardisation?

Anastasia Kynighou

BACKGROUND

BankCo[1] is a large European bank and operates in three key businesses: retail banking and financial services; global investment management and services; and corporate and investment banking. BankCo was founded more than 120 years ago and is well into the maturity stage of its life cycle. Currently the firm employs almost 150 000 members of staff in more than 80 countries. In the late 1990s, a subsidiary company, FinanceCo, was created and aimed to focus on BankCo's operations outside the country-of-origin. Overall, BankCo's corporate mission is to increase its profitability through an effective growth strategy for economies and individual clients. The basis for this vision, as it has been claimed, is a vigorous model that the parent company attempts to diffuse to all parts of the Multinational Corporation (MNC). BankCo also aims to disseminate a set of core corporate values, namely professionalism, team spirit and innovation, to all employees in all subsidiaries. The goal is that these values will govern worldwide operations, even if practices differ amongst subsidiaries.

BankCo expanded into Eastern Europe and Africa through the acquisition of local banks. Thus, BankCo prefers to acquire local knowledge and expertise since the banking sector is sensitive to local and global market pressures and is frequently regulated by national legislation and financial institutions as well as national central banks.

HISTORY OF THE LOCAL SUB-UNIT

BankCo started operating in Cyprus in the early 1980s through a partnership between BankCo and two other foreign banks. In the early 1990s, BankCo bought out the other two partners, resulting in a majority ownership of 51 per cent. Subsequently, the name of the parent company was adopted and used in Cyprus in an attempt to transfer the corporate model from the home country to the Cypriot market. Under the legal status of an 'offshore' company, the only form of legal entity allowed by the Cypriot government at the time for foreign banks, BankCo served non-Cypriot clients only. During this time, the banking sector's trade union had no legal rights in the workplace.

Ten years later, and following an amendment in the local legislation after Cyprus joined the European Union, BankCo Cyprus started operating as a fully licensed local bank, catering to residents in addition to a non-resident clientele. BankCo Cyprus has three key business units: the international business unit, the corporate unit and the private banking unit. According to the corporate website of the local unit, BankCo Cyprus aims to use capabilities found at both the Headquarters (HQ) and local level in order to provide creative solutions that cater to the needs of the local market, with customer needs driving the local strategy. However, at the same time this seems to be conflicting with FinanceCo's strategy, whose reason-for-being is to *control* subsidiaries (through explicit guidelines and set targets) and to ensure that the bank's image and reputation are maintained and protected.

SIZE AND MARKET POSITION

The Cypriot subsidiaries, like all foreign subsidiaries, are also part of FinanceCo and are expected to adopt the home country strategies and practices in the host country. BankCo currently employs over 100 people in four branches in Cyprus, down from 200 and seven branches in 2010, possibly due to the major financial crisis of the Cypriot economy in 2013. The Chief Executive Officer (CEO) of the local company is, and traditionally has been, a home-country national, a practice often used by MNCs from that country. This is a strategic choice by the parent company to appoint home-country nationals to the positions of GM and deputy GM in all foreign subsidiaries to ensure a greater extent of standardisation across all subsidiaries (Bartlett and Ghoshal 1989; Perlmutter 1969; McNulty and Brewster 2017). A key requirement by any expatriate who is appointed as a CEO in BankCo in foreign subsidiaries is to have at least five years of work experience abroad. However, the heads of all three business units are local managers, while ten non-Cypriots, who have become Cypriot nationals marrying Cypriots, work at BankCo. This indicates that the vast majority of employees and top management are Cypriots or even non-Cypriots who have personal reasons for living on the island and are not on short-term international assignments – with the exception of the CEO and his deputy.

BankCo's actual market position is difficult to pinpoint, especially in recent years after the downturn of the Cypriot financial sector and the closing of two of the biggest financial institutions of the island. Overall, this sector has seen a significant number (considering the Cypriot market's size) of foreign banks, some of them Greek, entering in recent years – especially since 2004 when Cyprus entered the EU, and despite the recession. Indeed, EU membership forced Cyprus to open up its market, reduce barriers to entry and promote competition between firms by limiting oligopolistic or monopolistic tactics used until then.

In turn, competition for staff among banks changed because, prior to EU membership, a 'gentlemen's agreement' amongst the Cypriot banks existed: the implicit expectation was that 'you don't poach my employees, I don't poach yours', which resulted in extremely low to non-existent staff mobility and turnover as well as jobs for life. As competition became fiercer, the agreement was disregarded and employees were allowed, and expected, to move from one bank to another. This newfound competition in the labour market led the banks to adopt more formal HR practices to manage and retain employees and become more strategic when making employment-related decisions, especially in terms of workforce size, employee turnover and labour costs. Currently,

BankCo's employee turnover is considered to be quite high due to the sectoral mobility of staff but also because of the wave of redundancies, voluntary and compulsory, which occurred after the recession in 2013.

HR DEPARTMENT AND HR PHILOSOPHY

Interestingly enough, employees own 7 per cent of the firm's capital, making them an important stakeholder group. BankCo's HRM philosophy, as explained by the top management of the subsidiary, is to ensure that the 'bank employs high calibre, knowledge-intensive individuals who will lead the firm to more successful paths'. As a result, learning and development is extremely important for BankCo, and the aim of the HR Department is to develop staff and talent further since their expertise will affect the services provided to clients.

HR within BankCo is no longer seen merely as a low-level bureaucratic management tool and has become much more strategic in recent years. This is consistent with an overall trend in Cyprus to switch to a more strategic position of the HR function as well as the professionalisation of the HR function there Brewster and Mayrhofer (2014). This is reflected in the sub-unit's new structure and which indicates that HRM is currently perceived as strategic.

> [In the past] I was reporting to the Administration and Support Director. The HR was perceived as something administrative, something bureaucratic. This year I am reporting straight to the CEO – because he believes in the strategic role that HR has to play in the subsidiary. I also sit on the management committee. Still, we are more of an HR function at the moment rather than a strategic HRM department but things are changing. (HHR)

Despite that, the HR department is still at its infancy stage and is relatively small. It comprises the head of HR, a staff facilitator (who is responsible for financial loans provided to BankCo's staff), one training officer and two recruitment and performance officers. This is summarised in Figure 35.1.

Figure 35.1 Structure of HR department – BankCo Cyprus

The local workplace of BankCo Cyprus is also greatly affected by the sectoral Trade Union (ETYK) and the collective bargaining agreement which is in place. In fact, more than 95 per cent of the workforce are members of ETYK, and as HHR claims, 'ETYK is so strong and there is not really much point in managers trying to resist them. It's a case of "if you can't beat them, join them".'

Working hours caused a serious conflict and friction between local staff and home country management concerned. Working hours, as well as pay, promotions and job security, are agreed and regulated by the collective bargaining agreement, giving little autonomy to banks to make their own decisions. As the HHR explained:

HQ said that we have to work from 8 am until 5 pm like everyone else in Europe. The answer from Cyprus was simple: NO. Collective agreement says banking sector employees have to work between 7.30 am and 2.30 pm and it was very hard for them to accept that. They would ask us 'but when do you actually work then?' This is actually one of the things that makes the bank sector attractive for employees and there was nothing that BankCo could do to change it.

IMPLEMENTATION OF HRM PRACTICES: LOCALISATION VS STANDARDISATION

The major question when examining HR implementation within MNCs is the extent to which HR practices are transferred from the top level to the bottom (standardisation) or adapted to fit the local market and context (localisation).

In the case of BankCo, and according to local managers, guidelines are imposed by HQ but the design and implementation of HRM practices, if these are not governed by the collective bargaining agreement, for example recruitment and selection or training and development, are quite localised – unlikely operational practices which are highly standardised. At the same time, the relationship between the subsidiary's management and HQ is very formal and the CEO of the Cyprus subsidiary reports directly to the board of directors and the retail banking manager of BankCo in the home country. This depicts how home and host country interplay to shape the implementation of HRM practices at the local level (Edwards et al. 2007; Rees and Edwards 2009; Yahiaoui 2015; Edwards et al. 2016; Chiang et al. 2017).

This interplay is also evident when comparing the key tasks of the HR department at the top and at the local level. The corporate HR department is mainly preoccupied with recruiting, promoting and retaining staff. However, in Cyprus this logic does not exist, either because of collective agreements or because of the local culture. For example, whereas recruitment in the country-of-origin is very rigid, in Cyprus, '[…] you still get calls from people who put [social] pressure on you to hire their daughter or their nephew etc' (HAF).

However, there is a very fine line between adaptation and standardisation of practices and this is not a straightforward phenomenon as one would expect. Despite the above comments, it was also claimed that 'The main framework is the same. Minor adaptations depend on differences in culture. […] HQ gives us an overview of their expectations' (HRI).

These indicate there is potentially extensive scope for adaptation of internal procedures. This is welcomed by HQ as long as the final outcome is consistent with standards set out in the main framework. Adaptations in terms of HR practices often take place in Cyprus since most line managers are host-country nationals. This is, in turn, due to high educational levels of local managers, which offers more scope for greater understanding of global targets. In contrast, in countries like Greece, where culture is quite similar but the national business system is quite different, all line managers are home-country nationals, and are 'assigned and sent' there by the parent company (HAF).

In addition, many control mechanisms are used and put in place by the parent company and are used consistently across all subsidiaries. For example, HQ controls all subsidiaries through 'audit missions', where people from the country-of-origin of FinanceCo visit Cyprus at regular intervals. Moreover, once a year there is a general audit and each department prepares reports that are then sent to HQ. Results from each subsidiary are then compared to those of other subsidiaries. This benchmarking technique creates internal competition among subsidiaries but also sets performance standards throughout the organisation.

The (expatriate) general managers have functional roles in all subsidiaries and are expected to carry out the same tasks in all locations. In fact, HAF claims that, 'If we get a new CEO, this will not affect how the bank works at all. Their approach might be different but practices will remain the same. They actually try to have the least possible impact on our local practices as possible.'

From this statement, and based on the local managers' perceptions, it can be assumed that CEOs are used as yet another control mechanism. They allow local managers to shape their HR practices according to the demands of the local market/ workforce. However, at the same time they play a critical role in acting as a conduit between HQ and the local level, transfer key global objectives to the local market, transfer wider organisational culture and values and validate procedures and processes so as to ensure that service standards and strategic objectives are met.

Nonetheless, local HR practices are also shaped by the Operations Directive, a global framework which is diffused to all parts of the organisation. The Operations Directive includes all guidelines of BankCo under which all subsidiaries are expected to operate and with which they are required to comply. In addition, it provides frameworks which local managers need to use when developing their local HR policies. The Directive explicitly outlines key objectives and tasks, which are standardised in all subsidiaries. This is especially important since the firm is growing through mergers and acquisitions. When acquiring brownfield sites these usually carry with them their own culture, practices and business system; hence a common framework exists to ensure internal consistency.

The Operations Directive has three main uses. First, it can be used by subsidiaries as a tool for communication between FinanceCo business departments and the various subsidiaries in order to exchange support on the organisational issues and projects, shared concepts and vocabulary. In addition, it is used as a tool of organisation, to help in setting up organisational projects and draft job descriptions, and to provide a style guide for writing instructions and procedures. Third, it can assist with change management processes as well as for training support when putting in place new principles of organisation or new structures, or for the implementation of information systems and so forth.

BankCo also uses training as a mechanism to increase consistency throughout subsidiaries. Training courses for the local trainers are frequently organised either in the home country or in other countries in the region. Their purpose is to support local subsidiaries, develop local levels of expertise, to diffuse 'best practices' to subsidiaries and to keep people up-to-date. To sum up, FinanceCo provides strong frameworks/tools that local managers use to accommodate the needs of their own subsidiaries, while at the same time meeting FinanceCo's objectives and leading to increased consistency of internal processes within the MNC.

Examples of HR practices that are adapted to suit local standards include recruitment and selection as well as training and development. For instance, the Staff Training Guide (which is inspired by the Guide to Training prepared by FinanceCo) states that regardless of the local unit's size or structure, and over and above the local regulations, the efficient implementation of a training plan requires the involvement of a number of key players, and by 'players' they mean local managers. General management, along with HR, set the priority objectives of the company and domains, while HR itself is responsible for delivering the training. Thereafter, HR works with the heads of the various functions in order to identify their collective needs, as well as the needs of individual employees. These are then prioritised and a training plan is established. The management team and HR then validate the training plan which is then designed, delivered and evaluated by HR. It is evident that local managers (i.e. Heads of Functions) make decisions based on the local department's needs. Nonetheless, these needs derive from the strategic planning set and validated by general management in Cyprus. Keeping in mind that the CEO is always an expatriate, the attempt by HQ to exercise control on how these needs are shaped and to control the plans before being implemented becomes apparent.

Likewise, for staff recruitment, the policy states that the HR function of the bank holds the responsibility for all matters relating to the recruitment of new staff. However, recruitment and selection policies are developed and implemented in consultation with the relevant head(s) of function(s) of the Bank, that is, the line managers. Eventually, for a practice to be implemented, the approval of the general manager is required. Again, the role of the CEO as a 'gatekeeper' is evident.

SUMMARY

The case study of BankCo Cyprus illustrates how different pressures are exercised on the MNC to ultimately shape HRM at the local level. In addition, it is evident that these influences can be both internal to the firm (or even internal to the specific sub-unit) as well as external. The case study highlights how the MNC strives to legitimise its actions in the host environment, while ensuring that internal procedures and processes are consistent in all parts of the organisation (Kostova and Roth 2002; Rosenzweig and Nohria 1994). On the one hand, the use of a number of internal control mechanisms (i.e. global policies, expatriate managers etc.) facilitate attempts to transfer practices from the top (HQ) to the bottom (subsidiary) level of the organisation. These mechanisms not only make local managers accountable to HQ but also, through the benchmarking technique, create internal competition between various sub-units of the MNC. Moreover, expatriate managers play a critical role, not so much in shaping local practices, but in ensuring that these are within corporate expectations and that they do not bear any financial or other liability. In addition, evidence from this case study highlights how internal parameters, such as the subsidiary's own age, size or even type of ownership, can have a significant role in moulding HR practices.

Further, external contingencies such as the national culture and institutions shape the implementation of HRM. Despite distinctive attempts by HQ to transfer certain employment practices to Cyprus (i.e. working hours), this attempt was undermined by the presence, and relative strength, that the sectoral Trade Union enjoys. Yet it appears that sectoral patterns are changing due to global pressures. Moreover, the host-country's national culture, sometimes implicitly, affects how employment decisions are made in the local subsidiary. Customer expectations, employee expectations, employee preferences and ultimately the demand and supply of workforce are shaped to a certain extent by local culture and this will be reflected in the choices of local management as well. As such, the expatriate manager's role is to ensure that either the local culture or institutions will not jeopardise the local unit's performance or damage the MNC's global brand.

Hence, actors at both the top and local level should appreciate how these various factors interplay to ultimately shape the set of HR practices implemented in foreign parts of MNCs.

QUESTIONS

1   A number of factors appear to influence the implementation of HRM in local sub-units of MNCs. The literature tends to classify these into institutional, cultural and organisational factors. Identify the key influences, whether internal or external, that shape HRM at the local level of an MNC and classify them according to these clusters.

2   In your opinion, how does the MNC achieve internal consistency while at the same time gaining external legitimacy in the host-country environment? Do you think that there is a conflict between these two pressures?

3   Critically assess the role of expatriate managers in the local unit. To what extent can they ensure that home-country HR practices, specifically, are transferred at the local level? What other roles do they serve in terms of people management?

END NOTES

1   Respondents: Head of Administration and Finance Domain (HAF), Head of Human Resources (HHR), HR Officer I (HRI), HR Officer II (HRII).

REFERENCES

Bartlett, C.A. and Ghoshal, S. (1989), *Managing across Borders: The Transnational Solution*, Boston, MA: Harvard Business School Press.

Brewster, C. and Mayrhofer, W. (2014), 'Comparative human resource management', in A. Harzing and A. Pinnington (eds), *International Human Resource Management*, 4th edn, London: Sage.

Chiang, F.F.T., Lemański, M.K. and Birtch, T.A. (2017), 'The transfer and diffusion of HRM practices within MNCs: lessons learned and future research directions', *International Journal of Human Resource Management*, **28**(1): 234–58.

Edwards, T., Colling, T. and Ferner, A. (2007), 'Conceptual approaches to the transfer of employment practices in multinational companies: an integrated approach', *Human Resource Management Journal*, **17**(3): 201–17.

Edwards, T., Sanchez-Mangas, R., Jalette, P., Lavelle, J. and Minbaeva, D. (2016), 'Global standardization or national differentiation of HRM practices in multinational companies? A comparison of multinationals in five countries', *International Journal of Business Studies*, **47**: 997–1021.

Kostova, T. and Roth, K. (2002), 'Adoption of an organizational practice by subsidiaries of multinational corporations: institutional and relational effects', *Academy of Management Journal*, **45**(1): 215–33.

McNulty, Y. and Brewster, C. (2017), 'Theorising the meaning of "expatriates": establishing boundary conditions for business expatriates', *International Journal of HRM*, **28**(1): 27–61.

Mohan, A. (2006), 'Variation of practices across multiple levels within transnational corporations', in M. Geppert and M. Mayer (eds), *Global, National and Local Practices in Multinational Companies*, London: Palgrave Macmillan.

Perlmutter, H. (1969), 'The tortuous evolution of the multinational corporation', *Columbia Journal of World Business*, January–February: 9–18.

Rees, C. and Edwards, T. (2009), 'Management strategy and HR in international mergers: choice, constraint and pragmatism', *Human Resource Management Journal*, **19**(1): 24–39

Rosenzweig, P.M. and Nohria, N. (1994), 'Influences on human resource management practices in multinational corporations', *Journal of International Business Studies*, **25**: 229–51.

Yahiaoui, D. (2015), 'Hybridization: striking a balance between adoption and adaptation of human resource management practices in French multinational corporations and their Tunisian subsidiaries', *International Journal of Human Resource Management*, **26**(13), 1665–93.

36
Global talent and mobility in a decentralised multinational enterprise

Anthony McDonnell, Stefan Jooss and Hugh Scullion

INTRODUCTION

This case examines several key issues and challenges faced by a European-owned, building materials sector multinational enterprise (MNE) that has grown rapidly over the past four decades based largely on an international strategy of cross-border acquisitions. The case highlights links between the business strategy and global talent management and, more particularly, the role of the corporate human resource (HR) function in the context of a company with a culture committed to delivering superior performance through a highly decentralised approach to managing international business operations. The case illustrates some of the complexity of global staffing and talent management issues in developed markets and also in the emerging markets of Central and Eastern Europe (CEE) and Asia. The talent management challenges are arguably more acute in these regions due to greater cultural and institutional differences, which results in a particular demand for a distinctive type of managerial talent which can operate effectively in these culturally complex and geographically distant markets (Skuza et al., 2013).

BACKGROUND AND CONTEXT

European Building Materials Company (EBMC) is a large, publicly listed, European headquartered MNE operating in the building materials industry. In particular, EBMC targets three core businesses covering residential and non-residential customer bases:

1. Primary Materials (e.g. cement, aggregates and asphalts);
2. Building Products (e.g. precast concrete products and fencing);
3. Distribution (e.g. builders' merchants and specialist distribution).

The EBMC strategy is one of vertical integration in terms of manufacturing and horizontal integration through servicing the breadth of building material product customers. EBMC operates multiple organisational structures consisting of global business functions, geographic regions, and international product divisions. Each of the three core businesses reports to a European or American structure who report to the seven group functions (finance, HR, risk management, corporate social responsibility, investor relations, environment, and health and safety). These functions then report to the chief executive officer. There is a mixed product- and region-based organisational structure which fits well with the decentralised approach allowing for a high level of flexibility for local conditions. This approach is regarded as 'business critical' for building materials companies due to the localised nature of the industry. Consequently, the development of a strong senior management team sensitive to the local market and cultural context is vital to EBMC.

Over the past 40 years, the company has developed from a small local player to a global enterprise, with operations in 30 countries and a global workforce of approximately 80 000 people. Some 90 per cent of this employment is accounted for outside of EBMC's home country. The company has developed a major presence in mature markets in Western Europe and North America, which accounts for approximately 85 per cent of business and more recently there has also been considerable growth in a number of emerging markets including CEE, South America and Asia, with a growing focus on the Chinese and Indian markets. The relatively limited nature of these operations in developing regions is illustrated by the organisational structure which sees the Indian and Chinese operations reporting to the European division. However, significant investment in South-East Asia in the next five years may require EBMC to restructure their organisation and develop an additional regional market focusing on Asia.

INTERNATIONAL BUSINESS GROWTH STRATEGY

Since the formation of the company in the early 1970s, EBMC has followed a focused and consistent business development and growth path with a strong emphasis on performance and results, which has involved internal/ organic growth. However, the main engine of growth has arrived through the success of the cross-border acquisitions strategy which has taken place across regions and products. Over the past decade, the level of growth has been remarkable, witnessing the emergence of the company as a global leader in the industry, which is reflected in its rise to the top 100 non-financial services MNEs in the world. In recent years, acquisition activity has been in the range of 70 to 75 per annum, primarily small- and medium-sized firms. However, due to the global recession, there was less emphasis on riskier acquisitions and more focus on operational and commercial competitiveness.

The company has a well-developed methodology in selecting firms for acquisition. First, target companies must be market leaders commanding first or second positions in their domestic market. Second, they should preferably be mid-sized, high-performing companies. Third, the quality of the local management team should be high and the local managers committed to growing the business. While the main foreign market entry strategy has been acquisitions of wholly-owned subsidiaries, international joint ventures have also been used on occasion as a stepping stage to full ownership, particularly in the emerging markets where investments are riskier. There is a high failure rate of cross-border mergers and acquisitions (CBMAs). Recent research shows that 83 per cent of all CBMAs fail to deliver additional shareholder value and 53 per cent even destroy value (Marks and Mirvis, 2011). The main reasons for failure in CBMAs are related to cross-cultural and human resource management (HRM) issues including the fact that managers are often unknowingly influenced by human biases and structural problems (Friedman et al., 2016). Hence, cross-cultural management and HRM are increasingly viewed as critical to the successful implementation of CBMAs. This reflects the complexity of integrating the HRM systems from the different organisations and national contexts. Generally, in the implementation phase of CBMAs, the tensions between the need for global integration and local responsiveness influence issues such as the level of integration the acquirer seeks and the extent to which the parent company seeks to introduce a common corporate culture. However, in our case study the company operated a highly hands-off approach to senior subsidiary management, allowing local managers a very high degree of autonomy to develop the business using their local knowledge and networks. The role of the corporate HR function in this context is limited to a few key areas, which we examine below.

THE CORPORATE HR FUNCTION

As organisations internationalise, the corporate HR function is faced with the challenge of establishing effective structures and processes. This may take one of three forms (Scullion and Starkey, 2000): centralised, decentralised, or transitional HR approaches. EBMC operates a highly decentralised approach with a very small corporate HR staff at headquarters (HQ) which undertakes a narrower range of functions than centralised global firms. This reflects the highly decentralised corporate structure which has been in place at EBMC since the early days of internationalisation. As the company operates in a relatively simple, locally based industry, HR policies and practices are devolved to the business unit level to support the business strategy, and senior management recognise that sustainable competitive advantage will derive from securing high-quality local management who are able to respond effectively to changing conditions in each host environment. Consequently, the overall role of the corporate HQ is one primarily of support services and coordination.

Shortages of managerial and professional talent have emerged as the key HR challenge facing the majority of MNEs and the growing difficulty of recruiting and retaining managerial talent has been noted as a significant constraint on the successful implementation of global strategies (Mellahi and Collings, 2010). In the last three years, EBMC lost some of their key talent to competitors and other industries, experiencing a turnover rate of 18 per cent due to the lack of opportunities for advancement in some of the established locations. MNEs increasingly need managers with the skills to operate in the new market conditions faced in foreign operations both in developed and emerging markets. Inherent in EBMC's market-driven growth approach is an acknowledgement of the importance of having a sufficient level and calibre of talent to grow the international businesses. Indeed, talent management is one of three identified strategic themes under the company's HR strategy (the other two being organisation development and systems and processes). EBMC operates three different leadership programmes, aimed at employees at different levels, to ensure there is a talent pipeline which will deliver the leadership capability to run an international business for the following five to ten years. There are strong links between all three strategic themes, the business strategy, and the corporate HR function. Recently there has been more focus on organisation development as the organisation begins to shift from a portfolio or conglomerate approach towards a more complex, integrated global organisation form. This will pose a new challenge for the corporate HR function, and the need to ensure the balance between global integration and local responsiveness will become even more critical particularly as the changing business environment is increasingly driving the structure of the business and the HR agenda. This also means a shift away from a heavily localised approach to one that incorporates a more global agenda.

MANAGING INTERNATIONAL TALENT IN EBMC

MNEs have three primary options with respect to staffing their foreign operations: employ parent country nationals (PCNs), host country nationals (HCNs), or third country nationals (TCNs). It is quite common for MNEs to use PCNs in the early years of a foreign operation to help transfer the company's culture and establish the preferred reporting and control systems of the parent company and for purposes of establishing control in the foreign market (Dowling et al., 2008). This approach has been used sparingly by EBMC other than on occasion in the early stages of internationalisation in some of the emerging markets. Here, PCNs may fill the top two or three positions in the foreign subsidiary. The continued use of an ethnocentric management approach with the use of PCNs in the top positions is likely to limit an organisation's ability to attract and retain high-calibre local managers and professionals. The staffing approach will also vary depending on whether an organisation enters the foreign market through establishing a new greenfield site or through acquisition. In addition, the location of the foreign operation may have a very practical effect on the staffing strategy. Research suggests a growing need for MNEs to select and develop managers with distinctive competencies and a desire to manage in culturally and geographically distant markets (Caligiuri and Tarique, 2012). These global leaders must be able to build relationships across cultures, cope with ambiguity, understand complex information, and adapt to new contexts. However, there may be staff availability issues in terms of high-quality managers and professionals with the required knowledge in some emerging markets and managers from established locations must learn to understand how different cultures communicate, lead, decide and persuade (Meyer, 2017). Also, it is more difficult to get PCNs to accept assignments in some emerging markets and the preparedness of leadership talent to move to new strategic markets cannot be guaranteed. Research suggests that mobility across borders, and particularly to higher risk locations in Africa, Asia and Latin America, is proving increasingly difficult to achieve (Yeung et al., 2008). The use of PCNs, albeit quite limited, has raised concern among some locals in countries where these individuals have a short-term focus in their roles. There is also concern over the opportunities for local managers, especially in cases where the acquired firm's management team have been moved on.

Talent management in high-growth acquisition MNEs

The growth of interest in global talent management reflects the growing recognition of the critical role played by international managerial talent in ensuring the success of MNEs. This also reflects the intensification of global competition and the greater need for international learning and innovation in the MNE (Bartlett and Ghoshal, 1989). Recent research argues that MNEs increasingly need to manage talent on a global basis to remain competitive and that talent can be located in different parts of their global operations (Stahl et al., 2007). The difficulties of implementing effective global talent management strategies are accentuated in highly decentralised MNEs adopting a rapid-growth, acquisition-based business strategy model. When a firm is acquired, it comes with staff who may or may not be wanted by the acquiring organisation. EBMC's acquisition strategy involves specifically targeting high-performing companies with high-quality local management. EBMC's post-acquisition staffing strategy is generally to continue with the existing local management as they tend to have a demonstrated track record and strong entrepreneurial flair. Hence, a key element of the talent management strategy in EBMC is acquiring good managerial and leadership talent and indeed the availability of high-quality local management is one of the key criteria used when selecting companies for acquisition.

In practice, the acquired firms' management are allowed a very high degree of autonomy to run the subsidiary operation so long as they reach the performance targets that reflect the local nature of the industry and the highly decentralised approach of EBMC. This approach has consistently produced high performance and growth to date. However, one corporate initiative was the introduction of a performance incentive scheme which seeks both to reward senior local managers and to retain them as their know-how, networks and knowledge would be attractive to other MNEs. There seems to be little issue that the HCN managers are relatively unknown to HQ management and there is little indication of the loyalty of these employees to the company. To date, EBMC has not established clear metrics around engagement and retention of these managers. There appears to be a lack of transparency as there is no global talent pool which would allow a long-term strategic view to managing talent (Sparrow, 2007). Moreover, there is very limited mobility of managers between the HQ and the subsidiary, which may limit international management development opportunities and the ability to develop talent at the global or regional levels. It seems that a global talent strategy requires better integration of global mobility aspects (Collings, 2014). As long as the global talent management strategy continues to support the business strategy and the present business model is achieving excellent results, there is little pressure on EBMC to change. However, as the company increasingly looks to the emerging markets as the high potential areas for business growth, there may be a greater need in the short term to use more expatriates to establish the business in the foreign markets. In addition to the more traditional mid- and long-term appointments, an increased use of international short-term assignments may be considered. That being said, there is little evidence that an overall approach which depends on high-quality local management to grow the market with very successful results will significantly change in the near future. The particular global talent management challenges in the emerging markets are discussed below.

Talent management in developing economies

The increasing investment in the emerging markets by EBMC in recent years has resulted in a growing demand for a distinctive type of managerial talent which can operate effectively in these challenging markets (Meyer and Xin, 2018). The talent management challenges for EBMC are more complex and acute in these emerging markets. While these markets have high-growth potential, they also involve higher risk. These cultures are considerably different from the home culture of EBMC and indeed much of their other foreign operations. A means by which EBMC has sought to reduce some of the risks of development in these countries is to first engage in international joint ventures and then look at a full acquisition.

However, despite the growth of unemployment during the global recession in countries like India and China, recent research suggests there is still a significant gap between the supply and demand of talent with high-level knowledge and skills in these countries (Cooke et al., 2014). In addition, the inability of these countries to produce graduates of the quality needed by MNEs has resulted in acute skill shortages in key areas (Farndale et al., 2010). Reports have highlighted that MNEs in India only take between 15 per cent and 20 per cent of available graduates because they do not fit the requirements of Western economy MNEs. The retention of managers and professionals in their emerging markets is a major talent management challenge for EBMC. There is intense competition for scarce managerial and leadership talent in these markets and the tight labour market for such talent allows individual managers to move easily to other MNEs or even to domestic organisations. Finally, organisational loyalty is not particularly strong in some of the emerging markets (Bhatnagar, 2007).

In the mature markets of North America and Europe, the vast majority of EBMC's senior managers are HCNs, reflecting the company strategy to localise the management. By contrast, the emerging market operations have a number of expatriates, particularly in the early years, as a means to develop the markets and also for control purposes. With many of these senior managers being close to retirement, another key challenge for EBMC is the retention of knowledge within the organisation. Successfully transferring knowledge to younger managers across regions is therefore a strategic priority.

The CEE region is an area of growing importance for the company since their first investment into Poland in the mid-1990s. Expatriates have been used in this region to develop the market, but more recently there has been a greater drive to implement a localisation strategy. In recent years EBMC has developed businesses in a number of other CEE countries and interestingly has used Polish graduates who were integral players in developing the Polish operations to lead the development of these markets (a localisation strategy would follow the initial set-up of the market). This suggests an emerging talent strategy of moving high potential managers between countries of a particular region (TCNs), namely the CEE region. However, there was virtually no mobility of managers between different regions of the world, which is an issue EBMC may need to address if they wish to evolve from being a highly decentralised conglomerate organisation to becoming more of an integrated international business.

The selection criteria for managers in the emerging markets involve a number of elements. Effective cross-cultural management skills and a strong motivation and desire to go and work in the emerging markets (not solely monetary) are important. In addition, managers accepted for these international assignments must be on the high potential list as the developmental aspect of these assignments is increasingly important for developing international leadership capability. In EBMC high potentials are viewed as individuals having the potential of being promoted two levels or crossing two functional areas. A key element of global talent management in EBMC is that mobility did not always mean moving upwards but could also be sideways. EBMC wishes to see lateral moves becoming more important as they help give individuals a better understanding of the entire business and position them better for taking on a range of roles rather than a very narrow role. Also, in a highly competitive business where cost reduction is increasingly important, lateral mobility allows development opportunities and develops a team approach. While this core idea is strongly presented in EBMC, the organisation lacks a clear reward strategy to foster mobility among key managerial talent.

One talent management challenge facing EBMC and many other MNEs is the growing difficulty in getting people to take up international assignments. There is growing evidence that families are less willing to accept the disruption of family and social lives associated with international assignments. Dual career issues are increasingly seen as a worldwide trend, which can pose significant restrictions on the career plans of multinationals. In the EBMC case a particular challenge was the failure to persuade US managers to move to other regions of the world. This reflects their polycentric approach to international management where until now managers were not expected to move across regional frontiers. Another peculiar feature of EBMC is that repatriation is not regarded as an issue. The practice of repatriation remains something relatively rare in EBMC. One important factor here seems to be the small size of the corporate head office. Also important is the balance of employees between domestic and international operations as over 90 per cent of employees are based outside the home country in EBMC. In practice, international assignments are essentially a one-way ticket and opportunities for a post in the parent country following an international assignment are extremely limited. Hence, the company is very careful not to raise expectations about the prospects of a job on return from international assignments.

SUMMARY

EBMC is an international success story through its high-growth acquisition development strategy. A highly decentralised management approach has been adopted thus far in the management of its international operations. With high-quality international managers, an increasingly scarce resource, the acquisition of high-performing companies with high-calibre managers and employees has many benefits although it brings many challenges. There is little doubt that their highly decentralised international management approach has stood them well. However, with the worldwide economy in a state of flux and the greatest business growth opportunities in diverse, culturally different developing economies there are question marks over whether the current approach is best suited in the future.

QUESTIONS

1. What are the strengths and weaknesses of the decentralised management approach adopted in EBMC? Is it feasible to maintain a decentralised approach as the firm continues to expand and internationalise? Why/Why not?

2. What are the benefits and weaknesses of the 'one-way ticket' approach to the use of PCNs? How might this approach fit with the need to increase the use of international assignments in EBMC?

3. What role does corporate culture play in developing leaders as part of a global talent management approach at EBMC?

4. How can EBMC foster collaboration among subsidiaries and develop a network of knowledge-sharing talent teams?

5. Discuss how EBMC can assure a strong alignment between business and talent strategies. How can the organisation assess, predict and plan the supply and demand of talent in the future?

6. To what extent does EBMC use integrated and strategic talent management approaches?

7. Discuss the issues/challenges in developing a dynamic talent management strategy which supports changing organisational priorities in a decentralised business such as EBMC.

REFERENCES

Bartlett, C.A. and Ghoshal, S. (1989) *Managing across borders: The transnational solution*, Boston, MA: Harvard Business School Press.

Bhatnagar, J. (2007) Talent management strategy of employee engagement in Indian ITES employees: Key to retention, *Employee Relations*, **29** (6): 640–63.

Caligiuri, P. and Tarique, I. (2012) Dynamic cross-cultural competencies and global leadership effectiveness, *Journal of World Business*, **47** (4): 612–22.

Collings, D.G. (2014) Integrating global mobility and global talent management: Exploring the challenges and strategic opportunities, *Journal of World Business*, **49** (2): 253–61.

Cooke, F.L., Saini, D.S. and Wang, J. (2014) Talent management in China and India: A comparison of management perceptions and human resource practices, *Journal of World Business*, **49** (2): 225–35.

Dowling, P.J., Festing, M. and Engle, A.D. (2008) *International human resource management* (5th edn), London: Thomson.

Farndale, E., Scullion, H. and Sparrow, P.R. (2010) The role of the corporate HR function in global talent management, *Journal of World Business*, **45** (2): 161–8.

Friedman, Y., Carmeli, A., Tishler, A. and Shimizu, K. (2016) Untangling micro-behavioral sources of failure in mergers and acquisitions: A theoretical integration and extension, *The International Journal of Human Resource Management*, **27** (20): 2339–69.

Marks, M.L. and Mirvis, P.H. (2011) Merge ahead: A research agenda to increase merger and acquisition success, *Journal of Business Psychology*, **26** (2): 161–8.

Mellahi, K. and Collings, D.G. (2010) The barriers to effective global talent management: The example of corporate elites in MNEs, *Journal of World Business*, **45** (2): 143–9.

Meyer, E. (2017) Being the boss in Brussels, Boston, and Beijing, *Harvard Business Review*, July/August: 70–77.

Meyer, K.E. and Xin, K.R. (2018) Managing talent in emerging economy multinationals: Integrating strategic management and human resource management, *The International Journal of Human Resource Management*, **29** (11): 1827–55.

Scullion, H. and Starkey, K. (2000) In search of the changing role of the corporate HR role in the international firm, *The International Journal of Human Resource Management*, **11** (6): 1061–81.

Skuza, A., Scullion, H. and McDonnell, A. (2013) An analysis of the talent management challenges in a post-communist country: The case of Poland, *The International Journal of Human Resource Management*, **24** (3): 453–70.

Sparrow, P.R. (2007) Globalization of HR at function level: Four UK-based case studies of the international recruitment and selection process, *The International Journal of Human Resource Management*, **18** (5): 845–67.

Stahl, G.K., Björkman, I., Farndale, E., Morris, S.S., Stiles, P., Trevor, J. and Wright, P.M. (2007) *Global talent management: How leading multinationals build and sustain their talent pipeline*, Fontainebleau: INSEAD.

Yeung, A.K., Warner, M. and Rowley, C. (2008) Growth and globalization: Evolution of human resource practices in Asia, *Human Resource Management*, **47** (1): 1–13.

37
Strategy and people management in China – Haier as an example

Fang Lee Cooke

BACKGROUND AND CONTEXT OF HAIER[1]

Multinational companies (MNCs) emerged and developed in various ways and different timeframes, in part reflecting the specific political, economic, institutional, cultural and industrial context of the parent country. These contextual characteristics also influence the evolution of corporate strategy and culture, as well as patterns of international expansion. In this case study, we look at the transformation of a collapsing Chinese state-owned enterprise into one of the world-leading MNCs and contemplate its strategy and implications for people management.

Founded in 1984, the Chinese-owned Haier Group Corporation (Haier hereafter) is one of the largest consumer electronics and home appliances companies in the world. Haier's previous life began in the 1920s as a privately-owned refrigerator manufacturing company. The company was taken over by the government and became a state-owned enterprise following the founding of socialist China in 1949 and a strong wave of nationalisation of private businesses. Like many other state-owned enterprises, Haier suffered from poor management, dilapidated infrastructure, backward technology and uncompetitive products, and was making a loss by the mid-1980s. In order to rescue the company, in 1984 the Qingdao government appointed Mr Zhang Ruimin, who has later become one of the legendary CEOs of contemporary Chinese businesses, to take over the company and turn it around. A series of radical changes were implemented to raise the product quality, to increase the product range, and to be more customer-oriented.

Headquartered in Qingdao, Shandong province, Haier has since grown into a multinational company with an expanding global footprint of markets and a growing range of innovative products that offer better life solutions. It designs, develops, manufactures and sells products including air conditioners, computers, microwave ovens, mobile phones, refrigerators, televisions and washing machines. Haier has ten R&D centres, 24 industrial parks, 108 manufacturing plants and 66 marketing centres across the world. It is currently one of the world leaders of smart home appliances, with customisation ('smart home customised for a better life') at the core of its business strategy. Haier's rapid international expansion has been achieved through acquisitions of electronic appliance companies as well as by building greenfield subsidiaries in developed and developing countries. In 2018, Haier Group's global turnover reached 266.1 billion yuan, with a year-on-year increase of 10 per cent.

CORE VALUES

Quality and customer focus are the core values of Haier. Underpinning these values are the assumption that users are always right and 'we [Haier employees] need to constantly improve ourselves', and a strong development concept driven by entrepreneurship and innovation spirits. Haier adopts a 'successful enterprises move with the times' philosophy. Platforms are created to attract talent to continuously create value for customers.

BRAND

Haier's branding is to be the global leader of future life styles and at the same time a socially responsible corporation to improve its environmental performance by constantly designing products and services that incorporate new concepts, new technology and innovative solutions. Haier espouses to be committed to the 'Green Concept' throughout the whole value chain from conception, manufacturing, servicing to logistics and recycling, and involves a broad range of stakeholders in environmental protection.

CULTURE

Two spirits – entrepreneurship and innovation – run deep in Haier's corporate culture. Employees are expected to constantly challenge themselves and develop innovative ideas and solutions to provide users with more choice. These, Haier believes, are the two important characteristics (i.e. innovation and user choice) of Haier's sustainable development.

TECHNOLOGY

In 2015, Haier started to explore how the internet of things (IoT) could be integrated into its products and how it could extend the company's core market in large appliance products to small electronic devices through the introduction of smart appliance products.

TECHNOLOGY-ENABLED BUSINESS INNOVATION STRATEGY AND PEOPLE MANAGEMENT

From 1984 to 2019, Haier has experienced five stages of strategic development: 'brand building' (1984–91); 'diversification' (1991–98); 'internationalisation' (1998–2005); global branding (2005–12); and 'networking' (2012–now) (http://www.haier.net/en/about_haier/). In particular, Stages 4 and 5 have had the most profound impact on innovation and human resource management (HRM).

Stage 4: The 'Win–Win Model of Individual–Goal Combination'

In Stage 4, the 'Win–Win Model of Individual–Goal Combination' (Rendanheyi, 人单合一), a key management initiative, was introduced in 2005 in which employees' value realisation is integrated with the value realisation of the customer and the organisation. 'Individual' refers to the employees with two spirits emphasised by Haier: entrepreneurship and innovation. 'Goal' is the users' value. Each employee establishes a goal with users by joining a ZZJYT (*zi zhu jing ying ti*, self-autonomous operational body) and signing a contract with users. Each ZZJYT supported by the Individual–Goal Combination model is provided with resources and mechanisms to enable employees to carry out their creative activities within the entrepreneurship and innovation spirits. Each employee creates value for users in a ZZJYT to fulfil their own values. As a result, the value of the company and stakeholders are fulfilled naturally. The theoretical assumption underlying the platform ecosystem of ZZJYT is the need to shift from a Tayloristic approach of 'scientific management', characterised by traditional corporate strategy and rigid organisational structure, to a humanistic approach to management characterised by employee autonomy and empowerment in the pursuit of economies of scale and scope.

The Individual–Goal Combination model requires employees to become their own master in independent innovation. It changes the dynamics of the relationship between the employee, the company and the user. Instead of following instructions from the company, employees now follow user demand, and in many cases create users and user demand and fulfil these demands. This, Haier believes, will release the employees from being managed by corporate bureaucracy, allowing them to become self-managed with maximum autonomy, and instead of working in a large operation, being operated, they will be working in a small unit with independent operation. This model is thus perceived by Haier to be a most humanistic model. Haier's Individual–Goal Combination model aims to make innovation meet the challenges in the Internet Age. Driven by the 'user personalisation' management concept, the focus on customisation requires employees to be constantly innovative in providing tailored customer solutions. Here, value alignment between the individual employee, the company and the customer/user is the key to success.

State 5: Networking strategy

Building on Stage 4, a key management initiative in Stage 5 ('networking strategy') was for Haier to transform itself from a traditional enterprise manufacturing household appliances to a platform organisation (deemed as an ecosystem) that enables employees to become entrepreneurs and business partners (see Figure 37.1). Haier's networking strategy is essentially a customer-centric, open innovation system (co-innovate and co-create value) in response to an increasing desire for customised products and services. Its intention is to accelerate product innovation, harvest innovative ideas from the smartest minds out there, and shorten the R&D cycle by reducing the information asymmetry between the company and the user (http://www.haier.net/en/research_development/rd_System/). The deployment of the Internet (mechanism) makes this possible. The core management thinking behind this business model is to build a co-creation and win–win platform to generate values for interested parties (http://www.haier.net/en/about_haier/haier_strategy/network_strategy/).

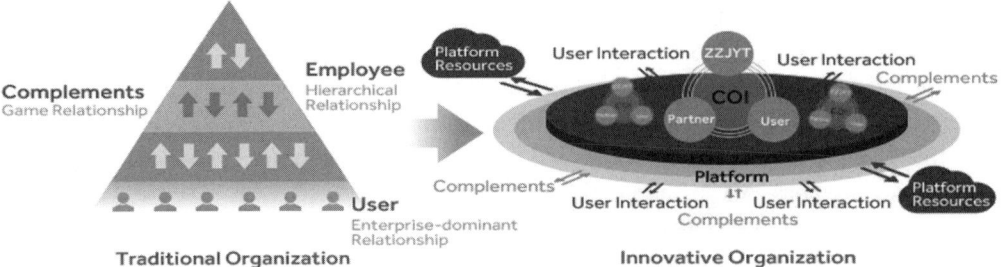

Source: http://www.haier.net/en/about_haier/one_person_alone/ (accessed on 17 February 2019, copyright of Haier).

Figure 37.1 Haier's networking system of innovation

Impact on employees and implications for HRM

In the process of Haier's transformation from a closed bureaucratic structure to an open network structure, over 100 000 managerial and supervisory employees were displaced. Employees are required to be connected through the Internet and the market, and to think of solutions continuously in order to remain in the game. To do so, employees are given autonomy to make decisions and have zero-distance interactions with co-workers and customers globally. Accompanying this fundamental shift of business model is the compensation/reward model from 'paid by the enterprise' to 'paid by the user' for the employees. Under the platform organisation model, resources are mobilised and dispersed on demand and employees become interfaces linked to resources rather than waiting for instructions from their superiors. Taking the household appliances R&D in Haier as an example, the R&D personnel have become the interface people connected to outside resources. As of 2018, Haier has over 1150 R&D interface people tapping into more than 50 000 R&D resources worldwide. In other words, many are not employees registered at the company, but 'employees' that can be consolidated online. The future for these interface people is to set up micro-enterprises as independent enterprising ventures (http://www.haier.net/en/about_haier/one_person_alone/).

Haier's objective for its latest business model is to use employees' knowledge as the capital and to allow them to become 'business partners' so that risks and profits are shared. It has practically fragmented a large organisation into many micro-entrepreneurial businesses in which employees enjoy operational autonomy and share profits, thus achieving business sustainability. Haier's platform organisation model fundamentally altered the employment relationship between the organisation and the employees. It dismantled the bureaucratic structure and the related job security, career paths and other HR benefits traditionally associated with working for a large prestigious firm. While it is unclear how successful Haier's platform organisation business model is, this model practically brings to an end the corporate career design and shifts all the risks and responsibility to individuals. Under this business model, employees become more motivated as their performance is directly related to their revenue. However, they need to develop new skills and competences, including: budgeting skills, market awareness, and an innovative and competitive mindset.

At the organisational level, a number of questions need to be asked: can platforms like this create core competitive advantage for the enterprise in a sustainable manner? Can the extension of the value chain to the market extend the lifeline of the business? Can/should a world-leading corporation place its future – innovation capability (core competence and core to its competitiveness) – in the hands of the market through its employees grouped in small teams? Who is responsible for the skill and competence development of the employees to ensure that they remain competitive? What might the implications be for the HR function? To what extent will corporate intangible resources be lost (e.g. tacit knowledge, know-how and corporate memories) when a large proportion of the managerial and supervisor workforce have been laid off? Under the business partnership model, the relationship between the employees and Haier has effectively changed from a traditional employment relationship to a transactional, contractual relationship. Without corporate shared values that bind employees together, how can collective wisdom be generated and pooled together to create more values? Who will be responsible for brand building, corporate image maintenance, and resource generation and integration?

SUMMARY

The recent changes in the business and employment model introduced by Haier, one of the world's largest white goods manufacturing companies, show that the adoption of a technology-enabled business innovation strategy may trigger business and work re-organisation, which may fundamentally impact employees' ways of thinking and working. Less bound by legal constraints and operating in a more flexible labour market, radical changes in HRM practices, including employment contracts and the labour process, may be achievable by Haier in China. Although Haier's Individual–Goal Combination model, which allows frontline employees in the company to be their own boss, is premised on Peter Drucker's motto that 'everyone can be a CEO', the long-term business and employee benefits and harms of such changes may not be evident for some time.

QUESTIONS

1. As an MNC from an emerging economy (emerging MNC), how may Haier's internationalisation and diffusion of the HRM model differ from, or even challenge, existing MNC theories?

2. What implications does Haier's business strategy have for managing its global workforce in different parts of the world?

3. What impact might Haier's core corporate value of 'users are always right and we need to constantly improve ourselves' have on employees' well-being?

4. What implications might the Individual–Goal Combination model have for employee commitment and employee engagement when a large organisation is being hollowed out?

5. In what ways may the Haier business model and HRM strategy and practices challenge existing HRM and employment relations theories?

END NOTES

1. Readers are encouraged to visit Haier's corporate website for more information: http://www.haier.net/en/about_haier/.

38
Emiratization: Benefits and challenges of strategic and radical change in the United Arab Emirates

Rachid Zeffane and Linzi Kemp

INTRODUCTION AND BACKGROUND

The United Arab Emirates (UAE) embarked on a very ambitious program of modernization, coupled with the need for major growth-driven business changes. Because of this and because of the small national population and the severe shortage of qualified local workforce, the UAE government was induced to adopt a more flexible immigration policy – hence allowing greater numbers of foreign workers into the country. These (the expatriates) now constitute the overwhelming majority of the workforce, with nationals being in the minority (Al-Waqfi and Forstenlechner, 2014).

Also, amidst its move for modernization, the UAE government also embarked on an "Emiratization" initiative in both the public and private sectors, aimed at enhancing the employment of its citizens in a meaningful and efficient manner (AME Info, 2007). As a result, multiple governmental initiatives have been actively promoting Emiratization through training and institutionalized initiatives such as the establishment of "Tawteen UAE"; the "Abu Dhabi Tawteen Council"; "Emirates Foundation"; a "Centre for Emiratization Research & Development" (Emiratization Research Foundation, 2009).

On 29 November 2010 the Ministry of Labour released Ministerial Resolution 1187 of 2010 (MR 1187), which represents a strong effort to increase the participation of UAE nationals in private sector professional roles through Emiratization. MR 1187 provides a "carrot-and-stick" approach, as while providing incentives to organizations which comply and participate, it also provides for severe penalties for non-compliance (Daleure, 2017; Ali, 2018). In essence, Emiratization is a strategy that seeks to use the country's human resources in the most favorable way in the economic process, through the transfer of skills and knowledge from expatriates to UAE nationals (citizens). Thus, Emiratization affects both public government agencies as well as private businesses. Expatriates in the UAE are currently the overwhelming majority in the working population, where non-nationals constitute 2.4 million (91 percent) of the working population (Al-Ali, 2008). An argument is that this domination in expatriate numbers in the workforce has led to insufficient emphasis on education, English, employment skills and even trust amongst the UAE nationals. It is believed that as a result the UAE nationals suffer from poor career advancement in their own country (Al-Ali, 2008). The strategic move for Emiratization, however, presents a series of challenges and issues (Toledo, 2013; Al-Waqfi and Forstenlechner, 2014).

The significant reliance on foreign workers created a distortion and segmentation of the labor market whereby the national workers became concentrated in the public sector, while close to 99 percent of the jobs in the private sector are staffed by expatriate workers. An unemployment problem among nationals started to appear despite the workforce Emiratization policy which has been implemented since the late 1990s (Al-Waqfi and Forstenlechner, 2014). In other words, the employment of a high number of non-national workers has created economic and social problems in the UAE labor market. A significant imbalance between the numbers of UAE nationals and non-nationals in the UAE labor market, in both private and public sector organizations, is considered to be a major impediment to socio-economic progress. The issue of an unbalanced labor composition was also coupled with an unemployment rate among Emiratis that by 2009 had risen to 13.4 (Gulf News, 2009a). In addition, the majority of Emiratis are currently engaged in employment in the public sector. However, the private sector controls 52 percent of all jobs in the UAE, but the Emirati strength in this sector was just 1 percent in 2009, with the exception of the banking and insurance sectors (Gulf News, 2009a). As the private sector drives the engine of business growth, it was considered imperative that more Emiratis be encouraged to join private companies.

EMIRATIZATION: FEMALES IN THE WORKFORCE

The Emiratization initiative also aimed to encourage national women into employment. The UAE Constitution states that

> social justice should apply to all and that, before the law, women are equal to men. They enjoy the same legal status, claim to titles and access to education. They have the right to practice the profession of their choice....[and] the family is the basis of society which shall be responsible for protecting childhood and motherhood. Laws shall be formulated in all fields to observe this protection and care in a way which safeguards the dignity of women.... and suitable work [for them]. (Kemp, 2008)

According to census data from 2005, 49.3 percent of the Emirati population is female, they contribute $3.4 billion to the UAE economy, and represented 13.9 percent of the total workforce in 2008 (Shallal, 2008). The literacy rate among women in the UAE rose to 88.7 percent in 1995, and by 1997, 72 percent of tertiary students were female (Kemp, 2008). However, many UAE national women do not choose to take up employment after education; legal and societal forces in the culture contribute to this scenario. Although law in the UAE states that there is equal pay for males and females, there have been claims that "at work women remain deprived of equal benefits such as housing and promotion" (Kemp, 2008). There is a suggestion that a factor in the low numbers of women in the workforce is "company restrictions on the numbers of females employed" (Shallal, 2008). A permit has to be issued by the husband before a wife can take up employment initially. There may be a personal preference to avoid the inconvenience of a career whilst running a household; also the family may raise objections to a wife, sister or daughter working. Hence, Emirati women overwhelmingly prefer public sector employment, and generally remain unemployed if their employment conditions are not met. UAE female citizens employed in the Ministry of Education and the Ministry of Health outnumber national male employees, and account for 27 percent of the civil servants within the 24 government ministries (Kemp, 2008).

Females have mainly taken up employment in the civil service, teaching, medicine, and in family businesses. In the rural and remote parts of the UAE, women's roles have been traditionally restricted to occupations where the genders do not mix, such as teaching. There are opportunities in nursing, a career where national women are not involved probably because of relatively low pay, long hours, and possibly cultural barriers of working in a mixed gender area in a rather intimate setting. In the health services, women (national and expatriate) account for 54.3 percent of the total number of employees, "one out of every three doctors, pharmacists, technicians and administrators is a woman" (Kemp, 2008). Engineering is also a career field where Sheikha Lubna Al Qasimi, a prominent UAE female politician, notes women are already established and doing well. Recent research, regarding the influences on job satisfaction amongst Emirati women, reveals that "modern Emirati women" are beginning to take up "untraditional jobs that demand they work side by side with men" (Shallal, 2008). Older Emirati women are more satisfied with their jobs than younger females, and those females with education at a higher level than secondary schooling were also more satisfied than those with only high school education (Shallal, 2008).

EMIRATIZATION: THE DRIVING FORCE FOR CHANGE

The World Bank and the International Monetary Fund have long identified unemployment as a major hindrance to development in the Gulf countries. The Gulf countries are joined together in a confederation for economic purposes called the Gulf Cooperation Council (GCC). In response to the problem of unemployment, the GCC countries, and the UAE in particular, introduced economic policies to direct national labor markets and promote their citizens' employment. In the early 1990s the UAE's council of ministers adopted Emiratization to apply to both public and private sectors, the former representing the vast majority of the workforce. Emiratization, as a strategy, is the shared responsibility of the Ministry of Labor and Social Affairs for policy matters, and the National Human Resources Development and Employment Authority ("Tanmia"), which provides UAE nationals with employment, training and development opportunities (Al-Ali, 2008).

In their endeavor, the UAE government put in place industry-based quotas for the employment of nationals. Other moves to encourage private sector Emiratization included wage subsidies, and wage restraint for government employees, as well as quotas on expatriate labor in the private sector, and employment targets for UAE nationals as a whole (TRA-Government News Services, 2010). The big push for Emiratization seems to have been met with some success over the years. For instance, Du (a telecommunication provider) recently announced that 20 percent of its workforce was now Emirati. Lloyds in the UAE also reported that just over one third of their employees are local. More recently, the National Bank of Abu Dhabi (NBAD) plans to recruit

300 UAE nationals in 2010, and increase Emiratization to 38 percent compared to 36 percent in 2009. NBAD also announced 50 percent Emiratization of its top management positions in 2009 (TRA-Government News Services, 2010). These achievements in the workforce composition have been attributed largely to the significantly higher pay levels enjoyed by nationals by comparison to expatriates performing similar jobs.

To further reinforce its drive and commitment towards Emiratization in the private sector, by June 2006 the UAE government declared that private companies must recruit nationals as human resource managers and secretarial staff (Dubai Memoir, 2006). This move created over 21 000 jobs, including the opening up of close to 700 managerial positions for nationals (Gulf News, 2009a). Private businesses were given 18 months to replace their existing non-national Human Resource and Personnel Managers with UAE nationals. Also, no further work permits were to be available for non-national secretaries. It needs to be considered that all "foreign workers" are only allowed to work in the UAE through the allocation of work permits. These permits are issued by the UAE government, and applied for by employers. The employer is then a "sponsor" of the employee; such sponsorship, once withdrawn, causes the employee to lose their right to be in the country. Foreign secretaries currently holding job contracts were allowed to remain in their jobs until the end of their limited period contracts. Furthermore, private companies would not be allowed to transfer sponsorship of secretarial staff to another employer, and they would not be issued temporary or part-time work permits. Secretaries sponsored by their husbands or parents were no longer to be issued labor cards (work permits). Following this move, the UAE Labor Ministry then announced that companies wishing to recruit UAE national secretaries would need to coordinate the changes through "Tanmia" and other human resource development programs in the Emirates.

BARRIERS TO EMIRATIZATION

Despite all the measures above, the private sector failed to meet the targets set for Emiratization. Although well received in many quarters, and to some degree successful in the public sector, the Emiratization policy was met with some resistance from various perspectives, as described below.

A barrier to private sector employment for a wider group of UAE underemployed is a negative attitude to physically demanding work. That type of work is usually performed by migrant workers, particularly in the building, roads and maintenance trades. Emiratization did not cater for the shift needed in attitude towards employment as opposed to running one's own business affairs. Employability is not a prime consideration in the minds of many local Emiratis, especially amongst young people. Even though many are willing to serve as business owners in their own economy, young Emiratis often prefer to work in the public sector (Gulf News, 2009a). The public sector is far more attractive for Emiratis as it provides superior employment conditions: remuneration, job security, hours of work, work content and generous vacations. The attractions also include an opportunity to work in the native language (Arabic), as well as an opportunity to practice "wasta" (using networks and connections) to get a job.

Work days and working hours play a part in the resistance to work in the private sector. Nationals may find unacceptable the private sector's working conditions of long and irregular hours, coupled with some restrictions on time spent on cultural and religious observances, short periods of leave, and a relatively more stringent approach to employee performance. In the UAE, the official weekend is Thursday and Friday; however, many of the UAE's smaller private workplaces close only on Friday, and perhaps for a half day on Thursday. By contrast, government offices run on relatively shorter working hours (7.30 am to 2.30 pm) Saturday to Wednesday. Furthermore, private sector offices tend to keep longer hours (often 8 am to 5 pm). Such time considerations are important in a nation that culturally places commitments to family above working obligations.

There is also the issue of retention or attrition of national employees. Due to the low numbers of available Emiratis in the population, demand exceeds supply. Qualified Emiratis can easily move from job to job as they are sought by employers throughout the economy. It is claimed that over 10 percent of Emiratis resigned from the private sector in 2008 because of social and cultural factors (Al-Ali, 2008). A study conducted by "Tanmia" reported that three out of five Emiratis resigned from corporate positions due to a lack of career progression and the absence of a mentoring culture.

OVERCOMING RESISTANCE TO EMIRATIZATION

In order to build Emirati nationals' leadership and management potential, to manage the country's future development, the public service retreated from its habitual full employment policy. This then forced new graduates to seek work in the seemingly less attractive/less financially beneficial private sector.

A preference for the public sector is overwhelming, and has been demonstrated by several studies on attitudes and preferences of Emiratis towards employment (Al-Ali, 2008). Most of these studies have shown that in addition to the work style preferences, compensation was an important obstacle to private sector employment of Emiratis. To reinforce its commitment, the government allowed wage disparities, enabling Emirati citizens to earn more than expatriates who performed the same job role in private sector firms. This earnings differential is implemented by adding a substantial pay allowance to the earnings of citizens working in the private sector. The head of Emiratisation at Lloyds claims Emiratis receive, on average, 35 percent of their basic salary as a national allowance (Sakhri, 2010). This is considered to be good practice for the purpose of increasing the number of UAE citizens working in the private sector, especially in jobs based in an office environment and in a management position. Several sectors (such as insurance) run a separate Emirati salary structure, which affords higher pay to nationals in order to attract them. This strategy is controversial and there are various viewpoints. To some, adding a national allowance to the salary of citizens working in the private sector makes the jobs more lucrative and will help the UAE in the long run, as the economy diversifies away from its reliance on oil/tourism/hydrocarbons. Others see a salary differential as a hindrance (or burden) to the principle of equity and fairness, which may trigger lower motivation of expatriates performing similar jobs, particularly at managerial levels. The views on this point vary greatly. While some are supportive of the policy, some express neutrality, and others are reserved or critical of the policy. Below are sample excerpts of the viewpoints (Gulf News, 2009b).

Viewpoints in support of the initiative

It makes sense when you recruit UAE nationals and pay them more. They add value, they are productive in the long run and they have a lot to contribute to the organization.

Hiring Emiratis in the private sector and paying them more makes great sense because they are better at navigating bureaucracy, have contacts in government and are more proficient at interpreting the country's changing labor laws.

This is a good chance for UAE nationals. UAE is their country and they should be the ones to serve it to their best abilities. Provided they have the drive and are really willing to work in all fields, and not choosy with regards to the time, pressure at work.

As a UAE citizen, I salute the government for this decision. For all expatriates: you should be grateful this country took you on its peaceful grounds for so long and gave you jobs and packages you wouldn't get in your own country. We are not responsible for your future, your country is.

What a great decision. I am a post graduate with 10 years' experience, currently working in the construction industry. All nationals are most welcome to take my job. Salary Dhs. 3500. Working Hours: 12 hrs/day and 6 days/week.

Neutral viewpoints

Expatriates say that the move will leave them jobless, while others say it will help train UAE nationals to become competitive in various fields of work.

Emiratization needs to be implemented on a broader horizon without causing loss to other people. At the end of the day it is the nationals who have to take care of their country.

Well this is a great opportunity for all nationals to contribute their knowledge and abilities to their own country, but why only as HR managers or secretaries? The best thing we could do is to "give and take" so that everyone can work for a living. Hiring manpower in general requires knowledgeable capacity to do the job and move the organization on for individual growth.

I'm in favor of Emiratization. It will be beneficial for the government but have an adverse effect on the private sector. Salaries, days of work per week and training are likely to be affected. The government should give a gesture of goodwill to all affected expatriates and allow them to renew their visa for other available jobs that may suit them best.

Viewpoints expressing reservations about the policy

The government has to challenge mentalities and change many wrong perceptions of the aspiring UAE nationals as well as that of the private sector. They should do this by engaging both and not imposing heavy-handed decisions.

Emiratization at any cost might not pay off at the end. Qualification and experience should be looked at as well, not only nationality.

This type of plan will never resolve the employment problem nor will the younger generation want to do anything creative with their lives. The current generation of nationals should be given opportunities but not things served on a plate, such that they don't improve or aspire or dream.

The most qualified person should be the one who receives the job opportunity. All the effort exerted into selling "Dubai as a World friendly place", has just been reduced to, "Go home, we don't want you here".

As a HR professional, I would have had a more positive reaction to the announcement if the government had instead proclaimed their affiliation with colleges and universities in the Gulf to offer Human Resource Management courses and programs to properly train prospective managers in HR.

I think it's unfair for the people who have been working for the development of the UAE for many years. They spend their life here. There should be opportunities for nationals to get a job but not if it means replacing people.

I am not against the concept of prioritizing UAE Nationals when it comes to hiring but replacing the people already working for a company by an Emirati is unjust.

Employment should be given on the basis of qualification and capabilities irrespective of race and culture.

CONCLUSION/SUMMARY

National change strategies designed to encourage and support the employment of nationals are quite prevalent throughout the Middle East, with countries such as Oman, Saudi Arabia and the United Arab Emirates adopting such initiatives (Rees et al., 2007).
    In the case of the UAE, it still seems that despite the great efforts made, the situation remains more or less the same and the issue remains a challenge (Rees et al., 2007; Toledo, 2013). The reality is that most private companies in the Arabian Gulf still do not hire nationals and changing

that attitude will take more time. Nationals continue to shy away from the private sector because of long working hours, lower pay, and relative insensitivity to their religious customs. When seeking employment, UAE nationals are often loath to consider the private sector's working conditions and compensation levels. More recently, government officials complained that private firms were failing to live up to their Emiratization commitments and were unable to retain nationals. The complaints were that private companies often hired Emiratis as quota-fillers, "following the letter of the law but not its spirit" (Shaheen, 2008).

It seems that employers faced complicated situations with the younger and inexperienced Emiratis who often assume that expatriates in general are more willing to work long hours at a substantially lower wage (AME Info, 2006). Emiratization to some degree has failed in the task of instilling effective work habits in young Emiratis, particularly in some industries. UAE companies may need to reconsider strategies currently in force internally to grow a more skill-based Emirati workforce. Some of the broader and more complex challenges are also issues relating to effective organizational commitment, quantitative evaluation methods, resistance to change and the role of expatriates in implementing Emiratization programs (Rees et al., 2007).

Action, and more importantly, preparation, needs to be undertaken by businesses now in order to achieve desirable success in Emiratization. While there is general agreement over the importance of Emiratization for social, economic and political reasons, there is also some contention as to the impact of localization on organizational efficiency. It is yet unknown whether, and the extent to which, employment of nationals will generate corporate and economic returns. Clearly, Emiratization is not always seen as advantageous for the corporate sector as the take up/ follow through is insignificant. The effectiveness of an Emiratization strategy is not yet evident as its success depends largely on the array of contingent factors discussed above.

QUESTIONS

1. What change management considerations arise for public and private sector managers as a result of the Emiratization policy?

2. If you were a private employer, what would your internal strategies be to retain nationals in your workforce?

3. Imagine yourself as an expatriate manager. How would Emiratization affect your role with your national managerial colleagues?

4. What are the steps needed to adopt an effective policy of Emiratization, taking into account the barriers perceived by younger and female generational citizens?

REFERENCES

Al-Ali, J. (2008), Emiratisation: drawing UAE nationals into their surging economy. *International Journal of Sociology and Social Policy*, **28**(9/10), 365–79.

Al Awadhi, A. (2010), Emiratisation of workforce "pillar of growth", accessed May 2010 at http://www.uaeinteract.com/docs/Emiratisation_of_workforce_pillar_of_growth/41096.htm.

Al-Waqfi, Mohammed. A. and Ingo Forstenlechner (2014), Barriers to Emiratization: the role of policy design and institutional environment in determining the effectiveness of Emiratization, *The International Journal of Human Resource Management*, **25**(2), 167–89.

Ali, Ahmed (2018), New UAE emiratisation regulations, International Briefings, IFLR/March 2011, accessed November 2018 at http://www.afridi-angell.com/items/limg/uaeemiratisation1.pdf.

AME Info (2006), accessed May 2010 at http://www.ameinfo.com/79535.html (March).

AME Info (2007), accessed May 2010 at http://www.ameinfo.com/133128.html (September).

Daleure, G. (2017), Emiratization progress and challenges. In: *Emiratization in the UAE Labor Market*. Singapore: Springer.

Emiratization Research Foundation (2009), Newsletter, accessed May 2010 at http://www.jumeirah.com/en/Jumeirah-Group/The-Emirates-Academy/Emiratization-Research--Development/.

Gulf News (2009a), New emiratisation drive, accessed May 2010 at http://gulfnews.com/news/gulf/uae/employment/new-Emiratization-drive-1.242285.

Gulf News (2009b), Have your say: Emiratisation move, accessed May 2010 at http://gulfnews.com/opinions/your-say/have-your-say-Emiratization-move-1.242277.

Kemp, L.J. (2008), Tejari.com, "the Middle East Online Marketplace", under the leadership of Sheika Lubna Al Qasimi, *International Journal of Leadership Studies*, **4**(1), 22–37.

Rees, Christopher J., Aminu Mamman and Aysha Bin Braik (2007), Emiratization as a strategic HRM change initiative: case study evidence from a UAE petroleum company, *The International Journal of Human Resource Management*, **18**(1), 33–53.

Sakhri, R. (2010), Pay Gulf nationals more than expats – experts, *Gulf News*, 28 April.

Shaheen, K. (2008), Government attacks Emiratisation laggards, *The National*, May.

Shallal, M. (2008), Jobs for Emiratis, accessed May 2010 at http://emiratisation.org/index.php?option=com_content&view=article&id=275%3Awomen-shattering-job-barriers&catid=96%3Aaugus-2009&Itemid=67&lang=en.

Toledo, H. (2013), The political economy of emiratization in the UAE, *Journal of Economic Studies*, **40**(1), 39–53.

TRA-Government News Services (2010), Mohammed instructs government entities to open door for national job-seekers, 30 March 2010, accessed May 2010 at http://www.uaeinteract.com/docs/Mohammed_instructs_government_entities_to_open_door_for_national_job-seekers/40351.htm.

39
Survival and outsourcing in the South African clothing and textiles industry: The changing fortunes of ClothTran

Christine Bischoff and Geoffrey Wood

THE CONTEXT

Many developing and mature economies (including the UK and Australia) have come to accept industrial decline as an irreversible fact. Yet, although industrial production has increasingly become concentrated in a handful of economies (most notably, China and Germany), a number of other economies have managed to retain significant industrial sectors. South Africa's relative fortunes have been mixed. Whilst the country has been very successful in the exports of minerals, food products (notably deciduous fruit and wine) and motor cars and components, many other sectors have not fared nearly as well. Historically South Africa had an extremely large clothing and textile industry; however, in recent years, many firms have been forced to close, and others to radically downsize in the face of low-cost Chinese imports.

Under apartheid, the government relied very heavily on gold exports; when the gold price declined in the 1980s, serious economic problems resulted, exacerbated by successive waves of popular resistance, sanctions and the inefficiencies of the system. The apartheid government had pursued an active industrial policy, leading to a heavily protected and often inefficient manufacturing sector. Although the latter provided large-scale employment, low wages, racial discrimination and associated inequalities in skills and access to training led to relatively low productivity. As one South African HR manager remarked, firms used to solve problems 'through throwing cheap labour at it', rather than using labour intelligently (cf. Wood and Els, 2000). Domestically manufactured goods were often of low quality, outdated and expensive.

The rise of independent trade unions in the 1980s, and the increasing inefficiencies of the system, challenged the dominant production paradigm. This led to a shift from very low-wage unskilled production centring on a racial division of labour to higher wage production, with the associated skilling of the black labour force. Hence, South Africa was shifting from a low-wage, low-skill economy to a more intermediate one. This process has been marked by large-scale job shedding, as employers reap the rewards of very much higher productivity and as less competitive firms went under.

Democratization in 1994 led to the principal liberation movement, the African National Congress (ANC) attaining power. Despite union backing, the economic policies adopted were largely neo-liberal. The ANC committed itself to the liberalization of trade in line with WTO regulations, the phasing out of import tariffs and export subsidies. In some areas – such as motor car manufacturing – the process was carefully managed, leading to the sector becoming highly competitive; in others, such as clothing and textiles, this was not the case (Wood and Glaister, 2008). The South African economy has enjoyed sustained growth despite the global recession from 1994 onwards; yet some estimates of South African unemployment are as high as 36.7 per cent, which is using the expanded definition of unemployment and includes people who have stopped looking for work (Statistics South Africa, 2018).

THE INDUSTRY

The South African clothing and textile industry has faced major problems, not only as a result of reduced tariff barriers, but also because of large-scale illegal imports. More specifically, the industry has had to contend with a flood of Chinese imports, in some instances at prices that appear difficult to comprehend, even in terms of the costs of raw material inputs only; one employer has claimed that at one stage, Chinese made T-shirts were being landed in Cape Town for as little as 1 GBP, and men's suits for 10 GBP.

Moreover, certain constituent fabrics can be imported duty free by manufacturers. Such fabrics can constitute up to 40 per cent of the cost of the finished production item. Although in theory it is only constituent fabrics that are not produced in South Africa that may be imported duty free, this is very difficult to police. There are many small and medium sized textile factories in the country and officials lack the capacity to inspect the usage of imported materials regularly. This means that much of the value generated in production accrues abroad. In addition to wholesale smuggling, Chinese fabrics and finished garments are often under-invoiced to reduce the amount of import duties payable.

In order to compete with Chinese imports, many South African clothing manufacturers need duty-free fabric and so agreed to the Southern African Development Community's (SADC) two-stage conversion process (that is, a local manufacturer has to source the fabrics within the region as well as manufacture the product locally). However, many clothing manufacturers in South Africa have moved away from this as Mauritius, one of the SADC countries, are yet to adhere to the process (Muradzikwa, 2001). Mauritius has also lifted restrictions on the employment of foreigners and now imports labour from Bangladesh. In some Mauritian clothing manufacturing companies, such as Firemount Textiles in Goodlands, northern Mauritius, Bangladeshi employees outnumber local employees (Ackbarally, 2016), which contravenes the SADC agreement, making the two-stage conversion process a difficult one to police.

To stabilize employment levels in clothing manufacturing companies and to increase competitiveness, the South African Department of Trade and Industry introduced the Clothing and Textiles Competitiveness Programme (CTCP). Funding assistance is provided via the Industrial Development Corporation to clothing manufacturing companies who need to invest in their competitiveness. Under the Competitiveness Improvement Programme (CIP) incentive programme, manufacturing clusters are created, which aim 'to build and improve capacity and competitiveness in manufacturers and designers through related value chains to effectively supply their customers locally and internationally'. The Ordinary Cluster is composed of a group of a minimum of five manufacturing companies or a mixture of manufacturing and associated organisations, for example, retailers, design houses and component manufacturers (Industrial Development Corporation).

The South African clothing and textiles industry has historically been very heavily unionized. The dominant union in the industry, the South African Clothing and Textiles Workers Union (SACTWU) represents a merger of several unions, from both the radical independent union tradition (notably from the Johannesburg region), and a large, bureaucratic service-orientated and compliant union (with a strong base in Cape Town and to a lesser extent, Kwa-Zulu Natal). SACTWU has faced major challenges owing to an imploding membership base as a result of large-scale job losses in the sector. SACTWU is a member of the Congress of South African Trade Unions (COSATU), which is in formal alliance with South Africa's ruling party, the African National Congress. Relations between unions and government have in recent years been somewhat variable. The unions played a central role in the ousting of President Mbeki, but relations with the former President Zuma were, at times, also fraught; the ANC remains wedded to broadly neo-liberal macro-economic policies, even under President Ramaphosa. Whatever political influence SACTWU enjoys does not appear to have been sufficient for the government to take concerted action against the dumping of textiles by Chinese producers into the South African market. SACTWU's membership includes large representation by members of ethnic minorities (coloured/mixed racial origin and Asian); the majority of the latter do not vote for the ANC, and this may have diminished SACTWU's political clout. SACTWU is committed to supporting local goods.

SACTWU is a major shareholder in Hosken Consolidated Investment Limited (HCI), which is a black empowerment company. HCI has investments in many industries including hotel and leisure, interactive gaming; media and broadcasting; transport; mining and properties. HCI purchased a clothing company called Seardel in 2008, which gave the trade union an indirect stake in the company. When Seardel closed their remaining apparel divisions, SACTWU resolved to safeguard jobs in the sector and so a company called TCI Apparel was established in 2014, protecting 2274 jobs in the sector. The Seardel assets are now accommodated in Trade Call Investments Apparel (TCIA) and SACTWU is the owner.

Ebrahim Patel, currently serving as the Minister of Economic Development, is also head of the Industrial Development Corporation, and its Development Funds Department administers the CTCP. Minister Patel was General Secretary of SACTWU from 1999 to 2009. In 2008 he was instrumental in obtaining the R250 million capital injection needed to rescue the Seardel Group from insolvency.

In 2018, South Africa celebrates the centenary birth of the first president of democratic South Africa, Nelson Mandela. A 'Mandela centenary T-shirt' has been made for this special event. The manufacturing of the T-shirt is interesting: most of the value added was concentrated in a factory in Mauritius which is owned by SACTWU, called Star Knitwear, which was bought in 2015. The cotton for the T-shirt was grown in Madagascar, it was spun, knitted and dyed in Mauritius and finally the cloth was cut and stitched in South Africa. The wages of Mauritian workers are far lower than South African wages and they are paid per item produced. Workers in South Africa are paid by the hour (Arde, 2018).

THE CASE STUDY ORGANIZATION

The case study organization, ClothTran, historically was a medium sized company. The company was heavily unionized. Over the period 2005–2006, the company was forced to undergo a major downsizing exercise, ending up as a Small Enterprise. The owner of the firm blames this forced downsizing on high labour costs, and what, he claimed, was a 'negative' attitude by the union. The company also moved most production away from the Gauteng Province (the greater Johannesburg/Pretoria region), South Africa's major industrial centre, where wages are relatively high. Some operations were outsourced to the Durban area of KwaZulu Natal, and others to Swaziland. The company retained its design operations in-house in Johannesburg.

Swaziland is a geographical neighbour of South Africa and is one of the last absolute monarchies in the world. The Swazi government has a very poor reputation when it comes to labour and general political rights. The country is significantly poorer than South Africa, and, with high unemployment and poor social protection, workers are in a very poor bargaining position. In order to circumnavigate the remaining protective tariffs, a number of Chinese clothing manufacturers have set up operations in Swaziland; many such operations have a reputation for extremely poor labour standards which, arguably, have had the effect of driving labour standards down further in established locally owned competitors (Similane, 2008). Even though the Taiwanese companies are major employers of Swazi labour, ClothTran has increased its labour force in Swaziland but restricts its unionized South African labour force to just 80.

ISSUES IN EMPLOYMENT PRACTICES

The firm currently pays wages somewhat higher than the industry norms; in part this represents a historical legacy from when the organization was very much larger and the union in a stronger position. ClothTran's owner claims that the current wage levels paid to his blue collar South African employees are far too high. In addition, in South Africa, employers have to extend certain fringe benefits – for example, paid public holiday leave and paid sick leave – that were again 'far too high' in relation to those enjoyed in competitor producing nations. He furthermore believes that, in response to this situation, most employers simply choose not to obey the law and that it is the Cut, Make and Trim (CMT) companies which are most guilty of this. Those who choose to play by the rules of the game reap few rewards and are simply penalized; enforcement mechanisms are weak.

Despite intense competition from China, South African textile employers lack unity. Indeed, a major employer association ceased operations in 2009. ClothTran's owner argues that the dominant union in the sector, SACTWU, lacks strategic vision and is primarily concerned with protecting jobs. However, SACTWU also faces competition from other trade unions. The National Union of Metalworkers of South Africa (NUMSA) is recruiting clothing manufacturing workers and so encroaching on SACTWU's territory. This is due to the fact that NUMSA was part of COSATU and it adopted an industrial approach to organizing workers. NUMSA was expelled from COSATU in 2014 and is now part of a new federation, namely the South African Federation of Trade Unions. NUMSA now adopts a 'value chain' approach to organizing workers. NUMSA justifies its position by citing an international example of a metal trade union, namely IF Metall in Sweden, which also organizes workers in the clothing sector.

The owner of the case study organization argues that SACTWU goes direct to government when confronted with a problem, rather than negotiating with employers; hence, the union appears unresponsive to the legitimate concerns of owners. On the other hand, it is clear that the union's position has been greatly weakened through downsizing across the industry, and it would, perhaps, have been surprising had it not sought all the assistance it could get from whatever quarter.

ClothTran's owner claims that employers are over-burdened with too many restrictions under the law. This includes restrictions on the ability to fire, union organizing rights, and leave entitlements. More specifically, he argues that the statutory dispute resolution mechanism, the Commission for Conciliation, Mediation and Arbitration (CCMA) 'goes too far' in protecting the interests of workers. Little heed is taken of the interests of employers and the difficulties firms face in surviving. Yet, whilst employers are restricted by what they can do under the law, little is done to control cut-throat competition from abroad.

Despite reservations towards both the union and the CCMA, ClothTran pays above the legally binding minimum wage for the industry and the owner reports that salaries for clothing manufacturing workers have increased by 7 per cent year on year. In contrast, many other employers do not comply with the law in this regard. The owner notes that most Cut, Make and Trim (CMT) operations do not comply at all. High unemployment means that there are many desperate job-seekers who are prepared to conspire with employers in breaching the law. Moreover, whilst ClothTran does provide leave for statutory holidays, as well as vacation leave, this is often not the case. ClothTran's owner claims that many smaller employers in the industry work 234 days a year, including over weekends during busy periods without necessarily granting over-time pay. In some respects, he believes the latter is justified, in that firms face intense pressures, and regulatory authorities take little notice of the need for firms to remain cost-competitive during busy periods. As a result, 'the only compliant companies are big firms'. The owner says that Trade Call Investments have become the largest clothing manufacturer in South Africa, employing approximately 2500 workers.

Collective bargaining within the clothing and textiles industry in South Africa is centralized and takes place within the statutory Bargaining Council. In practice, the Council is dominated by larger employers and the principal unions; smaller employers believe the body is unresponsive to their concerns and lack vision in promoting the viability of the industry, or, indeed, taking action when major firms close. In response, many smaller employers have partially disengaged from the process, giving up on hopes to impact on bargaining outcomes and, in return, ignoring aspects of agreements, even if, formally speaking, this is illegal.

ClothTran's owner believes that the principal HR problem his firm faces is still the sheer cost of labour. Whilst the union is seeking to narrow wage gaps across the industry, around what is known as the 'Newcastle wage', wages are already, he believes, far too high in South Africa. In neighbouring Lesotho, wages are still lower than they are in South Africa and similar wages rates are the norm in Swaziland, making relocation 'very attractive for South African employers': a significant number have exercised this option.

KEY ISSUES

A number of issues emerge from the case study. First, the firm – and the industry – have a historical legacy of high unionization. Indeed, during the late apartheid years, the union was able to extract significant gains from employers. Whilst wholesale job losses have undermined the position of the union, it has been able to leverage its residual position to mount a rearguard action in defence of labour standards. From a management perspective, this is 'unrealistic' given the grave competitive pressures facing the industry. Yet, from a union perspective, the central aim remains defending labour standards and jobs. And, if employers disengage from the collective bargaining system and are only hostile to unions, their chances of extracting concessions and promoting the industry at large may diminish even more. Nonetheless, it could be argued that, given that both employers and the union are so occupied with survival, there is little time for long-term strategic planning at both industry and firm level.

The case study organization's people management strategy can broadly be described as *contingent*, rather than benchmarked against an abstract set of *best practices*. It has two central dimensions. The first is to retain core knowledge in-house, retaining established HR policies and procedures, including paying more than industry norms. The latter reflects first a desire to retain specific sets of core competencies and, secondly, owing to a historical legacy of adversarial employment relations, a desire to avoid sustained confrontations with the union. The second – given perceived difficulties in dealing with the union, perceived over-regulation, wage costs, and the unresponsiveness of the Bargaining Council system – has been to outsource as much of the production as possible. In other words, to resolve HR problems by 'getting rid of them'. In the end, it is design and ideas that remained firmly in-house, with as much as possible of the process of production being outsourced to low-cost, more peripheral producers. This model has become increasingly common in a wide range of industries. Indeed, this has led some commentators to argue that there has been a rise of 'virtual firms', which have increasingly little to do with products that bear their name and incorporate their ideas. Outsourcing does, of course, impose a range of costs, ranging from a potential loss of skills and expertise, less direct control over quality, a less close integration between design and production, and low morale among remaining employees as a result of redundancies. However, in a context of intense competition from abroad, and apparent regulatory failures, the range of policy alternatives appears limited.

QUESTIONS

1. To what extent are the problems experienced by ClothTran really the fault of unions? Why do you think the employer blames unions for the problems experienced?

2. Critically discuss the risks associated with outsourcing production to Swaziland and Durban? What alternatives could there be?

3. Are there any alternative HR strategies that the firm could have employed to the ones presently utilized? What would these be?

4. 'Governments should have no role in protecting industries that cannot compete on global markets'. Critically discuss this statement.

REFERENCES

Ackbarally, N. (2016). 'Mauritius: Migrant workers driving manufacturing', *African Business Magazine*, 21 November, accessed at https://africanbusinessmagazine.com/sectors/finance/mauritius-migrant-workers-driving-manufacturing/.

Arde, G. (2018). 'Mandela centenary T-shirt should surely be 100% South African', *Business Day*, 8 June, accessed at https://www.iol.co.za/capetimes/news/million-sales-target-for-must-have-mandela-t-shirt-15368754.

Muradzikwa, S. (2001). 'Prospects for the clothing and textile industry in Zimbabwe: The implications of the SADC trade protocol'. *Policy Brief* No. 00/P7. Development Policy Research Unit, University of Cape Town.

Similane, X. (2008). 'Textiles and employee relations in Swaziland', *Employee Relations*, **30**(4): 452–65.

Statistics South Africa (2018). 'Quarterly Employment Statistics (QES), March 2018'. *PO277 Statistical Release*. Pretoria.

Wood, G. and Els, C. (2000). 'The making and remaking of HRM: The practice of managing people in the Eastern Cape Province, South Africa', *International Journal of Human Resource Management*, **11**(1): 112–25.

Wood, G. and Glaister, K. (2008). 'Union power and new managerial strategies', *Employee Relations*, **30**(4): 436–51.

40
Cultural and logistical preparation of expatriates

William Despotovic

BACKGROUND

HerbalCeuticals was established in 1986 to manufacture and sell high quality herbal supplements and vitamins within the Australian market. Over the last 10 years their Australian operations have been performing well. HerbalCeuticals' growth has been possible due to their capacity to keep up with market trends and use of evidence-based research in the development of their herbal supplements and vitamins. HerbalCeuticals' product line is highly regarded by both consumers and their respective suppliers. Until 2010 HerbalCeuticals operated from Brisbane; however, they have since expanded operations, with several smaller offices and distribution centres located across the country. In 2013 HerbalCeuticals attempted to enter the market in the People's Republic of China but failed due to a number of bad business dealings with suppliers, which left their small sales office and distribution centre with a poor reputation. HerbalCeuticals had failed to understand and acknowledge the cultural differences when working in a new context and struggled to form and sustain long-standing relationships with local stakeholders. The owners of the company, Bella and Sasha, admit they were very naive about the challenges of operating in new cultural environments and knew very little about the politics, business practices and social customs required to operate successfully in China. Bella and Sasha acknowledge that they were very aggressive in their business style and short-term focused, and did not work satisfactorily with their local partners in establishing trust and long-term relationships.

Following their success domestically within Australia, HerbalCeuticals now plan again to attempt to establish a presence within the Asian market and intend to start this new venture by setting up their first subsidiary in South Korea. Following a viability analysis and market analysis undertaken by HerbalCeuticals, South Korea was revealed to be the ideal location due to relative ease of establishment and high consumer demand for quality herbal supplements and vitamins. This new office will be responsible for first introducing their product range to the South Korean market and then in the long-term, for using South Korea as a base for expanding into the neighbouring countries of China and Japan.

CONTEXT

HerbalCeuticals has recently selected and promoted one of their Sales Managers, aged 27, to the role of Director of Asia-Pacific Sales. Prior to starting her role in HerbalCeuticals Mila had worked for a large Sydney-based pharmaceuticals company. Management at HerbalCeuticals felt that although Mila had not worked in South Korea previously, she was well suited to the role because of her knowledge about the company, experience in sales and also because her role at her previous employer required her to travel regularly to New Zealand and the United Kingdom. Mila was known to be assertive, to take pride in her work, and to complete projects on schedule, by any means necessary. Since her appointment to her new role at HerbalCeuticals, Mila has been tasked with starting up and managing the South Korean subsidiary. It was expected that Mila's role will require her to remain in South Korea for a period of at least two years. During this time Mila would be in charge of the whole office and would report to Sasha and Bella on a fortnightly basis. As expected, Mila has been advised that this promotion necessitates that herself and her fiancé, River, relocate to live and work in South Korea. Mila has always dreamed of living and working in Asia – a dream not shared by her partner River, who had imagined himself living in Europe.

PREPARING FOR THE MOVE

HerbalCeuticals offered to pay for Mila and River's personal belongings to be shipped from Australia to South Korea. While the company paid for the shipping, Mila had to pack and arrange all the logistics as well as complete the relevant import and export documentation with customs and border security. Throughout this process Mila continued to work in her old sales job and managed the process of training two Australia-based employees. Neither Mila nor River had sufficient time to really learn a lot about South Korea other than what they briefly saw on a travel show one evening. Beyond paying for shipping, HerbalCeuticals did not have any further involvement in the international move. Bella and Sasha felt that little assistance was required, given that Mila had sufficient technical expertise and had previously worked overseas.

CULTURE SHOCK

When Mila and River arrived at Seoul airport after their long flight from Brisbane they felt exhausted. They were greeted by one of the local business partners who offered to take them to their temporary accommodation. The first few months of starting up the new office were very busy for Mila. Her first order of business was to find a new office location and to recruit and select ten new staff members including administration support, a small sales team and a finance officer. Mila and River were also required to find their more permanent accommodation, which was difficult as all of the apartments they saw were either too small or were not very well kept and had mildew. They finally settled on a nice one-bedroom apartment near Mila's work.

Three months had passed since Mila and River had arrived in Seoul. Mila awoke one Monday. 'Time to get ready for work', she thought. She prepared toast and coffee for herself. She drank her bitter instant coffee and ate the bread, which was sweet. 'This is not like it is back home', she thought. Buying groceries was hard; River had complained numerous times about how difficult it was to find good quality breakfast food and how he really missed having vegemite and avocados on toast. Mila changed into her light jacket and stepped outside in the bitingly cold air. Neither she nor River had yet adjusted to the cold of winter. The winter clothes and personal belongings they had shipped from Brisbane hadn't yet arrived and they found this troublesome as most of the clothes in the shops in South Korea didn't fit them well. Things were tough beyond just the weather, she thought to herself. The food was unfamiliar and was often very spicy and fishy. It was hard trying to communicate that she had asthma and couldn't eat spicy food. Her thoughts ran on further. As she walked to work Mila thought to herself that there was a bizarre duality in Korean society. She thought about how ironic it was that technologically Korea was so well advanced yet as she walked she had to navigate the exposed electrical wires on the ground and hanging loosely overhead. 'That would never be allowed in Australia', she thought to herself. She also couldn't quite understand the dichotomy of how immaculately homes were presented yet the streets were littered with cigarette butts, empty bottles, urine and spit. Living in a non-English speaking environment was a daily challenge. Simple tasks such as shopping for groceries and asking for directions became burdensome chores.

River too was experiencing challenges. Since first learning about their relocation, River had intended on pursuing work in IT and was excited about the prospect of working in metropolitan Seoul. River had assumed that working in such a technologically advanced location would advance his career upon their return to Australia after two years. Unfortunately, prior to relocating from Australia, River had failed to realise that he required a special working visa. Once Mila and River had arrived in Seoul he struggled to apply for work. Most roles required Korean language proficiency and the limited roles that were in English-speaking organisations required a special working visa. Upon realising this, River commenced the visa application process. While waiting for the outcome, River thought he might be proactive and engage in the expatriate community. He found a local group that met socially every week. He attended two of the events but found that they were largely dominated by trailing female spouses and their children. He felt isolated and as if he didn't quite fit in. River never returned. Given his difficulties in making friends and obtaining employment, River was beginning to question the merit of relocating to Seoul.

Mila stood amidst the hustle and bustle of the Seoul Metropolitan subway system awaiting her train. Despite the enormous number of people surrounding her, she felt isolated. She silently pondered whether she had made the right decision to move. Mila was in two minds. Part of her enjoyed the thrill and challenge of being somewhere foreign but another part of her felt that this thrill and challenge was also weighing heavily upon her. Mila had been working long weeks and was feeling exhausted because of all of the after-hours socialising with clients and suppliers that was required as part of doing business in Korea. Mila hadn't had a chance to do any travelling and sightseeing and rarely spent quality time with River. Mila had also intended to attend language classes and make friends through various expatriate groups; however she found she just didn't have the time. Despite all of the long hours and hard work she was also finding that there were a number of work challenges that were adversely affecting her. She felt she wasn't being taken seriously or treated professionally because of her young age and gender. She found that communicating with Korean colleagues was difficult and she could never accurately gauge what they were thinking. She wondered whether her Korean male colleagues expected her to be more reserved, timid and submissive in her business dealings. She had seen many of her female colleagues be very subordinate towards their older male counterparts. 'Do I need to change who I am?', she reflected. There were other incidents, both big and small, that had made her last few months frustrating. To Mila it felt that living and working in Korea was like being on another planet. She had made a lot of sacrifices knowing that the career move might be of benefit for her when she returned to the home office. Mila thought deeply. 'Should I pack everything and return to the home office in Brisbane or should I somehow stay and try to finish the assignment?'. Mila was beginning to feel homesick and was missing being around her friends and family in Brisbane. Given how wonderful she thought things were to begin with in Seoul, it was a mystery to her as to how things had got to this point.

SUMMARY

Although Mila has relevant technical expertise and has previously worked overseas, Sasha and Bella now have some reservations about how well she is performing in South Korea. Sasha and Bella had received word from a trusted supplier that Mila was not coping so well. They have heard about the challenges faced at work and outside of work for Mila as well as River and are concerned that Mila might be struggling and experiencing culture shock. After failing in their expansion into China in 2013, Bella and Sasha are nervous about the prospect of making any further losses if Mila fails to adapt, which affects relationships with customers, suppliers and other business contacts and networks.

QUESTIONS

1. What are some of the work and non-work issues or challenges that Mila has experienced?

2. What cultural and logistical assistance could HerbalCeuticals have provided to better aid Mila's adjustment to life and work in South Korea?

3. What kind of factors might determine the extent to which training or support could be provided?

4. When should such training or support have been provided?

5. What could Mila and River have done themselves to aid their adjustment to life and work in South Korea?

6. Why is training or preparation necessary for life and work abroad?

SECTION VIII
GLOBAL LABOUR RIGHTS

41
Labor practices in Apple's supply chains in China

Jenny Chan

BACKGROUND AND CONTEXT

By early August 2018, Apple had transformed itself from a tiny producer of computers in a garage in 1976 to the world's most valuable publicly traded company, with a market capitalization that surpassed US$1 trillion. To put the US$1 trillion valuation in perspective, Apple's worth is more than the economies of Saudi Arabia, Switzerland and Taiwan. During fiscal 2018 (ended 29 September), Apple's fastest growth came in the Americas, followed by Europe, with annual gains surpassing 42 percent in the Americas and 23.5 percent in Europe, while Greater China generated nearly 20 percent of revenues (see Figure 41.1). Apple's net sales (US$265.6 billion) increased 16 percent or US$36.4 billion during 2018 compared to 2017, primarily driven by growth in services (digital content and customer services) and higher sales of iPhone.

Looking back, during the 1990s Apple had exported all of its manufacturing jobs overseas, its only remaining production site being a Mac assembly factory in Ireland. This outsourcing means that Apple's success is inseparable from the contributions of its suppliers and their workers to produce high quality products at high speed. But at all times, Apple, given its ownership of the commanding heights of both hardware and software and its ability to influence consumer choices, has remained in the driver's seat setting the terms and conditions for suppliers. Joshua Cohen, a faculty member of Apple University and University of California, Berkeley, explained that in 2015, Apple had as many as 2000 large and small suppliers in China alone, including first-tier and sub-tier suppliers. If, by this measure, China has risen to become an important site in electronics production "in the age of globalization," Sean Starrs highlights the fact that it is "more important to investigate who ultimately profits from the production and sale of goods and services" than to note "where their production or sale is geographically located."[1]

BUYER-DRIVEN VALUE CHAINS

In 2010, Apple's corporate prowess was demonstrated by its ability to capture an extraordinary 58.5 percent of the sales price of the iPhone, an unparalleled achievement in world manufacturing (see Figure 41.2). Particularly notable is that labor costs in China accounted for the smallest share, a mere 1.8 percent or nearly US$10 of the US$549 retail price of the iPhone 4 at that time. American, Japanese and South Korean firms that produce the most sophisticated electronic components

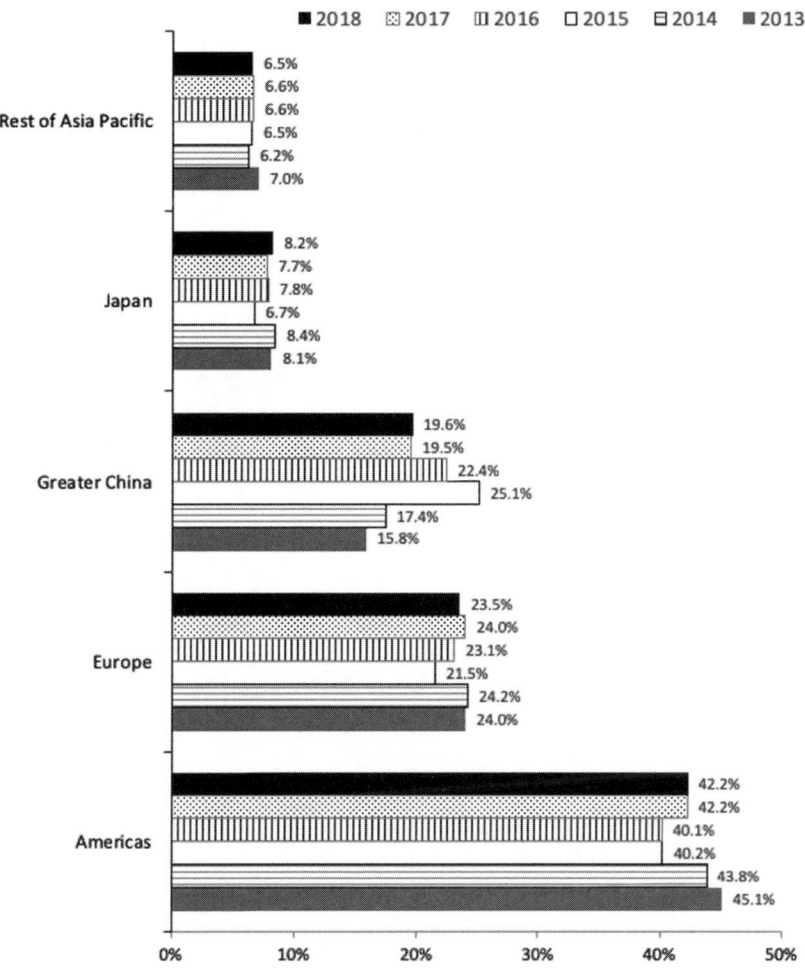

Note: The Americas includes both North and South America. Europe includes Europe, the Middle East and Africa. The rest of Asia Pacific includes Australia and Asian countries other than Japan and Greater China (comprised of mainland China, Hong Kong and Taiwan).

Source: Apple's annual financial reports (2015: 24, 2018: 23). Accessed at: https://investor.apple.com/investor-relations/sec-filings/default.aspx.

Figure 41.1 Apple's annual revenues by region, FY2013–FY2018

captured slightly over 14 percent of the value of the iPhone. The cost of raw materials was just over one-fifth of the total value (21.9 percent). In short, while the Taiwanese-owned Foxconn Technology Group has carved out a niche as the final assembler of the iPhone, the lion's share of the profits flow to Apple, followed by Japanese, Korean and American manufacturers who produce the key

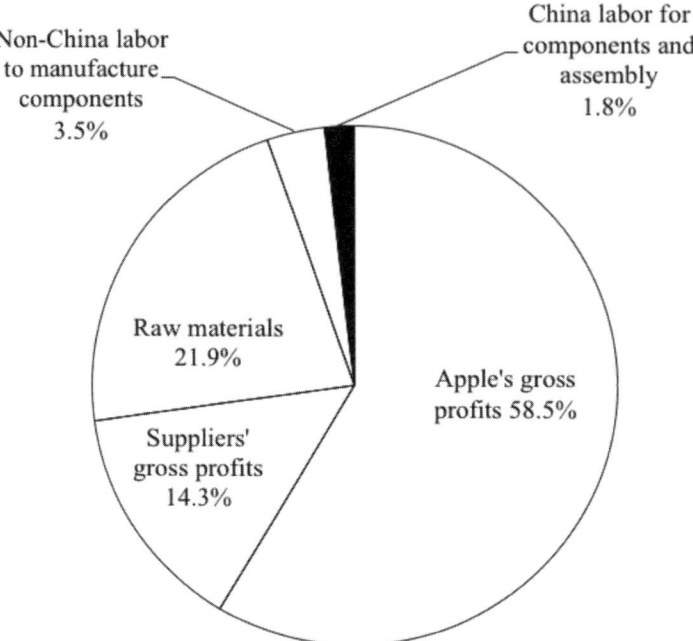

Note: The percentage is calculated on the iPhone 4's retail price at US$549 in 2010. No amount for "distribution and retail" is shown because Apple is paid directly by a cellular company, such as AT&T or Verizon, which handles the final stage of the sale.

Source: Adapted from Kenneth L. Kraemer, Greg Linden and Jason Dedrick, 2011, "Capturing Value in Global Networks: Apple's iPad and iPhone", p. 5. Accessed at: http://econ.sciences-po.fr/sites/default/files/file/Value_iPad_iPhone.pdf.

Figure 41.2 Distribution of value for the iPhone 4, 2010

components. In this international division of labor, little value is captured by Foxconn, and still less by workers in electronics processing and assembly.

Apple buys the most valuable components such as the touch screen display, memory chips and microprocessors from Intel, Sony, Samsung, and other American, Japanese and Korean firms, bringing the parts together for assembly and shipment from China. Jason Dedrick and Kenneth Kraemer observed that global technology brands generally prefer to "use fewer contractors and engage in long-term relationships with them" but they "still shift contracts for specific products amongst suppliers based on cost, quality, or unique capabilities."[2] In 2010, when Foxconn was confronted by a spate of worker suicides in its factories in China, the company was the sole maker of iPhones. Subsequently, Apple – following the common practice of pitting suppliers against each other to maximize profit – shifted some of its production to Pegatron, another Taiwan-owned supplier, where labor costs are allegedly even lower.[3]

By 2016 when the iPhone 7 was launched, Apple had maintained and even increased its grip on iPhone profits, despite intense competition from Samsung, Huawei and Xiaomi. Apple captured an estimated US$283 of the US$649 retail price of the 32GB model (nearly 44 percent of the total). By contrast, Chinese workers were estimated to earn just US$8.46 or 1.3 percent of the US$649 retail price.[4]

CHINESE LABOR PRACTICES IN APPLE'S PRODUCTION NETWORK

Apple's business model, characterized by its relentless pressure for just-in-time production of new models and fulfillment of holiday season rush orders, makes it directly responsible for the pressures experienced by workers in Foxconn's factories and its other contractors. Every second counts towards profit. Take a motherboard from the line, scan the logo, put it in an anti-static bag, stick on a label, and place it on the line. Each of these tasks takes two seconds. Every ten seconds an assembly-line worker finishes five tasks.[5] Electronics parts and components flow by, and workers' youth is worn down by the rhythm of the machines. New workers are often reprimanded for working too slowly on the line, regardless of their efforts to keep up with the "standard" work pace. The assembly lines run on a 24-hour, non-stop basis.[6]

In the context of China, the national labor law stipulates a 40-hour regular working week, which can be extended by a maximum of three hours a day or 36 hours a month, and only when workers consent. This translates to a maximum working week of 49 hours. While Apple requires its suppliers to meet the working hour standards stipulated by applicable laws, in reality it fails to monitor the working conditions. Workers at Foxconn reported that overtime work was compulsory. To meet the deadline, they were subjected to 13-to-1, and under extreme conditions, 30-to-1 work-to-rest schedules, that is, just one day off a month.

Just before Christmas in 2014, BBC's Panorama broadcast a one-hour feature entitled "Apple's broken promises".[7] The Panorama team, in multisite field investigations, found an exhausted Chinese workforce making Apple's iPhone 6s in Pegatron's Shanghai plant, as well as children toiling in tin mines in Indonesia to supply materials for the phones, facing the threats of landslides, injury and death. Excessive raw material extraction and illegal industrial practices have caused irreversible destruction to our planet and its people. With the corporate drive to produce every new iPhone and cannibalize all previous models, the green revolution proclaimed by Apple and its suppliers has been overwhelmed by corporate and consumer demand for new products.

Worse, teenage student interns, in China and in many programs throughout the world, have become a source of super-exploited labor. Foxconn student interns were subjected to the same working conditions as regular workers, including alternating day and night shifts, 10 to 12-hour workdays, six to seven days a week during peak seasons, and with extensive overtime. This was despite the fact that the Chinese educational law clearly stated that "interns shall not work more than eight hours a day", and that "interns shall not work overtime beyond the eight-hour workday". Not only must interns' shifts be limited to eight hours, all their training is required to take place during the day to ensure students' safety and physical and mental health, in accordance with the Law on the Protection of Minors.[8] Foxconn systematically violated the letter and the spirit of the law governing interns.

Good internship programs are practice-oriented and participatory, contribute to students' growth and development, and are related to their field of study. But interning students are like robots on the production lines. They repeat the same procedure for hundreds and thousands of times every day. And they are required to complete the "internships" to be able to graduate.

Under Chinese law, student interns are *not* classified as employees – even though they perform identical work to other production workers – and employers do not enroll them in government-administered social security (including old age pensions, medical benefits, maternity benefits, work-related injury benefits, and unemployment benefits). Just a quick look at the mathematics reveals that, for a total of 150 000 student interns working in various Foxconn factories during one month in the summer season, the savings from not providing them with social security alone is roughly 150 000 persons × 100 Yuan = 15 million Yuan. While this is a simplified exercise, it conveys a good sense of employer savings, and this is for only one month's insurance expenditure, while many interns work for a year. By dispensing with all these benefits, Foxconn saves money.

Foxconn is not the only black sheep. In a new school semester in the fall of 2018, nearly 200 student interns, with some as young as 16, were required to do excessive overtime through the night to build Apple Watches Series 4 at Quanta's factory in Chongqing, southwest China. They were placed in jobs unrelated to their studies.[9] "In electronics", Chad Raphael and Ted Smith comment, "lightning-fast product cycles and seasonal surges in consumer demand push suppliers to impose intense work hours and forced overtime, and to add droves of temporary workers to assemble the next new device to meet product launch deadlines determined by the brand owners".[10] Under this circumstance, students recruited from vocational schools are cheap labor on-demand. By law Chinese employers are permitted to pay student interns only 80 percent of the income offered to full employees on the job, regardless of whether the students' productivity is less than that of ordinary employees.

SUMMARY

The global sweep of outsourced production and sales of iPhones and smart wearables are defining features of capital and consumption in our digital world. From the labor perspective, the discrepancy between fair labor policies as enunciated by Apple in its supplier code of conduct and the reality on the supplier factory floor remains huge. Suppliers compete against each other for orders to maximize their own profits. The results include neglect of workers' need for rest time and their right to refuse overtime, and repression of workers' demand for higher income and better benefits. Benjamin Selwyn concludes that "chain governance represents a lead firm value-capturing strategy, which intensifies worker exploitation" in China and other economies.[11]

In this sense, the worker suicide tragedy, and subsequent strikes and protests, are best understood as collateral damage that are the product of the combined activities of international capital and the Chinese state in global capitalism. Student interns, along with many low-wage unskilled workers, face great pressures in the face of flexibilization of production of services and goods around the globe. It is a cruel irony that internship is not performed for the benefit of the intern. Some employers went as far as renaming "internships" as "social practice programs" and "service learning" to evade basic responsibility, while advancing their interests.

Different Chinese units such as the government trade union, the police, and the courts have responded to worker resistance in diverse ways, contingent in part on the actions of local and international labor organizations. To realize decent work in the global economy context, long-term monitoring of labor conditions, with workers' active participation in the decision-making process, is necessary.

QUESTIONS

1. How should Apple collaborate with its major suppliers (e.g., Foxconn, Pegatron and Quanta) to ensure adherence to high labor standards in China and other countries?

2. Is flexible employment and precarious labor prevalent in electronics manufacturing? Why?

3. Can the Chinese government hold Apple (and other tech multinationals) accountable to workers' rights in the manufacturing process?

4. How do Chinese workers, including student interns, seek to improve their working conditions at the supplier level?

END NOTES

1 Sean Starrs, 2015, "China's Rise is Designed in America, Assembled in China", *China's World*, **2**(2), 11–23.
2 Jason Dedrick and Kenneth L. Kraemer, 2011, "Market Making in the Personal Computer Industry", *The Market Makers: How Retailers are Reshaping the Global Economy*, edited by Gary G. Hamilton, Misha Petrovic and Benjamin Senauer, Oxford: Oxford University Press, p. 303.
3 Jenny Chan, Ngai Pun and Mark Selden, 2013, "The Politics of Global Production: Apple, Foxconn, and China's New Working Class", *New Technology, Work and Employment*, **28**(2), 100–115.
4 Jason Dedrick, Greg Linden and Kenneth L. Kraemer, 2018, "We Estimate China Makes only $8.46 from an iPhone – and That's Why Trump's Trade War is Futile", *The Conversation*, 7 July.
5 The usual time for completing the Standard Operating Procedure (SOP) in assembly is 25–30 seconds. Put it in context: 30 seconds is not long, and workers are working very hard on repetitive tasks.
6 There are exceptions. The assembly lines do not run during breaks or between shifts. Also, the time they run varies seasonally. Over a ten-month period at one of Apple's supplier facilities, for example, the median is 20 hours a day and the mean is 19. (Email communications with Professor Joshua Cohen on 28 November 2019.)
7 Panorama's "Apple's Broken Promises" on BBC One and iPlayer, 18 December 2014, accessed at http://www.bbc.co.uk/iplayer/episode/b04vs348/panorama-apples-broken-promises.
8 Jenny Chan, 2017, "Intern Labor in China", *Rural China: An International Journal of History and Social Science*, **14**(1), p. 88.
9 Students and Scholars Against Corporate Misbehavior (SACOM), 2018, "Apple Watch Series 4: Still Failed to Protect Teenage Student Workers", October. Accessed at http://sacom.hk/wp-content/uploads/2018/10/Apple-Watch-Series-4-Still-Failed-to-Protect-Teenage-Student-Workers.pdf.
10 Chad Raphael and Ted Smith, 2016, "The Future of Activism for Electronics Workers", *The Routledge Companion to Labor and Media*, edited by Richard Maxwell, New York: Routledge, p. 330.
11 Benjamin Selwyn, 2019, "Poverty Chains and Global Capitalism", *Competition & Change* **23**(1), p. 71.

42
Framing workers' rights internationally: The case of Volkswagen and transnational collective agreements

Stephen Mustchin, Miguel Martínez Lucio, Michael Whittall, Fernando Rocha and Volker Telljohann

BACKGROUND AND CONTEXT

How trade unions and workers respond to the growing pressures they face in terms of globalisation and rising levels of power among multinational corporations, firms who are increasingly producing and organising across a range of countries, has become a significant challenge. The fact remains that trade unions' role in representing workers, regulating their terms and conditions within specific national contexts, may be undermined by the scope of multinational corporations to relocate production and services to other countries where labour costs are lower. This obviously presents a challenge to trade unions and workers more generally, whose influence has historically been bounded and constrained within and by national contexts. Nevertheless, there is an emerging system of worker representation and forms of collective agreement that are steadily organising across boundaries and engaging with multinationals on (at or on) a transnational level; their aim, to create common standards and principles across counties regarding workers' rights (Hammer, 2005).

The German automobile manufacturer *Volkswagen* is an example of a high-profile company in which such transnational developments appear to be taking shape. A global player and Europe's largest car manufacturer, Volkswagen has over 119 production sites in 31 countries. Formed in the 1930s, in the post-war years it has developed close working relations with the IG Metall and plant level works council actors, a position towards organised labour that on the whole it follows outside of Germany, too. As we shall see below, though, some exceptions do prevail. The company has both Global and European Works Councils (the latter being regulated by various directives from the European Union). These are forums where trade union and worker representatives from various nations can meet senior management to discuss numerous developments and challenges emerging within the firm. Volkswagen was one of the first companies to develop an international and European framework agreement related to the general rights and working conditions of the company's workforce, as well as specific agreements to address a set of particular work-related issues. In terms of the latter, the aim has been to establish some ground rule procedures as to how management and trade union representatives could improve working conditions on specific issues within their national contexts. There have been various global and European-level agreements within the company covering issues such as union recognition and freedom of association, education and training, and health and safety, among others. For further details see Whittall et al. (2017).

TRANSNATIONAL COLLECTIVE AGREEMENTS (TCAS) AND AGENCY WORKERS

A major issue that has emerged in recent years is the development of more flexible forms of work, involving, for example, the use of temporarily contracted staff and workers from employment agencies. Companies are increasingly using such staff to cover gaps and smooth out variations in the production or service delivery process, though in many cases such workers have to contend with poorer working conditions and lower pay rates. Consequently, Volkswagen trade union leaders in a number of countries began to notice an expansion in use of this precarious model, a development they thought might have a much broader negative knock-on effect on the working conditions of the permanent workforce. They were concerned that it might lead to a growing fragmentation of work and an undermining of the rights and conditions that had been fought for and negotiated over many years. Because of this, there emerged a global and European-level agreement signed by trade union representatives and related levels of senior management designed to control and regulate the employment of agency workers. Primarily, it aimed to limit the use of agency workers, setting a 5 per cent cap on the proportion of the workforce employed through agencies, and to ensure that pay standards were harmonised between them and the rest of the workforce. Second, it sought to harmonise employment conditions between temporary and permanent workers, including the provision of equal pay. Finally, it attempted to ensure that, over time, such 'peripheral' workers would be offered permanent jobs.

The value of such agreements is that they are able to create a means by which challenges facing permanent employees and trade unions can be resolved through dialogue and negotiation, a process that can lead to more harmonious forms of industrial relations. They also allow for a greater investment in the long-term development and commitment levels of the workforce, as these workers, in turn, internalise the company's commitment to provide better and safer working conditions. The value to companies of such agreements is their ability to manage and possibly reduce conflict, and provide an opportunity to include the workforce in strategic discussions on developments in terms of production.

TCAS IN CONTEXT: THE UK AND GERMANY

Agreements such as these allow workers and their representatives from different countries to engage with management through discussions that address sensitive and potentially problematic questions in a coordinated and organised manner.

In the case of Volkswagen in the United Kingdom (the Bentley Motors plant at Crewe), trade unions were able to reference and use TCAs by accessing agency workers and offering them trade union membership, something that would allow them to be represented and seek advice on a range of problems that might arise at work. This agreement also allowed the trade unions to ensure that there was never more than 5 per cent overall of the workforce employed through agencies – the figure rising and falling slightly over time, but the overall average being sustained at that level across the year. Since Volkswagen had acquired Bentley, the trade unions were able to engage with senior management in a more productive manner, and gather information and insight into the firm and its future plans through the presence of their UK trade union representatives on the European and Global Works Councils.

There were similar developments in Germany, where the local trade union officers and works councils were able to use the TCA to ensure that staffing from employment agencies remained low. In addition, there were times when some parts of the company in Germany – the Audi plants, for example – were able to ensure that only 2 per cent of those employed were engaged by employment agencies. Generally, this reflects the stronger traditions of negotiation and workers' rights within the German context. There was variation across the different Volkswagen divisions and plants in Germany but overall it created a framework whereby the absolute maximum number of agency workers would be 5 per cent. Even within such an advanced system of industrial relations, with more effective systems of collective rights and worker conditions compared to the UK, the agreement was able to frame a more proactive relation between management and worker representatives. The agreement was also useful because it was able to create a common framework of interest and engagement between trade union representatives across the different national contexts. Specific challenges facing the global workforce created a dialogue and a common set of interests across the different national systems through the language and practice of 'better' and 'decent' employment conditions, leading to a range of agreements and common positions that underpinned a new form of trade union internationalism.

ISSUES AND CHALLENGES

Various challenges can emerge from such developments. In the first instance, countries still have very different systems for regulating employment conditions, and trade unions clearly have a weaker voice in some countries compared to others. The role of such agreements may be of greater value in those countries where there are fewer or weaker worker rights and participation within firms. To that extent, while these agreements may raise the platform of rights and participation within related workplaces linked to them, they may not be supported by the national legal frameworks of regulation, and be susceptible to manipulation. There might have to be greater scrutiny by trade unions in cases where they cannot implement such company-specific agreements in any systematic manner because of an absence of institutional involvement within these companies at the national and local level.

It may be that such agreements and internationally coordinated approaches to working conditions require greater levels of awareness and training among local trade unionists at the national level, as they may not always be aware of such developments. In fact, there are examples from other firms where this has been the case. Of course this applies to management as much as to trade unionists as management are sometimes out of the communication loop regarding such innovations.

Such agreements may also be developed in a context of distrust, in particular where local management seeks ways to circumvent agreements by possibly outsourcing or offshoring aspects of the work. In such cases agreements may increasingly take into account these counter-developments by ensuring that all workers engaged in a firm's production value chain, directly or indirectly, are covered by such agreements (though this may not be so straightforward).

In addition, within management and its hierarchies there may be uncertainty as to the viability of such agreements. One cannot assume that an internal consensus within management is always achievable on such developments, as local managers may feel that they do not have sufficient resources to avoid or limit the use of employment agency staff.

Another issue is that such agreements depend very much on the nature of the company and its organisational culture. In the case of Volkswagen there has been, relatively speaking, a long tradition of comparatively stable and productive trade union–management relations. One could argue that this is not the case for many firms, and that their internal cultures may vary tremendously, especially if they are a more decentralised and fragmented firm with competing approaches to human resource management. It is for these reasons, among others, that though these agreements are becoming more common the number of companies establishing such TCAs is not as large as it could be.

In fact, even in some of the more engaged and socially oriented firms, such as Volkswagen, there may be some operations where the commitment to the participation and role of the workforce is compromised: there could be cases of malpractice (Greer and Hauptmeier, 2015) and broader concerns operationally as in the scandal regarding emission tests (Elson et al., 2015). Furthermore, in the case of the company's Chattanooga plant in Tennessee (USA), the more skilled workers voted in 2015 for the right to join an American union – the United Automobile Workers (UAW) – which was opposed by local management, and in 2016 Volkswagen unsuccessfully appealed to the courts against the decision. This eventually led to the international coordinating trade union structures for this and related industrial sectors to call for a suspension of its overarching international framework agreements with the company (IndustriALL, 2019). The case of this car plant represents some of the limits of such agreements, as the local federal state context of Tennessee has a political leadership which is critical of trade unions and has introduced many obstacles to hamper the formation of trade union branches. There is much competition between American federal states for inward investment, and in the case of Tennessee, the local authorities have tried to make the area more attractive to companies seeking cost advantages in terms of wage levels and the general cost of labour, among other things. Whether Volkswagen felt disinclined to alienate the local authorities by accepting the anti-union stance or whether the local management were more vociferous in their questioning of the established corporate culture internationally, is a matter of conjecture. However, the clear differences in industrial relations cultures and systems across different geographical areas is a real test for the attempts to create a more coordinated approach to worker participation and rights, as discussed earlier.

SUMMARY

The development of such TCAs is an increasingly global part of the transnational system of industrial relations. We are seeing new and more engaged forms of social dialogue and negotiation between management and workers at a much higher corporate level. Such developments represent a way of creating a more coordinated and enhanced approach to workers' rights. They allow for a minimum floor of rights to be established across the operations of a multinational corporation. They can also be quite specific by focusing on particular issues facing workers, including the use of agencies, union recognition, training, health and safety and others (Mustchin and Martínez Lucio, 2017). These agreements and their corresponding participative structures can play an important role in enhancing social dialogue with regard to production, service delivery and human resource management. Nevertheless, there remain challenges in terms of: (1) ongoing national systems of industrial relations and national legal approaches to industrial relations; (2) the history and character of a company in terms of how worker-friendly it is; and (3) the reality of increasingly competitive economic markets. Yet in recent decades there have been more examples of TCAs being signed as workers and their representatives become increasingly aware of the global context in which they live and work, and therefore also of the need to coordinate attempts to improve working conditions transnationally.

QUESTIONS

1. Why is globalisation leading to these kinds of industrial relations developments?

2. Why are TCAs of value to the (a) workforce, (b) trade unions and (c) management?

3. What did the agreement discussed above do in relation to the use of agency staff?

4. Why do such agreements vary in terms of their implementation across different national contexts?

5. What are the main challenges facing the development and deepening of such agreements?

6. What could be done to enhance such agreements?

REFERENCES

Elson, C., Ferrere, C. and Goossen, N. (2015) The bug at Volkswagen: lessons in co-determination, ownership, and board structure. *Journal of Applied Corporate Finance*, **27**(4), 27–43.

Greer, I. and Hauptmeier, M. (2015) Management whipsawing: the staging of labor competition under globalization. *ILR Review*, **69**(1), 29–52.

Hammer, N. (2005) International framework agreements: global industrial relations between rights and bargaining. *Transfer: European Review of Labour and Research*, **11**(4), 511–30.

IndustriALL (2019) IndustriALL suspends global agreement with Volkswagen. Accessed 11 April 2019 at http://www.industriall-union.org/industriall-suspends-global-agreement-with-volkswagen.

Mustchin, S. and Martínez Lucio, M. (2017) Transnational collective agreements and the development of new spaces for union action: the formal and informal uses of international and European framework agreements in the UK. *British Journal of Industrial Relations*, **55**(3), 577–601.

Whittall, M., Martínez Lucio, M., Mustchin, S., Telljohann, V. and Rocha, R. (2017) Workplace trade union engagement with European Works Councils and transnational agreements: the case of Volkswagen Europe. *European Journal of Industrial Relations*, **23**(4), 397–414.

43
Labour rights and global standards: What the Ali Enterprises fire tells us about social accountability and labour conditions in an international supply chain

Jean Jenkins

This case study uses the example of a fatal fire at the Ali Enterprises garment factory in Pakistan in 2012 to explore issues around the realisation of labour rights and enforcement of voluntary codes of corporate social responsibility in today's international garment sector. While the case example is taken from one sector, the issues it raises have broader application in global value chains characterised by labour-intensive, low-skilled and low-paid work where workers have low associational and structural power. Thus, for example, similar employment relations issues pertain in light electronics assembly, the shoe and leather sectors and may also be seen in low-skilled service sectors. Furthermore, weak enforcement of regulation, be that private or statutory, is a matter of concern wherever workers face considerable barriers in organising to defend their interests in work and employment. The intensified exploitation of workforces, particularly where workers enter employment already socio-economically disadvantaged and casualisation and informalisation of employment contracts is a feature of workplace relations, is not limited to a single sector or place.

BRIEF BACKGROUND TO THE ALI ENTERPRISES CASE

Ali Enterprises drew much of its workforce from Baldia town which is located in the western part of the city of Karachi, in Pakistan. One of the factory's main customers was a European brand, Kik. At around 6 pm on 11 September 2012, fire broke out in the factory. Though Ali Enterprises denied the allegations, survivors claimed that factory doors were locked, windows were barred, fire exits were blocked and there was an absence of fire-fighting equipment. What is undisputable is that somewhere in the region of 500 workers found themselves trapped by the blaze, with just one viable exit from the premises. As a consequence of the fire, it is estimated 262 people were officially recorded as having died and a further unspecified number of people – perhaps around 50 – were injured as they tried to escape. All this happened in a factory that had been awarded its SA 8000 certification – a recognised international standard for social compliance and safety – a short time before the fire occurred.

THE INTERNATIONAL GARMENT SECTOR

Some contextual information about garment manufacture in the twenty-first century may be helpful in understanding how this situation came about. Garment assembly, also referred to as 'apparel manufacture', is a specific phase of production in the making of our clothes. The chain of production begins with the design process, moves on to the sourcing of raw materials and textiles, and next comes the 'cut, make and trim' processes that comprise the garment assembly phase. In the international supply chain, the clothing brands we see on our high streets are typically described as 'manufacturers without factories' as they generally subcontract the garment assembly phase of production to supplier factories located across the globe. This model of production – the sub-contracting of manufacture to different producers – has traditionally been a means of accommodating the seasonal nature of fashion at minimal cost (Phizacklea, 1990). In recent decades the trends to fast fashion and the quick turnaround and general disposability of clothing has intensified the pressures in the supply chain.

Historically, mature economies like the UK, continental Europe and the US had relatively large garment sectors and sub-contracting was likely to be more contained within national borders. However, the liberalisation of markets associated with the expansion of global capital has also contributed to the internationalisation of the garment sector supply chain. The collapse of mass manufacture of ready-made clothing in high-wage, mature economies was associated with the import / export quota system imposed by the Multi-Fibre Arrangement (MFA) (1974–2005) under the overall supervision of the World Trade Organisation (WTO). The MFA was intended as a temporary protectionist measure to prevent mature economies being flooded with low-cost clothing imports as trade was liberalised and garment assembly internationalised. However, quotas varied according to location and it had the perverse effect of initiating the 'great garment war' (Birnbaum, 2010), as international buyers for brands and their agents pursued new sites of production with favourable quotas, fiscal incentives and low labour costs. Brands forsook production in high-wage economies and it was said that the main ambition of garment importers was '[t]o find a place where workers [were] paid less than ten cents per hour' (Birnbaum, 2010: 124).

Thus, trade liberalisation allowed high street brands, who are the ultimate lead firms in the buyer-led value chain (Gereffi, 1994) in garments, to access suppliers across a far greater range of production sites across the world. The incentives in doing so were, and remain, considerable. First, social taxes and employment costs are normally significantly lower in emerging economies. Second, governments seeking inward investment may provide attractive fiscal incentives and facilitate access to land, power and water at low cost. Third, the nature of the value chain means that local manufacturers have to compete against one another to be selected as suppliers to the brands or their agents. In order to do so they have to be the best and cheapest as they fight to secure contracts for work. In a labour-intensive industry, local suppliers' battle to cut their own costs and derive economic rents – profit – from their point in the value chain inevitably makes labour costs and working conditions a key factor in their competitive strategy. In this context, trade union activity is fiercely and consistently opposed by employers throughout the sector, no matter what commitments to freedom of association or 'employee voice' are made in statements of corporate social responsibility.

It would be a mistake to characterise all suppliers to high street brands as small operations. Supplier factories may be graded along a scale of up to five tiers according to their size and proximity to the international buyers and brands who allocate them contracts for work (Hurley, 2005). Tier five workshops will most likely be very small, conforming to stereotypical representations of the 'sweatshop' and hidden from scrutiny deep within the subcontracting chain. However, 'tier one' factories are usually large (employing many thousands of workers) and have the closest and most direct contacts with international brands and buyers. They are more likely to have to engage with brands' voluntary codes of corporate social responsibility (CSR) and may be required to present evidence of international certification of their employment practices – such as, for example, SA 8000 certification – as a condition of being chosen as a supplier. 'Sweating' is a long-established term which describes the driving down of workers' conditions to the lowest possible level, and working in a tier one factory is no protection from 'being sweated'. No matter what the status of the premises, workplace power relations are likely to provide the conditions for exploitation to thrive. In garment workplaces today, research shows us very clearly that various forms of harassment, low pay and abuse of working time are the norm rather than the exception throughout the industry (for example, Anner, 2015; Jenkins, 2015; Hammer et al., 2015). As a matter of note, Ali Enterprises was a tier one establishment.

Garment assembly's focus on cost minimisation is associated with the automation of the sector and the feminisation of its workforce. The sector has generally exploited the typically lower socio-economic status of young workers and women, who have been a perennially attractive labour resource for the industry wherever it has settled. Allowing for regional and skill-based variations (see Mezzadri, 2014), the supposed female attributes of being cheap and compliant have secured for women their place as the international sewing machinists of choice and around 80 per cent of the workforce worldwide is female (Hale and Wills, 2005). Thus, employers across the international garment sector consistently target workers who are new and unused to paid industrial work and those, like women and young workers, who are economically disadvantaged, socially conditioned to comply and less likely to collectively organise in defence of their interests.

FIRE, TRAGEDY AND THE GARMENT SECTOR

Fire and the garment sector have a long and bitter history. With its low barriers to entry and relatively simple technology, the garment sector is typically a country's 'first step in building an export-based industrial economy' (Birnbaum, 2000). Yet, while garment production may bring a source of much-needed paid employment, it is an industry that has traditionally profited from workers' skill and sweat while abrogating responsibility for their conditions of work, including their safety and well-being. Tragedies of the past, such as the Triangle Shirtwaist Factory Fire in New York City in 1911, for example, 'called [public] attention to employers who lack[ed] concern for the lives of their workers … [and allowed poor conditions] … to continue despite the toll in suffering and human life' (Rosen, 2002: 1).

One hundred years later, it is apparent that garment sector employers still do not value their workers enough to keep them safe from harm. Despite ubiquitous corporate sustainability programmes, voluntary corporate codes of conduct and claims for ethical production, working conditions in the sector are generally poor. The economic and social *downgrading* of conditions for labour remains a key concern (Selwyn, 2013). From time to time, brands are exposed to public scrutiny – usually by some crisis or scandal. For example, the Rana Plaza building collapse of 2013 caused death and injury to thousands of garment workers and exposed employer practices to public view and attendant censure. The case of Ali Enterprises (see for example, Nieuwenkamp, 2014) has received rather less international attention, but the issues it raises have major implications.

SOCIAL AUDITING AT ALI ENTERPRISES

The Ali Enterprises factory order book was mainly dependent on KiK, a German brand that produces 'attractively priced clothing'. As the factory's main identified customer, Kik has therefore faced legal challenge from campaigners to accept responsibility for its supply chain and pay compensation to the families of those who died as well as to survivors of the fire.

The 2006 version of KiK's Code of Conduct (CoC), still applicable at the time of the Ali Enterprises fire, stated that in its supplier factories 'The workplace and the practice of the work must not harm employees' or workers' health and safety' (KiK Code of Conduct, 2006). (The Kik Code of Conduct was amended in 2015 but this wording remained the same.) Kik had undertaken several audits of its Code of Conduct at Ali Enterprises in 2007, 2009 and 2011. In addition, Ali Enterprises had itself sought international recognition of its standards of social compliance in the form of SA 8000 certification (Terwindt and Saage-Maass, 2016).

The SA 8000 standard was developed by the organisation Social Accountability International, which is a global non- governmental organisation. On its website, SAI declares its mission in unequivocal terms:

> SAI's vision is of decent work everywhere – sustained by an understanding that socially responsible workplaces benefit business while securing fundamental human rights. SAI empowers workers and managers at all levels of businesses and supply chains ... SAI is a leader in policy and implementation, working together with a diverse group of stakeholders, including brands, suppliers, governments, trade unions, non-profits, and academia.

Its website further explains the SA 8000 standard as follows:

> SA8000 measures social performance in eight areas important to social accountability in workplaces, anchored by a management system element that drives continuous improvement in all areas of the Standard. It is appreciated by brands and industry leaders for its rigorous approach to ensuring the highest quality of social compliance in their supply chains, all the while without sacrificing business interests ...

In the Ali Enterprise case, SAI delegated the task of *certifying* SA 8000 compliance to an Italian auditing firm, RINA, whose website describes its role thus,

RINA is the excellence behind excellence, a global corporation that leads industries to success. We work closely with customers, assisting them in the most effective, safe and sustainable way across the Energy, Marine, Certification, Transport & Infrastructure and Industry sectors. […] RINA third party certification services give an independent guarantee of compliance with associated regulatory standards.

RINA used one of its Pakistani subcontractors to undertake the required auditing processes. SA 8000 certification was successfully awarded to Ali Enterprises – just weeks before the fire took place.

The detail of how certification was awarded has been the subject of investigation, contestation and ongoing legal action (Terwindt and Saage-Maas, 2016). It is not the intention of this case study to explore the detailed claims and counter claims that are ongoing in this specific case. However, it is undeniably the case that failures at Ali Enterprises reflect broader concerns on the part of activists and researchers that social auditing processes may offer *at best* 'simplified, decontextualised versions of truth' in the absence of robust inspection and enforcement (Bartley, 2018; see also Locke et al., 2013).

THE NIGHT OF THE FIRE

When fire broke out at Ali Enterprises on the night of 11 September 2012, it spread rapidly. Though contested by the firm, investigations following the fire suggested that all exit doors except one had been locked, the majority of factory windows were barred and fire exits were obstructed. It was later confirmed that training in fire procedures had not been undertaken at the factory. Though some workers were able to find unbarred windows and jumped from the building, injuring themselves in the process, most victims could not – hence the 262 confirmed deaths from the fire. Accounts of the dead noted that 85 per cent of the victims were between 14 and 30 years of age. The Baldia community lost a generation of its young in just one night.

That this tragedy did not remain hidden from sight deep in the garment supply chain is largely due to the determination of victims' families, supported by local and international civil society. The struggle for some form of justice began while families grieved, but as many workers had never been issued with copies of contracts or proof of employment and some bodies were so badly burned they could not be identified, the first challenge for victims' families was to prove their loved ones had been workers at the site. Many families were initially unable to 'prove' their loss and were unable to get help from official channels. With support from local NGOs, notably the local Pakistan Institute of Labour Education & Research (PILER) and the trade union movement in the form of the National Trade Union Federation of Pakistan (NTUF) they formed the Ali Enterprises Factory Fire Affectees Association and began to campaign. The Association also gained support from international allies such as IndustriALL Global Union (to which NTUF is affiliated), the international Clean Clothes Campaign (CCC), and lawyers at the European Centre for Constitutional and Human Rights (ECCHR).

Some months after the fire, KiK paid US$1 million to a relief fund for victims and their families under the supervision of a Pakistan High Court Commission. The payment was termed 'immediate relief'. As the campaign for full, fair and meaningful compensation continued, the coalition of national and international civil society cooperated in support of the local campaign for access to remedy. In addition to legal cases lodged in Pakistan, lawyers also filed a claim against KiK in Germany, to try to establish its liability for what had happened within its supply chain.

Inevitably, 'remedy' has had to be framed in monetary terms. In September 2016, negotiations facilitated by the International Labour Organization (ILO) between IndustriALL, CCC and KiK, at the request of the German Federal Ministry of Economic Cooperation and Development yielded a further contribution from Kik of an additional US$5.15 million to fund loss of earnings, medical and allied care, and rehabilitation costs to the injured survivors and dependants of those killed in the disaster. However, as one campaigner put it, this should not be regarded as the 'monetisation of grief' … rather … 'it is the only justice we can get'.

On 13 September 2016, the struggle to hold KiK to account for practices in its supplier factory moved a step forward. An agreement was reached that KiK would pay an additional US$5.15 million to supplement Pakistan's social security payments to victims and meet compensation levels required by the ILO Employment Injury Benefits Convention 121. It is instructive that the brand's agreement took no less than four years to accomplish and was not a natural outcome of its own social accountability commitments or social auditing processes. Rather, the agreement for this additional payment to victims was entirely due to pressure and legal action by organisations of workers at the local and national level within Pakistan, supported by a dedicated coalition of international campaigners. It was only by means of their combined efforts that victims' voices were eventually heard and victims and their families secured some form of redress. In this case, as in a host of others, the struggle to hold firms accountable continues. For victims and families who have had to fight every step of the way for recognition and remedy, the effects of the fire will be life-long. A working community has been collectively bereaved and, of those who survived, many suffered injuries that have left them with permanent disabilities. For them, no amount of money can repair the damage done.

QUESTIONS

1. What social, economic, political and supply chain factors contributed to the Ali Enterprises Case?

2. Is this an isolated case of a bad employer or indicative of wider issues around labour and human rights in global supply chains?

3. Freedom of association is described as a 'foundational right' by the UN and the ILO. If we accept this is the case, how might the collective organisation of workers be part of *preventing* abuses in global supply chains?

REFERENCES

Anner, M. (2015), 'Social downgrading and worker resistance in apparel global value chains', in K. Newsome, P. Taylor, J. Bair and A. Rainnie (eds), *Putting Labour in its Place: Labour Process Analysis and Global Value Chains*, Basingstoke, Palgrave Macmillan, pp. 152–70.

Bartley, T. (2018), *Rules without Rights: Land, Labor and Private Authority in the Global Economy*, New York: Oxford University Press.

Birnbaum, D. (2000), *Birnbaum's Global Guide to Winning the Great Garment War*, Hong Kong: Third Horizon Press.

Birnbaum, D. (2010), *Birnbaum's Global Guide to Winning the Great Garment War*, New York: Fashiondex Inc.

Gereffi, G. (1994), 'The organization of buyer-driven global commodity chains: how US retailers shape overseas production networks'. In G. Gereffi and M. Korzeniewicz (eds), *Commodity Chains and Global Capitalism*. Westport, CT: Praeger, pp. 95–122.

Hale, A. and Wills, J. (eds) (2005), *Threads of Labour: Garment Industry Supply Chains from the Workers' Perspective*, Oxford: Blackwell.

Hammer, N., Plugor, R., Nolan, P. and Clark, I. (2015), 'A new industry on a skewed playing field: supply chain relations and working conditions in UK garment manufacturing', Report (University of Leicester/CSWEF, Ethical Trading Initiative).

Hurley, J. (2005), 'Unravelling the web: supply chains and workers' lives in the garment industry', in A. Hale and J. Wills (eds), *Threads of Labour: Garment Industry Supply Chains from the Workers' Perspective*, Oxford: Blackwell, pp. 95–132.

Jenkins, J. (2015), 'The significance of grass-roots organizing', in K. Newsome, P. Taylor, J. Bair and A. Rainnie (eds), *Putting Labour in its Place*, Basingstoke: Palgrave Macmillan, pp. 195–212.

KiK Code of Conduct (2006), Available at http://www.kik-textilien.com.

Locke, R.M., Rissing, B.A. and Pal, T. (2013), 'Complements or substitutes? Private goods, state regulation and the enforcement of labour standards in global supply chains', *British Journal of Industrial Relations*, **51** (3): 519–52.

Mezzadri, A. (2014), 'Backshoring, local sweatshop regimes and CSR in India', *Competition and Change*, **18** (4): 327–44.

Nieuwenkamp, R. (2014), 'Corporate leaders: Your supply chain is your responsibility', *OECD Observer*, Paris Iss. 299: 7–8.

Phizacklea, A. (1990), *Unpacking the Fashion Industry: Gender, Racism and Class in Production*, London: Routledge.

Rosen, E.I. (2002), *Making Sweatshops: The Globalization of the US Apparel Industry*, Berkeley and Los Angeles, CA and London, UK: University of California Press.

Selwyn, B. (2013), 'Social upgrading and labour in global production networks: a critique and an alternative conception', *Competition and Change*, **17** (1): 75–90.

Terwindt, C. and Saage-Maass, M. (2016), *Liability of Social Auditors in the Textile Industry*, Berlin: Friedrich-Ebert-Stiftung, available at https://www.ecchr.eu/fileadmin/Publikationen/Policy_Paper_Liability_of_Social_Auditors_in_the_Textile_Industry_FES_ECCHR_2016.pdf.

Index

'#996 approach' 1

ability practices 47
Achmea
   background and context 45
   HPWS
      in practice 47
      questions 51
      reasons for adoption 46
      summary and overview 49–51
   partnership approach 45, 49–50
   renewal of HR policies and practices 46
   results 48
   top managers and frontline supervisors 48
aerospace sector
   airline business models 80
   forecasting future jobs and skills 124–5
   see also Airbus; Ryanair; Southwest Airlines (SWA)
AfC *see* Agenda for Change (AfC)
aged care services *see* Jacaranda House
Agenda for Change (AfC) 60–61, 62, 63, 65
Airbus
   background and context 124
   competence forecasting and planning
      final version 126–7
      introduction 125
      lessons learned 127
      planning and simulation process 125–6
   initial competence management framework 125
Ali Enterprises
   background and context 277
   night of fire 281–2
   questions 282
   social auditing 280–81
   tier one establishment 279
Amazon
   background and context 191
   competitiveness of HRM 191–2
   ethical HRM as form of cultural control 195–6
   ideology of 'hard' leadership 192–4
   leadership principles 193–4
   questions 198
   sustainability of corporate model 198
   unethical HRM 196–8
Apple
   annual revenues by region 267
   background and context 266
   buyer-driven value chains 266–9
   Chinese labour practices in production networks 269–70
   distribution of value for iPhone4 267
   summary and questions 270–71
Apprenticeship Levy 8, 12
apprenticeships 7–8, 11, 12, 15

Argentinean Female Sex Workers' Union (AMMAR) 142, 143–6
Ashton, G. 129, 133, 135
austerity 40
Australian Manufacturing Workers Union (AMWU) 100, 101, 103–4
autism
  case study 21–3
  prevalence 20
  public discourse 20–21
  questions 24
AutoParts
  background and context 25
  flexible employment model 25, 27–9
  New Build business 27, 28
  recession
    prior to 26
    questions 30
    recovery from 27–9
    responses to 26–7, 28

banding supplements 61
BankCo
  background and context 222
  history of local sub-unit 222–3
  HR department and philosophy 224–5
  implementation of HRM practices 225–7
  size and market position 223–4
  summary and questions 227–8
BDMs *see* Business Development Managers (BDMs)
Bezos, J. 191–3, 195, 196–7, 198
bilateral air service agreements (BASAs) 80
body art industry *see* tattoos
Boselie, P. 45, 49
brand
  clothing 278–80, 282
  Ford Motor Company 201, 203, 204, 205
  Good to Great 185, 186, 188–9
  Haier 240, 243
  and people types 179
  of PubCo 178, 180
  use of tattoos in building 180–82

of WKG and JGC 101, 104
brand ambassadorship 93
brand protection 35–6
breathing apparatus (BA) training 113–14, 115–17
BritCo
  background and context 76
  double-breasting voice
    in Ireland 76–7
    practice and challenges of 77–9
  questions 79
  voice and transnational regulation 77
Brunei Darussalam
  background and context 207–8
  organisational change
    role of organisational members in maintaining existing practices during 210–12
    and stability after introduction of PM system 208–10
  summary and questions 212–13
building materials company *see* European Building Materials Company (EBMC)
bullying *see* workplace bullying
Business Development Managers (BDMs)
  Do Not Call (DNC) Registers 53–4
  incentives
    general 54–5
    rationale for competing plans 56
    resulting poor performance 57–8
  metropolitan
    incentives 55
    in Sprooker Perth structure 52
  pitch delivered by 54
  regional
    incentives 55–6
    in Sprooker Perth structure 52
  three task role 53
buyer-driven value chains 266–9

career stage profiles 151
case studies
  evidence-based 1–2, 4

importance of 4–5
   overview 2–4
   themes 5
change
   cultural, at Ford Motor Company 202–3
   driving force for in UAE 247–8
   HRM structural 217–19
   managing at Jacaranda House 163
   organisational
      in hierarchy 157
      and performance management 208–12
   Sports Direct plc under pressure for 108–9
Chartered Institute for Personnel and Development (CIPD) 20–21, 106, 137
China *see* Apple; Haier
Citizens UK 67, 68, 70
clinical excellence awards 61–2
clothing and textiles industry 255–9
ClothTran
   background 256–7
   employment practices issues 257–8
   people management strategy 259
   questions 259
   unionization
      high levels of 258–9
      issues with 257–8
Coffee Chain
   brand protection 35–6
   business overview 32–3
   compliance 33–5
   determining best approach to HRM 36–7
   Learning and Development (L&D) Manager 33–4
   summary and questions 37–8
collective bargaining
   BankCo 225
   BritCo 76
   New Zealand 67
   public sector authority 39–40
   South African clothing and textiles industry 258–9
   SWA 82

WeKnowGin 101
Collins, J. 185–9
colours test 15–16, 17
commonality 148, 150, 151, 154
community-led living wage campaign 69–70, 72
competence
   aerospace sector 124–5
   Airbus 124–7
   breathing apparatus 114
   broad definition 123
   European approaches to 123–4
   Haier 242–3
   policy instruments 124
   questions 128
competency model 151
competitiveness of HRM 191–2
compliance environment 33–5
computer gaming *see* gaming industry
continuity 164
contribution based pay
   adoption of 40
   goals 40–41
   main elements 41
   relation to performance 41–2
   summary and questions 43–4
   union view of 42–3
Cooke, F.L. 235
corporate social responsibility (CSR) 277, 278–9, 280
County Council
   austerity and pressures to reform 40
   background and context 39–40
   pay and performance 40–42
   summary and questions 43–4
   union perspective 42–3
cultural change
   at Ford Motor Company 202–3
   relation to PM principles 209
cultural control, ethical HRM as form of 195–6
culture
   Amazon's unique 191–8
   bullying 98

of discrimination 152–3, 154
of employee voice 96
Ford Motor Company
    improvement 205–6
    unhealthy 202–3
gossip 163
Haier's corporate 240
inclusive 82, 97
localisation vs standardisation 225–6, 228
managing international talent 233, 235
masculine 132, 133, 135
obedience 209, 212
performance 41
popular 91, 178–81
preparation of expatriates 261–4
results-obsessed 57
of suspicion 163
unhealthy 163, 165, 202–3
Volkswagen 275

Department of Public Service (DPS)
    background and context 95–6
    Director's Brown Bag Lunches 96–7
    employee voice mechanisms
        effects 97
        impact 97–8
        initiatives 96
    Federal Employee Viewpoint Survey 95–7
    focus groups 96–8
    pulse surveys 96–8
    summary and questions 98–9
developing country *see* Brunei Darussalam
disability 20–23, 131
Disability Discrimination Act, 1995 20
discrimination
    and commonality 148, 150
    culture of 152–3, 154
    intentional 148
    people with disabilities 20–21
    Victoria State Police 129, 131, 133–4
disparate impact 148, 154
disparate treatment 148, 154

diversity
    in law firm
        as best practice 9–11
        challenges 11
        context 7–9
        summary 12
    at Microsoft Corp. 153
    one size fits all approach 11
Doctors' and Dentists' Review Body (DDRB) 61
double-breasting voice
    in Ireland 76–7
    practice and challenges of 77–9
    questions 79
drivers as employees, issue of 92–3
Dundon, T. 1

Early Talent 8, 9–10, 12
'earn as you learn' pathway 8
EBMC *see* European Building Materials Company (EBMC)
educational institution 20–24
electronic devices components *see* Apple
Emiratization
    background and context 245–6
    barriers to 248–9
    driving force for change 247–8
    females in workforce 246–7
    overcoming resistance to 249
    summary and questions 251–2
    viewpoints
        expressing reservation 251
        neutral 250
        supportive 250
employee engagement
    background and context 95–6
    employee voice mechanisms 96–8
    summary and questions 98–9
employee voice
    at Amazon 196
    double-breasting
        in Ireland 76–7
        practice and challenges of 77–9

INDEX

    questions 79
    mechanisms
        BritCo 76–7
        effects 97
        impact 97–8
        initiatives 96
        questions 99
    and transnational regulation 77
employment contracts *see* zero hours contracts
employment security/insecurity
    Ryanair 85
    at Sports Direct plc 105–10
    SWA 81
'entertainment' games 172–3
Equal Pay Act 1970 59
Equality Act 2010 20, 59, 60
European Building Materials Company (EBMC)
    background and context 230–31
    corporate HR function 232–3
    growth strategy 231–2
    managing international talent 233–6
    summary and questions 236–7
European Credit transfer system for Vocational Education and Training (ECVET) 123, 124
European Qualifications Framework (EQF) 123, 124
evidence-based management 203–4
expatriates
    Australian
        background and context 261–2
        culture shock experienced 262–4
        preparation for move 262
        summary and questions 264
    at EBMC 224, 225
    managers 223, 226–8, 252
    in United Arab Emirates 245–6, 247–8, 249–50, 252

facilities management and infrastructure company *see* Neptune Plc
Fair Work Ombudsman 36
'family of concepts' surrounding job quality 167–8
Fells, R. 71

females in workforce 246–7
    see also gender
financial constraints 164
financial services *see* Saltire Brokers (SB)
fire
    at Ali Enterprises 277, 281–2
    in international garment sector 279–80
    and KiK 277, 280, 281–2
Fire Brigades Union (FBU) 113
fire service *see* Red Watch firefighters
flexible employment model 25, 27–9
flexible working
    as motivation practice 47
    and organisational hierarchy 158–9
focus groups
    Department of Public Service 96–8
    Scottish workers 169
Ford Motor Company
    background and context 201
    cultural change 202–3
    evidence-based management 203–4
    increased focus 204–5
    new CEO
        appointment 201–2
        first task 202
        leadership 202–6
        personality 202
    summary and questions 205–6
Foxconn Technology Group 268–70
franchises
    business overview 32–3
    compliance environment 33–5
    determining best HRM strategy 36–7
    and HRM policy 32
    protecting brand 35–6
    summary and questions 37–8
freelancers
    gaming industry 174, 175, 176
    Uber 93

GameCoal
    background and context 172–3

business model 174
HR strategy 175
job quality aspects 176
gaming industry
   background and context 172
   cases 172–3
   HR strategies 174–5
   job quality aspects 176
   project-based business models 172–4, 177
   questions 177
   variety in 173
GenCo
   background and context 216–17
   corporate HQ relations and communication 219–20
   HRM
      main role for 220
      structural changes 217–19
   summary and questions 220–21
gender bias 148, 152
gender discrimination
   Microsoft Corp. 149, 153
   Victoria State Police 134, 135
gender diversity *see* Victoria State Police (Australia)
gender pay gap
   definition 59–60
   Microsoft Corp.
      alleged culture of discrimination 152–3
      alleged statistical evidence 151–2
   possible contributions to 61–2
   questions 66
   reporting regulations 60
   SUHT report
      AfC plus pay grades and workforce segregation 65
      hourly pay 64
      pay quartiles 64
      workforce gender split 63
gig economy 92–3, 106
gin manufacturer *see* Jad-Gin Co. (JGC)
GMB 39, 70–72, 92
Good to Great 185–9

'good work' *see* job quality
Gunnigle, P. 83

Haier
   background and context 239
   brand 240
   business strategy and people management 240–43
   core values 240
   culture 240
   impact of open network structure on employees and implications for HRM 242–3
   networking strategy 241–2
   summary and questions 243–4
   technology 240
   'Win–Win Model of Individual–Goal Combination' 241
Harvey, G. 83
healthcare, sex workers' access to 145–6
HerbalCeuticals
   background and context 261–2
   expatriates
      culture shock experienced 262–4
      preparation for move 262
   summary and questions 264
hierarchies *see* organisational hierarchies
High Performance Organisations (HPOs) 50–51
High Performance Work Systems (HPWS)
   ability practices 47
   contextual factors 49–50
   definition 49
   implementation actors 50–51
   motivation practices 47
   multi-stakeholder creation 45
   opportunity practices 47
   overview 49
   process 50
   questions 51
   reasons for creation 46
   results of implementing practices 48
   role of supervisors and managers 48, 50

INDEX

HRM
  aligning with relationship marketing 179–82
  competitiveness 191–2
  ethical, as form of cultural control 195–6
  implementing in MNC
    HR department and philosophy 224–5
    localisation vs standardisation 225–7
    summary 227–8
  implications of open network structure 242–3
  in South African clothing industry 257–8, 259
  technology 120–21
  (un)ethical 196–8
HRM function
  BankCo Cyprus 224, 226, 227
  Coffee Chain 33
  corporate 232–3
  ProfessionalCo 118
  strategic or operational 220
  structural change to 217–19
  at subsidiary level 216, 217–19, 220
HRM strategy
  Achmea 49–50
  built on cooperative collectivism 82
  in China 239–44
  determinants in coffee shop franchise 32–8
  Emiratization 245, 247–52
  gaming industry 174–5
  localisation 235
  people management 240–43
  Ryanair 86–7
  in South African clothing industry 259
  talent management 119, 232, 234–6, 237

ideology of 'hard' leadership 192–4
incentives
  for BDMs
    general 54–5
    metropolitan 55
    regional 55–6
  competing
    poor performance related to 57–8
    rationale for 56

  in international garment sector 278
  need for clear 41
  pizza parties as 95–6
inclusion
  recognition of sex workers 144–5
  as recruitment strategy 9–11
Informing and Consulting Employees (I&C) Directive 77
insecurity *see* employment security/insecurity
Institute of Student Employers (ISE) 7–8, 12
insurance company *see* Achmea
international business growth strategy 231–2
international garment sector
  background and context 278–9
  fire and tragedy in 279–80
  see also Ali Enterprises
international staff mobility
  background and context 230–31
  corporate HR function 232–3
  growth strategy 231–2
  managing international talent 233–6
  summary and questions 236–7
internet of things (IoT) 240
interview process and types 16
iPhones 266, 268–9, 270

Jacaranda House
  background and context 161
  financial constraints 164
  gossiping 163
  impact of organisational issues on worker wellbeing 162
  investigation 162–4
  management perspectives 164
  managing change 163
  summary and questions 165
  training 163
  trust and safety 163
  workforce demographics 162
  workload and continuity 164
Jad-Gin Co. (JGC)
  background and context 100

new ownership structure and management
    control 100
  questions 103–4
  restructuring and redundancy 103–4
  work intensification and workplace
    misbehaviour 101–2
Jenkins, J. 279
job quality
  approaches to 166–7
  aspects in gaming industry 176
  extrinsic and intrinsic attributes 167, 170
  'family of concepts' surrounding 167–8
  'good jobs' 167–8
  for low-waged workers 168–70
  minimum standards initiatives 170–71
  nature of 166
  summary 170–71

Kemp, L.J. 246–7
key performance indicators (KPIs) 207–12
KiK 277, 280, 281–2
knowledge-based services delivery company *see*
    ProfessionalCo
knowledge exchange 157–8
knowledge-intensive firm *see* KnowledgeLtd
KnowledgeLtd
  background and context 156
  organisational hierarchy
    changes in 157
    and flexible working 158–9
    internal and external face of 159–60
    relations and exchange of knowledge 157–8
  summary and questions 160

labour standards 86, 90, 257, 259
law firm *see* Pinsent Masons (PM)
leadership
  Amazon's principles 193–4
  background and context 185–6
  embedded autocratic style 209
  Good to Great analysis 185–6, 188–9
  ideology of 'hard' 192–4

Level 5 186–8, 189
  meaningless 188
  New Public Management 207
  summary and questions 188–9
  transformational 202–6
learning by doing and telling 114–17
legal services *see* Pinsent Masons (PM)
Lehman Brothers 26
Level 5 leadership 186–8, 189
Living Wage campaigns
  background and concept 67
  community-led campaign at UEL 69–70
  development of 68–9
  effectiveness 72
  GMB, UNISON and Unite 70–71
  questions 73
local government sector
  contribution based pay 39–44
  Living Wage campaign 70–72
localisation vs standardisation 225–7
low fares airlines (LFAs) 80, 83, 85
low-waged workers
  decent work for 168–71
  in South Africa 254

Magic Circle 11, 12
management
  evidence-based 203–4
  perspectives at Jacaranda House 164
management control 101
management style 138–9
managers
  expatriate 223, 226–8
  top 48, 50
manufacturing firms *see* AutoParts; Jad-Gin Co.
    (JGC)
Martínez Lucio, M. 276
McCann, L. 185, 188
medical academics pay 61–2
mental health 21–3
Microsoft Corp.
  alleged culture of discrimination 152–3

alleged statistical evidence on gender pay and promotion gaps 151–2
background and context 148
calibration process 148, 149–51, 153, 154
cases of Ms Moussouris and Ms Muenchow 148, 149, 155
competency model and career stage profiles 151
denial of class action and movement to appeal 154
people conversations 148, 150–51
questions 154
misbehaviour at work 101–2
MNCs *see* multinational corporations (MNCs)
motivation
    and career advancement 157
    goal alignment for enabling 210
    intrinsic 174, 176
    leaders vs workers 189
motivation practices 47, 49
Moussouris, K. 148, 149, 155
Muenchow, H. 148, 149, 155
Mulally, A. 201–6
multinational corporations (MNCs)
    employee voice in 76–9
    implementing HRM within
        background and context 222
        history of local sub-unit 222–3
        HR department and philosophy 224–5
        localisation vs standardisation 225–7
        size and market position 223–4
        summary and questions 227–8
    managing international staff mobility
        background and context 230–31
        corporate HR function 232–3
        growth strategy 231–2
        managing international talent 233–6
        summary and questions 236–7
    strategy and people management
        background and context 239
        core values, brand, culture and technology 240
        summary and questions 243–4

technology-enabled business innovation 240–43
subsidiary level
    background and context 216–17
    corporate HQ relations and communication 219–20
    HRM strategic or operational role 220
    HRM structural changes 217–19
    summary and questions 220–21
Mustchin, S. 276
mutual gains principle 49, 51, 168
Myers–Briggs 16

National Autistic Society 20
National Minimum Wage (UK) 67–8, 72–3, 85, 107–9
National Vocational Qualifications 123
Neptune Plc
    background and context 137
    management style 138–9
    problematic team relationships 137–8
    questions 141
    team dynamics 140–41
networking strategy 241–2
new ownership 101
New Public Management (NPM) leadership 207
NHS pay determination 60–62
Nixon, C. 131–3, 135
Northern Fire *see* Red Watch firefighters

one size fits all approach 11, 120
opportunity practices 47
organisational change
    after introduction of PM system 208–10
    role of organisational members in maintaining existing practices during 210–12
organisational hierarchies
    changes in 157
    and flexible working 158–9
    hierarchical relations 157–8
    internal and external face of 159–60
    partnership structure 156

summary and questions 160
tensions caused by 160
organisational issues, impact on worker wellbeing 162
O'Sullivan, M. 83
outsourcing 39, 52, 257, 259, 266, 270, 274–5
Oxfam 168–9, 170

Pakistan *see* Ali Enterprises
partnership approach 50
pay and remuneration
    contribution based 40–44
    and performance 40–42
    performance related 39–40, 43
    progression 61
    underpayments 35–6, 108
    see also gender pay gap
pay determination
    within NHS 60–62
    at SUHT 62–3
pensions, sex workers' access to 145–6
people management strategy 240–43, 259
performance and pay 40–42
performance management
    implementing in developing country
        background and context 207–8
        difference between reality and rhetoric 212
        organisational change and stability after 208–10
        questions 213
        role of organisational members in maintaining existing practice 211–12
        timing and model of 208
    ProfessionalCo 120–21
    Sprooker Inc.
        incentives 54–6
        induction training 53–4
        resulting poor performance 57–8
performance related pay (PRP) 39–40, 43
Pinsent Masons (PM)
    challenges 11
    diversity context 7–9
    as law firm 7
    recruitment strategy 9–11
    summary and questions 12
PM *see* performance management
police *see* Victoria State Police (Australia)
pre-interview tests 15–16
PRIME alliance 8
Procter, S. 30
product-based business models 173
production networks, Chinese labour practices in 269–70
ProfessionalCo
    background and context 118
    summary and questions 121–2
    talent management
        factors influencing 119–21
        importance of 118–19
project-based business models 172–4, 177
Protecting Vulnerable Workers Bill 2017 34
Prowse, P. 71
PubCo
    aligning HR with relationship marketing 179–81
    background and context 178–9
    summary and questions 181–2
    target demographic 179
    tattoos as asset 181–2
public sector authority *see* County Council
public sector employee engagement *see* Department of Public Service (DPS)

Rare 10
Rashid, F.R. 207–10, 212
recession (2008)
    acquisition activity 231
    AutoParts
        prior to 26
        questions 30
        recovery from 27–9
    responses to
        Achmea 48, 50
        AutoParts 26–7, 28
        ProfessionalCo 118–19

unemployment growth in India and China 235
recruitment
    advertising 17
    of apprentices 7–8
    in BankCo Cyprus 224–5, 227
    contextualised 10
    diversity and inclusion as strategy 9–11
    job applicants with tattoos 181–2
    police officers 130, 134
Red Watch firefighters
    background and context 112–13
    breathing apparatus training 113–14
    learning by doing and telling 114–15
    in practice 115
    questions 115–17
    training session 115–17
redeployment policy 22
redundancy
    at AutoParts 27, 28
    and employee voice 78
    and HRM function 217, 218, 219, 220
    as response to workplace misbehaviour 103–4
reform, pressures for 40
regulation
    gender pay gap reporting 60
    lack of formal guiding employment relations in Ireland 220
    transnational employment 77
    Uber's reluctance to be bound by 90, 91, 93–4
regulatory arbitrage 90–91, 93–4
regulatory constraints, successful 91–2
relationship marketing 179–82
representation
    Amazon 192–3, 194, 197–8
    in autism case 21–3
    BAME 11
    BritCo 76–7
    SACTWU 256
    for women 152, 154, 159, 194
resistance *see* workplace resistance
restructuring
    at Britco 78
    at County Council 40, 43
    at Ford Motor Company 201, 205
    HRM function 205, 218–19, 220
    and Level 4 leaders 187
    as response to workplace misbehaviour 103–4
Rhineland model of capitalism 45, 49
Rhineland perspective 46
Russell Group 8, 12
Ryanair
    employment insecurity 85
    high productivity 86
    HR strategy and employment relations 86–7
    low-cost business model 82–3
    low wages 85–6
    minimum skill 86
    union avoidance 83–4
    union recognition 84–5, 87

Said, T.F.H. 207–10, 212
Saltire Brokers (SB)
    background and context 14–15
    CEO 14–18
    as financial services firm 14
    HR/Accounts manager 14–16, 18
    pay 15
    questions 18
    selection process
        current practice 15–16
        issues with 16–17
    staff performance issues 14
    succession planning 15
Scullion, H. 232
selection
    in BankCo Cyprus 225, 227
    criteria for managers in EBMC 235–6
    interview process and types 16
    issues with 16–17
    pre-interview tests 15–16
'serious' games 172–3
SeriousEst
    background and context 172
    business model 173–4

HR strategy 174–5
job quality aspects 176
sex discrimination
   Microsoft Corp. 148, 151
   Victoria State Police 134
sex workers
   access to healthcare, pensions and welfare 145–6
   background and context 142–3
   summary and questions 146
   violence and repression against sex workers 143
   worker recognition 144–5
sexual harassment
   Microsoft Corp. 148, 149, 153, 154
   Victoria State Police 133–4, 135
SkateCo
   aligning HR with relationship marketing 179–81
   background and context 178–9
   summary and questions 181–2
   target demographic 179
   tattoos as asset 181–2
skills
   Airbus 125
   communication 149, 164
   and competence 123–4
   cross-cultural management 232, 235
   of firefighters 112, 115–17
   freelance workers 175
   gaps in 11
   Ryanair 86
   SWA 81–2
   and talent 9, 118, 119
smartphone components *see* Apple
social auditing 280–81, 282
South Africa
   background and context 254–5
   clothing and textiles industry 255–6
      high unionization 256
   ClothTran
      background 256–7

      employment practices issues 257–8
      high unionization 258–9
      people management strategy 259
      questions 259
   outsourcing 257, 259
South African Clothing and Textiles Workers Union (SACTWU) 256, 257–8
Southern Works Committee (SWC) 77
Southside University Hospital Trust (SUHT)
   background and context 59
   gender pay gap 59–60, 63–6
   pay determination
      in NHS 60–62
      at SUHT 62–3
   questions 66
Southwest Airlines (SWA)
   employment security 81
   HR strategy and employment relations 82
   low-cost business model 80–81
   productivity 82
   profitability and rankings 81
   skills 81–2
   wages 81
Sports Direct plc
   agency workers 107–9
   background and context 105
   business strategy 105
   divided workforce 105–7
   employee turnover rates 106
   pressure for change 108–9
   punitive employment practices 107
   resulting initiatives 109
   summary and questions 109–10
   zero hours contracts 106–7, 108
sportswear and equipment retailer *see* Sports Direct plc
Sprooker Inc.
   background and context 52–3
   incentives
      for BDMs (metropolitan) 55
      for BDMs (regional) 55–6
      general 54–5

INDEX

rationale for competing plans 56
induction training 53–4
resulting poor performance 57–8
standardisation vs localisation 225–7
stories and narrative
    firefighters 114–15, 116–17
    leadership 184–5, 187
SUHT *see* Southside University Hospital Trust (SUHT)
supervisors, frontline 48, 50
supply chains
    garment sector 278–82
    labour practices in Apple's 269–71
    labour standards in 90

talent
    defining 9, 120
    measuring 120–21
talent management
    in developing economies 234–6
    differing perceptions as challenge 121
    EBMC
        international 233–6
        as strategic theme for 232
    factors influencing 119–21
    in high-growth acquisition MNEs 233–4
    importance of 118–19
    questions 122, 237
talent pools 10–11
target demographic, establishing 179, 180
tattoos
    aligning HR with relationship marketing 179–81
    as asset in case study organisations 181–2
    background and context 178–9
    summary and questions 181–2
    target demographic 179
team (workplace bullying)
    dynamics 140–41
    impact of management style 138–9
    problematic relationships 137–8
technology
    Amazon 194

Haier 240–43
HRM 120–21
    and talent 9
    and Uber 91, 92
technology-enabled business innovation strategy 240–43
telemarketing firm *see* Sprooker Inc.
temporary workers
    in flexible employment model 25
    recession
        removal as response to 26–7
        situation in recovery from 28–9
Timming, A.R. 182
trade unions *see* unions
training
    breathing apparatus 113–14, 115–17
    Jacaranda House 163
transformational leadership 202–6
transnational collective agreements (TCAs)
    and agency workers 273
    issues and challenges 274–5
    summary and questions 275–6
    in UK and Germany 273–4
transnational employment regulation 77
triptyque 123
trust
    at Jacaranda House 163
    leaders earning 194
Turnbow, T. 126, 127
Turnbull, P. 83

Uber
    background and context 90–91
    issue of drivers as employees 92–3
    regulatory arbitrage 90–91
    successful regulatory constraints 91–2
    summary and questions 93–4
UEL *see* University of East London (UEL)
underpayments 35–6, 108
union avoidance
    Amazon 197–8
    BritCo 78

Ryanair 83–4
union recognition
   BritCo 78–9
   Ryanair 84–5, 87
   Sports Direct plc 108
   SWA 81, 82
   Volkswagen 273, 276
unions
   for Argentinean female sex workers 142, 143–6
   heavy presence in South African clothing industry 256, 257, 258–9
   local government membership 39
   and transnational collective agreements 272–6
   view on contribution based pay 42–3
UNISON 39, 42–3, 69–72
'unitarist' conception of work 189, 192–3, 197
Unite 70–72, 84, 108–9
United Arab Emirates (UAE) see Emiratization
University of East London (UEL) 69–70, 72

value chains
   buyer-driven 266–9
   characteristics of global 277
Victoria Equal Opportunity and Human Rights Commission (VEOHRC) 129–30, 131, 133–5
Victoria State Police (Australia)
   female Chief Commissioner, experience of 131–3
   introduction to 129–30
   questions 135
   and VEOHRC 133–5
   women in 130–31
voice see employee voice
Volkswagen
   background and context 272–3
   trade union actors 272–6
   transnational collective agreements
      and agency workers 273
      issues and challenges 274–5
      summary and questions 275–6
      in UK and Germany 273–4

voluntary codes of corporate social responsibility 277, 279, 280

Warhurst, C. 167–8
WeKnowGin (WKG) 100–104
welfare, sex workers' access to 145–6
wellbeing at work
   Achmea 48, 49
   autism case study 21–4
   as driver of productivity and customer service standards 82
   growing recognition of issues 21
   impact of organisational issues on 162, 165
   at Jacaranda House 161–5
WellbeingCo 162–5
Whittall, M. 273
Wilkinson, A. 1
'Win–Win Model of Individual–Goal Combination' 241
Wood, G. 254–5
work intensification 101–2
work quality see job quality
worker safety 163, 279–80
workload
   Airbus calculation 125
   Jacaranda House 164
   managing fluctuating 174, 177
   Neptune Plc 140
   and peer pressure 176
   self-reporting 175
Workplace Behaviour Survey 20
workplace bullying
   background and context 137
   Department of Public Service 98
   impact 138–9
   management style 138–9
   problematic team relationships 137–8
   questions 141
   team dynamics 140–41
Workplace Equality Index 8–9
workplace misbehaviour 101–2
Workplace Relations Act 1996 33

workplace resistance
   background and context 100
   management responses 103–4
   MNC examples 198
   new ownership structure and management control 101
   questions 104

work intensification and workplace misbehaviour 101–2
workplace wellbeing *see* wellbeing at work
Wright, S. 30, 167

zero hours contracts 106–7, 108